# The Bliss and Blisters
# of
# Early Career Teaching

A Pan-Canadian Perspective

# Praise for *The Bliss and The Blisters*

As a former school administrator and someone who teaches about leadership, I am pleased to see a book about early career teacher induction and mentorship across Canada. We need Canadian examples for us to better understand our own challenges and strengths. With their background and expertise, Keith Walker and Benjamin Kutsyuruba have provided us with an engaging and enlightening collection. – *Ann Sherman, PhD, Dean of Education, University of New Brunswick.*

Canada in the 21st century is changing. As a nation, we are experiencing significant shifts to our social, demographic, cultural, technological, economic and political contexts. New teachers in Canada are entering a profession which is tasked with interpreting these new realities for our children and youth, who are facing a world where globalization and tribalism are now vying for power. Unfortunately, many new teachers are unable to cope with these challenges, and drop-out rates are high. In this important new book, educators from many parts of Canada examine the issues facing new teachers and explore how early career teacher induction and mentorship programs might assist in keeping more new teachers in the profession. – *J. Tim Goddard, PhD, Professor of Education, University of Prince Edward Island*

Bliss and blisters indeed! With over 40 authors from across Canada contributing to 25 chapters, this book offers the reader a pan-Canadian perspective on our differing approaches to schooling, mentorship and teacher education. Noting provincial differences sheds light on inequities and suggests new directions for the retention of the newest members of our profession. – *Olenka Bilash, PhD, Professor of Education, University of Alberta*

This volume addresses the essential topic of Early Career Teachers within the Canadian context. It will be an important read for educational administrators, teacher educators, field-based mentors, and for early career teachers themselves. – *Jacqueline Kirk, PhD, President, Canadian Association for the Study of Educational Administration*

This book is long anticipated by those of us who work with early career teachers. For the first time, we will have a Canadian compilation of the realities of this group of colleagues along with some real suggestions as to what might be done to support them. The editors have invested significantly in timely and thoughtful research to compile this important and well-worth-spending-time-with book. It will leave you more committed than ever to supporting this sometimes vulnerable group of our teacher colleagues and equipped with ideas on how to do so. – *Beverley Park, Senior Administrative Officer, Newfoundland and Labrador Teachers' Association*

L'entrée dans la profession enseignante présente de nombreux défis qui s'intensifient d'année en année. Par la diversité et la pertinence des expériences partagées, cet ouvrage offre une mine riche en pistes d'éclairage et de solution pour toute personne que ces défis interpellent. – *Claire Lapointe, PhD, professeure titulaire, Faculté des sciences de l'éducation, Université Laval*

I am thankful to Benjamin and Keith for guiding this important and timely contribution to the literature surrounding the education, induction and mentorship of early career teachers. The voices presented within this book should help those of us who work in teacher education to gain an improved understanding of the impact on early career teachers of a teacher development model that assumes education programs are just one step in the development of teachers. – *Mark Hirschkorn, PhD, Former President of the Canadian Association for Teacher Education (CATE)*

Collaboration, change, and diversity are normal features of today's classrooms for beginning teachers. This work spearheaded by Kutsyuruba and Walker makes a significant contribution to our understanding of early career teaching by giving space to the voices of beginning teachers and by providing information to school leaders about support models and practices in use across Canada. It is especially significant that this book emphasizes the creation of a culture of both collaborative and self-directed professional learning for early career teachers. – *Ken Brien, PhD, President, Commonwealth Council for Educational Administration and Management (CCEAM)*

Sound, research-based professional induction processes for teachers are of significant importance to professional teacher organizations. This pan-Canadian review of the experiences of beginning and early career teachers is welcomed. My hope would be that the research itself, but more importantly the voices of teachers that contributed to the research, will inform the development of a broad array of robust supports for new and experienced teachers and administrators. Congratulations to all of the contributors to this valued volume of work. – *Gwen Dueck, Executive Director, Saskatchewan Teachers' Federation*

In the aptly titled *The Bliss and Blisters of Early Career Teaching: The Pan-Canadian Perspective,* Drs. Kutsyuruba and Walker have provided essential solutions to the puzzle of how we support, or should support, new teachers. Too many new teachers leave our teacher development programs to become stranded in the purgatory between graduation and first contract known as the substitute pool. These highly motivated and well trained novice teachers deserve more from the system that ultimately hires them, and this pan-Canadian perspective on early career teaching is a direct contribution to this process. – *Kirk Anderson, PhD, President, Association of Canadian Deans and Directors of Education (2017-2019)*

Combining the lessons learned from a national study as well as the textures of individuals immersed in the field, Kutsyuruba and Walker have produced a thorough collection of initiatives in, experiences of, and perspectives on early career teacher induction and teaching from across the country. This collection has much to offer to the field—from beginning teachers in the classroom to policy-makers, alike. – *Michelle Prytula, PhD, Dean of Education, University of Saskatchewan*

This book is a valuable resource for teacher unions committed to mentorship for early career teachers. Within this pan-Canadian collection, readers can explore mentorship research, programs and practices that empower beginning teachers through collaborative professional development and affirm the centrality of place and community in teacher work. – *Glen Hansman, President, British Columbia Teachers' Federation*

I am so pleased, excited, and thankful to the contributors of this book. As teacher education continues to be challenged by the rapidly changing contexts teachers face every day, this work is much needed and timely. Its Canadian coverage adds to my excitement. I look forward to reading the work. – *Randolph Wimmer, PhD, Dean (interim) and Professor of Education, University of Alberta*

This vital book is a unique collection of the Canadian research on teacher induction and mentoring. It makes a timely and valuable contribution by bringing together the pan-Canadian voices of authors who are passionate about the development of early career teachers. It is an excellent guide to scholars, practitioners, and policymakers who want to make a difference. – *Rebecca Luce-Kapler, OCT, PhD, Dean of Education, Queen's University*

# The Bliss and Blisters
## of
# Early Career Teaching

## A Pan-Canadian Perspective

**Benjamin Kutsyuruba**
and
**Keith D. Walker**

EDITORS

Foreword by **Megan Tschannen-Moran**

Word & Deed Publishing Incorporated
1860 Appleby Line, Suite #778
Burlington, Ontario, Canada, L7L 7H7

Edited by Benjamin Kutsyuruba and Keith D. Walker
Book design by Jim Bisakowski – www.bookdesign.ca

ISBN  978-0-9918626-9-6

Word & Deed Publishing Incorporated
1860 Appleby Line, Suite #778
Burlington, Ontario, Canada, L7L 7H7
(Toll Free) 1-866-601-1213

Visit our website at
www.wordanddeedpublishing.com

# Contents

## Part I
## The Voices of Early Career Teachers

## Part 2
## Programmatic Support for Early Career Teachers Across Canada

## Part 3
## School and School System Support for
## Early Career Teachers

# Dedication

We dedicate this book to our wives and families – our core support groups who continue to put wind in our sails, help us stay rooted in our values, and encourage us to have grounded hope in and for the future. Benjamin dedicates this book to his wife Olichka and to their awesome sons, Kevin and Jason. Likewise, Keith dedicates this book to his wife Viv and to their adult children by birth and marriage: James (teacher), Martha, Eric (teacher), Sarah Jane (teacher), Graham, Stacie, Gillian, and Cody.

We also dedicate this book to the early career teachers across Canada, along with those who help, support, form, mentor, sponsor, and advise them in their journeys as professional educators.

Finally, as we've worked on this project and listened to the stories of others, we've been reminded, with gratitude, of the many exceptional people in our lives who have been so generous and patient with us in our educator journeys. Their timely mentorship and wise presence has brought much encouragement and many benefits to us and those with whom we've worked.

# Acknowledgments

First and foremost, we would like to acknowledge the funding from the Social Sciences and Humanities Research Council of Canada that has made possible both research project and the publication of this volume. One of the overarching purposes of this research project was to initiate and sustain long-term pan-Canadian conversations among scholars, practitioners, and leaders whose work is related to the development of new and early career teachers across all provinces and territories. Conducting pan-Canadian research for us has meant engaging with various partners across provinces and territories who work directly and indirectly with early career teachers. To this end, we would like to acknowledge the significant contributions to this research and this volume from the partners listed below.

**The Pan-Canadian Expert Panel**

The pan-Canadian expert panel established as part of our research project consists of scholars (university deans, faculty, and graduate students) who conduct research on teacher induction and mentorship; teacher induction program coordinators (at the ministry, teacher association, school board, or school levels); school principals; and, representatives of provincial and territorial teacher associations, federations, and unions. The panel's role was instrumental in providing advice and support in all phases of the project. We thank the following expert panel members for their timely and invaluable contributions:

- Alison Davies (British Columbia Teachers' Federation)
- Ann Sherman (University of New Brunswick)
- Barbara Lepp (University of Manitoba)
- Beverly Park (Newfoundland and Labrador Teachers' Association)
- Ching-Chiu Lin (University of British Columbia)
- Jim Strachan (Ontario Ministry of Education)
- Kathy Collis (Winnipeg School Division, Manitoba)

- Ken Brien (University of New Brunswick)
- Laurie-Ann Hellsten (University of Saskatchewan)
- Noel Roche (Prairie Spirit School Division, Saskatchewan)
- Rien Meesters (New Brunswick Department of Education)
- Rita Irwin (University of British Columbia)
- Robert Smilanich (University of Alberta)
- Ruth Kane (University of Ottawa)
- Sylvie Fontaine (Université du Québec en Outaouais)
- Trista Hollweck (Western Quebec School Board)

## Teacher Associations, Federations, Unions, and Professional Organizations

We have been blessed to partner with representatives of teacher organizations in all provinces and territories, who provided us with vital support in advising on and piloting, translating, and disseminating the pan-Canadian early career teacher survey. These partners have sent out invitations in English, French, and Inuktitut languages, and the survey was offered in English and French through their communication channels. We would like to express our gratitude to the following organizations and their representatives (whose names are too numerous to be listed here): Newfoundland and Labrador Teachers' Association (NLTA); British Columbia Teachers' Federation (BCTF); Ontario Teachers' Federation (OTF) and its affiliates, AEFO, OECTA, ETFO, and OSSTF; Saskatchewan Teachers' Federation (STF); Northwest Territories Teachers' Association (NWTTA); New Brunswick Teachers' Association (NBTA); Manitoba Teachers' Society (MTS); Alberta Teachers' Association (ATA); Nunavut Teachers' Association (NTA); Nova Scotia Teachers Union (NSTU); Prince Edward Island Teachers' Federation (PEITF); and Quebec's Carrefour national de l'insertion professionnelle en enseignement (CNIPE).

## Ministries and Departments of Education

A number of ministries and departments of education across Canada have been involved with providing input and with survey dissemination efforts. We would like to acknowledge the tremendous support we have received from the Ontario Ministry of Education, New Brunswick Department of Education, Yukon Department of Education, and Nunavut Department of Education.

## Graduate Students

In line with the mentorship focus of our research, the graduate students have been involved and mentored in their roles as project managers and research assistants in all aspects and phases of this research project, including data collection, data analysis, presenting, and writing. We would like to express our sincere gratitude to and acknowledge the valuable contributions of the Project Manager, Dr. Lorraine Godden (who has recently graduated from Queen's University PhD in Education program) and Research Assistants, Ian Matheson, Paul Godden, Maha Al Makhamreh, Rebecca Stroud Stasel, John Bosica, Lindsay Heggie, Stefan Merchant (all Queen's University), and Erin Lashta (University of Saskatchewan).

# Foreword

*Megan Tschannen-Moran*

In many schools, veteran teachers take a decidedly unfriendly approach to welcoming their novice colleagues. As class lists are drawn up in the spring for the following fall, they often load up the roster of the new teachers with the more difficult or troublesome students. They may also put their thumbs on the balance of class size, giving the novice teachers the larger share of students. If there is not enough classroom space, they are likely to keep the prime real estate for themselves and give itinerant status to the neophytes, consigning them to a cart wandering from one classroom to the next throughout the day, with no classrooms to call their own. Or they may place them in the dingy "temporary" classrooms parked behind the school or in the parking lot that are long past their expiration dates. In a culture of scarcity, they may regard a classroom left unoccupied over the summer as unguarded territory and invade that classroom to pilfer any supplies, curriculum materials or other "loot" that looks good. They may swap out classroom desks that wobble from their own classroom for sturdier ones in the empty classroom, along with broken chairs, bookcases or clocks. Things don't improve once the novice teachers report for duty. They may find few of their veteran colleagues willing to lend a hand or a listening ear; rather, these veterans may snicker just a little as they watch their junior colleagues dash for the exit at the end of the day, struggling to hold back tears until they reach the safety of their cars. A graduate student once told me her middle school students reported to her that an older teacher had encouraged them to deface the beautiful interactive bulletin board she had put up one weekend, presumably because it made the efforts of the rest of the staff look paltry by comparison. She was studying administration, in part to learn what might be done to change the mean-spirited culture in schools like hers. It has been said that teaching is the only profession that eats its young. Indeed, the poor quality of most teacher induction programs is part of what causes teaching to fall short of what it fully means to be a profession.

A profession is characterized by members who possess specialized expert knowledge and pledge their first and primary responsibility to the welfare of those they serve. Professions are bound together by a code of conduct and a set of ethics that guide decision making in meeting the needs of clients. In schools, professionalism is oriented toward a collective focus on student learning. As novice teachers are socialized into the norms of the profession, their beliefs, attitudes, and actions are expected to demonstrate a strong sense of accountability to the shared mission of service to students and their families. This socialization, however, is not well served by the norms of isolation, autonomy, and equal status that have characterized the teaching profession. Nor are they served by the kinds of hazing rituals described above that allow and encourage veteran teachers to torment their novice colleagues, or to subject them to the most disagreeable and challenging tasks. The veterans may justify their actions, asserting that they paid their dues, and it is only fair for their young colleagues to do the same.

Professionalism in schools is fostered through productive collaboration, rigorous inquiry, de-privatized teaching practice, and reflective dialogue (Seashore, Kruse, & Marks, 1996). Professional educators continually seek best practices to better serve their students through rigorous, disciplined inquiry both individually and collectively. A hallmark of a profession is the application of professional judgment in non-routine circumstances, taking relevant considerations into account. Where certainty about practice does not exist, practitioners continually seek to discover the most responsible course of action (Darling-Hammond, 1988). Families expect that teachers will have the knowledge to make a thorough assessment of their child's learning needs, and that they will have at their disposal an array of evidence-based strategies tailored to meet those needs. Darling-Hammond noted the need for ongoing inquiry to uphold the standards for professional practice:

> Norms of inquiry and ethical conduct are extremely important. But because knowledge is constantly expanding, problems of practice are complex, and ethical dilemmas result from conflict between legitimate goals, these requirements

cannot be satisfied by codification of knowledge, prescriptions for practice, and unchanging rules of conduct. ... These norms must be accomplished by socialization to a professional standard that incorporates continual learning, reflection, and concern with the multiple effects of one's actions on others as fundamental aspects of the professional role. (p. 67)

Because the decisions made by teachers are complex, the quality of those decisions is enhanced by collective deliberation in which differences in perspectives are valued and problems are openly discussed and resolved (Tschannen-Moran, 2009).

Professionalism stems from education and socialization processes which demand that entrants to the profession demonstrate that they possess knowledge of the principles, theories, and procedures that undergird appropriate decision making, and that they continually seek to enhance their knowledge through professional development. The rigorous training and selection of teachers helps ensure that all individuals permitted to practice are adequately prepared to do so responsibly (Darling-Hammond, 1988). The standards of practice and professional ethics are articulated, transmitted, monitored, and enforced by the profession itself through a process of peer review. Thus, the teaching profession needs mechanisms to see to it that unethical or inappropriate practice is not allowed to persist. And to be effective, this scrutiny and support must begin during the induction process. There need to be means to intervene when teachers fall short of accepted instructional practice, or when they engage in teacher aggression, meaning teachers who yell at students, who use sarcasm, humiliation, or group punishments for individual misdemeanors as means of student control. These processes, then, create the conditions that support student learning.

The successful induction of new teachers into the teaching profession is supported where empathy and trust are fostered, and where a strengths-based orientation cultivates a robust sense of self-efficacy among novice teachers (Tschannen-Moran & Tschannen-Moran, 2010). Empathy allows veteran teachers in the role of mentors, coaches, or colleagues to create a safe space for the novice to share the myriad emotions and needs that are stimulated as they engage in the very complex work of teaching. Training in communication processes that facilitate empathy helps to equip those charged with supporting and guiding novices with the skills necessary to extend empathy, even in situations when they have observed a less-than-stellar, or even a cringe-worthy, teaching performance. Trust is also essential to a successful induction process. If the novice fails to develop a sense of trust in his or her mentor or colleagues, he or she is unlikely to fully embrace the norms, ethics, and standards of the teaching profession. Without trust, the process of collective inquiry, if it happens at all, will be impaired by self-protection and problem-hiding rather than creative problem solving. What's more, research evidence suggests that the trust teachers hold for their colleagues and school leaders is related to the level of trust they are likely to extend to their students. This has far-reaching implications because the trust between teachers and students is such a strong predictor of student learning (Tschannen-Moran, 2014).

Adopting a strengths-based orientation in the induction of novice teachers is a powerful strategy to allow novices to build on the things that they do well in order to improve in areas that are more of a challenge for them. In this way, it helps to bolster their sense of self-efficacy. Nurturing a strong sense of self-efficacy during the first three years of teaching is crucial for several reasons. First, those who fail to establish a belief in their own capabilities to teach are more likely to exit the profession early, resulting in a loss on the investment that both they and the profession have made in their training, and also contributing to more students being taught by struggling, novice teachers, especially in hard-to-staff schools. A robust line of research has also demonstrated that teachers with stronger self-efficacy put forth more effort in their teaching, set more ambitious goals for themselves and their students, and are more resilient in the face of setbacks. They are more innovative and open to trying new instructional methods. Moreover, they are less likely to blame students for poor learning outcomes or to display negative affect toward students. Once established, however, these self-beliefs about one's capabilities tend to be resistant to change (Tschannen-Moran & Hoy, 2007). There is a window of opportunity in the first few years of teaching, when the novice teacher's self-efficacy beliefs are pliable, that closes as those beliefs become established. Thus, when novice teachers are not well inducted, when they are given the most challenging and undesirable assignments, when they are unsupported by their colleagues, and not given adequate resources to be successful, they are likely to come away from their early years with a diminished sense of efficacy that will lead to a career of less effort, less challenging goals, less resilience and less positive relationships with students. Alternately, neo-phyte teachers who are well supported, and who come away from their early years believing that they have what it takes to be a successful teacher, are more likely to put forth the effort that ongoing inquiry requires, to be more hardy in the face of the challenges they face, as well as more enthusiastic and innovative. The differential between these contrasting outcomes is magnified by the hundreds of students these teachers will impact over the course of their career.

The work of supporting teachers in their early years in the profession is critically important for the profession and for society as a whole because the work of education is so fundamental to the well-being of a society. The Teacher Induction and Mentoring Forum that was held September 21-23, 2016 in Kingston, Ontario, provided an engaging and meaning-ful space for professionals deeply engaged in this work across Canada to come together to share their best thinking and successful practices. It was the conversations and workshops at this Forum that provided the starting place for this volume. Dr. Benjamin Kutsyuruba of Queen's University and Dr. Keith Walker of the University of Saskatchewan had the vision to see the importance of hosting this pan-Canadian conversation, the first of its kind, and then the forethought to create this volume so that the insights and good work shared at the Forum could reach an even broader audience. We owe them a debt of gratitude for their efforts in hosting this important conversation, both the face-to-face one that happened in Kingston, and the one between authors and readers hosted here between the covers of this volume. I am confident that if you are a person who cares about the future of the teaching profession, and of schools and schooling in Canada, your imagination will be stirred.

Happy reading and imagining!

*Megan Tschannen-Moran, PhD, The College of William & Mary*

# References

Darling-Hammond, L. (1988). Policy and professionalism. In A. Lieberman, A. (Ed.). *Building a professional culture in schools* (pp. 55–77). New York, NY: Teacher College Press.

Seashore, K., Kruse, S., & Marks, H. M. (1996). School-wide professional community: Teachers' work, intellectual quality, and commitment. In F. W. Newman & Associates (Eds.), *Authentic achievement: Restructuring schools for intellectual quality* (pp. 179–203). San Francisco, CA: Jossey-Bass.

Tschannen-Moran, M. (2014). The interconnectivity of trust in schools. In D. Van Maele, P. B. Forsyth, & M. Van Houtte, (Eds), *Trust and school life: The role of trust for learning, teaching, leading, and bridging* (pp. 57–81). Rotterdam, Netherlands: Springer. DOI 10.1007/978-94-017-8014-8_3

Tschannen-Moran, B., & Tschannen-Moran, M. (2010). *Evocative coaching: Transforming schools one conversation at a time.* San Francisco, CA: Jossey-Bass.

Tschannen-Moran, M. (2009). Fostering teacher professionalism: The role of professional orientation and trust. *Educational Administration Quarterly, 45*(2), 217–247.

Tschannen-Moran, M., & Hoy, A. W. (2007). The differential antecedents of self-efficacy beliefs of novice and experienced teachers. *Teaching and Teacher Education, 23*(6), 944–956.

# Introduction:
# Exploring the Pan-Canadian Terrain of Early Career Teaching

*Benjamin Kutsyuruba, Keith Walker*

Much attention needs to be given to the development of novice teachers because the quality and abilities of a child's teacher are considered to be the most important school-based factors determining how much that child learns (Cochran-Smith, 2006; Darling-Hammond, 2006; Rivkin, Hanushek, & Kain, 2005). However, reviewing the extant research literature on early career teachers, one can't help but notice the reports of increasing numbers of beginning teachers leaving the profession around the world: despite their initial enthusiasm, far too many novice teachers abandon the profession, depressed and discouraged (Boreen, Johnson, Niday, & Potts, 2009), with the most talented beginning teachers among those most apt to leave (Colb, 2001). The notion of teacher attrition seems to span the international boundaries, whereas dauntingly low numbers of teachers remaining in the profession have been reported in the United Kingdom (Smithers & Robinson, 2003), Australia (Stoel & Thant, 2002), the United States (Darling-Hammond, 2001; Ingersoll & Smith, 2003; Smith & Ingersoll, 2004), and other countries (Organization for Economic Co-operation and Development [OECD], 2005). Indeed, despite their heavy financial and educational investment in pursuing a teaching career, most teachers quit the profession in their first two to five years; in some extreme cases, teachers drop out even before the end of their first year (Black, 2001). Internationally, the argument is that the first three to four years after initial training are the most crucial for a teacher's decision whether to remain in the profession or not (Jones, 2003).

# Early Career Teacher Attrition, Retention, and Development in Canada

In relation to early career teacher attrition across Canada, the recent statistics are often inconsistent, contradicting, and incomplete. As reported by the Canadian Teachers Federation (CTF, 2003), only 6 in 10 of the 1995 graduates from elementary and secondary teacher education degree programs in Canada were employed as full-time teachers five years after graduation; almost one quarter of them never went into teaching at all. Contrastingly, Canada's teacher attrition rate in 1999 was deemed to be at 3-6% (OECD, 2005). In 2004, the estimated teacher turnover rate in Canada was approximately 30 percent in the first five years of service (CTF, 2004). Significant variations also exist across the country, whereas some Canadian jurisdictions post very high early-career attrition rates (Clandinin et al., 2012; OCT, 2012), while others indicate much lower rates (e.g., Ontario's statistics showed 6.7% turnover (OCT, 2004) and 10% (Clark & Antonelli, 2009)). Furthermore, certain segments of the teaching profession in Canada have significantly higher attrition rates (e.g., French Immersion or French as a Second Language teachers (Karsenti, Collin, Villeneuve, Dumouchel, & Roy, 2008)). In addition to the inconsistent statistical information of the pan-Canadian picture, there is also limited research on understanding the problem of early-career teacher attrition (Schaefer, Long, & Clandinin, 2012). It must be said that we do not know the actual and up-to-date figures and details of new teacher attrition, but there are enough indications in the evidence above to draw our warranted concern and to suggest attention must be paid to supporting early career teachers. Summarizing the exhaustive review of the literature, Karsenti and Collin (2013) concluded that there are four main factor types for teachers who leave the profession: a) task related factors; b) individual factors; c) social environment factors; and d) socioeconomic conditions. They posited that the interdependence of attrition factors suggests that teacher attrition is usually the result of a set of factors rather than a single factor. Therefore, much research is needed on these factors within the pan-Canadian scope.

While a certain level of attrition within the profession is both necessary and healthy (Ingersoll, 2001; Ryan & Kokol, 1988), the early-career loss of teachers is neither desirable nor sustainable (Plunkett & Dyson, 2011), as it is generally costly to schools and detrimental to student learning (Guarino, Santibañez, & Daley, 2006). Borman and Dowling (2008) noted that, despite an increased research and policy rhetoric to explore the factors that may help retain a greater proportion of the existing teaching force, attrition and its associated costs to the system have not always been systematically addressed by formal policies and interventions. Clandinin et al. (2012) urged for increased focus on how to sustain new teachers in their teaching life-careers, rather than upon merely retaining them in the profession.

Researchers (Darling-Hammond, 2003; Huling-Austin, 1986, 1988; Huling-Austin & Murphy, 1987; Laitsch, 2005; Strong, 2005, 2006) claimed that induction programs with effective mentoring in the early teaching years are capable of positively affecting beginning teacher retention and student achievement, and reducing the waste of resources and human potential associated with early-career attrition. Scholars found that induction programs and high-quality mentoring programs have positive impacts through increased teacher effectiveness, higher satisfaction, commitment, improved classroom instruction and student achievement, and early-career retention of novice teachers (Glazerman et al., 2010; Guarino et al., 2006; Henry, Bastian & Fortner, 2011; Ingersoll & Strong, 2011; Odell & Ferraro, 1992; Richardson, Glessner, & Tolson, 2010).

As education is a provincial/territorial responsibility in Canada (afforded by Section 93 of the *Constitution Act*), with attendant variations in school systems and policies, induction and mentoring responses to attrition concerns tend to be compartmentalized, such that lessons learned from one jurisdiction remain unavailable to other jurisdictions experiencing similar teacher retention issues. Recognizing the vast geographical, political, and contextual factors of the Canadian systems of education, we embarked on a pan-Canadian research journey to explore not only *why* early career teachers across the country consider leaving, or in fact leave, the profession, but also to understand *what* supports exist for them across provinces and territories that are aimed at retaining the novice teachers. In 2012, we started a multi-year pan-Canadian research project funded by the Insight Grant we have received from the Social Sciences and Humanities Research Council of Canada (SSHRC), entitled "Understanding Teacher

Attrition and Retention: The Role of Teacher Induction and Mentorship Programs."

## The Pan-Canadian Research Project

The purpose of this research project was to explore the differential impact of teacher induction and mentorship programs on the early-career teachers' retention, as perceived across the provinces and territories. The following research questions guided our research study:

1. What are the organization, evolution, mandates, and efficacy of teacher induction programs in each jurisdiction?
2. To what extent and to what benefit have jurisdictions established policies and/or programs of mentorship as an aspect of teacher induction programs?
3. What administration and leadership practices at the system and school levels in the area of teacher induction and mentorship are conducive to teacher retention?
4. What are beginning teachers' perceptions of induction and mentorship programs, especially with respect to retention and career issues?

To meet the objectives of the study, we have completed a number of research activities and deliverables over the four-year period (please note that the key findings from our research deliverables are detailed in several chapters in this volume).

1. A multi-function research website was developed in 2012 with the purposes of communicating research focus, engaging with partners, and disseminating research products and deliverables (see www.earlycareerteachers.com);
2. A multi-year document analysis study was conducted in 2013 and then updated in 2016, reviewing the policy and program documents publicly available from provincial education authorities, teacher associations/federations, teacher unions, and individual district school boards websites across Canada (see Chapter 10);
3. An international systematic review of research literature was conducted in 2014-2015 to explore the varied and diverse contextual

challenges faced by beginning teachers and identify how successful induction programs address these contextual factors (see Chapter 21);

4. An online survey in English and French was developed, piloted, and conducted in 2016 with over 1300 new teachers from all provinces and territories who were within the first 5 years of employment in publicly funded schools in Canada (see Chapter 2);

5. Telephone interviews were conducted with a selected survey – 36 teachers – all in their first five years of teaching from nine provinces and three territories (3 in French, 33 in English) (see Chapter 7).

As a culmination for the project's activities, a First Pan-Canadian Teacher Induction and Mentoring Forum was organized in Kingston, Ontario in September, 2016. This forum was the first ever attempt to initiate pan-Canadian conversations among the interested parties who work with early career teachers from all provinces and territories in Canada. We welcomed leaders, scholars, administrators, teacher induction and mentoring program coordinators, representatives from teacher associations, ministries/departments of education, universities, school boards, schools, and community organizations across Canada. The forum was attended by over 70 attendees representing eight provinces of Canada. This edited volume is the direct product of the collaborative efforts between the scholars, practitioners, and policy makers across the Canadian jurisdictions generated by our research project in general and by the first pan-Canadian Teacher Induction and Mentoring Forum in particular. Most of the chapter authors have also participated as presenters and engaged in conversations at the Forum. Through the Forum and this edited book, we are hoping to disseminate the wealth of research studies, deliberations, reflections, and understandings, as well as encourage the sharing of insights on the vital topics of attrition, retention, induction, mentoring, and development of early career teachers within the Canadian contexts. Despite our geographical and contextual differences, we have much to share with, and learn from, each other.

It should also be noted here that our research on early career teaching, theoretically and conceptually, has been positioned within the ecological perspective on organizations. Schools and other educational organizations are living and breathing systems or, as we prefer to say: "ecosystems." They are not merely problems to be solved or mechanically tuned, but are mysteries to be embraced, and wonderfully complicated and intricate settings where the addition of each unique person exponentially and beautifully complexifies the life-world of those who host the school environment (Bronfenbrenner, 1994). This ecological perspective results in our seeing schools as living systems – inherently unstable, interdependent networks that cannot be understood through mechanical analytical processes. Instead, we envision a holistic interpretation of how a school's social systems are created by the people within: interconnected, developing, and progressing (Clarke, 2000; Mitchell & Sackney, 2011; Wheatley, 1999). In this ecological view, no one aspect of a system is thought of as a separate entity from other parts; instead there is an emphasis on connectedness, relationships, and contextual interdependency. There are symbiotic relationships everywhere: the difficult times for some will implicate others, and the celebrations of some or one will have ramifications on the lives of others. Furthermore, such an ecological perspective regards relationships amongst the members who comprise the school organization as essential to creating the sustainability of the learning community and its members. This ecological perspective permeates not only our research conceptualization, approach, and methods, but also the graphic and visual representations associated with our research. We have attempted to capture this in the colours and images chosen for our project's various deliverables, including this book. The cover of this book represents the road to success that is often difficult, and may require getting through a thick, dense bush and possibly treacherous terrain in the forest. Hence, the title of this book denotes the successful and challenging experiences of early career teachers through the ecologically metaphorical symptoms of bliss (harmony) and blisters (discord).

## Chapter Overview

The book is divided into three sections. **Part I** of the volume describes the experiences of early career teachers, offering various venues like poems, comics, and research analysis for their voices to be heard.

In **Chapter 2**, Benjamin Kutsyuruba, Keith Walker, Ian Matheson, and John Bosica outline the results from a pan-Canadian *Teacher Induction Survey* (N=1343) that explored beginning teachers' perceptions of induction and mentorship programs, with particular interest in retention and career issues, from all provinces and territories in Canada. Along with demographic information about early career teachers, including their experience with non-permanent work, experience by grade level and subject area, the location and setting of current employment, the chapter provides the data analysis of the early career teachers' experiences with induction and mentorship supports, administration, the work environment, and their own career and professional development.

Sarah Barrett's qualitative case study, detailed in **Chapter 3**, describes the induction of a new working class science teacher, Samuel, into the community of practice of an affluent suburban high school. Over the course of two years of observations and interviews, four themes emerged: a rough initiation, a conservative but supportive professional culture, a conservative but affluent community, and bids for full community membership. Through these themes, this case provides an example of the ways in which structural aspects of society, such as social class, impact the agency and professional identity of a classroom teacher. Implications for mentorship of new teachers are provided.

The poem, included in **Chapter 4**, is written by Rebecca Stroud Stasel about her calling as a new teacher. Although the poem was written a long time ago, musing about her teaching career, she noted that the calling still rings loud and true in her mind as she remembered the exhilaration, the trepidation, and the hope that she felt in being called to be a teacher – a new teacher.

In **Chapter 5**, Ching-Chu Lin, Julian Lawrence, Amber Lum, and Rita Irwin aim to demonstrate the implications of comics as a mode of inquiry into teachers' stories of challenges and professional growth. Through comics, they invite readers to experience imaginative insight into new teachers' stories that offer reflections on their experiences of becoming teachers, provoke conversation around educational issues, and articulate the complexity of pedagogical relationships among teachers and their professional learning communities.

Matthew McIntyre, in **Chapter 6**, shares his experiences of being a new elementary school teacher in the Western Quebec School Board's Teacher Induction Program. Through the lens of his challenging, stressful and rewarding experiences, he explains the systems put in place to support new teachers, and the impact that the induction program has had on him as a new teacher.

In **Chapter 7**, Keith Walker, Benjamin Kutsyuruba, Maha Al Makhamreh, and Rebecca Stroud Stasel examine the data from 36 interviews with new teachers as part of a pan-Canadian study. Teachers shared how they developed themselves, what experiences led them to persevere, what leadership supports they had, and what advice they had for new teachers. Corroborating extant literature, the findings show that relationships are essential to thriving: teachers need to establish multi-pronged strategies, passion and resilience along with consistent, non-judgmental, support from administrative teams; conversely, lacking such relationships leads to high levels of stress. The teachers recommended a good work-life balance, a positive mindset, engaging in reflective practices, and collaboration with other teachers.

Another poem, included in **Chapter 8,** is written by Keith Alcock about his experiences as a new teacher. It conveys his thoughts on searching for and finding opportunities for teaching and learning, looking for mentorship that comes naturally, taking ownership of teaching, dealing with frustrations, and persevering and hoping while doing what he truly loves.

In **Chapter 9**, Kathryn Broad and Stefanie Muhling address the lived experiences of early career teachers and the colleagues who support them on their route to permanent teaching in Ontario. The provincial context for entry to the profession is briefly outlined. Voices of new teachers in daily and long-term occasional positions, colleagues and mentors, and the teacher educators, policy-makers and school district leaders who support them are shared. These new and experienced colleagues describe practices and relationships that develop and sustain optimism, agency and continued growth in challenging circumstances. Implications that may further foster collaborative, reciprocal learning are offered.

**Part II** represents a selection of chapters that address programmatic support for early career teachers across Canada. This section is structured in such a way as to first offer the pan-Canadian overview of teacher induction and mentoring policies and programs and then detail programmatic research efforts in different Canadian jurisdictions.

In **Chapter 10**, Benjamin Kutsyuruba, Keith Walker, Ian Matheson, and Lorraine Godden describe the findings from a multi-year document analysis study (2013 and 2016) that examined the organization and mandates of teacher induction programs, the role of mentorship as an aspect of teacher induction programs, and the mandated roles, duties, and responsibilities of school administrators in teacher induction and mentorship processes in each Canadian jurisdiction. Four different types of programmatic support were identified. The chapter tracks the development and changes in provision of support in the form of teacher induction, mentoring, and both induction and mentoring programs at the provincial and district levels. Although evidence of mentoring was seen in all provinces across Canada at some level, the role of the school administrator in induction and mentoring efforts was inconsistently identified.

In **Chapter 11**, Joséphine Mukamurera and Sylvie Fontaine focus on beginning teachers working in the province of Québec. The results presented are drawn from two studies financed by SSHRC; one conducted in the fall of 2013 by Mukamurera and Martineau, and the other conducted by Kutsyuruba and Walker in 2016. Results from both studies provide an indication of the current professional reality faced by many beginning teachers (job insecurity, teaching subjects outside their specialty, professional instability, feeling incompetent, etc.), and stress the need for support as more important in the first two years of teaching. Furthermore, authors note that although some forms of support are more appreciated than others, their relevance is improved when they are linked with the teacher's specific needs.

Trista Hollweck, in **Chapter 12**, outlines the context and composition of the Teacher Induction Program (TIP) in the Western Quebec School Board. Conceptualized as a patchwork quilt, TIP's three key pillars of professional growth, a Mentoring and Coaching Fellowship (MCF), and evaluation are discussed against international mentoring, coaching and induction research literature. Importantly, this chapter defines and visually depicts mentoring and coaching as distinct, yet complementary, approaches in effective induction programs. Now in its eighth year, TIP remains an unfinished project, but an exciting pattern is beginning to emerge, with some lessons learned that may be useful to other Canadian districts interested in mentoring, coaching and induction programs.

In **Chapter 13**, Sylvie Fontaine, Ruth Kane, and Thursica Kovinthan consider the ways in which new teachers are prepared for the responsibility of assessing their students' learning in the provinces of Quebec and Ontario. Using evidence from two provincial studies of new teachers, they ask: How is the development of teachers' competency regarding the assessment of students being addressed in teacher education and induction programs to ensure new teachers are ready to take on these responsibilities in their classrooms? New teachers have responsibility for ensuring that assessment activities foster and support ongoing learning, and provide evidence for students and their parents and/or caregivers. Yet research demonstrates that new teachers graduate from their teacher education programs feeling unprepared to undertake this responsibility. Their findings have implications for both teacher education and induction programs.

In **Chapter 14**, Jim Strachan, Kate Creery, and Aggie Nemes describe the Ontario's New Teacher Induction Program (NTIP) that supports the growth and professional learning of new teachers. It is the second job-embedded step along a continuum of learning and growth for new teachers building upon the first step of initial teacher education. They share their learnings about the key factors that contribute to the growth of new teachers, along with the emerging understandings of the power of building what they term a "mentoring web", not just for new teachers but for all educators.

Many experienced teachers are excellent in teaching but are not automatically skilled in mentoring new teachers. In **Chapter 15**, Annette Ford presents insights from Israel's mentor preparation program, discusses the importance of understanding cultural and societal contexts in international educational research, describes Ontario's New Teacher Induction Program, and proposes an adaptation of the Israeli program that could enhance new teacher induction in Ontario and other parts of Canada.

In **Chapter 16**, Francine Morin, Kathy Collis, Gail Ruta-Fontaine, Cathy Smith, and Jennifer Watt describe a mixed methods evaluation study that examined the experiences of early service teachers (ESTs) with a formal learning partnership model of mentorship employed by one large urban school division in Manitoba over a two-year period. Two primary sources were used to generate data—online exit surveys and focus group interviews. Overall, ESTs valued the mentoring feature of the program and benefitted from the trusting learning relationships that evolved over time with their trained mentors. ESTs reported acquiring a range of pedagogical knowledge and skills, as well as improved teaching practice as a result of the mentoring process. Shared teaching contexts and close proximity were found to be important factors for effective mentoring relationships. Challenges experienced by ESTs and recommendations for improving future iterations of the program are identified.

In **Chapter 17**, Laurie-Ann Hellsten, Lynn Lemisko, Carol Demchuk-Kosolofski, and Tracy Dollansky investigated one approach to the induction and support of beginning teachers in rural school divisions in Saskatchewan, where new teacher migration and wellness are continuing challenges. The authors explored the impact on novice teachers of a mentoring model that provided release time for mentor-teachers to work one-to-one with beginning teachers in their classrooms. They found that the induction-through-mentorship model supported the creation of collaborative relationships which, in turn, provided co-learning and supportive professional and personal development for beginning teachers.

In **Chapter 18**, Laura Servage, Jaime Beck, and Jean-Claude Couture present key conclusions drawn from a five-year longitudinal study of beginning teachers (2008-2013). Funded by the Alberta Teachers' Association, the study examined the impacts of school cultures and induction supports on novice teachers over the first years of their practices. The study was conducted in the Province of Alberta, Canada, and included the experiences of an initial cohort of over one hundred teachers. In reflecting on the qualities of effective teacher induction and on the consequences of induction experiences, this paper explores the ways in which the quality of professional growth in established teachers is contingent upon the quality of their professional learning experiences early in their career.

Alison Davies and Anne Hales detail in **Chapter 19** how a pilot mentorship initiative in British Columbia — the New Teacher Mentorship Project (NTMP) — attempts to conserve spaces that encourage new teachers to become themselves as educators, while honouring the diversity and significance of the places they inhabit, and building collaborative opportunities for organizational leadership. The writers explore the ways in which a provincial mentorship framework can create and hold generative space for 'new' teachers to become ethical educators and decision-makers within diverse contexts. The chapter narrates how the NTMP supports the cultivation of wisdom and attentiveness to place, while still attending to the provision of specialized knowledge and technical proficiency of beginning teachers. In doing so, the authors wish to contribute to the characterization and examination of mentorship programs in Canadian research by documenting how local program cultures evolve, and what and whose needs mentoring programs and activities actually serve.

In **Chapter 20**, Tashi Kirincic tells the story of Delta School District's mentorship program with the intention of highlighting what others can learn from its successes and challenges. The author hopes to spark conversation and uncover possibilities for mentorship program design. The chapter is organized around four core beliefs that ground the mentorship program in Delta. These core beliefs posit that an effective mentorship program: is aligned with the vision and goals of the district; is a means to build the leadership capacity of teachers; is responsive to learner needs; and promotes and develops innovative teaching practice.

**Part III** is comprised of chapters that address school and school system support for early career teachers as evident from international and Canadian research studies and personal reflections.

In **Chapter 21**, Keith Walker, Benjamin Kutsyuruba, Lorraine Godden, and Ian Matheson present the findings of an international systematic review that explored the implementation of induction programs in different contexts, and identified how successful induction programs have responded to the contextual challenges affecting early career teachers worldwide. The authors offer an international geographic mapping of empirical research (written in English) that details the varied and diverse contextual challenges faced by beginning teachers; describe the formal programmatic responses of support provided to beginning teachers; synthesize the known evidence for the effects of the roles of mentors or induction programs for beginning teachers on their professional practice, with attention to attrition and retention rates; and contribute valuable information to support policy makers and educational leaders on the role of school administrators in supporting beginning teachers. The findings of this review warrant continuing research into the multifaceted nature of organizational and contextual factors that shape the roles and responsibilities of all stakeholders' participation in induction and mentoring programs.

In **Chapter 22**, Carmine Minutillo explores elementary teachers' motivation for, and the school principal's influence on, their engagement in self-directed PD by examining the following questions: a) What motivates teachers to engage in self-directed professional development? b) What are the conditions necessary for promoting teachers' engagement in self-directed professional development? c) What are teachers' perceptions of the principal's role in supporting, fostering, encouraging, and sustaining the professional development of teachers? The study's findings suggest that satisfaction of external motivational factors, such as salary increases and good fit into a new school, motivates novice teachers to engage in PD; whereas satisfying all teachers' needs for competency, relatedness, and autonomy within the positive school culture increases the probability of teachers to take on self-directed PD.

In **Chapter 23**, Terry Kharyati reflects on his learning journey as the school administrator, working to ensure that all teachers, including new or novice teachers, are truly supported pedagogically, socially, emotionally, and individually. This chapter conveys his thoughts and notes jotted down during that journey as perceived through the music and lyrics of The Tragically Hip, and especially through their notion of *phantom power*. His reflection has led him to believe that, ironically, to be effective in supporting new teachers as a principal requires no phantom power at all.

In **Chapter 24**, Jenny Gonyou-Brown and Katina Pollock describe how Ontario elementary principals can draw from their teaching experience and resource networks to facilitate supports for the new teachers in their school. Driven by data collected from interviews with twelve elementary principals, this chapter considers principal work in dispatching supports to meet a range of individualized new teacher professional learning needs. Challenges that some principals identify in developing supports for new teachers are discussed, including the principals' intensifying workload, along with engaging new temporary, short-term teachers in supportive school-based collaborative learning. This chapter considers the merits of establishing supportive professional collaborative learning opportunities for all early career teachers.

Finally, in **Chapter 25**, we offer our editorial epilogue, summarizing the forum and authors' deliberations with attention to their insights and scholarly descriptions. We take comfort at the sight of various initiatives that take place across Canada to understand and support the needs of early career teachers, and seek to expand knowledge and understanding of the contextual and programmatic elements affecting their development. We anticipate that this book will generate even more interest, dialogue, and research among scholars, practitioners, and policy makers with regard to enhancing early career teaching scholarship and practice. We aspire to see this book used widely to encourage and to inspire hope for the readers, the advocates for early career teacher support and, of course, for those who are beginning their adventures as educators.

# References

Black, S. (2001). A lifeboat for new teachers. *American School Board Journal, 188*(9), 46–48.

Boreen, J., Johnson, M. K., Niday, D., & Potts, J. (2009). *Mentoring beginning teachers: Guiding, reflecting, coaching* (2nd ed.). Portland, ME: Stenhouse Publishers.

Borman, G., & Dowling, N. (2008). Teacher attrition and retention: A meta-analytic and narrative review of the research. *Review of Educational Research, 78*(3), 367–409.

Bronfenbrenner, U. (1994). Ecological models of human development. In T. Husen & T. N. Postlethwaite (Eds.), *International Encyclopedia of Education* (2nd ed., Vol. 3, pp. 1643–1647). Oxford, England: Pergamon Press.

Clandinin, D. J., Schaefer, L., Long, J. S., Steeves, P., McKenzie-Robblee, S., Pinnegar, E., & Downey, C. A. (2012). *Early career teacher attrition: problems, possibilities, potentials.* Edmonton, AB: Centre for Research for Teacher Education and Development, University of Alberta.

Clark, R., & Antonelli, F. (2009). *Why teachers leave: Results of an Ontario Survey 2006–08.* Toronto, ON: Ontario Teachers' Federation.

Clarke, P. (2000). *Learning schools, learning systems.* London, UK: Continuum.

Cochran-Smith, M. (2006). *Policy, practice, and politics in teacher education.* Thousand Oaks, CA: Corwin Press.

Colb, N. M. (2001). A survival guide for the teacher shortage. *Independent School, 61*(1), 72–77.

CTF. (2003). Teacher supply and demand series: Volume III. *CTF Economic and Member Services Bulletin* (2003–3).

CTF. (2004). Recruitment and retention of teachers: Why teachers entering the profession remain or leave. *CTF Economic and Member Services Bulletin* (2004–5), 1–20.

Darling-Hammond, L. (2001). The challenge of staffing our schools. *Educational Leadership, 58*(8), 12–17.

Darling-Hammond, L. (2003). Keeping good teachers: Why it matters, what leaders can do. *Educational Leadership, 60*(8), 6–13.

Darling-Hammond, L. (2006). Constructing 21st-century teacher education. *Journal of Teacher Education Policy Analysis Archives, 57*(3), 300–314.

Glazerman, S., Isenberg, E., Dolfin, S., Bleeker, M., Johnson, A., Grider, M., & Jacobus, M. (2010). *Impacts of comprehensive teacher induction: Final results from a randomized controlled study (NCEE 2010–4027)*. Washington, DC: National Center for Education Evaluation and Regional Assistance, Institute of Education Sciences, U.S. Department of Education.

Guarino, C. M., Santibañez, L., & Daley, G. A. (2006). Teacher recruitment and retention: A review of the recent empirical literature. *Review of Educational Research, 76*(2), 173–208. doi:10.3102/00346543076002173

Henry, G. T., Bastian, K. C., & Fortner, C. K. (2011). Stayers and leavers: Early-career teacher effectiveness and attrition. *Educational Researcher, 40*(6), 271–280.

Huling-Austin, L. (1986). What can and cannot reasonably be expected from teacher induction programs. *Journal of Teacher Education, 37*(1), 2–5. doi:10.1177/002248718603700101

Huling-Austin, L. (1988). *A synthesis of research on teacher Induction programs and practices*. Paper presented at the Annual Meeting of the America Educational Research Association, New Orleans, LA.

Huling-Austin, L., & Murphy, S. C. (1987). *Assessing the impact of teacher induction programs: Implications for program development*. Paper presented at the Annual Meeting of the American Educational Research Association, Washington, DC. http://www.eric.ed.gov/ERICWebPortal/recordDetail?accno=ED283779

Ingersoll, R. M. (2001). *Teacher turnover, teacher shortages and the organization of schools*. Seattle, WA: Center for the Study of Teaching and Policy, University of Washington.

Ingersoll, R. M., & Smith, T. M. (2003). The wrong solution to the teacher shortage. *Educational Leadership, 60*(8), 30–33.

Ingersoll, R. M., & Strong, M. (2011). The impact of induction and mentoring programs for beginning teachers: A critical review of the research. *Review of Education Research, 81*(2), 201–233.

Jones, M. (2003). Reconciling personal and professional values and beliefs with the reality of teaching: findings from an evaluative study of ten newly qualified teachers during their year of induction. *Teacher Development, 7*(3), 385–402.

Karsenti, T., & Collin, S. (2013). Why are new teachers leaving the profession? Results of a Canada-wide survey. *Education, 3*(3), 141–149. doi:10.5923/j.edu.20130303.01

Karsenti, T., Collin, S., Villeneuve, S., Dumouchel, G., & Roy, N. (2008). *Why are new French immersion and French as a second language teachers leaving the profession? Results of a Canada-wide survey.* Ottawa, ON: Canadian Association of Immersion Teachers.

Laitsch, D. (2005). The effect of new teacher induction programs on teacher migration and attrition. *Association for Supervision and Curriculum Development, 3*(5).

Mitchell, C., & Sackney, L. (2011). *Profound improvement: Building learning community capacity on living system principles* (2nd ed.). London, UK: Routledge.

OCT. (2004). *Transition to teaching report.* Toronto, ON: Ontario College of Teachers.

OCT. (2012). *Transition to teaching 2011: Early-career teachers in Ontario schools.* Toronto, ON: Ontario College of Teachers.

Odell, S. J., & Ferraro, D. P. (1992). Teacher mentoring and teacher retention. *Journal of Teacher Education, 43*(3), 200–204.

OECD. (2005). *Teachers matter: Attracting, developing and retaining effective teachers.* Paris, France: Organization for Economic Co-operation and Development Publishing.

Plunkett, M., & Dyson, M. (2011). Becoming a teacher and staying one: Examining the complex ecologies associated with educating and retaining new teachers in rural Australia. *Australian Journal of Teacher Education, 36*(1), 32–47.

Richardson, R. C., Glessner, L. L., & Tolson, H. (2010). Stopping the leak: Retaining beginning teachers. *Australian Journal of Teacher Education, 32*(2), 1–8.

Rivkin, S. G., Hanushek, E. A., & Kain, J. F. (2005). *Teachers, schools, and academic achievement.* Princeton, NJ: Econometrica.

Ryan, K., & Kokol, M. (1988). The aging teacher: A developmental perspective. *Peabody Journal of Education, 65*(3), 59–73.

Schaefer, L., Long, J. S., & Clandinin, D. J. (2012). Questioning the research on early career teacher attrition and retention. *Alberta Journal of Educational Research, 58*(1), 106–121.

Smith, T. M., & Ingersoll, R. M. (2004). What are the effects of induction and mentoring on beginning teacher turnover? *American Educational Research Journal, 41*(3), 681–714.

Smithers, A., & Robinson, P. (2003). *Factors affecting teachers' decisions to leave the profession.* Nottingham, UK: DfES.

Stoel, C. F., & Thant, T.-S. (2002). *Teachers' professional lives - A view from nine industrialized countries.* Washington, DC: Milken Family Foundation.

Strong, M. (2005). Teacher induction, mentoring, and retention: A summary of the research. *The New Educator, 1*(3), 181–198. doi:10.1080/154768.80590966295

Strong, M. (2006). Does new teacher support affect student achievement? *New Teacher Center at University of California Research Brief, 6*(1).

Wheatley, M. J. (1999). Bringing schools back to life: Schools as living systems. In F. M. Duffy & J. D. Dale (Eds.), *Creating successful school systems: Voices from the university, the field, and the community* (pp. 3–19). Norwood, MA: Christopher-Gordon Publishers.

# Part I

# The Voices of Early Career Teachers

# Mapping Out the Early Career Teachers' Needs: Findings from the Pan-Canadian Survey

*Benjamin Kutsyuruba, Keith D. Walker,*
*John G. Bosica Jr., Ian A. Matheson*

## Introduction

The quality and the abilities of teachers who work with our children and youth are commonly cited as the most significant school-based factors contributing to student achievement and educational improvement (Cochran-Smith, 2006; Darling-Hammond, 2006). Therefore, understanding new teachers' experiences with developing their quality performance and abilities through transition and socialization into school contexts and into the profession are pivotal (Howe, 2006; Kauffman, Johnson, Kardos, Liu, & Peske, 2002). This chapter outlines the results from a pan-Canadian *Teacher Induction Survey* (N=1343) where we explored beginning teachers' perceptions of induction and mentorship programs, with particular interest in retention and career issues. Along with demographic information about early career teachers, we also gathered information about teachers' experiences with mentorship, administration, the work environment, and their career and professional development. This initiative represents one of the phases in a multi-year pan-Canadian research project centered on exploring the differential impact of teacher induction and mentorship programs on the early-career teachers' retention, as perceived across the provinces and territories.

# Methodology

As one of the data collection instruments for the project, the online *Teacher Induction Survey* was developed by the researchers, based on suggestions and recommendations from an expert panel of researchers and practitioners, the relevant literature, and adapted items from related instruments. Overall, the survey contained 77 closed and 12 open-ended questions. The instrument was field-tested with the expert panel, principals, and teachers prior to distribution. The invitation to participate in the online survey for new teachers within their first five years of employment in a publicly funded school in Canada was distributed through various venues (e.g., teacher associations, ministries, community organizations, social media), across all provinces and territories in the spring-summer of 2016. With various degrees of completeness, the researchers received over 2000 responses to the survey from early career teachers, from all Canadian jurisdictions. Before engaging in data analysis, the researchers removed surveys with minimal responses or missing data that did not allow for further analyses. For the final sample (N=1343), the researchers obtained descriptive statistics, including percentages, means, and standard deviations for questions in the demographics section. For questions where respondents had been asked to use a Likert scale to indicate their response, means and standard deviations were calculated. For all open-ended qualitative responses, the researchers engaged in thematic coding; in addition, codes were developed to create categories based on emergent themes. In the presentation of data, quantitative data are complemented by direct quotations wherever possible throughout this chapter.

# Demographics

The demographic data for the study included six categories: age, gender, academic credentials, institution and province where respondents had received their accreditation, and the province where the respondents were living and teaching at time of survey completion. The mean age of the respondents was 29, with 19% being male and 81% being female. Significantly, 96% of the respondents had a Bachelor of Education degree, and 27% of the respondents had other forms of credentials (M.Sc., B.A., B.Sc., etc.). While the current teaching location for the majority of participants represented three provinces, Ontario (33 percent), Alberta (27 percent), and British Columbia (18 percent), all of the provinces and territories were represented in this study. This trend reflected the province in which the respondents obtained their teacher certification/accreditation: 33% of the respondents in Ontario, 27% in Alberta, and 18% in British Columbia. In regards to the institutions, fifteen percent of the respondents received their accreditation from the University of Alberta, 13% from Queen's University, 8% from the University of British Columbia, and 5% from Simon Fraser University; while the rest (61%) represented graduates from other universities across Canada and worldwide (See Table 1 for detailed demographic information).

**Table 1**
*Demographic Information*

| Province Currently Teaching In | | Province of Accreditation | |
|---|---|---|---|
| Ontario | 33% | Ontario | 38% |
| Alberta | 27% | Alberta | 23% |
| British Columbia | 18% | British Columbia | 18% |
| Quebec | 5% | Quebec | 5% |
| Manitoba | 4% | Manitoba | 5% |
| Saskatchewan | 6% | Saskatchewan | 4% |
| Newfoundland and Labrador | 2% | Newfoundland and Labrador | 3% |
| New Brunswick | 0.38% | New Brunswick | 1% |
| Nova Scotia | 0.38% | Nova Scotia | 1% |
| Prince Edward Island | 0.38% | Prince Edward Island | 1% |
| Nunavut | 1% | Nunavut | 0.3% |
| Northwest Territories | 1% | Northwest Territories | 0.15% |
| Yukon | 1% | Yukon | 2% |
| **Age Range** | | **Accreditation Program** | |
| 19-22 | 1% | University of Alberta | 13% |
| 23-26 | 34% | Queen's University | 13% |
| 27-30 | 35% | University of British Columbia | 8% |
| 31-34 | 14% | Simon Fraser University | 5% |
| 35+ | 17% | Other | 61% |

According to respondents from all provinces, 85% have had experience as an Occasional Teacher, with 28% being in service for less than 1 year, 19% for a full year, 22% for 2 years, 15% for 3 years, 8% for 4 years, and 9% for 5 years. As for the overall years of teaching experience, data showed almost equal distribution: 20% were in their first year, 23% in their second year, 21% in their third year, 16% in their fourth year, and 20% in their fifth year. The question of grade level experience continued this trend of equal distribution, with each individual grade having had over 35% of the respondents having taught at that level. Grade 10 was the most highly taught grade with 26% of active respondents indicating that they had taught at that level. Again, each grade, except for Kindergarten at 16%, had a similar representation with Grade 1 to Grade 12 having over 21% representation (See Table 2). Surprisingly, when asked how many teachers were teaching outside of their subject area, 37% noted they were teaching outside of the area that they had been prepared for, and for every three teachers who were teaching inside a grade level that they had been trained for, one teacher was teaching outside their grade level. Two-thirds (67%) indicated that they were teaching outside of the typical classroom setting, of which special education accounted for 37%, French Immersion for 24% and tutoring for 23%.

**Table 2**
*Experience as An Occasional Teacher*

| Yes | 85% | No | 15% |
|---|---|---|---|
| **Length of Service as Occasional Teacher** | | **Overall Years Teaching** | |
| Less Than One Year | 28% | In Their First Year | 20% |
| Full Year | 19% | In Their Second Year | 23% |
| Two Years | 22% | In Their Third Year | 21% |
| Three Years | 15% | In Their Fourth Year | 16% |
| Four Years | 8% | In Their Fifth Year | 20% |
| Five Years | 9% | | |
| **Grade Level Experience** | | **Current Grade Level** | |
| Kindergarten | 35% | Kindergarten | 16% |
| Grade One | 41% | Grade One | 21% |
| Grade Two | 41% | Grade Two | 21% |
| Grade Three | 41% | Grade Three | 20% |

| | | | |
|---|---|---|---|
| Grade Four | 43% | Grade Four | 21% |
| Grade Five | 45% | Grade Five | 21% |
| Grade Six | 45% | Grade Six | 21% |
| Grade Seven | 46% | Grade Seven | 23% |
| Grade Eight | 47% | Grade Eight | 23% |
| Grade Nine | 44% | Grade Nine | 25% |
| Grade Ten | 42% | Grade Ten | 26% |
| Grade Eleven | 40% | Grade Eleven | 25% |
| Grade Twelve | 37% | Grade Twelve | 22% |
| Other | 14% | Other | 16% |

Over a third of the respondents (37%) had been at their current school for less than a year. Twenty-three percent had been at their school for a full year, 22% for two years, 10% for three years, 5% for four years, and 4% for five years. Moreover, the majority of these schools were in a small city (examples provided included Saint John, Drummondville, and Red Deer).

# Research Findings

In the following sections, we present key findings from select questions from the survey. These are grouped into the following themes: the type and nature of support, mentorship experiences, administrator engagement in induction processes, working environment, and career and professional development. Wherever appropriate, we offer verbatim quotes from the participants' open-ended responses (with indication of province) to complement the statistical data analysis from closed survey items.

## Type and Nature of Support

When asked about the type of support they had received as a beginning teacher, 82% said they had received professional development, with 73% receiving informal mentorship, compared to only 27% receiving formal mentorship. Over 40% of the respondents noted having received the most beneficial support from their informal mentors, 14% from professional development, 10% from resource sharing amongst peers, and 6% from networking with other teachers (See Table 3). The majority (37%) of their support came from their school, 35% came from their school board and

18% came from their teacher association or union.

**Table 3**
**Support for New Teachers**

| Type of Support | | Most Beneficial Support | |
|---|---|---|---|
| Professional Development | 82% | Informal Mentorship | 44% |
| Informal Mentorship | 73% | Professional Development | 14% |
| Formal Mentorship | 27% | Resource Sharing with Peers | 14% |

When asked whether or not the support they had experienced met their needs as a beginning teacher, participants' responses varied among those that were exclusively positive, exclusively negative, and mixed. Regarding *formal programming*, some beginning teachers believed that the new teacher orientation and professional development they received had been helpful in meeting their needs, and that they had been given adequate planning time to prepare for teaching. Others indicated that the formal programming took too much time away from the classroom and that the professional development and orientation were insufficient or unhelpful. Some participants indicated that they had not been given enough planning time to prepare for teaching. A number of beginning teachers indicated that they did not qualify for formal support, given their non-permanent status or because their position at a school had commenced after the formal support had begun. Many of the respondents also shared that they had to seek out their own support, instead of support being provided to them by someone else's initiative. The following quotations illustrate respondents' experiences:

> There is a wealth of information available and as a new teacher having access to professional development has helped me with my planning and delivery of lessons. (Alberta)

> The New Teacher Induction Program I completed in my very first year of teaching I found to be very overwhelming. It involved a lot of time away from the classroom, and there-fore lots of booking and preparing for sub teachers. I didn't 'click' with my mentor teacher so I didn't feel very motivated or encouraged by them. Overall I found the program added more work and didn't add value. (Alberta).

*Colleague support* emerged as a positive source for beginning teachers, where colleagues listened, collaborated with beginning teachers, observed beginning teachers' practice, and provided resources. These were examples of how colleagues met beginning teachers' needs. Beginning teachers indicated that formal experienced mentors were helpful in meeting their needs, and many also indicated that they had developed their own informal mentors in their colleagues who had supported their growth. Respondents who said they felt that colleague support was non-existent or not helpful indicated that they had not received nor benefited from observation of their teaching from a mentor or colleague, that they had a poor relationship with their formal mentor, or that their mentor had not provided them with resources. For example:

> Yes, I have been very lucky to have many colleagues provide me with advice, materials, and support. (Alberta)

> My NTIP Mentor was too busy to mentor me, and actually worked against me by talking to my Principal behind closed doors despite it being against the rules. (Ontario)

The perceived *level of formal support* was directly related to their satisfaction with the support or the lack thereof. For beginning teachers who felt that they were well supported, administrators were commended for their support and feedback, as were the district and teachers' union personnel. New teachers who felt their needs had not been met indicated that administrators were not supportive of them, that formal support systems were poorly implemented, and that they were not receiving support from above to meet their students' needs. Two differing perspectives – positive and negative perceptions - are described in the following quotes, typical for each of the points of view:

> Definitely. The administration is very active and played a large part in my growth. As did the division's supervising teacher. They gave me a lot of advice that was largely helpful. Also every co-worker was more than willing to share resources. (Alberta)

... No one has supported me in my classroom to deal with management issues. My students who require additional learning/behaviour supports are not receiving them, despite many requests. It is all falling to me to deal with on my own. (British Columbia)

Beginning teachers identified elements of their teaching experience that had either *met* or *not met* their needs. Some cited feelings of comfort and confidence within their school environment as an indication that their needs were being met. Others noted that they were made to feel that they were a part of the school community, and some shared that they felt comfortable to communicate issues they had experienced with colleagues and administrators.

Elements of beginning teachers' personal experiences that did not meet their needs included feelings of isolation and of being undervalued within the school. Some felt that expectations of them had not been communicated, and some beginning teachers shared that they were afraid to seek help within their school. Several beginning French teachers pointed out that formal support did not seem to be designed for their unique needs, and many beginning teachers actually felt that the formal support provided added more stress to their lives.

I think it has, because I have become more comfortable and a lot more confident over the course of this year. (Alberta)

... it has been very minimal as an [occasional teacher], and it's really up to me to ask for help if I need it. Otherwise there's no real organized initiative to support us. (Ontario)

## Mentorship Experiences

Over two thirds of the respondents (67%) noted that they had had a mentor. Of that number, 77% had an informal mentor, 55% reported rarely or never having their mentor observe them in class, 44% reported that their mentor encouraged them to try different teaching approaches often or very often, and 66% of the respondents reported that at least sometimes they had worked with more experienced teachers to plan collaboratively (See Table 4)

**Table 4.**
*Mentorship Experiences*

| Question/Statement | N | R | S | O | VO | N/A |
|---|---|---|---|---|---|---|
| How frequently do you and your mentor meet? | 4% | 15% | 30% | 21% | 12% | 18% |
| My mentor provides constructive feedback about my practice. | 9% | 15% | 29% | 20% | 8% | 20% |
| My mentor provides constructive feedback about my students' learning. | 10% | 16% | 30% | 18% | 5% | 21% |
| My mentor clearly communicates school expectations. | 9% | 9% | 22% | 26% | 10% | 23% |
| My mentor observes my teaching to enable more effective practice. | 34% | 20% | 16% | 6% | 3% | 21% |
| My mentor encourages me to try out different teaching approaches. | 7% | 8% | 22% | 29% | 15% | 19% |
| My mentor guides me to set goals related to student learning. | 11% | 11% | 22% | 25% | 10% | 21% |
| My mentor and I have professional conversations. | 3% | 4% | 15% | 32% | 28% | 18% |
| I work with more experienced teachers to plan collaboratively. | 7% | 12% | 24% | 23% | 19% | 16% |
| My mentor and I discuss my ongoing career planning. | 16% | 18% | 21% | 16% | 9% | 20% |
| My mentor helps me to communicate with school administration. | 18% | 15% | 20% | 14% | 10% | 23% |
| Mentoring helps me with my personal development. | 9% | 9% | 21% | 25% | 18% | 19% |

*Note.* N = Never, R = Rarely, S = Sometimes, O = Often, VO = Very Often, N/A = Not Applicable.

Three major themes emerged from the open-ended responses of Canadian beginning teachers regarding the different ways that mentors had been valuable to them and their teaching, indicating value through *general collaboration, guidance for teaching, and non-teaching guidance.* Responses that involved the mentor and mentee working together were considered to be collaboration, and responses that involved the mentor providing material or modelling behaviour were considered to be guidance. Mentors who provided value through collaboration with beginning teachers did so in helping with report cards, co-planning for teaching, and co-developing resources to use in teaching. Mentors who guided beginning teachers in teaching provided resources, modeled their own teaching practices, and modeled communication practices to students. Mention was made of a number of instances where mentors guided beginning teachers in non-teaching contexts. For example, it was shared that mentors provided general career feedback and advice, and assisted with a number of first-time experiences, including speaking with parents and how to handle students failing courses. The following quotations illustrate some of the respondents' experiences:

> Collaboration within lesson planning, decoding the curriculum, making me aware of policies and regulations, and finding resources. (Alberta)

> As a model for building positive relationships with students and classroom management. (Ontario)

> By supporting me in situations where I've had to make tough calls -- failing a student, contacting parents about plagiarism, etc. (Alberta)

Beginning teachers also shared challenges that they had experienced with mentoring *processes, structure, and relationships*. Challenges related to mentoring processes included finding time to meet and understanding responsibilities within the mentor-mentee relationship, and many also indicated that the mentoring process had added more stress. Overall, the sentiment was that there was not enough time to meet together during the school day/week.

In terms of structural challenges with mentoring, many beginning teachers indicated that they had wanted but had not received observation of their teaching or had not received feedback from their mentor. Beginning teachers felt that having a mentor either out of the subject area or grade presented a structural challenge, as did having a mentor from outside of their school or community. Some beginning teachers shared that a lack of budget for funding their mentor-mentee meet-ups presented a structural challenge, and that there were not enough formal activities related to mentorship. Some beginning teachers felt the relationship created a power dynamic challenge in that they felt beneath the mentor. Some non-permanent beginning teachers indicated that they had structural issues with general access to a mentor.

> I was formally matched with a mentor who had never taught the same grade level as me. She was also assigned to a different school. It was difficult to connect with her as we had very little in common and did not interact regularly. I feel like mentoring partnerships should be developed more naturally between two people who can connect more authentically. (Ontario)

In terms of relationship challenges with mentoring, beginning teachers shared that having a different style and/or personality than their mentor had created challenges, as had the feeling that they had become too much of a burden through their relying on the support of their mentor. Some beginning teachers indicated that their mentor had not shared resources with them, and in some cases, that they felt their mentor did not care about them.

> Just being told sometimes the way that I must do something even if I don't necessarily agree. I understand that the other teachers are very experienced but sometimes I would like to try out a new idea and not worry about the other grade teachers being upset with me planning something different. (Ontario)

The mentor-mentee relationship, whether formal or informal, had a wide-reaching impact on the induction of beginning teachers into the profession. The combination of positive and negative experiences shared by respondents suggests that individual differences impact how mentoring support was received.

## Administrator Engagement in Induction Processes

The role and importance of the administrator in the induction process yielded mixed responses across Canada. A considerable number of participants (35%) could not comment about the administrators' engagement due to a lack of direct experience. Across Canada, one-fifth of the respondents (21%) strongly disagreed that their school administrator had played a key role in the relationship between them and their mentor. Almost 45% agreed or strongly agreed that their school administrator took an active interest in their successful induction into teaching. As part of this active interest, 53% of respondents were in agreement that their administrator had observed their teaching, with approximately 47% agreeing that these observations had led to feedback that helped improve their teaching. When asked if they were encouraged to question their beliefs about teaching, 45% of respondents agreed and 40% indicated that they were given the opportunity to observe other methods of teaching. Additionally, 60% of the respondents agreed or strongly agreed that their school administrator shared leadership and promoted a collaborative culture in their school. Over half (63%) of the respondents agreed or strongly agreed that they felt comfortable talking to their school administrator about problems they were experiencing, with 59% agreeing or strongly agreeing that overall they felt supported by their school's administrative team (See Table 5).

**Table 5**
*Administration Support*

| Statement | SD | D | D/A | A | SA | N/A |
|---|---|---|---|---|---|---|
| My school administrator plays a key role in the professional relationship between my mentor and me. | 21% | 17% | 14% | 8% | 4% | 35% |
| My school administrator has taken an active interest in my successful induction to teaching. | 12% | 15% | 18% | 28% | 16% | 11% |
| My current school administrator clearly communicates school expectations. | 6% | 13% | 15% | 38% | 22% | 8% |
| My current school administrator values the role my mentor plays in my induction to teaching. | 8% | 8% | 24% | 17% | 8% | 36% |
| I believe my working conditions are appropriate for a beginning teacher. | 15% | 20% | 14% | 31% | 12% | 8% |
| I am encouraged to question my beliefs about teaching. | 6% | 16% | 26% | 34% | 11% | 7% |
| I am given opportunities to observe models of good teaching and learning. | 14% | 25% | 15% | 30% | 10% | 6% |
| I have adequate time to reflect on student learning. | 12% | 27% | 20% | 29% | 7% | 5% |
| My mentor and I are given adequate time to meet. | 15% | 18% | 15% | 13% | 6% | 33% |

| | SD | D | D/A | A | SA | N/A |
|---|---|---|---|---|---|---|
| My current school administrator shares leadership and promotes a collaborative culture in our school. | 8% | 10% | 15% | 36% | 24% | 7% |
| My current school administrator observes my teaching. | 12% | 17% | 11% | 37% | 16% | 8% |
| My school administrator gives me feedback based on observation(s) to help me improve my teaching. | 13% | 18% | 12% | 31% | 16% | 11% |
| My current school administrator is part of the reason I am still a teacher. | 21% | 16% | 21% | 19% | 14% | 9% |
| I feel comfortable talking to my school administrator(s) about problems I am experiencing. | 10% | 12% | 11% | 38% | 25% | 5% |
| As a new teacher, I feel supported by my current school's administrative team. | 9% | 10% | 17% | 34% | 25% | 5% |

*Note.* SD = Strongly Disagree, D = Disagree, D/A = Neither Agree nor Disagree, A = Agree, SA = Strongly Agree, N/A = Not Applicable.

In the open-ended responses, beginning teachers shared mixed feelings when asked about their school administrator and whether or not this person had wanted them to succeed. Some beginning teachers provided a *neutral* response by indicating that they did not know whether or not their administrator wanted them to succeed, but some felt their administrator did not care. Some non-permanent beginning teachers shared that they did not have an administrator, given the nature of their current employment. The following quotations illustrate respondents' experiences:

> I honestly don't know that. I feel my administrators have their own agendas and I am just a piece of their puzzle. I feel that I am replaceable. I do have a good relationship with them and feel that I can ask them questions or advice, but I honestly feel that they only want me to succeed to make them look better, not for my own personal growth. (Manitoba)

Beginning teachers shared that their administrator had *espoused* their desire for beginning teachers to succeed. Espoused desires entailed administrators giving beginning teachers advice, encouragement, and positive feedback. Some beginning teachers noted that their administrators had explicitly expressed their desire to keep them on staff and many beginning teachers also noted that administrators were clear about their goals and hopes for beginning teachers. Administrators also verbally assured beginning teachers that it was OK when things did not go as planned in the classroom.

> She has checked in and asked about my future teaching plans/goals, where do I see myself, encouraging comments about my rapport with students and teaching style, offered positive and constructive feedback following an interview. (Alberta)

Beginning teachers also shared that their administrator had *demonstrated* their desired intentions to help beginning teachers succeed. Demonstrated desire included administrators providing support, collaborating with beginning teachers, observing their teaching, and assisting them through the evaluation process. Administrators who demonstrated this desire were available to talk, checked-in regularly, listened to beginning teachers' concerns, and generally cared about them. Administrators also demonstrated desire by offering a contract, recommending a beginning teacher for work, and by covering classes and offering relief time when possible. Administrators gave beginning teachers opportunities for professional development, pushed and challenged them to improve, trusted them to succeed, and gave them freedom to experiment with their teaching. Some beginning teachers also reported that administrators wanted them to succeed because they wanted the school and students to succeed.

> They check in on my classes, and ask what I need. They volunteer their time to talk with me about challenges I might be facing with my kids. They're kind and involved. My current administration is awesome ... (British Columbia)

The mixed responses to why beginning teachers knew their administrator wanted them to succeed shed light on the types of relationships administrators had with their novice staff members, as well as the styles with which they operated in leading their school.

## Working Environment
Over 70% of the respondents agreed or strongly agreed that they had felt integrated into their school, and 80% agreed or strongly agreed that other teachers listened to their thoughts and opinions. Furthermore, over 80% agreed or strongly agreed that they had felt respected as a colleague in their

school. Over 80% agreed or strongly agreed that their school had an overall inclusive and supportive culture. The majority of teachers (79%) agreed or strongly agreed that in general they had thrived as a teacher. Over 90% agreed or strongly agreed that as a teacher they know their strengths and weaknesses, and 87% agreed or strongly agreed that they are proud to tell others that they are a teacher. Unfortunately, 71% agreed or strongly agreed that their first year of teaching was experienced as "trial by fire." But when asked if they regularly considered leaving the teaching profession it was good to hear that 31% responded that they disagreed with that statement and 33% had never thought this. Additionally, over 90% of the respondents from all provinces agreed or strongly agreed that caring for their students was what kept them coming into work each day (See Table 6).

## Table 6
### Working Environment

| Statement | SD | D | D/A | A | SA | N/A |
|---|---|---|---|---|---|---|
| I am expected to focus on student learning. | 1% | 2% | 9% | 56% | 29% | 3% |
| My successes are regularly acknowledged. | 7% | 17% | 24% | 36% | 12% | 4% |
| I've had opportunities to observe models of excellent teaching and learning in my current school. | 13% | 25% | 15% | 32% | 11% | 5% |
| I am expected to engage in professional learning and development. | 1% | 4% | 9% | 49% | 32% | 4% |
| In my school, teachers take responsibility to develop and improve their own teaching practice. | 1% | 5% | 13% | 55% | 21% | 5% |
| At my school, we have professional learning and development that encourages career-long learning. | 4% | 13% | 22% | 37% | 16% | 9% |
| I have participated in professional development specific to new teachers. | 8% | 15% | 6% | 42% | 24% | 5% |
| There is informal peer-mentoring (or group mentoring) in my school. | 11% | 16% | 14% | 34% | 15% | 9% |
| As a teacher, I know my strengths (things I do well). | 0% | 2% | 6% | 53% | 39% | 0% |
| As a teacher, I am aware of my weaknesses (things I don't yet do well). | 0% | 2% | 2% | 57% | 38% | 0% |

| I have taught students from diverse backgrounds. | 0% | 6% | 6% | 38% | 49% | 1% |

*Note.* SD = Strongly Disagree, D = Disagree, A/D = Neither Agree nor Disagree, A = Agree, SA = Strongly Agree, N/A = Not Applicable.

Factors that had been instrumental in beginning teachers remaining in the teaching profession emerged as *internal* and *external* factors. Beginning teachers noted that self-reflection of practice, reminding oneself of one's own limitations, having a hope that things would improve and change, and having had passion for teaching a subject area, and/or for helping students were all internal factors. Many beginning teachers noted that having had a balance between work and life was instrumental in their continuing in the profession. Other internal factors included feeling that teaching was part of their identity, enjoying the lifestyle of both the hours and having summers off, and that the job was very rewarding. Beginning teachers also indicated that their enjoyment of the profession, feeling capable within it, and having both a desire to improve and not to give up were instrumental in them remaining as teachers. Some beginning teachers also indicated that the challenge of teaching kept them coming back, and others identified their own faith as an instrumental factor in them that helped them to continue within the teaching profession: "I love kids and I enjoy what I do tremendously. I love the people I work with and am passionate about education in general" (Alberta).

Beginning teachers identified support from colleagues, administration, the school community, family, and friends as external factors that were instrumental in their continuing within the teaching profession. Many beginning teachers emphasized that the students had been the most instrumental factor in them continuing in the teaching profession: "The daily satisfaction I get from my students" (Alberta), said one. Other external factors included professional development, counselling, and income as instrumental factors to encourage their remaining within the profession.

Beginning teachers identified *personal* factors, *staff*, and *structures* as examples of what had allowed them to sustain their own well-being and to "flourish" or "thrive," as a beginning teacher; though some beginning teachers indicated that they had not felt they were thriving or flourishing, but merely *surviving*. Having a balance between work and life, getting a good sleep, engaging in regular physical activity, and faith were all cited as personal factors that had allowed some beginning teachers to thrive. Other beginning teachers mentioned having confidence in their abilities, passion for the profession and/or their teaching subject, having perspective and tempering expectations of what was possible as a new teacher, and taking time to reflect. Beginning teachers also indicated that recognizing daily successes, staying organized, having a strong work ethic, and taking time to prepare were reasons they had thrived. Some beginning teachers indicated that to thrive they needed to work nights (and weekends) to plan their material for teaching.

> Making sure I have healthy work-life balance. This is something that I have struggled with since the start of my teaching career. I only recently started to take more time for my life and relationships outside of work. Having the balance helps me feel rejuvenated and gives me the motivation to continue learning and thriving as a teacher. (Alberta)

In terms of staff-related supports, beginning teachers were able to thrive thanks to staff mentoring, resource sharing, collaborating with others, and feeling generally supported by colleagues. Beginning teachers also mentioned that being able to ask for help and feeling supported by administrators allowed them to thrive, as did experiencing a positive work environment within the school community.

> Formal and informal mentoring from teachers on staff- good conversations/encouragement. Regular massage and exercise for balance and a healthy lifestyle ... (Alberta)

> Structures including part-time work, sick days, and professional learning time all were mentioned as reasons undergirding beginning teachers in their thriving. A number of beginning teachers attributed their thriving to the impact that their students had on them: "[It's due to] My students and seeing their aha moments" (Quebec).

Beginning teachers reflected on how the intensity and pace of the profession had affected their induction and socialization, and for this they provided both *personal* and *work*-related examples. Wanting more downtime at home, feeling a general sense of fatigue, both physically and mentally, and the negative influence on social life were mentioned by a number of beginning teachers as personal examples. Others indicated that the profession had affected their family time, made them become introverted over time, and had increased their feelings of isolation. Others indicated that things had improved over time, and some beginning teachers indicated that the profession had had no effect on their induction and socialization: "I have struggled in my 1st year to work less than 10 hours a day and felt extremely tired and burnt out some days" (Saskatchewan).

In terms of work-related examples, beginning teachers indicated that they had become increasingly busy, that they had no time for extra-curricular activities within the school, and that there were always extra jobs for them to do, including various forms of supervision. Some beginning teachers indicated that their social life within the school community had increased; while their personal social life had dwindled, and some even claimed that they no longer had a social life because of the profession. Many felt that work was all consuming and that the workload was too intense, especially at certain times of the year (e.g. report card production period). Some beginning teachers mentioned that they felt staff rooms were zones of negativity, and that they had become more negative because of the profession; though many also indicated that other teachers had become friends because they truly understood the demands of the profession and their influence on personal lives.

> It has had a negative effect. Everyone is just too busy and too stressed. I have learned to avoid staff rooms at most schools, as they are often negative energy zones with overworked teachers constantly airing concerns in an unproductive manner. (Alberta)

Beginning teachers were asked to put themselves in the shoes of mentors, and to comment on what they would do as mentors to support beginning teachers. Responses included gestures that had to do with the mentor-mentee *relationship* and gestures that were *teaching or school-related*. Beginning teachers indicated that they would be encouraging, honest, supportive, approachable, and confidential in order to support their mentee. Many beginning teachers mentioned that they would regularly check-in with their mentee to see how things are going, and to particularly check-in about their mentees' personal health, as this can become an issue with the stresses of teaching in the early-career stages especially. Other beginning teachers indicated that they would find something to do with their mentee outside of work to build their relationship, and some indicated that they would ask mentees what they needed. A number of beginning teachers mentioned that they would make sure to just listen to their mentees about their needs and concerns: "Ensure their personal health is high, check in often to see how they are doing. Plan together every now and then. Meet regularly" (Alberta).

Related to teaching and school, beginning teachers suggested a number of gestures, including: sharing resources, helping to build their mentee's network, and helping with the general transition to the school and with routines. Other beginning teachers indicated that they would observe the new teacher and/or give the mentee an opportunity to observe them teaching, and that they would provide feedback. Many beginning teachers reported that they would team-teach with their mentee, collaborate with them in planning and using classroom strategies, show them different teaching styles, and edit their plans if desired. Some beginning teachers indicated that they would help mentees with time management, help them deal with administration and advocate for them, and generally discuss the profession together.

> Give them an entire unit plan that is ready to teach. Offer them support in their personal lives as well as their professional lives. Act as their champion and advocate to administrators and colleagues. Tell them often, in no uncertain terms, the great things they are doing. (Alberta)

Beginning teachers' responses regarding the ideal role of the mentor provided insight into the areas in which novices could have used more support during their first few years of teaching.

## Career and Professional Development

When asked if they were expected to engage in additional professional development, over 80% agreed or strongly agreed and over 75% agreed or strongly agreed that, at their school, teachers take responsibility to develop and improve their own teaching practice (See Table 7).

**Table 7**
*Career and Professional Development*

| Statement | SD | D | D/A | A | SA | N/A |
|---|---|---|---|---|---|---|
| I feel I am well integrated into my current school community. | 2% | 9% | 14% | 44% | 27% | 4% |
| Other teachers listen to my thoughts and opinions. | 1% | 5% | 11% | 55% | 25% | 2% |
| I feel respected as a colleague in this school. | 1% | 5% | 10% | 53% | 28% | 3% |
| I feel I have earned the trust of my fellow staff members in this school. | 1% | 3% | 12% | 52% | 29% | 4% |
| My school has an inclusive and supportive culture. | 3% | 7% | 15% | 45% | 26% | 4% |
| In my school, teachers are engaged in decision making processes about matters that affect them. | 6% | 12% | 15% | 43% | 17% | 6% |
| In general, I thrive as a teacher. | 1% | 6% | 13% | 47% | 32% | 1% |
| Teaching experiences in my first years can be described as "trial by fire". | 1% | 9% | 16% | 38% | 33% | 2% |
| I regularly consider leaving the teaching profession. | 33% | 31% | 14% | 15% | 8% | 1% |
| I am proud to tell others that I am a teacher. | 1% | 3% | 8% | 36% | 51% | 1% |
| Caring for students keeps me coming into work each day. | 0% | 2% | 6% | 38% | 54% | 1% |

*Note.* SD = Strongly Disagree, D = Disagree, A/D = Neither Agree nor Disagree, A = Agree, SA = Strongly Agree, N/A = Not Applicable.

Beginning teachers identified three sources of an expectation for them to engage in professional learning and development—*colleagues, personal, and senior*. Colleagues made explicit recommendations to beginning teachers in terms of their engagement in professional learning and development. Many beginning teachers identified a personal desire to help students, to grow as an educator, and to stay current as sources of their expectation to engage in professional learning and development. Beginning teachers indicated that administration was a source through both pressure and encouragement, and that some expectations were felt coming from the school board, high teaching quality standards, and their provincial governments—all examples of senior sources. The following quotations illustrate respondents' experiences:

> It's always available and other colleagues share opportunities they're aware of, so others can take part. (Ontario)

> Myself, I want to be a better teacher. My responsibility [as] a teacher is to learn new ways to help my students learn. (Alberta)

> Administration encourages collaboration and provides opportunities, suggestions and support to attend and participate in PD opportunities. (Alberta)

Beginning teachers identified examples of *personal ventures* and *external factors* as the best and most effective sources for their own professional development. Personal ventures included the use of social media and online resources. Many beginning teachers indicated that the best and most effective sources for their professional development were times spent in the classroom with their students and times spent reflecting and focusing on their own personal growth, without any pressure from others to do so.

> The classroom. That is it. The failures and successes made in the classroom on a daily basis and the reflection upon them. The formal PD sessions and get-togethers have taken away from my much-needed prep time. I am trying to survive the day to day and learn how to just get through. The essentials are the beginning point and much of what is being discussed and emphasized at PD is going beyond what I am currently capable of and taking time away from the practical in order to get theoretical and abstract when that is not what I currently need. (Alberta)

External factors included other teachers, in cases where beginning teachers identified observations of and from other teachers, conversations, collaborations, and informal mentorship as effective sources of professional development. Others noted formal, embedded professional development sessions as effective sources of professional development, including conferences, a variety of content sessions, mentorship sessions, school-based professional development, and new teacher programs. Some beginning teachers indicated that resource sharing, school district publications, teachers' associations and external learning sessions had provided them with effective professional development.

> Having a colleague look at my lessons, assignments, etc., and make suggestions. [Discussing] classroom management techniques with colleagues. (Saskatchewan)

When asked about what advice they might give to teachers who were just starting their career, they provided advice that was both *personal* and *work-related*; although many beginning teachers' advice was to avoid the profession and find another career. For personal advice, beginning teachers suggested that new teachers should work to just make it through a certain amount of time (first few months, first year) before making major decisions about their career; but that at some point new teachers should reflect on whether or not the profession was truly for them. Other beginning teachers suggested tempering expectations, pacing themselves, not taking things personally, not expecting affirmations, and expecting both change and criticism. Other personal advice included taking risks, advocating for oneself, prioritizing, exercising, and generally having fun with it.

> Pace yourself and enjoy every moment of it ... (Alberta)

> Don't teach unless you really feel the calling to do so. It is a difficult field to get into and you don't want to wait x amount of years to get true experience as a classroom teacher. (Ontario)

Work-related advice included asking questions, planning, going electronic with resources, finding good resources, and using hands-on activities. Other beginning teachers suggested finding balance, not being afraid to teach differently than colleagues or mentors, knowing the curriculum and the students, and staying organized. Some beginning teachers recommended that new teachers try substitute teaching. Other work-related advice included picking your battles with students and colleagues, getting involved with the school community and living close to the school, if possible. As well, they mentioned communicating with parents, observing other teachers, and developing a network of colleagues. A number of beginning teachers emphasized the importance of finding a mentor, whether formal or informal: "Find a good mentor. Develop a close relationship with your administration. Avoid the negative teachers in the staff room!" (Alberta).

To conclude the survey, beginning teachers were asked if there was anything else that they felt the researchers should know. A variety of responses were provided that fit within the themes of *support*, the *profession*, and *mentoring and induction*. Related to support, beginning teachers pointed out that administration could really make a difference for better or for worse, as can the school community. Some expressed concerns and frustrations that evaluations were unfair, there were a lack of resources and support, and that beginning teachers were given unfair class assignments. Some beginning teachers expressed their beliefs in a need for more team teaching.

> New teachers are put into the positions that other teachers don't want. I don't believe that experienced teachers should have to take undesirable assignments either, but offering more part-time contracts would make difficult assignments more manageable, especially for new teachers. (Alberta)

In terms of the profession, beginning teachers also reported a number of concerns and frustrations, including: that expectations for teachers are too high, that there are a lack of jobs, that hiring systems are poor and inconsistent, and that class sizes needed to be smaller. Many new teachers expressed frustration about teacher training, feeling that it needs improvement, and many even suggested that the profession should adopt an apprenticeship model for new teachers to ease transition. Other beginning teachers expressed that teachers are not paid enough and easily burnt out, and many also cited a lack of focus on teachers' mental health. Some beginning teachers expressed frustrations with the government, specifically with the perceived emphasis on students passing, frequent shifts in education initiatives and focuses, and the introduction of Regulation 274 (Ontario). Beginning teachers' frustrations and concerns also related to the lack of opportunity for teachers to specialize in a subject or a few subjects, that not enough prep time is given to teachers, and generally about the difficulties related to dealing with parents. While many of the profession-related responses were negative, a number of beginning teachers emphasized that teaching is an incredibly rewarding profession.

> Beginning teachers are often the first people to devalue their role in a school. We need consistent and positive feedback. We also won't know about burnout until we are in the midst of it. Our mentors and administrators need resources and support to recognize the signs of burnout in beginning teachers and to help us to manage and rectify our burnout. (Alberta)

Beginning teachers provided a variety of responses related to the mentoring and induction of new teachers, including that mentor teachers needed more training, and that many wanted extended mentoring and support beyond the initial year or two years provided. Some beginning teachers expressed frustrations about the lack of mentoring and induction support; specifically in Northern Canada, where some teachers went without mentors, and with non-permanent staff that were not able to access support given their status. Some beginning teachers felt that the mentoring and induction support provided to them was too vague, and many felt that they needed specific services such as observation of their teaching for their growth. Other beginning teachers expressed that they were given no induction program, and some who were given induction programs felt these were too time consuming. A large number of beginning teachers expressed that mentoring, whether formal or informal, made a huge difference in their personal growth and induction into the profession.

> The first few years of teaching are incredibly difficult because your job is not steady. Most of the time you are just a substitute and are waiting for a contract. At this time there is no support. The year where I had a contract, it seemed as if there was no one I could turn to. I felt like I had to do most of everything on my own. My teacher partner was also young and did not provide adequate support. A teacher with a lot of experience is needed to provide the support necessary. It doesn't matter if they are teaching the same grade or cycle. (Alberta)

It was evident that most respondents felt grateful and appreciative to have had the opportunities to voice their concerns, both with formal questions in the survey and in the final open-question; hoping that change was possible and that their voices might be heard.

# Summary of the Findings

The majority of the respondents came from three provinces—Ontario, British Columbia, and Alberta. Most beginning teachers had spent time as occasional teachers, and there was a good split of beginning teacher representation across grade levels taught, and distribution of respondents over the first five years of teaching. Over one third of respondents reported that they were teaching outside of their subject area, and one quarter reported that they were teaching outside of their grade level. Three quarters of the respondents reported that they had received support from an informal mentor, and one quarter of the respondents reported that they had received support from a formal mentor. When asked about whether or not support had met their needs, beginning teachers commented on formal systems, colleagues, and their own personal experiences.

Beginning teachers shared the importance of the strength of the relationship in mentoring, regardless of whether it was an informal or a formal mentoring relationship. Many shared struggles with mentoring processes, including finding time to meet for collaboration, as well as with mentoring structures related to the nature of the relationship, and how mentors were supporting new teachers. The influence that administrators had on the induction processes was felt to be very powerful by new teachers. Many cited that positive support from administrators was the most important determinant of how inclusive and supportive the culture of their school would be.

Most beginning teachers indicated that they had felt integrated into their school and that they had been respected by colleagues. Most respondents also indicated that they generally thrived as a beginning teacher, though the first year was cited as an extremely trying one. Beginning teachers commented on the expectation of them to engage in professional development; indicating that this had come from a variety of sources and that they had engaged in a variety of sources of professional development, including personal ventures. They also commented on both internal and external factors that had kept them in the profession, though the pace of the profession evidently had taken a toll on their socialization. Beginning teachers provided personal and work-related advice to new teachers entering the profession, and indicated how they might support new teachers if they were acting as mentors.

The findings from this pan-Canadian survey offer a glimpse into the reality for beginning teachers across Canada. While we might examine the structures and systems in place to successfully induct teachers into the profession and retain them, it is important to consider how these structures and systems have been received and how their use was perceived by the very individuals they were designed to serve. Overall, our findings provide insight and feedback about what was working well and what might be improved upon. Hopefully these insights and descriptions will serve as a guide for scholars, practitioners, and policymakers in their design and improvement of policies, initiatives and processes for mentoring, induction, and retention practices for the early career teachers in Canada.

# References

Cochran-Smith, M. (2006). *Policy, practice, and politics in teacher education.* Thousand Oaks, CA: Corwin Press.

Darling-Hammond, L. (2006). Constructing 21st-century teacher education. *Journal of Teacher Education Policy Analysis Archives, 57*(3), 300–314.

Howe, E. R. (2006). Exemplary teacher induction: An international review. *Educational Philosophy and Theory, 38*(3), 287–297.

Kauffman, D., Johnson, S. M., Kardos, S. M., Liu, E., & Peske, H. G. (2002). "Lost at sea:" New teachers' experiences with curriculum and assessment. *Teachers College Record, 104*(2), 273–300.

## Chapter 3

# "Wealth That I Can't Even Imagine:" The Relevance of Social Class to New Teacher Induction

*Sarah E. Barrett*

This chapter describes a longitudinal qualitative case study, which focused on the induction of a new working class science teacher, Samuel, into the community of practice of an affluent suburban high school. Although a great deal of research has described the plight of the working class student straining under middle-class values (see, for example, Freeman, 2010; Jones & Vagle, 2013; McGrew, 2011), there is very little research on the plight of the working class teacher who works in an affluent school. Yet I suspect that this juxtaposition is a common occurrence. I use this case study to explore the extent to which social class is an important consideration in the induction of new teachers.

The process of new teachers' induction may be seen as a process of developing their professional identities, a key project for any new teacher. If we imagine identity as an ongoing social negotiation, then we can view a professional identity on three sociological levels: the micro level (between individuals), the meso level (between an individual and a local community), and the macro level (between an individual and the larger society). The mentor-mentee relationship is a one-on-one relationship at the micro level that can transform and heavily influence the development of the professional identity of a teacher. However, I seek to understand the impact of factors beyond the mentor-mentee relationship. Therefore, in this chapter I focus on the meso and macro levels. In the case of a new teacher, the meso level is at the level of the school and its community, and we know that the school community is heavily influenced by the macro structures of society.

# Conceptualizing the Meso:
## Wenger's Communities of Practice

A new teacher's professional identity is negotiated within the community of a teacher's school. Professional culture is communicated to a teacher both formally and informally. The goals of formal teacher induction tend to be oriented to help new teachers to become familiar with procedures and workplace culture (Luft, 2009). Scholars (Luft, Bang, & Roehrig, 2007; McCormack, Gore, & Thomas, 2006) have found that the informal induction received from work colleagues has the biggest influence on the new teachers' teaching practice. Knowing that the new teachers' professional work cultures affect their curricular choices (McGinnis, Parker, & Graeber, 2004), taking note of how a new teacher chooses to teach can tell us a great deal about the professional culture into which they are trying to assimilate. Indeed, Wenger (1998) contended that professional cultures are defined by their practice. These communities of practice are spaces where identities are negotiated through activity; where people derive their identity, partly from the way they see themselves in relation to those with whom they presently work professionally, and those with whom they expect to be working in the future. He describes this conception of identity in terms of five components: learning trajectory, community membership, nexus of multi-membership, relation between local and global, and negotiated experiences.

*Learning trajectory* is the part of identity that is based on who one wishes to be in the future. For new teachers, learning trajectory relates to where they see themselves in their professional futures. There are four trajectories: peripheral, inbound, inside, and boundary (Wenger, 1998). A person with a *peripheral* learning trajectory does not feel part of the community of practice, but is interested in what the community has to say. A teacher with an *inbound* learning trajectory indicates that she sees herself belonging to the community in the future. Individuals with an *insider* or a *boundary* trajectory will feel like they are a part of the community in question; however, those in the boundary trajectory see themselves in liaison roles between or amongst different communities.

*Community membership* is a person's recognition of the familiar and the unfamiliar; the culture and norms, which make one feel at home or in a foreign territory. The implicit values that we come in contact with in a given setting, and the way we define ourselves in relation to these, will form this part of the identity negotiation. New high school science teachers are attempting to become members of the community of science teachers, and will attempt to reconcile their personal values with the values they encounter in their work setting. *The nexus of multi-membership* is the complex interaction between a person's various community memberships, including, but not limited to, work communities. A *relation between local and global*, in Wenger's conceptualization, refers to how a new teacher might see his actions in the classroom fitting into the expectations of the community. *Negotiated experiences* derive from the way we view ourselves within specific contexts and how we believe others perceive us in those contexts. This aspect of identity is shaped by and, in turn, shapes the way we behave or intend to behave in given contexts. New teachers develop a perception of themselves as science students and teachers based on their past and present experiences. These five components connect identity to group membership and lend themselves well to an analysis of the meso-level of the mentorship of new teachers, from their pre-service internships to employment. However, I would like to also include the macro level in this analysis.

## Conceptualizing the Macro:
## Anyon's Schools and Social Class

Although each school has its own unique professional culture, that culture has been and will be influenced by macro social structures, including social class. The concept of social class can be hard to pin down (Bourdieu, 1987-88) but, as Freeman (2010) stated:

> Class relations, whether based on fact or fiction, shape our beliefs about ourselves and others. Class is therefore socially and culturally constructed and its constraining or liberating effects manifest themselves differently depending on the social, institutional, and cultural context. (p. 181)

What does this look like in practice? A classic study by Anyon (1980) provided an excellent illustration of this as she examined the culture and curricular choices of Grade 5 teachers and students in five different schools. Anyon categorized each school into one of four social classes based on the occupations and incomes of the parents – *Working Class*, *Middle Class*, *Affluent Professional*, and *Executive Elite*. The differences between the schools were striking (see Table 1), from the way courses were taught, to classroom management, to teachers' and students' attitudes toward the curriculum and each other. For example, in the two *Working Class* schools, pedagogy focused on teaching students to follow procedure. In response to that, the students actively resisted school in subtle ways – a phenomenon noted in subsequent research (McGrew, 2011). In contrast, in the *Executive Elite* school, the emphasis was on developing analytical powers. What I believe Anyon (1980) illustrated is the potential of social class to have a profound effect on the community of practice in a given school. Other research has demonstrated the effect these social class-mediated cultures have on students, including the internalization of oppressive hegemony (Freire, 1970/2000), low self-esteem for both the working class (Jones & Vagle, 2013) and the elite (Brantlinger, 2007), and the specific ways that subjects such as science continue to be taught with specific class-based pedagogies (Gorard & See, 2008) that closely match Anyon's scheme. Consequently, a new teacher who works at what might be categorized as a *Working Class* school will need to adjust differently to communities of practice than that teacher might if they worked at an *Executive Elite* school. Thus, Anyon's scheme provides insight into the influence of social class on new teacher induction because it connects social class to the day-to-day work of a teacher.

**Table 1**
*Anyon's (1980) Categorization of Schools by Social Class*

| Learning Goals | Working Class schools | Middle Class school | Affluent Professional school | Executive Elite school |
|---|---|---|---|---|
| **Overall** | Follow procedure | Get the right answer | Be creative | Analyze systems |
| **Mathematics** | Accept algorithms without explanation | Understand the algorithms | Apply math skills using real-world data | Derived procedures |
| **Language arts** | Learn punctuation | Learn practical grammar | Do creative writing | Do presentations |

| | | | |
|---|---|---|---|
| **Social studies** | Take notes | Gather information and "put in own words" | Relate current affairs to topics in lessons | Do independent research, and discuss concepts |
| **Science** | Follow instructions | Gather information and "put in own words" | Focus on comprehension of concepts | Begin with social problems and derive solutions |
| **Discipline** | Follow arbitrary rules | Follow established rules and regulations | Comply through negotiation | Behave according to requirements of the task, not of the rules |

## Samuel's Case

This case study was developed over the course of two years of email correspondence and monthly interviews, along with full-day classroom observations. I approached this work from the perspective of one who challenges the role of schools in reproducing and supporting inequitable and unjust social structures (Jones & Vagle, 2013). All names in this chapter are pseudonyms. In what follows, I will describe Samuel's initial years of teaching through four themes: a rough initiation, a conservative but supportive professional culture, a conservative but affluent community, and bids for full community membership. This will be followed by an analysis through the lens of Wenger's (1998) conception of identity.

## A Rough Initiation

Samuel is a 30-year-old white cis-male who grew up in a working class neighbourhood in an industrial city just outside of a large urban centre. He became interested in science in Grade 10 when his teacher recommended him for a high school science enrichment program at the local university because "I guess he saw something there." The program revolved around a proposed expressway. Through this program, the students discovered violations of environmental laws (including dumping raw sewage directly into the local bay):

... and I thought, "This is the coolest subject ever! This is amazing! Why are we not getting excited in school science every single day? Look what we're doing – we're changing the world!" And there were meetings. And there were hearings, because of all the research I did. So I thought, "Ok. I have to do this. This is awesome!"

As he judged his science teachers as "pretty substandard," Samuel learned how to be an enthusiastic teacher from his history, drama and English teachers:

[They] would just be in love with their subjects. All they could do was talk about their subjects. They'd be performers for their subjects and they would run the class through excitement and ... strict rules, but you don't necessarily see the strict rules ... because you're just going along with the ride that is the classroom ... And I learned what a classroom should look like from these sort of teachers that I had growing up. Not from the science.

When Samuel entered the Faculty of Education, he aspired to this professional identity, in spite of his lack of experience of it within a science education context.

Unfortunately, his experiences as a practice teacher were less than encouraging. Although he was placed in a working class school in the same city as the Faculty of Education, he said:

I just didn't see eye to eye in terms of classroom management .... And my practicum associates, through a complaint, threatened to fire me if I wasn't going to start yelling and screaming at the students like a barbarian.

Feeling uncomfortable with what was being asked of him, Samuel had no choice but to do as he was told:

They said I wasn't strict enough with the kids and it was a Grade 12 chemistry class, and they said you go in there tomorrow, because they all failed the quiz again, and my associate said to me "you either go in there and read them the riot act or I will fail you on your report."

The experience led to a great deal of emotional turmoil:

I actually dropped out of teaching for a full year after working with her. I hated teaching so much. I couldn't stand the thought of it.

Thus, Samuel's experience led him to temporarily abandon his ambitions to become a full-time teacher because he was unable to resolve his own values about how a science teacher should be, with the values he believed he would have to adopt as a classroom teacher. Instead, he became involved in a travelling science show that visited local schools.

## A Supportive but Conservative Professional Culture

At the end of that school year, by chance, he met a principal at a job fair who encouraged him to volunteer at her school – Eminent High – and to get some experience. He said, "… and I met this wonderful staff here and teaching at this particular school was what I always dreamed teaching was going to be." Samuel clearly saw that his values would not conflict with those he perceived at Eminent High "… and it wasn't until I started working with this department head, volunteering, that I realized teaching could actually be a pleasurable experience; it could be fun to do." It appears that volunteering at Eminent High gave Samuel the courage to be himself, "running the classroom the way I wanted to – not punitively, not angrily."

If you write your lessons right, if you give activities, if you plan, if you structure your labs, it takes care of the classroom management because you know where you're supposed to be. And kids want to succeed, so if you show them the path and you clearly outline it they'll succeed on their own.

Samuel eventually managed to get two short-term contracts at the school and, once he had his own class in his first limited term contract, everything changed for him. For the first time, he had full responsibility for the classes he was teaching. Even three years out of the Faculty of Education and with two years' experience, he still commented that, "…it feels like I just got out of teachers college." Although this particular jurisdiction has a new teacher induction program, he did not find it especially useful. Instead, he consulted with his senior colleagues and found that that was enough.

Samuel wished to provide for his students the same experience of relevance and empowerment that he had had as a student in the enriched science program, but it was a struggle because of the active resistance his colleagues displayed to the idea. He said, "I adore it but it's very difficult with the older teachers who just hate it." For example, in the second half of his first year with permanent part-time status, when he was given the opportunity to plan the electricity unit for a Grade 9 science course, he designed a unit that centered on power generation – investigating local power consumption and designing and running experiments to determine the efficiency and feasibility of different energy sources. At that time, he noted that his colleagues were "terrified" of trying to do this. When he included more advanced versions of these investigations in physics, his senior physics colleague would simply pick a different topic to teach on that day.

Regardless of his colleagues' attitudes towards issues-based teaching, Samuel expressed gratitude for their support. They had gone out of their way to support him through sharing resources and giving advice. He was also fortunate that his department head fully supported his goals and encouraged him to take part in school board-wide professional development on the approach. She essentially focused on the newer teachers coming into the department and left the senior teachers alone.

## An Affluent and Comfortable Community

Eminent High is a relatively large school with 1300 students, located in one of the most affluent communities in the province. As Samuel said:

> I have students come from wealth that I can't even imagine. From houses that would fit four or five of my parents' house ... It's that sort of extreme. In poorer schools that I've worked in, if I pull out a little technology trick everyone gets amazed. If I pull out a technology trick at this school, well, everyone's probably bought it last month. So you can't wow them with things. You can only wow them with yourself.

> This affluence also meant that, in spite of the fact that the school received no more provincial funding per student than any other in the province, the facilities were stellar. Samuel never worried about finding materials or equipment,

planning class trips, or seeking funds for professional development. Further, none of his students were working long hours in part-time jobs. Although the school was racially diverse, their parents were mainly professionals or high-level managers; thus, it was not socioeconomically diverse. The school mirrored Anyon's *Executive Elite* category of schools to such an extent that its high ranking in provincial standardized tests was almost universally explained to be the result of this affluence.

Samuel noted that students were different from those he had become accustomed to in his previous experience, both as a student teacher and as a student. These students were reluctant to ask questions even if they were confused:

> There is just such a culture of "You've got to get it perfect. You don't want to show imperfection."... There's a culture of not asking questions ... if they have a problem that is chemistry related, they'll hire a chemistry professor from [the local university] to teach it to them.

This aspect of things was described not only in Anyon's study but also by Brantlinger (2007), whose work on the double-edged sword of social class makes it clear that the affluent student is not so much better off than the poor one in terms of their experience of schooling because of the pressure to uphold a perfect image within a hypercompetitive system. Demerath, Lynch, Milner, Peters, and Davidson (2010) described several mechanisms by which upper-middle-class parents enhance the academic success of their children, including interventions in school, "manipulation of educational policies" (p. 2935), and explicitly coaching their children to extract the resources they need from the system.

At Eminent High the pressure exerted on students from their parents was high. This was equally so with teachers, with whom the parents were happy to engage. From the other side of the desk, the teacher's perspective, Samuel described this experience as "you sort of feel two inches tall when you deal with them." He referred to this sense of inferiority often in his interviews. In his work, direct encounters with parents were a constant. In his extracurricular work, he described feeling worn down by parents' micromanaging of the team's affairs, and he commented on how unwilling they were to allow their students to fail as they learned new skills. Further, indirect encounters with parents haunted his curricular planning as he felt a great deal of pressure was on him to avoid controversy. He envisioned the possible negative scenarios that might result if he was not careful:

> Let's say Student X hears me and really is upset because I say the power plant is a good idea – which I think it is. Student X is upset. Student X feels frazzled because he's a 15-year-old hormonal teenager. Student X goes home crying to his parents. His parents are on the phone before the end of the day demanding a meeting with the principal. This has not happened to me. It's happened to other teachers, for sure. At this point I have to have a sit down meeting with the parents and the principal, which begs the question of, "Why did you stir up this hornet's nest?"....It's a very conservative community. This is not what they want to see. They don't want to see some free-thinking young teacher polluting their child's mind. And all of a sudden I've got this issue because I have an out of control, upset student. And the principal is having to deal with something they shouldn't have to.

Samuel's anticipation of a situation like the above led him to be very cautious about which local issues he chose to bring into the classroom. For example, a power plant that was being proposed for the neighbourhood was an issue he was afraid to touch in his first year as a permanent teacher because of his status as a part-time teacher who was hoping for full-time employment.

## Bids for Full Membership

Samuel's employment status had a profound effect on the development of his professional identity. He had entered Eminent High as a volunteer and never left. He continued his second year there as a supply teacher and took on limited term contracts for a year before being hired in a part-time, permanent position in his third year of teaching. He became a participant in the study in his third year. Still hoping for a full-time position, Samuel dealt with his precarious job security, in part, through extracurricular involvement and avoiding controversy. At the end of his first semester as a permanent teacher, I asked him what he was most proud of:

Surviving the semester – that's the short answer. In between having a personal life, and extracurricular, I have never felt so overwhelmed at any task I have ever faced. It was much harder than anything I had experienced in my first year of teaching.

He reported that most of his students complained about his lack of availability – due to three-hour football practices every evening. Samuel also felt pressure to impress his department head: "I put a LOT of pressure on myself, since this was my first senior science course and I really want more in the future!" When pressed to discuss his predilection for over-extending himself, he stated: "This year has been much better than my first year …. I'm having more fun in my life; but the time I spend having fun is quite limited, since I work 60-70 hours a week." Still, I could not help but think that this workaholism was a point of pride for him, and served as evidence of his dedication as a teacher offered up both in word and deed, in the hope that he would be noticed and be given a more stable position. Indeed, conversations in the latter part of his second permanent year confirmed this.

In his first year of permanent status, as a part-time teacher, Samuel's strategy for avoiding controversy extended into questionable curricular choices. For example, in spite of the fact that the Grade 10 curriculum in this jurisdiction has a unit of study named, "Climate Change," he still worried about discussing the topic because he knew that many of the parents did not believe climate change was actually happening, and he feared he might offend them by suggesting otherwise. Students brought up their parents' arguments regularly, but he did not feel he could argue against them, too much:

What I'm saying is they are going to have to come to the classroom the next day and if they feel isolated and alienated nothing I'm going to say is going to be listened to anyways. At the end of the day they have to be able to have a trust in the classroom … They have to be able to listen to the argument and if you push it too hard then they shut down. Then the game's over…They're not listening anyways.

Samuel admitted that he was frustrated by this. Although he, himself, had been turned on to science because of local issues and the controversies surrounding them, he did not feel safe engaging his students in this way. He did not have a full-time position yet, and he had no intention of leaving the school; therefore he had to be careful. Samuel said, "I'd like to think it doesn't stop me. It probably does come out, you know, worrying about losing my job."

He continued to pressure himself to impress his principal and, although he received positive feedback from students and parents, he still trod carefully and was very hard on himself:

> My lessons for the past month have either felt fantastic or awful, depending on how much time I put into the prep. As I wrote/reflected what I just said, I am starting to see the contradiction. Why am I feeling so crappy about the lessons, when the students were still responding well?

By his second year of permanent status, he had a full-time permanent schedule. Perhaps not by coincidence, he began to incorporate controversial issues and inquiry into all of his classes. He introduced the topic of the new power plant being built in the neighbourhood – the one he had been afraid to discuss the year before "... because it's so close to the neighbourhood, their opinions became based on what their parents said or other insults they hear through the media ..."

He began by having the students calculate the amount of energy their city used compared to the provincial average. He then continued by showing the students two videos – one supportive of building the power plant (by the company that would be building it), and one against (by a coalition of community parents). Students were very engaged in the topic and seemed glad to be given an opportunity to openly discuss an issue that had been prominent in the community:

> When I talk about local issues, it's a fine line. If I play devil's advocate too strongly they tune out, and there's anger, and there's complaints. But if I don't do anything then I'm not really doing my job. So I tread with caution. I'd rather be too cautious than too ambitious. We were talking about sources of greenhouse gases – what are the sources? Where are they

coming from? How are we affecting these? ...Well then this brings up; what about alternate fuel sources like windmills and solar panels? Well the obvious one there too is nuclear power plants ... But I have to tread lightly. I can't say [the new power plant] is a good idea because then half of the class gets offended and it becomes an argument.

This strategy worked well for him. Over the course of the school year, students seemed less tense when an issue was introduced. However, in the senior level physics, Samuel continued to struggle with introducing both inquiry and controversial topics. A colleague rejected even a brief project investigating different sources of energy, and Samuel did not feel comfortable pushing it further. Samuel also received a lay-off notice that winter that further complicated his situation.

## Intersections between the Meso and the Macro

To situate Samuel's story in the larger context of the school and society, I begin by looking at the meso level and Wenger's (1998) concept of identity as negotiation with the community of practice (including the facets of learning trajectory, community membership, nexus of multi-membership, relation between local and global, and negotiated experience).

During Samuel's initial years of teaching, his *learning trajectory* evolved from peripheral to inbound. During practice teaching, he could not find a way to join the teaching profession that felt comfortable, but he remained interested in science education. As such, he adopted a peripheral learning trajectory, marginalized from high school teaching but very much connected with teaching science in the travelling science show. Perhaps because of this connection, he continued to explore the possibility of teaching and adopted an inbound trajectory as he began to work at Eminent High.

*Community membership* was an important part of Samuel's experiences in his first two years. He explicitly contrasted the authoritarian stance expected of him in the lower income school during his practice teaching, with the much more relaxed stance expected at Eminent High. His values were so incongruous with the former that he almost gave up on the teaching profession, yet his value alignment in the latter maintained his motivation to belong, in spite of his precarious employment status. However, as a self-proclaimed working class man, he struggled with the teacher's social status in comparison to the status of the parents. In this *Executive Elite* school, the parents actively monitored the learning environment and expected the school to align with their values (even if it meant not teaching topics mandated by the provincial curriculum). This seemed to be a strange situation in his eyes. Samuel, who himself could not afford to live in the city where he worked, marveled at the resources and facilities available to the school, the almost total lack of behaviour problems, and the motivated student population.

*Nexus of multi-membership* takes Samuel's different community memberships into account. Samuel had grown up as a member of the working class, and some would argue that public school teachers are working class as well (Carlson, 1992; Dornbusch, Glasgow, & Lin, 1996). He was also a member of a supportive staff. However, the affluent community where the school was situated left him feeling insecure about his place in the school. He had no one who could help him financially should he lose his job. Further, rather than negotiate directly with the principal to secure his position, as he might have learned to do had he attended an *Executive Elite* school like Eminent High (Demerath et al., 2010), he worked as hard as he could in the hopes that he would be noticed, and awaited his fate (in a way reminiscent of temporary clerks in an office, hoping for a permanent job). The *relation between the local and global* is an extension of this. Samuel was keenly aware of how the larger school community perceived his curricular choices within his teaching practice, and how their perceptions were related to the predominant social class within the school. And so he deliberately monitored his own behaviour in order to join and remain in the community of practice of the school.

However, it is with his *negotiated experiences* that Samuel's working class upbringing comes most into conflict with the upper-middle-class status of the school's community. He described himself as feeling "two inches tall," and recounted worrying about upsetting students who might tell their parents about his transgressions. Clearly he believed himself to be expendable in the eyes of his employer, and as insignificant in the eyes of the parents. At the end of the study, when he was laid off, he was angry at the School Board for letting him go; but his anger was also directed at himself for not figuring out what he needed to do to stay. As he put it, throwing up his hands, "I don't know what more I can do."

The impact of social class on this teacher's experience of developing a professional identity within the community of practice at Eminent High was manifest in his curricular choices, relationships with parents, students and colleagues, and the material resources available to him. Yet it would be easy to overlook these effects or explain them differently. One could explain that his strategies for remaining employed were entirely due to his personality, or the community of practice could be construed as entirely the result of the unique collection of personalities that constituted it. But to do so would isolate Samuel and his struggles from larger societal structures (Demerath et al., 2010; Dornbusch et al., 1996; Jones & Vagle, 2013), and this would essentially blame him for circumstances largely beyond his control. It is precisely this warning that researchers such as Jones and Vagle (2013) invoked when they discussed working class students' experiences of schooling. I argue that if this understanding applies to students, there is no reason why it should not also apply to teachers. Teachers are subject to social class as a macro social structure in the same ways as students.

## Improving New Teacher Induction and Mentorship

It is a truism that teaching is a complex activity. New teachers in K-12 must cultivate mutually respectful relationships with individual students, parents and colleagues, and they must assimilate into an existing community of practice with the school's faculty. The rules, norms and procedures that govern these interactions are complicated and largely implicit. Formal and informal induction and mentorship programs have prioritized helping new teachers to become competent and confident at the micro and meso levels of their practice. Many school boards and faculties of education have also sought to expand teachers' understanding and recognition of the macro social structures that affect students and, therefore, need to be taken into account by teachers. However, what this case study illustrates is that the school itself is a microcosm of those macro social structures, such as social class, and that these structures can have a significant impact on new teachers' practices.

It would be helpful if formal and informal induction programs assisted new teachers to observe aspects of their school settings in terms that make social structures visible – acknowledging the impact of social class on teaching practice would make it easier for them to develop viable professional identities. Samuel's induction was successful, in spite of many setbacks, because of the support of his colleagues. However, he would have benefitted from an explicit acknowledgement of his context, extended beyond the micro level of interpersonal relationships and the meso level of procedures and norms within the school.

Explicit acknowledgement of social class as a significant factor in teachers' curricular choices would not only make it easier for new teachers to take it into account as they join the school's community of practice, but would also create space for critique. It would neither be appropriate nor practical for new teachers to bear the burden of interrupting the public school's role in maintaining social strata. However, formal new teacher induction and mentorship programs involve the participation of board and school administrators, senior teachers, and, in Samuel's jurisdiction, the provincial government. All of these individuals might take part in the discussion, and all might be afforded the opportunity to question the role of schooling with respect to this particular macro social structure. But the first step in dealing with the problem of social class and schools is to explicitly name it.

Finally, for the record, Samuel was eventually hired back and is currently employed on a full-time permanent contract at Eminent High.

## Acknowledgements

*This research was funded by grants from the Social Sciences and Humanities Research Council (Canada) and the Faculty of Education at York University, and was completed with help from the following graduate assistants: Warren Barden, Emma Biondi, Darren Hoeg, Ava Klemensberg, and Angelika Otfinowska.*

## References

Anyon, J. (1980). Social class and the hidden curriculum of work. *Journal of Education, 1*, 67–92.

Bourdieu, P. (1987-88). What makes a social class? On the theoretical and practical existence of groups. *Berkeley Journal of Sociology, 32-33,* 1–17.

Brantlinger, E. (2007). (Re)Turning to Marx to understand the unexpected anger among "winners" in schooling: a critical social psychology perspective. In J. Van Galen & G. W. Noblit (Eds.), *Late to class: Social class and schooling in the new economy* (pp. 235–268). Albany, NY: State University of New York Press.

Carlson, D. (1992). *Teachers and crisis: Urban school reform and teachers' work culture.* New York, NY: Routledge.

Demerath, P., Lynch, J., H. Richard, M. I., Peters, A., & Davidson, M. (2010). Decoding success: A middle-class logic of individual advancement in a U.S. suburb and high school. *Teachers College Record, 112*(12), 2935–2987.

Dornbusch, S. M., Glasgow, K. L., & Lin, I.-C. (1996). The social structure of schooling. *Annual Review of Psychology, 47,* 401–429.

Freeman, M. (2010). Knowledge is acting: Working-class parents' intentional acts of positioning within the discursive practice of involvement. *International Journal of Qualitative Studies in Education, 23*(2), 181–198.

Freire, P. (1970/2000). *Pedagogy of the oppressed* (M. B. Ramos, Trans. New Rev. 20th-Anniversary ed.). New York, NY: Continuum.

Gorard, S., & See, B. H. (2008). Is science a middle-class phenomenon? The SES determinants of 16-19 participation. *Research in Post-Compulsory Education, 13*(2), 217–226.

Jones, S., & Vagle, M. D. (2013). Living contradictions and working for change: Toward a theory of social class–sensitive pedagogy. *Educational Researcher, 42*(3), 129–141. doi:10.3102/0013189X13481381

Luft, J. A. (2009). Beginning secondary science teachers in different induction programmes: The first year of teaching. *International Journal of Science Education, 31*(17), 2355–2384.

Luft, J. A., Bang, E., & Roehrig, G. H. (2007). Supporting beginning science teachers. *The Science Teacher, 74,* 24–29.

McCormack, A., Gore, J., & Thomas, K. (2006). Early career teacher professional learning. *Asia-Pacific Journal of Teacher Education, 34*(1), 95–113.

McGinnis, J. R., Parker, C., & Graeber, A. O. (2004). A cultural perspective of the induction of five reform-minded beginning mathematics and science teachers. *Journal of Research in Science Teaching, 41*(7), 720–747.

McGrew, K. (2011). A review of class-based theories of student resistance in education: Mapping the origins and influence of Learning to Labor by Paul Willis. *Review of Educational Research, 81*(2), 234–266.

Wenger, E. (1998). *Communities of practice: Learning, meaning, and identity.* Cambridge, England: Cambridge University Press.

# New Teacher's Calling

*Rebecca Stroud Stasel*

Many people struggle over their career choice. I always knew I wanted to work with youth; I love kids and the energy and hope that they perennially plant in the world. I also believe in public service. Many secular and spiritual communities promote service as integral to society. Initially, I thought I would use my desire and capacity to help children as a social worker or a lawyer. Then, during my undergrad, when I found my studies in social psychology and criminology rather depressing, someone suggested that I might think of teaching. I knew that teachers hold great social and moral responsibility in their work. Although parents rarely get to know their children's teachers, beyond a meeting or two, they entrust teachers with the care of their children who, of course, mean everything to them. Over the span of school years, teachers will have immense influence on these children as they teach. Even though I put applications into bachelor of education programs, I continued my soul searching. The legal concept of *in loco parentis* terrified me. Yet, I thought that teaching might be transformational. After several months of soul searching, one morning, my direction became clear: my calling was to teach.

Teaching indeed is transformational. It is a privilege to be a part of the development and growth of youth; they are the future. I applaud all who are now choosing a career in education, in the service of children and on behalf of their parents and society. It is not an easy profession, but for those like me who have felt called to this noble vocation, there is no other way.

For years now, one way that I have made sense of the world has been by writing poetry. I have done this when I have celebrated the heights of joy; when I have beheld the beauty of nature; when I have experienced a moment of spiritual maturity; when I have felt sad and broken; and when I have been in need of direction. I wrote many poems in my early 20s, as I transitioned from a student to a professional, and as I found my footing as an adult in this world. Using words, I worked through my initial angst as I faced the prospect of teaching. I didn't know if I could rise to the challenge of all the meanings entailed in the notion of *in loco parentis*. This is not to say that my view of teaching or service reflects the views of others. However, as I listened to some of the new teachers sharing their insights for our team's research project, I did hear many diverse and unique voices of hope, of devotion, and of service to the children of today. Although the poem below was written a long time ago, it still rings loud and true in my mind as I remember the exhilaration, the trepidation, and the hope that I felt in being called to be a teacher, a new teacher…

> What is it to teach a child, be this craft or a skill,
> unlock these imagination ciphers: guarded or just paucity?
> To teach rather than give fish, to inspire, to invoke reciprocity,
> To shift the classroom from a drill to a thrill.
>
> What magic, what wisdom have sage teachers styled,
> How do they set minds ablaze with wonder?
> And do I have what it takes to be beguiled
> By the passion and wisdom to inspire like thunder?
>
> The oak tree, large, robust, king in the forest crew
> intimidates some with its large, bold presence;
> but generosity flows through its veins, it gives back too
> giving shelter, shade, stability to forest dwellers.
>
> I am a tiny young sapling, will never stand up to the oak.
> Soon charged to teach, inspire, in loco parentis cloak.
> Oh Oak, please share your secrets, your ever-growing awe.
> Please send filigrees of your cipher, to create that magical 'aha'!
>
> It is magical the way the child views the world.
> They are raw, honest, free of adult bunkum guile.
> Really, their teaching us should be rejoiced then unfurled.
> We could embrace past wisdom by reviving childhood's style.

## Chapter 5

# Mentorship Through the Comics

*Ching-Chiu Lin, Julian Lawrence, Amber Lum, Rita Irwin*

# VOICES OF EARLY CAREER TEACHERS: MENTORSHIP THROUGH COMICS

by Ching-Chiu Lin, Julian Lawrence, Amber Lum and Rita Irwin, University of British Columbia.

THIS IS YOUR INTREPID REPORTER *FLIP CHART*, AND IN THIS CHAPTER WE AIM TO DEMONSTRATE THE EFFECTIVENESS OF COMICS AS A VEHICLE FOR PRESENTING TEACHERS' STORIES OF CHALLENGE AND PROFESSIONAL GROWTH. COMICS HAVE THE POTENTIAL TO ILLUSTRATE, IN A LIGHT-HEARTED FASHION, NARRATIVES FROM EARLY CAREER TEACHERS ON THE SUBJECT OF PROFESSIONAL PRACTICE IN BRITISH COLUMBIA, CANADA. PRINTED COPIES OF THE COMIC BOOKLETS ARE WIDELY SHARED AMONG THE EDUCATIONAL COMMUNITIES IN BRITISH COLUMBIA, AS WELL AS THROUGH NATIONAL AND INTERNATIONAL CONFERENCE VENUES. THROUGH COMICS, WE OFFER TEACHERS AN IMAGINATIVE INSIGHT INTO NEW TEACHERS' STORIES, INVITING THEM TO REFLECT ON THEIR OWN EXPERIENCE OF BECOMING TEACHERS, TO ENGAGE IN CONVERSATION AROUND EDUCATIONAL ISSUES, AND TO ARTICULATE THE COMPLEXITY OF PEDAGOGICAL RELATIONSHIPS AMONG TEACHERS AND THEIR PROFESSIONAL LEARNING COMMUNITIES.

THIS SERIES OF COMICS IS PART OF THE BODY OF WORK FROM A RESEARCH PROJECT ENTITLED: *PEDAGOGICAL ASSEMBLAGE: BUILDING AND SUSTAINING TEACHER CAPACITY THROUGH MENTORING PROGRAMS IN BRITISH COLUMBIA (2014-2017).* THIS RESEARCH BUILDS ON THE NEW TEACHER MENTORING PROJECT (NTMP) THAT BRINGS TOGETHER THE TEACHER EDUCATION OFFICE (TEO) AT THE UNIVERSITY OF BRITISH COLUMBIA (UBC), THE BRITISH COLUMBIA MINISTRY OF EDUCATION, THE BRITISH COLUMBIA SCHOOL SUPERINTENDENTS' ASSOCIATION (BCSSA), AND THE BRITISH COLUMBIA TEACHERS' FEDERATION (BCTF) TO ADDRESS THE NEED FOR PROMOTING, BUILDING AND SUSTAINING A PROFESSIONAL CULTURE OF COLLABORATION THROUGH TEACHER MENTORING IN THE CONTEXT OF THE BRITISH COLUMBIA K-12 PUBLIC EDUCATION SYSTEM.

FOR MORE INFORMATION, VISIT MENTORINGBC.CA

TODAY I'M ASKING *EDUCATIONAL PROFESSIONALS* THIS QUESTION:

## WHY IS TEACHER MENTORSHIP ESSENTIAL?

**SD: 60, PEACE RIVER NORTH**

MENTORSHIP IS KEY IN NORTHERN REGIONS TO COMBAT GEOGRAPHIC ISOLATION.

**SD: 20, KOOTENAY-COLUMBIA**

IT BUILDS A CULTURE OF COLLABORATION AND CARE.

# MENTORSHIP CONFIDENTIAL!

JUNE 2010 MARKED ONE OF THE **MOST MEMORABLE** MOMENTS OF MY LIFE. AFTER MANY YEARS OF POST-SECONDARY EDUCATION, THOUSANDS OF HOURS OF VOLUNTEER AND GENERAL WORK, AND UNCOUNTABLE LATE STUDY NIGHTS, I WAS FINALLY IN MY CAP AND GOWN, WALKING TOWARD MY CONVOCATION CEREMONY TO COMMENCE MY *CAREER AS AN EDUCATOR.*

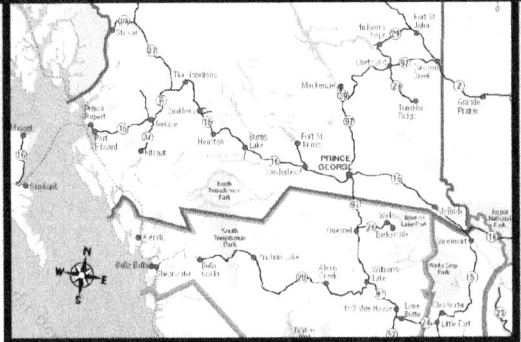

AFTER GRADUATION, I WAS FORTUNATE TO BE HIRED BY MY 'HOME' SCHOOL DISTRICT – THE DISTRICT THAT EDUCATED ME AND THE ONE I ULTIMATELY WANT TO GIVE BACK TO.

AFTER THREE MONTHS OF BEING A **TEACHER ON CALL,** A POSITION CAME UP IN ONE OF THE DISTRICT'S RURAL, ONE-ROOM SCHOOLS THAT I HAD BEEN EYEING FOR YEARS.

THREE MONTHS LATER, I WAS ECSTATIC TO FIND MYSELF IN A RURAL COMMUNITY WITH MY OWN K - 7 CLASSROOM.

YES, I HAD TAKEN A RURAL ELECTIVE IN MY EDUCATION PROGRAM, KNOWING THAT I WANTED *RURAL TEACHING EXPERIENCE.* THOUGH I WAS AWARE OF THE CHALLENGES I WOULD FACE, THE REALITY WAS VERY DIFFERENT FROM MY IMAGININGS! RURAL, MULTIGRADE TEACHERS FACE SIMILAR CHALLENGES TO ALL TEACHERS; HOWEVER, THERE ARE ALSO VERY *SPECIFIC CHALLENGES* FOR THOSE IN THESE ISOLATED TEACHING POSITIONS. WITHIN MY FIRST 4 MONTHS OF BEING A LONE STAFF MEMBER AT MY SCHOOL, I STARTED SEEKING SUPPORT!

I STARTED BY REACHING OUT TO *MS. FANTASTIC,* WHO HAD BEEN A GUEST SPEAKER IN MY RURAL EDUCATION ELECTIVE. AFTER TALKING WITH HER, I JOINED THE BC RURAL AND SMALL SCHOOLS PSA.

THIS OPENED THE DOOR FOR ME TO EXPAND MY PROFESSIONAL NETWORK AND MAKE EXTREMELY MEANINGFUL CONNECTIONS WITH TEACHERS ACROSS THE PROVINCE...

... WHO ARE IN VERY SIMILAR TEACHING ASSIGNMENTS TO MYSELF

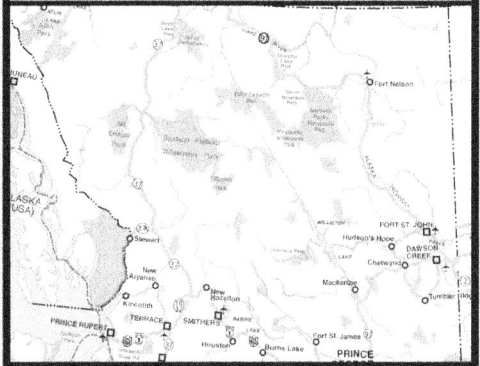

BEING ABLE TO COMMUNICATE WITH THESE *MASTER TEACHERS* OVER THE PHONE AND THROUGH EMAIL WAS, AND CONTINUES TO BE, A MAJOR STAPLE IN MY LIFE.

HOWEVER, NOTHING COMPARES WITH FACE-TO-FACE INTERACTION.

I ALSO STARTED CONTACTING AND QUESTIONING SPECIFIC PEOPLE WITHIN OUR DISTRICT ABOUT FUNDS FOR MENTORSHIP PURPOSES.

MY WORRY SURROUNDING THE ABSENCE OF THESE FUNDS SUBSIDED WHEN I WAS ADVISED BY A LOCAL PRO-D CHAIR THAT I COULD USE MY PRO-D FUNDS TO VISIT OTHER RURAL SCHOOLS.

AFTER TALKING WITH TWO RURAL TEACHERS, VISITING THEIR SCHOOLS, AND OBSERVING THEIR PROGRAMS AND STUDENTS, I NOTICED MY NEED FOR SELF-AFFIRMATION BEING FULFILLED...

BUT MY THIRST FOR OBSERVATIONAL AND COLLABORATIVE OPPORTUNITIES WITH SEASONED TEACHERS WAS NOT QUENCHED.

EARLY IN MY SECOND YEAR OF TEACHING, I WAS INFORMED ABOUT OUR DISTRICT'S PARTICIPATION IN THE NEW TEACHER MENTORING PROJECT...

THE MENTOR

AND I JUMPED RIGHT ABOARD!

NEW TEACHER MENTORING PROJECT

WHEN YOU ARE ALONE AND THE CLOSEST SCHOOL AND COMMUNITY IS OVER AN HOUR AWAY, CORRELATING STUDENTS' PROGRESS WITH THAT OF OTHER STUDENTS' FOR ACCURATE ASSESSMENT IS A CHALLENGE. THE SAME GOES FOR RECEIVING AND MAINTAINING SOCIAL HEALTH AND MORAL SUPPORT BY CONVERSING BOTH PROFESSIONALLY AND SOCIALLY WITH COLLEAGUES...

NOT TO MENTION MY OWN PERSONAL NEED TO SELF-ASSESS IN ADDITION TO MY DESIRE TO GROW AND IMPROVE AS AN EDUCATOR.

THE MENTORSHIP PROGRAM HAS FULFILLED THESE NEEDS AND HAS, MOST IMPORTANTLY, GIVEN ME THE TIME TO CONNECT WITH OTHER TEACHERS IN SIMILAR TEACHING POSITIONS.

THE SKILLS, STRATEGIES, AND RESOURCES I HAVE GAINED HAVE ACCUMULATED, SO MUCH SO THAT I AM FULLY CONFIDENT WHEN I OFFER HELP TO OTHER TEACHERS IN THE BEGINNING STAGES OF THEIR OWN RURAL OR MULTIGRADE TEACHING ASSIGNMENTS.

$?

I AM WELL ON MY WAY TO ACHIEVING MANY OF MY GOALS:

✓ TO BE A FOREVER LEARNER FOR MY CURRENT AND FUTURE STUDENTS

✓ TO MAINTAIN CONFIDENCE AND THE BELIEF IN MYSELF AS AN EARLY CAREER TEACHER

✓ TO NETWORK, CONNECT AND COLLABORATE WITH COLLEAGUES

✓ TO BE A RURAL SPECIALIST WITHIN OUR DISTRICT...

-- JUST TO NAME A FEW!

IT IS THE MENTORSHIP PROGRAM THAT HAS PROVIDED ME WITH THE OPPORTUNITIES TO GET TO THIS VITAL POINT AT AN EARLY STAGE IN MY CAREER.

START

CHANCE

I AM A SECOND YEAR PARTICI-PANT IN THE MENTORSHIP PRO-GRAM, AND THE AMOUNT OF KNOWLEDGE I HAVE GAINED FROM MY MENTORS IS *TRULY INDE-SCRIBABLE.* MY SECOND YEAR, IN PARTICULAR, HAS HAD A PRO-FOUND IMPACT ON MY PERSONAL GROWTH, AND I MUST CREDIT IT TO BEING PARTNERED WITH MASTER RURAL TEACHER, *MS. FANTASTIC,* WHO IS A *TRUE INSPIRATION.*

HI!

THE *MENTORSHIP PROJECT* GAVE ME *TIME* AND *OPPORTUNITIES* WITH A MASTER TEACHER BY MY SIDE - IT HAS GIVEN ME EVERYTHING I HAVE NEEDED, WAS LOOKING FOR, AND *SO MUCH MORE.* ABSOLUTELY NOTHING COMPARES WITH FACE-TO-FACE INTERACTION WITH OTHERS, ESPECIALLY FOR EARLY CAREER TEACHERS IN RURAL COMMUNITIES. IT HAS TRULY BEEN A *PRIVI-LEGE* TO BE PART OF THIS MENTORSHIP PROJECT, AND I *WHOLEHEARTEDLY* HOPE THAT IT CONTINUES FOR THE *BENEFIT* FOR *ALL TEACHERS ALIKE.*

# A Letter from a New Teacher to her District's Teacher Mentorship Steering Committee!

Dear members of the Steering Committee...

... and everyone else involved in setting up the mentoring program in our district - -

Thank you for giving me the opportunity and the release time to work with a mentor teacher.

As a teacher new to the profession, I have found the last couple of years rewarding, but extremely stressful and often isolating.

Working with my mentor and the entire mentoring group, knowing that there was someone with the time to help me, lifted a big weight off my shoulders.

Last year I was off for a few months with a nasty virus. I am sure it was because my immune system couldn't hack the stress I had been experiencing in my first and second year of teaching.

This has cost the district a lot of money. I think putting money into initiatives such as the mentoring program is a great preventative measure, giving teachers more of the support they need from the beginning of their careers.

So thank you very much. I am extremely grateful to work in this district and am continually amazed at the support that we're offered via professional development.

Sincerely,
Hannah

IT WAS SUCH A **RELIEF** TO HEAR I WAS ACTUALLY DOING FINE, BUT I DIDN'T KNOW THAT UNTIL ROBERT CAME INTO MY CLASSROOM AND OBSERVED MY TEACHING.

AS A TEACHER I WANT TO BE **CONFIDENT** IN MY ABILITY TO PROVIDE STUDENTS WITH **VALUABLE LEARNING EXPERIENCES.** I COULDN'T HAVE HAD ROBERT'S SUPPORT AND FEEDBACK WITHOUT BEING INVOLVED IN MY DISTRICT'S MENTORING PROGRAM. ROBERT'S PRESENCE IN MY CLASSROOM ALLOWED ME TO **REFLECT** UPON MY TEACHING AND **HELPED BUILD** MY INNER CONFIDENCE.

FOR EXAMPLE, HE WAS **SHOCKED** WHEN I SHOWED HIM MY WAY OF MARKING. I THOUGHT IT WAS BAD BUT HE SAID:

THAT'S **CLEVER**; I'VE NEVER SEEN THAT BEFORE IN MY LIFE.

IT WAS REALLY COOL TO BE **COMPLIMENTED** BY A WELL-RESPECTED TEACHER.

WHAT I VALUE MOST IS ROBERT'S VAST KNOWLEDGE BASE, AS HE HAS BEEN WORKING IN THE TEACHING PROFESSION FOR SEVERAL DECADES.
IT HAS BEEN AN AMAZING EXPERIENCE TO WORK WITH HIM AND GET SOME IDEAS FROM HIM WHILE KNOWING HE IS ALWAYS THERE TO HELP ME GROW. WORKING WITH MY MENTOR IS NOT ABOUT GOING INTO SOME-ONE'S CLASSROOM AND GRABBING A COUPLE OF LESSON IDEAS. ROBERT WOULD SAY:
LET'S DEVELOP SOME IDEAS AND LESSONS TOGETHER.
HE OPENED MY EYES TO HOW TEACHERS CAN BE LIFE-LONG LEARNERS THROUGH COLLABORATION. OUR MENTORING PARTNERSHIP CREATED THE OPPORTUNITY FOR US TO CONSTRUCT NEW LESSON IDEAS THAT SUIT MY STUDENTS' NEEDS.
I FEEL I'M ON MY WAY TO BECOMING A BETTER TEACHER BY MERGING MY PROFESSIONAL KNOWLEDGE WITH ROBERT'S PRACTICAL INSIGHTS.
AT THE SAME TIME, I'M SHOWING MY STUDENTS WHAT LIFE-LONG LEARN-ING IS THROUGH MY PRACTICE.

*CALVIN* AND I MET THE YEAR BEFORE HE MOVED TO OUR COMMUNITY. HE IS A *BRAND NEW TEACHER*. WE HAVE A LOT IN COMMON AND GET ALONG REALLY WELL. HOWEVER, IT MADE ME QUESTION WHAT CAUSES A PROFESSIONAL RELATIONSHIP TO SHIFT FROM A FRIENDSHIP TO--

# SOMETHING MORE STRUCTURED

SINCE WE ARE BOTH BASKETBALL COACHES I THINK WE WOULD HAVE NATURALLY COLLABORATED BUT THIS MENTORSHIP PROJECT GAVE US THE OPPORTUNITY TO FORM A MORE CONSTRUCTIVE RELATIONSHIP.

I'M DARREN.

HEY, I'M CALVIN.

IT WAS REALLY VALUABLE TO DISCUSS AND PLAN BEFOREHAND HOW WE COULD COLLABORATE TOGETHER.

DO YOU LIKE B-BALL?

DO I? *YOU BET!!*

WE DECIDED WE WANTED TO ACCOMPLISH SOMETHING THAT UNITED PEOPLE FROM THE SOUTH AND THE NORTH OF OUR COMMUNITY, BUT OUR EXISTING RELATIONSHIP WASN'T ESTABLISHED ENOUGH TO START IMMEDIATELY.

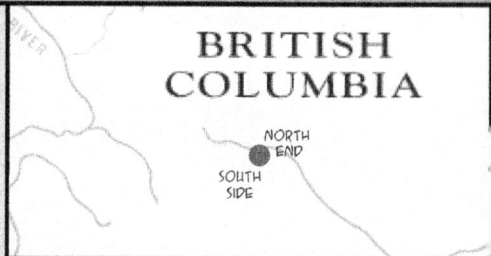

**BRITISH COLUMBIA**

RIVER

NORTH END

SOUTH SIDE

OUR FIRST COLLABORATIVE PROJECT WAS A COMBINED CAMPING TRIP WITH OUR TWO BASKETBALL TEAMS. WE NEEDED TO GET THESE KIDS TOGETHER SO WE COULD BOND WITH EACH OTHER'S STUDENTS.

WE EVEN ROASTED A DEER TOGETHER. THE TRIP NOT ONLY STRENGTHENED OUR RELATIONSHIP BUT I GOT TO KNOW CALVIN'S KIDS.

IT WAS A REAL HIGHLIGHT OF THE YEAR.

AT THE BEGINNING, WE WEREN'T SURE WHAT THE DYNAMIC WAS GOING TO BE. HOWEVER, AT THE END OF OUR TRIP, WALKING DOWN THE BEACH WE SAW OUR TEAMS MIXED, THE COACHES AND PLAYERS EXCHANGING INSIGHT.

IT WAS REALLY REWARDING.

ONCE A FRAMEWORK OF COLLAB-ORATION WAS IN PLACE IT WAS NO EXTRA EFFORT TO DO MORE COOPERATIVE WORK.

WE RECENTLY TOOK OUR GRADE 10 CLASSES CAMPING. IF STUDENTS SEE TWO TEACHERS WORKING TOGETHER IT TRIPLES THE EXCITEMENT FOR THEM.

THROUGH COLLABO-RATION THE TRIP BECAME MORE MEMORA-BLE.

THIS MENTORSHIP PROJECT HELPED US ESTABLISH A FOUNDA-TION THAT WAS THEN EASY TO BUILD ON.

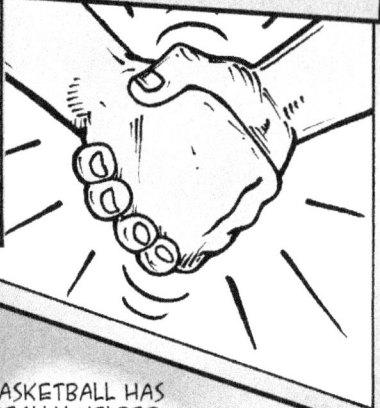

OUR MOST RECENT JOINT VENTURE IS A TRIP TO NEW ZEALAND WITH THE MEN'S BASKETBALL TEAM CALVIN AND I COACH TOGETHER.

BASKETBALL HAS REALLY HELPED STRENGTHEN CONNECTIVITY IN THE COMMUNITY. WHEN YOU GO TO THE GYM ON A WINTERY TUESDAY NIGHT, THERE ARE PLAYERS OF ALL AGES PLAYING TOGETHER.

MY TEACHING PRACTICE HAS BEEN INFLUENCED IN SUCH A POSITIVE WAY THROUGH THIS PROGRAM. HAVING A MENTOR LIKE DARREN WHO HAS SO MUCH EXPERIENCE PERTINENT TO WHAT'S HAPPENING IN MY EARLY CAREER AS A TEACHER HAS BEEN INVALUABLE. I REMEMBER DARREN SAYING:
"OKAY, YOU'RE GOING TO BE TEACHING P.E. SO HERE'S A FEW THINGS I THINK YOU SHOULD KNOW. YOU'RE GOING TO FIGURE OUT A LOT OF THIS AND YOU AREN'T GOING TO ADOPT ALL MY SUGGESTIONS, BUT YOU MIGHT FIND SOME OF THEM USEFUL."
C
D
THOSE WORDS HAVE BEEN SO VALUABLE TO ME. MY FIRST YEAR OF TEACHING WOULD NOT HAVE BEEN THE SAME WITHOUT THIS PROGRAM. DARREN AND I WOULD HAVE BEEN FRIENDS, BUT KNOWING WE HAD BEEN GIVEN TIME TO WORK TOGETHER REALLY ALLOWED US TO FOCUS ON COLLABORATION.

84

85

# PAPERWORK

THIS PROJECT HAS HAD A PROFOUND IMPACT ON MY PROFESSIONAL CONFIDENCE. TEACHERS IN SPECIALIZED POSITIONS SUCH AS LEARNING SUPPORT CAN BE LONELY, AND THERE IS A STEEP LEARNING CURVE.

THERE IS SO MUCH TO LEARN...

ESPECIALLY ALL OF THE PAPER WORK!

I E-MAILED KAREN FREQUENTLY, ASKING QUESTIONS ABOUT RESOURCES, ACTIVITIES, IDEAS, AND EFFECTIVE WAYS TO EXECUTE MY JOB.

THE RELEASE TIME THIS PROGRAM PROVIDED TO VISIT WITH OUR MENTORS WAS PARTICULARLY HELPFUL.

MY MENTOR HAS PASSED ON TONS OF KNOWLEDGE AND RESOURCES, INCLUDING HOW TO PROPERLY FILL OUT PAPERWORK AND TALK TO PARENTS IN A PROFESSIONAL AND COMPASSIONATE MANNER.

HI, JENNI...

HI, KAREN.

WHAT'RE YOU DOING?

PAPERWORK!

IT WAS BENEFICIAL TO COLLABORATE, SWAP IDEAS, SHARE RESOURCES AND OBSERVE HOW KAREN WORKED AT HER SCHOOL.

MOREOVER, I BELIEVE MY STAFF ALSO BENEFITED FROM THIS PROGRAM BECAUSE OF THE ACTIVE EXCHANGE OF KNOWLEDGE THAT WAS OCCURRING IN OUR SCHOOL COMMUNITY.

IF I DIDN'T HAVE A MENTOR, I WOULD HAVE ASKED FOR HELP BUT WOULD HAVE FELT BAD FOR TAKING UP SOMEONE'S TIME.

KNOWING KAREN HAD OFFERED HER TIME MEANT I DIDN'T HAVE TO FEEL GUILTY ABOUT ASKING QUESTIONS CONSTANTLY.

KNOWING SOMEONE HAD VOLUNTEERED TO HELP ME MADE ASKING FOR ADVICE SO MUCH EASIER.

FURTHERMORE, PROGRAM MEETINGS INTRODUCED ME TO OTHER NEW TEACHERS IN OUR DISTRICT. THIS WAS COMFORTING BECAUSE IT PROVIDED US ALL WITH A STRONG SUPPORT NETWORK THAT ALLOWED US TO LEARN AND GROW AS PROFESSIONALS.

MOST OF MY COLLEAGUES DON'T KNOW MUCH ABOUT THE MENTORING PROGRAM, BUT THOSE I HAVE ASKED SAY THEY WOULD HAVE LOVED TO JOIN IF THEY HAD BEEN AWARE OF IT. I ENCOURAGE MY COLLEAGUES TO GET INVOLVED, AS I BELIEVE TEACHER MENTORSHIP IS AN EFFECTIVE APPROACH TO ONGOING PROFESSIONAL DEVELOPMENT.

THIS PROGRAM HAS BEEN ABSOLUTELY INVALUABLE FOR ME FOR THE PAST TWO YEARS.

THE SUPPORT, KNOWLEDGE, AND CONFIDENCE I HAVE GAINED THROUGH THIS PROGRAM HAVE ALLOWED ME TO BECOME MORE QUALIFIED AND EFFICIENT AS A LEARNING SUPPORT TEACHER.

# The Nature Of How We Work

IN *HAIDA GWAII*, WE PREFER TO USE THE TERM 'TEACHER COLLABORATION PROJECT', RATHER THAN 'TEACHER MENTORING PROGRAM', TO SPEAK TO THE NATURE OF HOW WE WORK TOGETHER AS A PROFESSIONAL LEARNING COMMUNITY. THESE NAMES SIMPLY DESCRIBE DIFFERENT WAYS IN WHICH TEACHERS HELP EACH OTHER IN ORDER TO DEVELOP AND EXPLORE THE IDEAS OF TEACHING AND LEARNING.

COMING FROM ENGLAND AND BEING A *NEW TEACHER* IN HAIDA GWAII, I APPRECIATE THE OPPORTUNITY TO BE A PART OF THIS PROJECT.

I WANTED TO EXPLORE HOW I COULD TEACH CULTURALLY SENSITIVE PROCESSES AND THE USES OF ART IN MY CLASSROOM, BASED ON A CULTURE THAT IS NOT MY OWN.

I HAVE LEARNED SO MUCH ABOUT THE PROPER USE OF *HAIDA FORMLINE*...

... THUS BEING ABLE TO OFFER THAT KNOWLEDGE TO MY *STUDENTS.*

THE COMMUNITY ASSISTED ME TO PRESENT *CULTURALLY APPROPRIATE LESSONS.* OVER TIME, I HAVE OBSERVED THAT STUDENTS RESPECT THE FACT THAT THE HAIDA TEACHERS ARE BEING INVITED INTO MY ART CLASS AND THAT I'M INVITED INTO THEIRS. WE HAVE HELPED EACH OTHER TO PROVIDE STUDENTS WITH *MORE LEARNING OPPORTUNITIES.*

THIS PROGRAM MAKES TEACHER COLLABORATION **ACKNOWLEDGED IN SCHOOLS** – TEACHERS REALIZE THERE IS A STRUCTURE IN PLACE THAT ENCOURAGES YOU TO COLLABORATE WITH OTHER TEACHERS. IT GIVES TEACHERS A **STARTING POINT**, NOT JUST TO HELP EACH OTHER, BUT ALSO TO CONNECT AND LEARN TOGETHER.

WITHOUT THE TEACHER COLLABORATION PROJECT, TEACHERS WOULD BE **PRESSED FOR TIME.**

2:00AM

THIS PROJECT GIVES ME THE OPPORTUNITY TO BE **MINDFUL** AND **REFLECTIVE** ABOUT MY TEACHING.

PRESS

IT ALSO ALLOWS TEACHERS TO FOSTER A **CULTURE OF COLLABORATION**...WHERE THEY LEARN TOGETHER TO IMPROVE AND REFINE THEIR PRACTICES.

THE END

## Chapter 6

# A Year in the Life of a New Teacher

*Matthew McIntyre*

A teacher. That is who I am, through and through. I am someone who is often told how easy I have it. I am told that because I get every major holiday and the summers off, I don't deserve to be paid as much as I am. Why can't we put five more kids in your classroom? How big a difference can that make anyway? But, as every good teacher knows, we are not here for the money or the "time off." We are prepared to put up with parents, and those parts of society looking down at us, in order to help sculpt the future generations. Teachers change the world, one little mind at a time; that is why we're here.

Being a teacher is never easy; but being a new teacher is exceptionally tougher. It is a lot of late nights, a lot of uncertainty, and a lot of flexibility. You have to be quick on your feet and ready to go with the flow. This chapter is a small glimpse at some of my experiences as a new teacher in the Western Quebec School Board where I teach English subjects at the elementary level.

## The Support

It all starts with the interview, and the late August phone call saying that you have got the job. You have that brief minute of pure excitement before the gears start spinning and the anxiety kicks in. There is so much to plan! Just to scratch the surface, you have to get familiar with the curriculum you will be teaching, explore the layout of your classroom, and start gathering materials that are grade specific, as well as methods of evaluation. As you begin to plan, then panic sets in; you realize you have far more questions than answers. You begin to wonder what mess you have gotten yourself into. Where will your classroom be? Who will your students be? Will they have allergies? Where do you go if the fire alarm goes off? And the worst of all these panic inducers is: "Why did they hire me for *this* class? Are they so bad off that none of the other teachers wanted them?"

Luckily, at the Western Quebec School Board they start off all new teachers with a Teacher Induction Program that begins with a one-day workshop at our Board Office. At the end of August, we had one day where we got to meet with our program coordinators, network with fellow first-year teachers, and ask all of the questions we could. They had answers for most of these questions, and if they did not have the answers, they were eager to point us in the right direction, or note the questions and send the answers to us later. Also, as part of this day, there were two small group workshops. We got to choose from a number of options of course-specific workshops, such as English Language Arts or Math. The one I chose was based on Dr. Gordon Neufeld's work on child developmental science (Neufeld & Mate, 2013). Finally, we had a session that described how the hiring process and seniority processes worked in our Board. This day was incredibly valuable to me as a new teacher because it put my mind at ease. The day gave me a safe place to ask questions, and a network to lean on, should I experience difficulty along my way.

Loaded with all this information I was ready to get to school and start. The absolute best part about our Teacher Induction Program is the mentoring aspect. Every teacher in the first year of our two-year induction program is paired with a mentor-coach who is there to help you with anything you might need: where to look for resources, what strategies exist for reaching certain students, how to write IEPs and report cards, and so much more. In our Board they do the best that they can to get each teacher a mentor-coach from within his or her own school. Mine was an incredible colleague who also happened to be our resource teacher. For me that match was perfect. This is where my experience with our teacher induction program begins to differ from others' experiences. I was able to use my resource time every day to take the whole class to the resource room for 30 minutes and co-teach with my mentor. We used this time to do "Daily 5", which structures literacy time so students develop lifelong habits of reading, writing, and working independently. They do this through choosing an option such as reading independently, reading with a partner, writing, working with words, or working with media for 20 minutes per day.

Co-teaching with my mentor-coach taught me so many great strategies. This pattern allowed me to practice lessons and strategies of my own with immediate feedback, while at the same time doubling the teaching opportunity for my students so that we could work with small groups on very specific challenges that only a few were experiencing. This is not an opportunity that a lot of new teachers get, but one I feel has been instrumental to my success in our program. Our program also gives you and your mentor-coach a total of two days' worth of supply teacher coverage, between mentee and coach. We called this our M&M days (Mentor-Coach & Mentee days). You can use these days in any way that is considered professional development. For example, you could both take a day to go and observe experienced teachers at other schools, or each take two half days throughout the year to discuss strategies and unit building techniques used by teachers in your school.

## The Challenges

I love my job, and every single day I am grateful for having it; especially as so many of my friends and professional colleagues struggle to find employment in my home province of Ontario. As teachers, we live for the little moments, such as when a student of yours makes a breakthrough and begins to read like never before. Or, like in September this year, when I was introduced to a new student at our school. This was a special needs student who has been fully integrated into my Grade 6 Phys-Ed class. We shook hands, and he asked to carry my clipboard. He then took my hand and we walked together to the front of the line where he drew his hand up my arm, looked me square in the eyes and told me "Sir, your fur is just like a werewolf."

Unfortunately, these moments are not what make up the majority of a teacher's job. On a daily basis, we have a tremendous number of challenges that we must deal with: emails from parents, children who aren't engaged, the latest incident on the school yard, what we were supposed to have prepared for our staff meeting that day, and what one student said to another on Instagram last night. The list goes on and does not even mention the routines of lesson planning and marking. However, these are just the challenges of a teacher. New teachers get to experience all of these, and so many more.

One of the challenges I remember most was related to how much time I wasted trying to get to know my school. Things like fire drill and lock down procedures, how to book a supply teacher, who to call if I am sick, how to claim my classroom budget money, where I can find resources, how to file attendance electronically, and the list goes on and on. The answers were certainly worth the time I put into finding them; but I thought there must be a better way. Whenever one of these questions came up, I had to write it down, then head to the office to see if my principal had time to see me. Often it went quickly, but sometimes it took a day or more before I could get my answer. Some questions I could run through my colleagues or my mentor-coach; but this sometimes gave me multiple answers and left me with even more questions. In my second year of teaching, our principal created binders for each teacher. These binders included everything from our teaching and supervision schedules, to emergency procedures, and step-by-step guides for all of our online databases and more. This has been an invaluable tool for me, and retrospectively, would have saved me hours of time searching for answers had this been available in my first year.

Another challenge I experienced as a first-year teacher was being given a classroom which had previously belonged to a teacher who had changed careers, leaving his classroom 'as is' when he left: a full desk, full filing cabinets, and every closet filled with materials and resources. Some of these materials were useful, and some looked like they may have been there since the school was built. Even a year later, I have still not had a chance to go through everything that was left in that room. I was able to reclaim my desk, and I have gone through the closets and reorganized them, but there is still so much space being used by materials that I cannot use because I don't know what they are.

Starting my first year, it quite quickly became evident just how few resources I had compared to many of the other teachers. I felt my walls were barer, my book shelves emptier and my manipulatives were basically non-existent. I was okay with not having these materials myself, but I was not okay for my students' education to be impacted by this. I talked with my mentor-coach to see if she had any ideas, and she discussed it with our principal and helped me find some additional funding for my classroom library. With such limited classroom budgets, and the expectation to provide everything from art supplies to extra paper, a class library was next to impossible to build in my first year without this additional funding. However, most of the materials, such as manipulatives for math or workbooks in social studies, were around the school, or I could easily borrow what was needed from other teachers until my own resources were built up.

The last challenge I want to touch on is one that came up with a few of the teachers I spoke with. These teachers were thrilled with all of the resources that were in place for them through the teacher induction program and their mentor-coaches. However, quite a number of teachers began in the middle of the school-year; this had resulted from maternity leaves, injuries, illness, and so on. Our induction program only accepted people into the process as part of the year-long cohort. Therefore, the teachers who took over classrooms without formal support from the induction program, and with no mentor-coach, found it difficult to dive in. They did not have the network to lean on, nor did they have people they felt comfortable asking questions of as they did not want to bother anyone. This was a comment I heard a number of times when talking about teachers' experiences in our particular Board. If a way could be found to extend some of these services to those teachers as well, it would make their transition into teaching considerably easier.

## The Induction

In our Board, there are two aspects to our teacher induction program that are most controversial. Both of these aspects hold a lot of value and act as tools for monitoring progress, but also add a lot of pressure to an already stressful first year for many new teachers.

First is our portfolio. Now, I should preface this by saying that our program has drastically changed this year, and the portfolio is no longer a major aspect of our program. However, it was a major component of my first year, not to mention that over the past few years, hundreds of new teachers have experienced the portfolio in our program. I believe that it is worth mentioning. Our portfolios were designed to be separated into the 12 competencies of teaching that we follow in Quebec, and we had to contribute to 5 of them in our first year. Most people created binders for their portfolios; however, wanting to save myself some time and desiring to stick out from the crowd, I decided to create a website instead. I am so glad that I did; but, boy, was I wrong about it being a time saver. It was so much work to design it and lay it out just how I wanted it. In the end, it was worth it; to be honest, this resource has saved me several times already. One day when I thought I knew where an online video was, I just could not find it. I knew that I had uploaded a link onto my website, though, and I was able to get directly to it through that means.

I loved the fact that my program allowed us to communicate our reflections in any way that we felt most comfortable; whether by website, by binder, by blog or by YouTube videos. I chose the website method because this allowed me to combine all of these aspects into one. The reason everyone has been so conflicted on the value of creating a portfolio simply comes down to the preciousness of time. Teachers would inevitably pour countless hours of their time into the design and creation of their portfolios in order to impress their principals and coordinators. This was especially so at a point in our careers where there is already such a steep learning curve, and so much of this has to be done in so little time that adding such a substantive amount of work around these portfolios felt like too much to many.

The fact that our Teacher Induction Program no longer requires a portfolio is rather remarkable. This demonstrates the fluidity of our program. It is constantly adapting and changing to meet the needs of our teachers, based on instrumental feedback through the teacher fellows, mentor-coaches, administrators and program coordinators. Without that open door for communication, program growth and maturity is impossible. This year, teaching fellows (a term given to the teachers currently in our two-year induction program) will be responsible for meeting with our principals each term and laying out two goals. Like the portfolio, these goals should be centered in one of the 12 teaching competencies. For each goal we create, we must submit evidence at the end of the term on our progress toward meeting that goal. This evidence could be a written reflection, a video, or a song. Anything will do, so long as it acts as a supporting document to demonstrate our growth. Additionally, teaching fellows are required to create an end of year reflection piece to demonstrate their yearly growth.

The second most debated topic among my induction program colleagues has been related to our class observations. Once again, many teachers see the value in these, but the experience is one that is dreaded by most. For our induction program, the observation team consists of two members from our Induction program coordinators, as well as our principal. Often, a mentor-coach will sit in as well to help make the teaching fellow feel more comfortable. We get one full observation per year of our induction program, plus at least one more formal evaluation from our principal each year. For our observation with the Teacher Induction Program team, a new teacher is typically given 24-48 hours' notice of their visit. The idea behind this is that they do not want a teaching fellow to change anything about their teaching style; they just want to see the teaching fellows in their everyday work.

For these observations, the team joins us in our classroom for a period (or more often a part of a period) and quietly observes the classroom, our teaching styles, how the new teachers differentiate their teaching to meet the needs of all their students, and student engagement, to name a few. Once the students are up and moving as part of an activity, the observers will often ask a couple of the students a few questions to see if they have a good understanding of the activity, their expectations, and their objectives. Following the lesson, the observation team meets to discuss how the teaching fellow felt the lesson went, what went well, and what we would do differently when we do it again. They provide their direct feedback verbally at this point, but also in typed form within a week. The feedback comes in under a rubric of three points of "What Went Well" and three points of "Even Better If." It is important to note that the teacher is only evaluated on a "Successful/ Not Successful" scale. If a teacher receives an unsuccessful observation, they are able to have the team come in and visit again. Observers are flexible and reasonable people. They do appreciate the stress that observation sessions put on new teachers, and they are flexible with how they execute this function. The part they stress out about the most, and is sometimes the hardest part to remember as a teaching fellow, is that regardless of the outcome of the observations, the principal of your school always has the final say as to whether or not one is successful in the program.

# The Conclusion

In conclusion, my induction program experience has been incredibly rewarding. Despite inevitable challenges along the way and always looking for ways to make improvements, my first year of teaching would never have been so successful if it were not for the program put in place by my Board. My experiences with my colleagues and mentor-coach have been very positive, and I owe so much of my success to them. Without their constant support, feedback and ideas, I would never be where I am today. Although I am only in my second year of teaching, the foundation that this program has helped me build will undoubtedly help shape my entire career. After all, that is who I am...

A teacher.

# References

Neufeld, G., & Mate, G. (2013). *Hold on to your kids: Why parents need to matter more than peers* (3rd ed.). New York, NY: Ballantine Books.

## Chapter 7

# Exploring the Experiences and Perceptions of the Canadian New Teachers

*Keith D. Walker, Benjamin Kutsyuruba,*
*Maha Al Makhamreh, Rebecca Stroud Stasel*

## Introduction

Transition into the workforce, socialization processes, as well as efforts focused on acculturation to school contexts and the profession, are commonly noted experiences of teachers at the beginning of their careers (Halford, 1998; Howe, 2006; Kauffman, Johnson, Kardos, Liu, & Peske, 2002). Earlier research has demonstrated that teachers' expectations strongly influence students' achievements (Rosenthal & Jacobson, 1968). Thus it might be justified to generally assume that novice teachers enter the field knowing their powerful roles and the enormous responsibilities that the society places on their shoulders. Teachers choose this noble profession for different reasons; and for a lot of them, it is to make a positive change and to provide our societies with productive and well-educated young people (Ewing & Smith, 2003). But as a matter of fact, this is not an easy or stress-free occupation (Joseph, 2000) and new teachers often experience pressures and challenges during their initial inroads into the profession. They experience differing expectations from their employers (school boards), administration, fellow teachers, parents, and students. Teachers are expected to encourage the students' academic growth as well as to promote the students' emotional, social, moral, health and well-being development.

Added to all of this are the significant challenges faced by beginning teachers, often including: the egg-crate structure of schools, isolation, reality shock, cultural adjustment, inadequate resources and support, lack of time for planning and interaction with colleagues, difficult work assignments, unclear and inadequate expectations, intergenerational gap, dealing with stress, lack of orientation and information about the school system, and institutional practices and policies that promote hazing (Andrews & Quinn, 2004; Anhorn, 2008; Darling-Hammond, 2003; Johnson & Kardos, 2002; Patterson, 2005). Based on telephone interviews with 36 teachers from nine provinces and three territories, this chapter addresses two critical questions: 1) What are the experiences of the new teachers across Canada during their first years of teaching? and, 2) How do they deal with the requirements, expectations, and challenges?

# Methodology

This study represents one of the phases in a multi-year pan-Canadian research project that examined the differential impact of teacher induction and mentorship programs on the early-career teachers' retention, as perceived across the provinces and territories. Telephone interviews were aimed at inviting insights from early-career teachers about their experiences with, and perceptions of, the role of teacher induction and mentoring programs. Based on the participant sample from the survey that was distributed earlier, we contacted those teachers who expressed their willingness to participate in the follow-up interviews. In the summer of 2016, we conducted telephone interviews with 36 teachers, all in their first five years of teaching and from nine provinces and three territories (3 in French, 33 in English) (See Table 1 for pseudonyms and province/territory representation).

**Table 1**
*List of Participants*

| # | Pseudonym | Province/Territory | Language |
|---|-----------|--------------------|----------|
| 1 | Mike | NS | English |
| 2 | Lise | ON | French |
| 3 | Maira | NL | English |
| 4 | Kamille | ON | French |
| 5 | Mackenzie | ON | English |
| 6 | Evelyn | AB | English |
| 7 | Kandace | AB | English |

| 8  | Alli      | QC | English |
|----|-----------|----|---------|
| 9  | Stewart   | SK | English |
| 10 | Nick      | SK | English |
| 11 | Ashish    | NT | English |
| 12 | Charlotte | AB | English |
| 13 | Maribelle | SK | English |
| 14 | Christina | ON | English |
| 15 | Andrea    | ON | English |
| 16 | Mark      | AB | English |
| 17 | Ken       | ON | English |
| 18 | Lily      | NS | English |
| 19 | Lois      | NB | English |
| 20 | Myles     | MB | English |
| 21 | Cassie    | MB | English |
| 22 | Gladys    | ON | English |
| 23 | Tennae    | BC | English |
| 24 | Anya      | NU | English |
| 25 | Ruth      | ON | English |
| 26 | Ed        | ON | English |
| 27 | Shana     | NU | English |
| 28 | Jane      | NU | English |
| 29 | Marilyn   | YT | English |
| 30 | Noor      | BC | English |
| 31 | Helen     | BC | English |
| 32 | Alessandra| BC | English |
| 33 | Bob       | BC | English |
| 34 | Lebert    | BC | English |
| 35 | Shelle    | BC | English |
| 36 | Françoise | ON | French  |

Most of the interviews lasted approximately 15-20 minutes, were recorded and transcribed, and all proper names and identifiers were changed to pseudonyms. The interview protocol included five questions pertaining to development, resilience, mentorship, and leadership. The rich descriptive data were analyzed thematically and are presented below with direct quotations from our participants.

# Teacher Development

We asked our interviewees to think back over their experiences of the first years of teaching and tell us what had worked best for them regarding their development as teachers. Their perspectives are organized under three categories below: formal and informal learning from others, self-learning, and establishing good relationships.

## Informal and Formal Learning from Others

Having a mentor, both formally and informally, was the most frequently mentioned factor that was important for their professional growth. They noted that having one-on-one time with a mentor or another teacher had allowed them to expand their understandings and gain confidence in the decisions that teachers need to make on a daily basis. For example, Evelyn explained:

> I really appreciated having one-on-one time with a mentor or another teacher. Having somebody to bounce ideas back really benefitted me to expand my understanding, and just to gain confidence in the decisions that I was making.

Shelle highlighted a similar beneficial experience about formal mentoring: "I would say that, initially ... one-on-one time with someone in the district to orient me to how everything worked was the best possible practice for that experience." Those coworkers were described as knowledgeable, versed in research, and most importantly, willing to share those resources. It was evident that many of the novice teachers had come into the profession with limited resources, but were able to find support from others, which had helped them to "get back on their feet". As Anya explained, "They weren't assigned or anything; but they kind of took me under their wing and really helped me out with procedures; and, if I had any difficulties or any questions, I would usually go to them first." Christina was also appreciative of her mentor teachers, "Thanks to a few of my mentor teachers in the school, I thought it was pretty easy to get back on my feet, and they were very, very supportive about me starting teaching."

The participants described co-teaching as an exceptional learning experience; wherein they were able to co-teach, co-plan, and explore things they planned to do in the classrooms. For example, Evelyn noted, "That kind of co-teaching and co-planning was awesome ... he let me kind of explore things I wanted to do, but he was there as kind of support." Others mentioned that asking for help, getting tips and "profession tricks," and then incorporating what they had learned into their own classroom practices was an effective method for them, as new teachers. Ed described his experience by saying:

> I can do better, I can teach more, but I can't do it by myself, and so I had to go around and ask all the other teachers how they did things. I got little tips and tricks, and every little thing that someone had to offer; I was able to incorporate it into my own classroom practices.

Getting help from more experienced teachers was not the only source of help that novice teachers valued; they also expressed how interaction with other new teachers allowed them to feel that they were not alone in this challenge, and allowed them to meaningfully engage in formal professional learning and professional development activities. Shana suggested, "It was good to be able to do professional learning in the school while I was actually working, because, you know, you can actually apply it, and, you know, work it so that it fits with your students and your community, your classroom." Discussing the most beneficial factor for his professional growth, Ashish said, "I would say collaborating with coworkers, so working with the team around me, learning from them." There was a near consensus from our interviewees that collaborating, getting support from other teachers, and sharing materials had made a difference in their early years, and had provided them with the guidance they needed. Some of our interviewees also considered formal professional learning and professional development activities to be beneficial for them as new teachers.

## Self-learning

Self-learning was viewed by the participants as a developmental phenomenon that was beneficial to their socialization processes. This type of learning resulted from dedicated reflection time, acquiring or nurturing a proactive mindset, developing planning skills, gaining classroom experiences, and from independent work. Some interviewees described reflection as their best mechanism for improvement. When confronted with difficult situations, which is not unusual in this profession, the ability to think back and mentally prepare differently for the next time had helped many novice teachers to develop and grow professionally. However, it was unfortunate to hear that while some of these teachers valued reflection as an effective technique to progress, others said they had a challenge of not having enough time to reflect. Charlotte described it well: "There isn't enough time ... especially not enough time to reflect properly on what you're doing. So there's only enough time to kind of just survive from day to day, but I don't think there's enough time to improve." Proactive mindsets allowed these early career teachers to plan ahead and to be flexible. For example, Ken highlighted the following:

> I think what worked--actually, I know what worked best for me was being very proactive in taking advantage of every opportunity, and really being flexible ... I think my mindset was just to be very proactive, to be very flexible, and to be willing to do anything, because anything could eventually lead to something.

Other interviewees highlighted the importance for new teachers to be good planners, especially when preparing their curriculum outcomes. They shed light on the development that comes with experience in the classroom. As Myles said, "To be honest with you, the development probably just comes with the experience in the classroom ..." His words imply that teachers learn from their students, just as they learn from their mentor teachers and through professional development. Some participants shed light on their independent work that consisted of such activities as volunteering, attending workshops, acquiring knowledge through reading and by pursuing further qualifications. Gladys explained:

> I felt encouraged to know that there are different ways of doing the same thing and doing it well, if that makes any sense. And sometimes you find that out from learning and reading and taking courses, and sometimes you find that out just from talking with other colleagues.

These results suggested that being open to learning, from all people and all opportunities, worked best for our interviewees in their early years.

## Establishing Good Relationships

Establishing good relationships with colleagues, administrators, as well as with students, was found to be one of the main factors that had helped beginning teachers to excel in their development. Establishing relationships promoted collaboration and sharing materials among colleagues. They shared about feeling supported and having been encouraged to ask for help when needed; both were seen as results of the healthy relationship they had managed to establish in their schools. The kind of relationships that some of our participants had developed with other teachers, who ended up playing the role of informal mentors to them, had allowed them to enjoy informal dialogues with colleagues who were experienced in the field. When things did not go well for them, the novice teachers noted their need for space and the opportunities to share their frustrations. Under these circumstances, experienced teachers were there to provide novices with practical advice and help. Andrea noted:

> It was nothing formal. It was just more, like, after a class kind
> of debriefing with them, and saying, you know, maybe some
> of my frustrations or things that didn't go well, and based on
> their experience, they were able to offer me advice.

Moreover, experienced teachers played vital roles in the transitions of novice teachers. At the same time, it is worthwhile mentioning that our participants also highlighted the importance of developing relationships and networking with other new teachers. Christina elaborated:

> In my school, there were also a lot of first year teachers, too,
> so that was very helpful, not just having everybody who knew
> what they were doing and not everybody that was always giving
> me advice, but there are also teachers in the same boat as me
> ... I know there's a big emphasis on setting up the network of
> mentor teacher to new teachers, but I think it would be really
> great, too, to have just networking in terms of new teachers
> and sharing what's gone well and what hasn't gone well.

Having good relationships with students was another significant factor that benefitted some of our interviewees. As new teachers, they noticed the importance of being patient with students and maintaining a teacher/student relationship that was based on mutual respect.

Françoise explained that establishing good relationships, especially with the students, had helped her. She said that it was the reason why she had chosen this profession. She also described her bonds with colleagues, the department and the school:

> Ce qui a bien fonctionné, c'est surtout le lien avec les élèves. C'est la raison pour laquelle j'ai choisi la profession, donc le lien avec les élèves a bien été, en termes de développement professionnel, justement la gestion de classe, la question gestion du temps, ça a été assez bien, les liens avec les collègues aussi, le sentiment du département, de l'école.

Along with colleagues, Ashish explained the importance of developing collegial relationship with principals or vice-principals. This was something that had assisted him in his early teaching years. He also portrayed his principal as being patient, sympathetic, and someone who explained things well. Others also noted that teachers need supportive principals in order to build beneficial relationships with them (this point will be elaborated on below).

## Attrition and Retention of New Teachers

We asked the interviewees to share a significant story or particular moment in their first years of teaching that had played a part in convincing them to remain in the profession. Some teachers told us that the active roles of mentors and the support they had received from others in their schools had encouraged them to stay. Others shared about their passion, or their positive mindset, or the accumulation of nice moments that had convinced them that this was the profession they wanted to stay in. It was interesting to learn that for many teachers who shared their significant stories with us, these stories were often related to students. For example, their bonds with students, the struggles students had faced and worked through, and the resilience of their students had offered many teachers a sense of professional affirmation that they had made a positive difference.

At the same time, teachers shared their struggles and their frustrations, and it was unfortunate to hear that some of them were considering leaving the profession, and that one teacher had left already. Moreover, these teachers were keen to have these interviews as a venue to send a clear message about their challenging experiences as novice teachers. They wished to amplify their desire to make changes in the teaching profession. Overall, three categories of stories emerged: about staying, about considerations of leaving, and about leaving. These were predicated on two main influences: external and internal influences. Inductively, it became evident that the internal factors had to do with personal values, intrinsic motivation, thoughts, feelings, and beliefs; whereas external factors were related to structures, processes, or other individuals outside of the personal realm that exerted significant influences on teachers' decisions. Below, we have grouped the stories according to the type of influence.

### External Influences

In this section, we present the novice teachers' stories about how different external factors had either encouraged teachers to stay in their profession, or had led them to consider leaving the profession in order to find another career.

**External factors for retention**. In their stories about the external factors that had encouraged them to stay, teachers mentioned the pivotal role of their having a mentor, the support they got from people when faced with difficult situations, the encouragement and empathy they had received from others, their students' appreciation and positive feedback, and the supportive school climate in their respective schools.

Mentoring programs and mentor teachers were mentioned as having been enormously influential and had encouraged teachers to "stick to their passion," their profession, and to overcome the barriers that had been encountered in their early years of teaching. For instance, Noor indicated that mentorship was the key factor that kept him going: "Things that have kept me going, and as I go, is making those connections with others - with colleagues and that's again related to that mentorship that is so important."

Ed shared a challenging story about how the support from his principal encouraged him not to quit the supply teaching profession. He was supplying for a teacher "who went off on a stress leave again" from working with a very challenging class. When one day, Ed was about to go home, frustrated and very angry at a challenging situation that happened in class, thinking of quitting this "whole supply teaching business," the principal stopped him and had a positive conversation about the anomaly that he was going through, and this calmed him down. Ed added that the most positive moments of his job were related to the people who were in his school, supporting and helping others through various difficult experiences.

The impact of guidance and support of a person in a mentor role, be it formal or informal, left good effects on these new teachers. Nick shared his gratitude for a retired teacher who had stepped in to guide and supervise his work during a period of procedural fluctuation at the school board. He appreciated the feedback from this retired teacher in the larger context of what he called "an awful lot of negative feedback."

Several stories related to teachers leaving and coming back into the profession. Marilyn made a decision to leave teaching, based on an unsupportive environment where collaboration was rare and the lack of motivation was prevalent. As a result, the negative climate reduced her motivation to stay. However, rather than leave the teaching profession altogether (teacher attrition), she reconsidered and moved to another province (teacher migration). Having secured employment in the new locale, she experienced a positive work environment where colleagues were "in the habit of helping and you can bounce ideas off them." In addition to a collaborative work environment, she explained that the lifestyle in her new place of employment was different. For one thing, she now spent more time outdoors with her students and received support from the community.

**External factors for attrition.** Teachers shared with us their struggles and frustrations as a result of external factors that had led them to consider leaving the teaching profession. In fact, we talked to one teacher, Andrea, who had already left the profession at the time of the interview. Andrea started sharing her attrition story as follows:

> Well, the only thing I would say is I have actually left the teaching career, so I don't know how that will impact your data collection and study, but just in terms of full disclosure, yeah, I left a permanent teaching job which is difficult to get in Ontario, but I was very unhappy. So, I think the research you're doing is important because figuring out why new teachers leave the career I think can help with retention.

Andrea added that the school lacked structure and discipline, class sizes were constantly getting bigger, and demands were increasing; as a result, her well-being deteriorated and her sense of happiness at work decreased: "I was heavily involved with coaching; putting in 60 to 80 hours a week just took a toll on me." The combination of these conditions prompted her to leave teaching altogether.

Lack of a supportive system was a factor that made other teachers frustrated and moved them to consider changing their profession. Alessandra elaborated on this issue and described her frustration:

> I'm so interested in your study because, I mean, I heard when I went to teachers' college that, you know, one out of every - like, 50 per cent of teachers didn't stay in the profession, and I thought, well, that's impossible. That can't possibly be me, and here I am. I never thought - I mean, I thought what would be difficult was the kids, working with the kids, and sometimes the parents. And the kids are the best part of it. It was everything else that was at play ... We're dealing with large class sizes, class composition that's not manageable, major lack of supports within the system. And so, when you combine that systemic problem with a localized problem of a very difficult administrator, it just becomes impossible.

Some participants mentioned observing other teachers leave the profession because of the different regulations that were coming into place in different provinces. Some of the Ontario participants mentioned that new teachers were leaving the profession because of the Regulation 274, which they thought was hurting the teaching profession more than it was helping. For example, Ken explained:

> I really adamantly think that the regulation is not doing what it was intended to do. It, in fact, is hurting the teaching profession more than it's helping it, because nepotism still exists, the need for teachers to improve their skills is no longer there, and great, fantastic teachers that I know are leaving the profession, because there's no incentive out there for being a good teacher any more.

Stewart hoped to find employment in Ontario but had moved to Saskatchewan in order to teach full-time. His advice to teachers was to "be prepared to leave Ontario for the next decade, because the way the regulations are set up, the deck is extremely stacked against you." Ontario isn't the only province with hiring obstacles. Stewart elaborated, "I know people - at my school, there are 11 teachers and only six of them are from Saskatchewan because the other five of us moved from other jurisdictions - Ontario, Manitoba, Alberta - because Saskatchewan will hire you full-time straight out of school." While teachers are appreciating the employment opportunities in Saskatchewan, and abroad, in order to gain initial experience, teachers like Stewart preferred to reside closer to their extended families in provinces where full time, contract employment was not possible immediately upon graduation.

As a result of constricting regulations, one teacher, Gladys, emphasized that if novices are "... very, very frustrated and have not – and don't quite feel like it's enough of – a passion for them to hold out for five years to get a job, then they should consider other employment."

### Internal Influences

In this section, we highlight the novice teachers' stories about how their decisions to stay or leave were affected by internal influences. Interestingly, most of the internal influences, explicitly mentioned in relation to the decision to leave, were the direct result of external pressures and influences. As for retention, some teachers shared with us that it was their passion to teach and it was what they always wanted to do. Others described to us the feelings they enjoyed when changing their students' lives and how these enormous moments had influenced them to stay in their profession.

**Internal factors for attrition.** According to the data, high levels of stress, anxiety, and conflicting demands of the job, in a context of unsupportive parents and administration, lead teachers at all stages of their careers to leave the profession. Nick stated, "You're working those hours, huge hours a week, and you're dealing with stress and you're getting the parent phone calls, and the administration is down on you." The anxiety piles up "because, no matter what you do, there's always something more they wanted." The same teacher expressed a desire for support to help navigate the challenges; but instead felt unsupported, and burdened with the entire responsibility. Nick said:

> It always falls back on me, so that this differentiation and adaptation is great and ideal but what's happened is it shifted responsibilities to the point where there is a never-ending

well of responsibility on the teacher, because there's always a what if? What more?

Nick is conscious of the persistent and extra onus placed on teachers to take responsibility and to do the right thing. He spoke of the challenges associated with the indeterminacy that had characterized so much of his work. In terms of coping with similar experiences, Alli provided her perspective and recommended that teachers do not pretend to be okay if they are not. She suggested that new teachers should find "at least one person at the school, I think, that you can hopefully talk to."

**Internal factors for retention.** Passion was the most frequently mentioned internal factor that had encouraged teachers to stay in the profession, related to participants' internal desire to be teachers. As a strong intrinsic motivation factor that kept teachers going, passion to teach was often confronted with challenging circumstances, especially for the occasional teachers who were still without full-time contracts. Ken suggested that passion wins if teachers "remain patient," while Ed advised that new teachers who are not passionate enough about teaching, and for some reason ended up as teachers, tended to leave the profession. Ed explained the reasoning in a competitive way: "Quite frankly, myself and everyone else don't need the extra competition of people [who lack passion] trying to get employment as a teacher."

The internalized value of supporting students, and the positive impact that teachers have on students, was mentioned as a landmark point that encouraged and convinced teachers that they were in the right place. For example, Tennae said, "The convincing [factor] to stay is the student achievement; when students, particularly at-risk or high-risk kids, have breakthroughs or stay in school for that matter, that is - that is significant to me."

A touching story from Françoise represents the positive impact that teachers can have on special needs students. She described that working with a group of students, which no one wanted to teach because they had difficulties with learning, allowed her to create bonds with them and convinced her that she was in the right place. On her birthday, they pretended to all come to school, and then they hid under the stairs in order to bring her a cake and sing happy birthday. That was the moment when she realized that she gave them a challenge and a desire to learn, and this was the biggest affirmation for her:

> Cette année, l'année qui a passée était ma première année complète avec des groupes. J'ai eu un groupe avec des besoins particuliers, il y avait beaucoup d'élèves qui avaient des troubles d'apprentissage et justement les liens qu'on m'a créé ensemble avec le groupe-là, on a discuté que personne ne voulait les avoir, ça m'a vraiment convaincu tu sais, que j'étais à la bonne place. A ma fête, ils ont fait semblable de tous venir à l'école, et ils se sont cachés dans un escalier pour m'apporter un gâteau en chantant bonne fête .... C'était la quand j'ai réalisé que je leur avais donné une challenge et une envie d'apprendre, et ça d'était la plus grande réalisation.

Affirmations and recognition of achievements are wonderful when experienced. Françoise articulated her realization that this group of student had a desire to learn and her challenging them had led to what she called her greatest achievement. For teachers who demonstrated passion, experiencing tangible student learning in and through a challenging context appears to have fueled more passion. Lois described her experience:

> It made me believe in being a teacher to see a student who, when I first arrived, was having a very difficult time, didn't want to interact as much because he didn't want to say something wrong, but then was starting to take more risks by the time I left that classroom, and it was just an amazing - it really made me think I want to stay in this profession - this is why I'm doing this profession.

Lily experienced a similar boost in motivation from observing positive shifts in student attitudes when she and her team:

> were able to kind of change the self-deprecating words into words of encouragement on the part of the youth. So, for example, the youth would often say, 'I can't do this'. And the youth has become a leader in helping other kids believe in themselves and say, 'I'm having a hard time, but I can try instead of I can't'. And, yeah. So, that's been a big motivator to continue teaching and continue working with youth.

Lily expressed her increased sense of efficacy as she experienced her students transform before her eyes. She found this to be highly motivational, especially as those same students began to exert a positive influence on other students. Cassie stated that she did not consider leaving the teaching profession, but she had been through some moments where she felt appreciative that she was a teacher:

> Well, I wasn't really contemplating leaving the teaching profession, but certainly there are moments - yeah, of course there are moments when you - when I felt, like, thank goodness I was here. I had a suicidal student, for example. That was a big one, and I recognized it and talked to him about it and then got him to some help. And really, of course, at moments like that, you wonder if - if you - if I hadn't, would, in fact, anybody have noticed?

Similarly, Alessandra noted that there had been moments when she had felt like she had had a positive impact on students, but she added that this "generally has not overridden the stress and difficulty that [she] faced as a new teacher." In a similar vein, Myles experienced positive feelings of enjoyment when kids expressed their appreciation to him: "There are some nice moments, like when kids give you things, or they come up and they say oh, you're my favourite teacher … I feel relaxed and confident in my skills, and that's always a nice feeling."

Lise expressed that her nice moments are when she observes the students have learned something new and when they are curious, happy and show their affection to learn. For her, it was moments like these that explained why she teaches. She said:

> Enfin, chaque fois que je vois que les élèves apprennent quelque chose de nouveau, puis les élèves ont les poser, quand je vois que les élèves apprennent quelque chose de nouveau, et puis qu'ils sont heureux d'apprendre puis ils sont contents qu'ils apprennent, c'est les moments comme ça que j'enseigne…C'est vraiment les liens avec les élèves … Puis j'apprends toujours, il y a toujours des choses à apprendre, donc il y a des possibilités à l'apprentissage.

Lise articulates the reciprocity of learning. She is encouraged by her students' desire to learn and their happiness in learning. She realizes that her own learning and excitement of her students' learning gives her moments of special engagement with her students and her work. Finally, it was evident that having a positive mindset, being proactive, and being patient, have been instrumental factors that encouraged new teachers to stay in the profession, kept them going, and prompted involvement in professional development.

## Leadership and Support from School Administration

When we asked the study participants about the administrative relationships or behaviours that supported their development, some shared stories of how school leaders played a supportive role in their development, while some suggested that roles were supportive, but only in certain areas. Others indicated that their needs for support went unanswered. Analysis of their responses is presented below under two categories: *supportive roles* and *little or no support*.

### Supportive Roles

Our participants emphasized that varied supports were both needed and appreciated. Principals have a role to play in the support of new teachers, from being accessible, to providing resources, to guiding teachers. Many teachers, such as Myles, believed that principals should be approachable and accessible, responsive, and also be effective communicators. Maira appreciated judgment-free leadership. When she requested help, "they would give me every resource, and they would never judge me for saying I need help." Maira made the link between her needs as a teacher and sound pedagogy by stating, "That's the same thing I expect from my kids in my class. If I ask them a question, I want them … to feel comfortable enough to say, I don't know." Data showed that principals made a positive impact upon teachers in supporting them through "tricky" situations. Several teachers discussed the crucial role that the principal or vice principal had played in facilitating their interactions with parents. Jane stated that "having the principal stick up for you when the parents can be difficult; that's important." Christina appreciated the coaching that had taken place in her interactions with parents, "I had to make a few uncomfortable phone calls, and she [the principal] was very supportive about practising what I could say and making sure that I came off in the most professional way." Evelyn liked her vice-principal's proactive approach since he guided her on how "to properly answer emails or phone calls. If I ever had to phone home for a parent, he said he could be there with me just to be giving me tips and stuff, so I think that was great." Another participant, Charlotte, "really appreciate[d] that they make themselves available and they're always willing to take the time to help [her if she had] a problem."

For some new teachers, it was beneficial if principals checked in with them, visited classrooms, provided feedback, and challenged them to be better teachers. Ken praised his principals:

> They challenged me to be a better teacher, and they challenged me based on my individual goals. They didn't give me generic feedback ... Their comments were always authentic ... they really made me want to walk the extra mile for them.

Ken noted that when principals supported teachers it was really a strategy to put students first; this was the case of professional relationships that affirmed the teachers and benefitted students. A few teachers found their administration supportive with time and money for professional development. Cassie benefitted from a "budget that permitted (her) to attend one conference annually." Kandace benefitted from a mentoring program that her school district was offering, noting that administration "was very supportive, and I really appreciated that he allowed me ... to take that time to work with a mentor."

While many interviewees hoped for a supportive leadership team to assist them in finding their way; some teachers, such as Lise, identified having the freedom to experiment, and, indeed, to be able to make mistakes, as part of a learning curve, without fear of reprisal. When she made mistakes, Lise trusted that her administrator would support and guide her throughout the experimental processes: « elle est là pour me soutenir, mais elle me laisse quand même essayer de nouvelles choses ... qui nous soutiens si jamais qu'il y a des erreurs qui sont faits. « Similarly, Kamille wanted administrators to develop relationships of trust with teachers and to lead by suggestion and not by orders:

> Des relations de confiance, des relations de quelqu'un qui
> écoute à nos idées, mais ... j'ai besoin vraiment des personnes

qui suggèrent et qui font faire leur point de vue sans nécessairement donner des ordres.

In addition, most of the teachers in our sample appreciated the support of positive administrators: non-judgmental leaders who encouraged
good relationships, explained things well, and created favourable working
conditions. The willingness of experienced leaders to help, guide, share,
and support early teachers proved invaluable to developing their confidence and resilience.

### Little or No Support

Unfortunately, some of our interviewees received little, limited, or
no support in their early years of teaching. Their responses pointed to
the complex relationships between new teachers and administrators. For
example, Françoise believed that although most teachers aimed to please,
the relationship with the administration was not fully transparent, thus
causing problems. Her principal expected her to keep in touch; yet not
approach him with needs, since he expected this kind of support to be provided by her colleagues:

> C'est toujours bizarre la relation avec les directeurs, on veut
> absolument leur plaire ... J'ai pas l'impression que ce soit une
> relation à 100% transparent ... la responsabilité d'accueillir
> les nouveaux enseignants à d'autres enseignants plutôt que du
> directeur lui-même.

Françoise understood that her principal supported her growth by
using the mentorship program, thus delegating mentorship tasks to another
colleague; but the lack of transparency led her to pretend that she knew
what she was doing in order to avoid administrative disapproval, which
might, in turn, lead to nonrenewal of her contract. Lack of transparency
and mixed messages eroded Françoise's trust in her employers. When she
discovered her assigned mentor listening to her teaching her class out of
sight from the hallway and without her knowledge, she didn't know if the
mentor's secrecy was being used to support her growth or to be reported to
the school board for reprisal. Thus, she concluded that the best mentorship
support would come from a like-minded colleague with whom there were
mutual values and trust.

We heard from teachers who did not get a formal evaluation that might have helped them in terms of their development. Helen and Anya both needed more help than just daily routines. Anya projected frustration when she noted:

> I didn't get any professional development from them. They didn't come and check me as I taught ... I was in my first year ... I know that they're busy, but I really found that I didn't get ... any assistance with my actual teaching. No one ever came to watch me ever. No reviews or anything.

Nick received a formal evaluation, but not from his principal. A retired teacher was brought in to observe and write up the evaluation, because "the superintendents were overloaded."

Alli, Françoise and Maribelle each noted the work overload that characterized administrative roles, with the effect that leadership tasks became the obligation of colleagues. They observed that these supportive tasks were downloaded from administration to teachers who were already busy, but Alli speculated, "I don't think that responsibility really lies with my grade-alike teachers." Her experience echoed the sentiments of a number of participants that the principal was so busy that they had assumed that their teachers did not need support. For Mark, "it was more the other teachers in my department that really reached out and helped and gave suggestions and such." Teachers cited the lack of support in important areas such as low literacy, low SES, and special needs. For example, Ruth argued for her need of increased "support in special education as well as socio-economic awareness."

Finally, several teachers cited lack of support as the reason they had considered leaving the profession. At the time of interviews, one teacher had already left, and one teacher was in the process of a career change; while a few others were thinking about it. Alessandra, whose story was highlighted earlier in this chapter, shared with us that she considered leaving the profession because of the negative and challenging relationship she had had with her principal:

> The lack of support from my administrators was a major issue for me and has been the largest factor in me considering leaving the profession. My school principal was dismissive

of my concerns. She was not supportive. She did not set up any structure that would help a new teacher find her feet. Anytime I tried to take the initiative, I was shot down. Anytime I tried to ask questions, I was dismissed.

Alessandra's words are powerful and sad. She shares her terrible experience as a reminder to school administrators that words can foster life or yield destruction. Not listening, not providing timely support, dismissive comments and discouraging words can be devastating, as in this former teacher's case.

It is clear, then, that just as the supports new teachers received had led to a sense of increased confidence and resilience in the face of this demanding profession, the lack of supports was disempowering and demotivating. In our sample, supported teachers felt better able to meet the high demands of the profession; while unsupported teachers felt unsafe professionally and even considered leaving the profession.

## Advice to Other New Teachers

In one of the questions, we invited teachers to indicate the advice they would give to other new teachers regarding the development of resilience and well-being. Their pieces of advice were collated under the following themes: Work-Life Balance; Nurturing a Healthy Mindset; Reflective Inquiry; and, the 3 Cs: *Connect*, *Consult*, and *Collaborate*.

### Work-Life Balance

The most repeated pieces of advice that the interviewees offered were to maintain a work-life balance, to take care of mental health, and to do something that is not school related. They explained that when teachers need to prove themselves, they can easily become overwhelmed and unbalanced. For example, Christina explained the importance of self-care, from health to hobbies:

Getting enough sleep, making sure that there is a work-life balance, that you're not spending all of your time creating new lesson plans and thinking about work...take the time to pursue hobbies. Pursuing counselling ... because if you can't take care of yourself and if there's a problem with you, you can't take care of the students.

Lois echoed Christina, stating that teachers need to "step back and give themselves a life." Evelyn, who played basketball, believed that her involvement in community sports was good to "get away from school for even an hour, just to do something completely unrelated to work and just relax." Mike, who coached sports at his school, advised that when taking on a volunteer or extra-curricular activity, one ensure that it "needs to have an end date, so at least you get a bit of a breather before you get burnt out." Stewart suggested that teachers' work-life balance would benefit from doing something healthy outside of work. He explained it this way:

> Be prepared to take your work home with you, but you're definitely going to need some time for yourself. Take up running, do something, because if you go home and mark and plan until midnight every night, you're going to burn out pretty fast … You know, you love these kids, and you want to do your best for them, but you can't do the best for them if you're not in a good place mentally.

Lebert, on the other hand, advised teachers not to bring work home:

> When you're off work, you're off work. That's been very successful for me. I do my job when I'm at work, and if I have to stay late at work, I stay late at work, but I don't take it home, and there's a very clear separation between my home life and my work life.

Maribelle urged defining one's own healthy boundaries, even if this meant not always finishing a job. In a profession where the job is never fully done, Maribelle advised her peers "to draw a line and say, if I get it done, I do, and if I don't, I have to just sort of make do" in order to increase resilience for the long run.

## Nurturing a Healthy Mindset

Many teachers talked about the importance of mindset. They advised being proactive, patient, and realistic about what can be accomplished at first. Among others, Bob and Mackenzie encouraged teachers to be flexible and to seek help when unsure about how to handle situations. Bob added, "it's always better to go and ask for help when you think it's needed rather than try to handle a situation you aren't sure about." Bob further expressed the impact that caring for children has on one's career:

> You have to love children, and if you don't, you're not going to last five minutes. And you need to have an attitude of humility, and an openness to learning is huge. It's impossible to do it without that. You have to be constantly questioning your practice.

According to Lily, initiating requests for help leads to teaching success. She explained that when teachers "were very confined to their own classrooms, to their own ideas of education and to ideas of how to teach and didn't ask for much support, those were the teachers who were not as successful in their first year of teaching." For Alli, asking for help was pragmatic from a training standpoint, and preserves one's wellness. As mentioned earlier in this chapter, she advised "not to pretend that you're okay if you're not." To do so Alli interacted with retired teachers, who have "been really helpful ... I meet them for lunch, just getting their different points of view ... then you realize that other people feel the same way." Although this seems to be problematic from a school effectiveness and improvement standpoint, Nick highlighted the importance of "letting go" of certain policies and administrative norms that teachers have no control over, and focus instead on what teachers can do for their students.

These novices noted that keeping negative interactions in check helped with their resiliency. Shana advised teachers not to "internalize the negativity that you might feel, you know, with students or with other staff or parents or with administration." Myles thought that balancing negative interactions with positive thoughts helped "for developing resiliency, in any given position, it would just be to make sure that you interact with the other individuals, try to be positive in all ways, and always interact positively with others." In order to maintain a positive mindset, Christina and Shelle suggested that teachers without passion do not thrive. However, Lois warned of losing clarity because of too much passion: "I think that's the toughest thing about this profession ... If you are passionate about it, you lose sight of yourself." Last but not least, Kamille concluded with the following affirmation: « Aye confiance en toi. » [Believe in yourself.]

## Reflective Inquiry

The benefit of reflecting on one's work as a path to development was featured throughout the interview data. Anya suggested that teachers need to reflect upon their work:

> You need to keep things confidential but having someone you could confide in about situations ... I did a lot of talking ... how it made me feel, and how I felt, my goals, kind of reflecting on what a teacher does.

When developing pedagogy at the beginning of one's career, Marilyn advised teachers to be practical and learn from "bad days," but she warned teachers not to be too hard on themselves when they tried something and it did not work out:

> Remember that every lesson isn't always going to be a hundred per cent, it can't be. And so, if something goes wrong then ... deal with it, but not get down on yourself ... realize everybody has bad days, bad lessons and to just move on.

Reflecting on one's practice helped our teacher participants to take inventories of what worked, what did not work, and what needed adjusting; these reflective processes ultimately supported the second theme, above, to nurture a positive mind-set.

## Consult, Connect, and Collaborate: The Three Cs

Many interviewees recommended an approach that can be called "3 Cs:" consulting a mentor, connecting with colleagues, and collaborating with others. When choosing professionals with whom to consult, new teachers highlighted the importance of trust and accessibility. Being able to trust one another in consultation increases the impact of the connection and collaboration. Accessibility ensured that ongoing connection and collaboration would take place. Ruth suggested that beginning teachers "find a mentor ... to have somebody support you and know that you're the right person for this job, and that it's going to take time ... having somebody to talk to about the process." Kamille emphasized the importance of trusting relationships when it comes to choosing who to consult with. She advised teachers to make friends with teachers in other schools, and people who work with youth, and to ask as many questions of others as possible:

« Fais-toi confiance. Demande des questions même si tu penses qu'elles sont stupides ... trouve-toi quelqu'un à qui tu peux discuter ouvertement. » Tennae advised new teachers to be pragmatic and to find "one principal mentor or somebody you could go to." She conceded that many new teachers move from position to position, so it can be "hard to develop a sort of consistency in a relationship." Françoise advised teachers to find someone with similar values with whom to discuss matters, such as an older teacher, a classmate, a teacher in another school, and then ask questions and talk and explore, knowing that they will not be judged or belittled for your questions or what they are going through. She cautioned that the advice coming from teachers with different values can sometimes be very demoralizing: « Il y a certains profs qui ont pas la même vision...puis de s'entourer avec des personnes qui ne pensent pas pareille, ça peut être vraiment insécurisant. » For lesson planning, Alessandra prioritized efficiency: "get [colleagues] to share their resources with you." Marilyn shared advice that she was given and found helpful. The advice was to "beg, borrow, and steal everything you can." For the larger, more philosophical issues, our findings were that positive, affirming relationships with experienced educators who are accessible was the key to successful development of new teachers.

## Teachers' Needs, Concerns, and Hopes

Finally, in this section we detail the theme of early career teachers' needs and hopes. This theme emerged from our interviewees' responses to the question: "Is there anything else you would like to share with us?" To say the least, all of them greatly appreciated this open venue to share about their needs, concerns, aspirations, and hopes. Most of them further emphasized the benefits of having a formal mentorship program for new teachers, or at least some kind of orientation to help them. For example, Shelle, from British Columbia, suggested:

> I think if you are working in a district that doesn't have a mentorship program, or at least a mentorship program was supposed to be set up for new teachers that aren't on contract, I would really like to see at least some information for new teachers about pursuing a mentorship that isn't formalized, so some kind of suggestions or pieces or orientation that

talk about mentorship and accessing a mentor can happen, even if there isn't a formal program set up already.

When we asked the Ontario participants about their needs, concerns and hopes they expressed concerns about the contradictory nature of the LTO regulation and the associated challenges that they faced in their first years of teaching. The hiring processes and other regulations across Canada were highlighted among our participants, with the hopes of having their voices heard. The teachers highlighted the challenges of supply teaching and the lack of new teacher induction programs for occasional teachers. Several teachers reiterated that they were unable to define their mentorship programs, from selection criteria to objectives and goals, to scope. They appreciated the benefits of the program but also noted that the program was not available to all new teachers.

Many of these early career teachers reflected on the fact that new teachers had "enough on their plate already," and they wished that their administrations would embrace this idea. They suggested creating and communicating clear expectations about the number of classes and subjects that early teachers should teach, because they often got overwhelmed with unreasonable expectations. Kandace went as far as to assert that a regulation should be in place for early teachers, to limit the number of different classes that they were to teach:

> My first year, I taught eight different classes, and I teach in junior high, and I think that that really contributed to the amount of stress that I was experiencing. I think that it would be beneficial to have some regulations or rules in place for early teachers to limit the amount of different subjects that they have to teach, and maybe increase the amount of preps or spares that they get so that they have more time to plan and more time to work with mentor teachers.

Others highlighted their school's specific challenges (e.g., literacy skills, discipline, attendance) and suggested that decision makers should pay attention to these areas. Jane highlighted some of her school's challenges and said: "I'm shocked with the literacy skills. They're very low. Very, very low. Like, I'm talking these kids are in grade nine and can't write simple sentences." When we asked her about the reason behind this, the teacher answered: "Mainly attendance, but secondly, English is a second language. ... or their parents aren't educated and don't practise with them, or you know, support them in school. But a lot of it is attendance."

> Several have also shed light on funding issues. Alessandra said: I do actually think that the major piece of the problem is the lack of funding in public education ... the lack of supports that are available is hugely problematic, especially to new teachers, and the level of support that children need in order to be successful is so much higher than what is available to us.

Alessandra was able to look beyond her own circumstances to the larger system challenges and accompanying concerns with respect to the inadequacy of funding to a level that the learning needs of all children could be addressed.

Finally, the disconnect in communication between the university and the school boards was mentioned. The interviewees reminisced about their teacher preparation programs, noting the realization and recognition of being "less prepared in some areas" when they commenced their teaching, especially when it came to special education. In essence, while participants expressed their needs and concerns, the overall feeling was that they were placing these perspectives "out there" with the hope of bringing changes into their valued, respected, but highly demanding professional path of teaching.

## Discussion and Conclusions

The interview process was an enriching learning experience as we gathered insights from a cross-section of Canadian teachers on their early careers. While many of the findings do not come as a surprise, they do corroborate and add to the extant literature on early career teaching from the pan-Canadian perspective. Despite the geographic, contextual, and policy differences of the lived experiences of our participants, there were more similarities than discrepancies in their responses. The majority of them benefitted from formal supports from administrators, mentors, and guides, as well as informal support from colleagues and others. In both kinds of support, good relationships played a significant role in the successful development of teachers; whereas poor relationships affected new teachers dramatically, leading some to leave their profession. Overall, supportive relationships with peers, administration, and community help beginning teachers with socialization into the teaching profession (Fenwick, 2011; Long et al., 2012; Tillman, 2005).

The most frequently cited external factors influencing teacher retention were related to the support from experienced people in education, who had been willing to help, guide, share, and support in professional and interpersonal ways. When new teachers had faced a myriad of challenges, interpersonal supports could be of great impact (Friedrichsen, Chval, & Teuscher, 2007). However, as Andrews and Akerson (2012) noted, "the value of having a mentor teacher depends greatly on the mentor" (p. 10). Furthermore, friendship was found to be a helpful factor in successful mentorships (Achinstein & Barrett, 2004; Burris, Kitchel, Greiman, & Torres, 2006; Lee & Feng, 2007). This supports Françoise's suggestion that the pairing of mentors be based on similar values, which in turn builds trust (Gardiner, 2012). Some interviewees recommended the establishment of formalized mentorship programs. Clark and Byrnes (2012) maintained that administrative support embedded into mentorship relationships strengthens them. Good mentorship programs foster confidence in teachers, while reducing stress (Allen & Eby, 2007; Lacey, 2000), and also increase student achievement and teacher retention (Anhorn, 2008; Darling-Hammond, 2003; Wynn, Carboni, & Patall, 2007). Finally, our findings support the claim that a supportive school climate and good relations with parents (Castro, Kelly, & Shih, 2010; Perry & Hayes, 2011) further benefit new teachers.

The predominant internal influence for retention was the high level of passion that teachers felt for their profession. Many of these teachers had a strong desire to help students thrive. When teachers felt successful, they were affirmed in their choice of profession, suggesting a harmonious type of passion that increases adaptability (Carbonneau, Vallerand, Fernet, & Guay, 2008).

In contrast to those who felt supported, teachers who were frustrated by systemic obstacles within teaching spoke of leaving the teaching profession. We found that their lack of support resulted in these teachers battling anxiety over daily events. When administration was unresponsive to supporting teachers, this neglect affected their emotional health (Brindley & Parker, 2010), and increased their sense of isolation and frustration (Brindley & Parker, 2010; Cherubini, Kitchen, & Hodson, 2008; Frels, Zientek & Onwuegbuzie, 2013). Compounding the variety of demands upon teachers—such as those cited by these teachers—with a lack of resources, insufficient support and inconsistent communication, teachers felt ineffective, and this led to attrition (Moir, Barlin, Gless, & Miles, 2009). Andrea, who had already left her teaching position for the reasons cited above, was thankful for the opportunity to speak with us in hopes that the message will get out and that conditions might improve in the future.

New teachers' understanding of leadership roles in their schools echoed our discussion of retention and attrition. Leaders who are knowledgeable and supportive provided extra resiliency to teachers in their moments of vulnerability. In addition to supportive roles adopted by administrators, when new teachers experienced support from colleagues and delegated mentors, they clearly benefitted. Nonetheless, some of the teachers believed that administrators were too busy to give them the support that they need. On the one hand, the imperative for administrators to make time for such support (Catapano & Huisman, 2013; Certo, 2005) was compelling; and yet one must also consider the possible risks when blending mentorship with an evaluation role (Glazerman et al., 2008), which also lies squarely with the administrative team.

The importance of work-life balance featured prominently in our findings. It is fascinating and exhilarating to immerse oneself in teaching, but the demands upon new teachers are monumental. Work-life balance theory explores the complex interplay of opposing factors in pursuit of harmony (Poelmans, Kalliath, & Brough, 2008). Neglecting self-care takes a toll, as many new teachers had learned the hard way. Part of what makes the work-life balance so critical is the importance of maintaining a positive mindset and committing to reflective practices (Wood & Stanulis, 2009). Teachers advised consultation, connection, and collaboration, which were found to be beneficial (Abbott, Moran, & Clarke, 2009).

The extant literature speaks to the data that we collected in our interviews; however, in some cases, these data also open up complexities within this field to be further explored. We have limited our discussion to the key findings and insights from our interviews, but also note that some of the more specific findings, such as restrictive provincial policies and the role of communication between universities and school boards, also require further inquiry.

# References

Abbott, L., Moran, A., & Clarke, L. (2009). Northern Ireland beginning teachers' experiences of induction: the 'haves' and the 'have nots'. *European Journal of Teacher Education, 32*(2), 95–110. doi:10.1080/02619760802613313

Achinstein, B., & Barrett, A. (2004). (Re)framing classroom contexts: How new teachers and mentors view diverse learners and challenges of practice. *Teachers College Record, 106*(4), 716–746.

Allen, T. D., & Eby, L. T. (2007). *The Blackwell handbook of mentoring: A multiple perspectives approach*. Oxford, UK: Blackwell Publishing Ltd.

Andrews, N., & Akerson, A. (2012). Mentoring: A university approach. *National Teacher Education Journal, 5*(1), 29–34.

Andrews, B. D., & Quinn, R. J. (2004). First-year teaching assignments: A descriptive analysis. *The Clearing House, 78*(2), 78–83.

Anhorn, R. (2008). The profession that eats its young. *The Delta Kappa Gamma Bulletin, 74*(3), 15–26.

Brindley, R., & Parker, A. (2010). Transitioning to the classroom: Reflections of second-career teachers during the induction year. *Teachers and Teaching, 16*(5), 577–594. doi:10.1080/13540602.2010.507967

Burris, S., Kitchel, T., Greiman, B. C., & Torres, R. M. (2006). Beginning and mentor agriculture teachers' perceptions of psychosocial assistance, similarities, and satisfaction. *Journal of Agricultural Education, 47*(4), 64–75. doi:10.5032/jae.2006.04064

Carbonneau, N., Vallerand, R. J., Fernet, C., & Guay, F. (2008). The role of passion for teaching in intrapersonal and interpersonal outcomes. *Journal of Educational Psychology, 100*(4), 977–987. doi:10.1037/a0012545

Castro, A. J., Kelly, J., & Shih, M. (2010). Resilience strategies for new teachers in high-needs areas. *Teaching and Teacher Education, 26*(3), 622–629. doi:10.1016/j.tate.2009.09.010

Catapano, S., & Huisman, S. (2013). Leadership in hard-to-staff schools: Novice teachers as mentors. *Mentoring & Tutoring: Partnership in Learning, 21*(3), 258–271. doi:10.1080/13611267.2013.827833

Certo, J. L. (2005). Support, challenge, and the two-way street: Perceptions of a beginning second grade teacher and her quality mentor. *Journal of Early Childhood Teacher Education, 26*, 3–21.

Cherubini, L., Kitchen, J., & Hodson, J. (2008). Aboriginal epistemologies and new teacher induction: The context of a bi-epistemic research endeavour. *Brock Education, 18*, 79–89.

Clark, S. K., & Byrnes, D. (2012). Through the eyes of the novice teacher: Perceptions of mentoring support. *Teacher Development, 16*(1), 43–54. doi:10.1080/13664530.2012.666935

Darling-Hammond, L. (2003). Keeping good teachers: Why it matters, what leaders can do. *Educational Leadership, 60*(8), 6–13.

Ewing, R., & Smith, D. (2003). Retaining quality early career teachers in the profession. *English Teaching Practice and Critique, 2*(1), 15–32

Fenwick, A. (2011). The first three years: Experiences of early career teachers. *Teachers and Teaching, 17*(3), 325–343. doi:10.1080/13540602.2011.55 4707

Frels, R. K., Zientek, L. R., & Onwuegbuzie, A. J. (2013). Differences of mentoring experiences across grade span among principals, mentors, and mentees. *Mentoring & Tutoring: Partnership in Learning, 21*(1), 28–58. doi:10.1080/13611267.2013.784058

Friedrichsen, P., Chval, K. B., & Teuscher, D. (2007). Strategies and sources of support for beginning teachers of science and mathematics. *School Science and Mathematics, 107*(5), 169–181.

Gardiner, W. (2012). Coaches' and new urban teachers' perceptions of induction coaching: Time, trust, and accelerated learning curves. *The Teacher Educator, 47*(3), 195–215. doi:10.1080/08878730.2012.685797

Glazerman, S., Isenberg, E., Dolfin, S., Bleeker, M., Johnson, A., Grider, M., & Jacobus, M. (2010). *Impacts of comprehensive teacher induction: Final results from a randomized controlled study (NCEE 2010-4027).* Washington, DC: National Center for Education Evaluation and Regional Assistance, Institute of Education Sciences, U.S. Department of Education.

Halford, J. M. (1998). Easing the way for new teachers. *Educational Leadership, 55*(5), 33–34.

Howe, E. R. (2006). Exemplary teacher induction: An international review. *Educational Philosophy and Theory, 38*(3), 287–297.

Johnson, S. M., & Kardos, S. M. (2002). Keeping new teachers in mind. *Educational Leadership, 59*(6), 12–16.

Joseph, R. (2000). *Stress free teaching: A practical guide to tackling stress in teaching, lecturing and tutoring.* London, UK: Routledge.

Kauffman, D., Johnson, S. M., Kardos, S. M., Liu, E., & Peske, H. G. (2002). "Lost at sea:" New teachers' experiences with curriculum and assessment. *Teachers College Record, 104*(2), 273–300.

Lacey, K. (2000). *Making mentoring happen: A simple and effective guide to implementing a successful mentoring program.* London, UK: Allen & Unwin.

Lee, J. C., & Feng, S. (2007). Mentoring support and the professional development of beginning teachers: A Chinese perspective. *Mentoring & Tutoring: Partnership in Learning, 15*(3), 243–262. doi:10.1080/13611260701201760

Long, J. S., McKenzie-Robblee, S., Schaefer, L., Steeves, P., Wnuk, S., Pinnegar, E., & Clandinin, D. J. (2012). Literature review on induction and mentoring related to early career teacher attrition and retention. *Mentoring & Tutoring: Partnership in Learning, 20*(1), 7–26. doi:10.1080/13611267.2012.645598

Moir, E., Barlin, D., Gless, J., & Miles, J. (2009). *New teacher mentoring: Hopes and promise for improving teacher effectiveness.* Cambridge, MA: Harvard Education Press.

Patterson, M. (2005). Hazed! *Educational Leadership, 62*(8), 20–23.

Perry, B., & Hayes, K. (2011). The effect of a new teacher induction program on new teachers reported teacher goals for excellence, mobility, and retention rates. *The International Journal of Educational Leadership Preparation, 6*(1), 1–12.

Poelmans, S. A., Kalliath, T., & Brough, P. (2008). Achieving work-life balance: Current theoretical and practice issues. *Journal of Management & Organization, 14*(3), 227–238. doi:10.5172/jmo.837.14.3.227

Rosenthal, R., & Jacobson, L. (1968). Pygmalion in the classroom. *The Urban Review, 3*(1), 16–20.

Tillman, L. C. (2005). Mentoring new teachers: Implications for leadership practice in an urban school. *Educational Administration Quarterly, 41*(4), 609–629. doi:10.1177/0013161x04274272

Wood, A. L., & Stanulis, R. N. (2009). Quality teacher induction: "Fourth-wave" (1997–2006) induction programs. *The New Educator, 5*, 1–23.

Wynn, S. R., Carboni, L. W., & Patall, E. A. (2007). Beginning teachers' perceptions of mentoring, climate, and leadership: Promoting retention through a learning communities perspective. *Leadership and Policy in Schools, 6*(3), 209–229. doi:10.1080/15700760701263790

## Chapter 8

# Unentitled

*Keith Alcock*

I sit in my classroom.
Listening to my students play outside.
Some they frantically seek
While others cleverly hide.

There are those talking about projects.
And those applying their new knowledge of rocks.
There's a group playing soccer
And Chad will of course have muddy socks.

Some slide. Some swing.
Half of them have untied shoes.
But, I listen and smile
And write this poem for you.

Writing poems and teaching.
Well, they are rewarding and life's special treat.
To succeed with both you have to be
Honest, motivated and a little bit neat.

I was hired three years ago.
And it marked a major milestone.
A very happy moment
And I felt perfectly alone.

Yes, alone. On an island.
Just me. That's it and that's all.
But who ever said being alone
Was equivalent to a fall?

"Be confident," I said.
My aloneness leading to great introspection.
After all, you have the ability to steer yourself
In any direction.

So, I looked around the island.
I searched with openness and glee.
"Search," I said. "Search"
And sure enough, I found opportunities available for me.

Teaching and learning opportunities.
Are at the top of the trees and hidden under large sand dunes.
For they will not come to those
Who need to be fed by a spoon.

Regrettably or not, young teachers.
Always have to prove their worth.
But if you want an island
You have to shovel some earth.

Don't be mistaken. Mentorship chances.
Are available by ship.
But, if you are looking to create your own island,
Should you really leave on a trip?

Instead, I found mentorship naturally.
For it is always there.
The teacher beside me
Or the custodian, whose office is by the stairs.

So, when asked what supports help teachers.
What supports are the best?
Honesty and perspective from them
And you have to be willing to do the rest.

I will take ownership of my teaching.
And I ask that you create a learning environment for us all.
So, that all educational staff members
Can pick-up and answer the call.

I say, read books aloud and listen to conversations.
Even the ones that you have with yourself.
Build professional development bridges
And, perhaps, a shelf for that elf.

Meaningful support beams, after all.
Are those put up by your own desire.
Professional development and experiences are available
But, you have to be the one that says, "higher."

Yes, there will be problems and some.
Outside of the controllable doors.
Don't even get me started
On that Regulation 274.

It is sad. It is frustrating.
Watching young teachers depart.
Truth be told the situation—
Well, it hurts my very heart.

It is so unbelievably hard.
To look a parent, or worse, a student in the eye.
And tell them with a grin,
"I won't be back, but I'll try."

Try. That's what I tell myself. Try.
Don't let yourself be disposed of.
Because the fact is,
I'm doing something I truly love.

So, I will continue to build my island.
And make bridges out of palm tree wire.
I will seek out opportunities
And continually build my fire.

It is easy to create a smile,
On someone's face.
But it's far more rewarding to help students
Ignite and accomplish their own race.

With that, the recess bell has rung.
And soon, learning will be all about.
I walk excitedly to the door
I have no intentions of ever burning out.

## Chapter 9

# Voices of Hope: Sustaining Learning and Optimism Through a Protracted and Jagged Entry to the Teaching Profession in Ontario

*Kathryn Broad, Stefanie Muhling*

## Introduction

From 2013 to the present, while serving as Education Officers with the Ministry of Education, we have had the privilege of visiting faculties of education and school districts in Ontario to learn about the entry-to-practice experiences of, and supports provided for, new teachers. The courage and resilience of the new teachers, as well as the sensitivity and dedication of their mentors and school leaders, were evident from these conversations. We were continually inspired and humbled by the optimism, vitality, creativity and commitment of the new teachers. They had frequently encountered long and bumpy paths into their teaching careers. We were also impressed by the ideas and actions described by the mentors and colleagues with whom they had worked. In this chapter, it is our intention to provide a window into the lived experiences of early career teachers and the colleagues who support them on their routes to permanent teaching in Ontario. We do so by directly sharing the powerful voices of hope and experience of new teachers and mentors. We believe that these stories of learning and growth within particularly challenging contexts will have resonance and application for teachers and mentors in a multitude of settings.

We begin this chapter with an overview of the context of Ontario's entry to practice for teachers, and then move to a discussion of the questions and responses of new teachers and the mentors, colleagues, administrators and system leaders who supported their growth and transition into the profession. We conclude with a call to move forward in ways that honour and build upon the wisdom, actions, and learning shared by these educators.

## Entry to Practice in Ontario

### Oversupply of Teachers

For many early career teachers in Ontario, the route to permanent employment has been a long, and often circuitous and bumpy journey. Ontario has experienced a significant oversupply of teachers since 2005, which has resulted in a challenging job market for graduates from teacher education programs. The increasing oversupply has been documented by the Ontario College of Teachers (OCT), the regulatory body responsible for the licensing and certification of teachers, for regulation of the profession in the public interest, and for accrediting initial and continuing teacher education programs. Since 2001, the OCT has been conducting an annual survey of teachers in their first five years following graduation. The annual Transition to Teaching (T2T) study provides a longitudinal view of the trends in early teacher employment, and offers information about learning opportunities and supports for graduates of teacher education programs based upon samples of voluntary respondents. The 2010 T2T report outlines contextual factors that have affected employment opportunities for new teachers, including declining enrolments, declining rate of teacher retirements, and reduction in policy changes that necessitated additional teachers (such as implementation of primary class size caps, introduction of Student Success positions in secondary schools, and increases to preparation times). In addition, this report concluded that these factors have resulted in long "job queues …as new teachers compete with underemployed graduates of earlier years for the comparatively limited number of openings" (OCT, 2011, p. 1).

The authors of the 2015 T2T report suggested that the "teacher surplus peaked in 2013" (OCT, 2016, p. 1). However, the reality of a long path to a permanent position has continued for graduates of English-language programs, and particularly for those who are qualified to teach Junior Kindergarten – Grade 6. Many beginning teachers are still constructing their employment by piecing together occasional positions, part-time and short-term positions, and many are supplementing their incomes with work outside of teaching. At noted in the 2015 report, one third of early career teachers were still not fully employed within the first five years following graduation. As a contrast, Ontario graduates who leave Ontario report better employment outcomes. The OCT also reported that the number of early career teachers who do not renew their annual membership has increased (OCT, 2016).

Thus, it seems that under-employment, teaching in multiple schools, part-time and long-term occasional (LTO) positions are the norm for most graduates of English-language programs for the first couple of years. At the same time, the 2015 OCT Annual Report indicated that employment outcomes are improving, particularly for graduates of French-language programs and those qualified to teach French as a Second Language (for details, see http://reports.oct.ca/2015/en/statistics/index.html).

In 2014-15 and 2015-16, participants in focus groups at Ontario faculties of education and new teachers, as well as mentors and New Teacher Induction Program leads, corroborated the realities of a five year-long pathway into permanent teaching in publicly-funded school settings, with some variation due to region, language of instruction, and subject-area. In some districts, the vast majority, or in some cases all, newly employed teachers in permanent positions were in French Immersion or French as Second Language settings. This has resulted in differing needs for support and induction that are evident in the voices and stories to follow.

## Regulation 274: Hiring Practices

Another related factor affecting the hiring of teachers in Ontario is a regulation passed in 2012. In response to concerns that hiring practices and procedures varied across school districts, on August 13, 2012, "the government announced it will introduce a fair hiring regulation that will create a standardized, consistent and transparent approach to hiring occasional teachers for long-term occasional and permanent positions" (Ontario Ministry of Education, 2012)). The resulting Ontario Regulation 274/12 *Hiring Practices* stipulated a particular route to a permanent position in the teaching profession, and was described as an effort to increase clarity and to address concerns about the variability in employment practices, given the highly competitive job market. The regulation was passed in September 2012. However, as part of centrally negotiated agreements with the four provincial teacher federations, the Association des enseignantes et des enseignants franco-ontariens (AEFO) requested that they be exempted from the regulation. As of December, 2015, the regulation no longer applies to members of AEFO, nor to teachers seeking employment in French-language boards in Ontario.

Generally, the pathway for teachers seeking employment in English-Language School Boards according to O. Reg. 274/12 is outlined below:

1. All teachers wishing to apply for teaching positions must be successful in obtaining a place on an Occasional Teacher (OT) roster for each board in which they wish to seek employment;

2. Once successfully placed on the OT roster, an OT must complete 20 days of teaching within a 10-month period before being eligible to apply for placement on the Long Term Occasional (LTO) list;

3. Once successful in an interview to be placed on the LTO list, the OT can apply to LTO positions for which they hold the qualifications;

4. If not deemed unsuccessful in an LTO position of at least 80 days duration, the OT can apply for interviews leading to permanent positions for which they hold the qualifications; and

5. In the case of both LTO and permanent positions, the five qualified teachers with the greatest seniority on the roster or list are offered an interview. For LTO positions, the process of moving through persons with the required qualifications and greatest seniority continues until the position is filled.

While transparent, the process proved challenging to implement and has resulted in difficulties for both applicants and those involved in hiring. Consequences for early career teachers have been significant. The inclusion of seniority as a factor for determining which persons are to be considered for interviews for positions has meant that the individuals most recently added to the OT roster and LTO list (i.e., recent teacher education program graduates) have the longest wait to have an opportunity to apply. Given that each district maintains its own OT roster and LTO list, new teachers must complete the requirements within each district in which they hope to obtain employment. The requirements can complicate the efforts of early career teachers to manage several different occasional assignments and multiple locations. These and other challenges have been documented in a 2014 report (Directions Evidence and Policy Research Group, 2014) that summarized early implementation of the regulation. While this report indicated that having a clear developmental pathway into the profession provides benefits for applicants, concerns regarding discouragement of new graduates, based on the lack of availability of assignments, were identified.

## Support and Induction

Efforts to support teachers entering the profession in Ontario have been long-standing and retention of these teachers to the profession remains high. Since 2006, the New Teacher Induction Program (NTIP) has supported school districts to provide orientation, professional learning and mentoring to NTIP eligible teachers (http://www.edu.gov.on.ca/eng/teacher/induction.htm). NTIP eligibility has been amended in response to research and to the lengthier entry to the profession. Initially, the program was mandated for teachers in the first year of a permanent position. In 2009, based on research (Kane, 2009) and feedback from district school board partners, the program was extended to include teachers in their first Long Term Occasional assignment of 97 days or more. At the same time boards were permitted, at their own discretion, to extend support to teachers in their second year of contract employment, as well as to Continuing Education teachers. Supports for mentors have also been a critical and responsive element of NTIP, with focus on opportunities for job-embedded learning, learning-focused conversations and a growing understanding of mentoring as a web of support that involves and facilitates learning for all. Recently, additional needs for support for ongoing transitions have been identified in discussions with new teachers and board contacts. As described in this chapter, the current reality of a protracted entry into the teaching profession has engendered greater and more diverse needs for induction support. Two groups of teachers with increasingly recognized needs for support are those engaged in multiple and differing LTO positions over time, and those who may have held contract positions and been declared surplus before moving into yet another new position.

# Induction Journeys

As described above, these new realities have significantly impacted the journeys of the majority of early career teachers in Ontario and have resulted in a changed pattern of entry into the profession. This change has been recognized by teacher educators, policy-makers, school districts and, especially, by early career teachers, their mentors and their colleagues. As part of our roles as Education Officers, we conduct visits with different panels in various regions and settings across the Province of Ontario. To capture the lived experiences of the inspiring educators we had met during these visits, we invited a number of the new teachers and their colleagues to tell us about their journeys. Those educators who responded positively to an email invitation sent in late fall 2016 received a link to an online questionnaire comprised of a series of open-ended questions. The questions invited respondents to share their challenges and successes, the ways they continued to learn and collaborate, and the ways they were able to sustain optimism, energy and agency. Finally, we asked them to tell us about the learning they gained through these journeys.

## The Teachers

The early-career teachers who responded to our request to share their stories graduated from Ontario faculties of education between 2006 and 2014. They represented both elementary and secondary panels, with the majority holding elementary qualifications and one teacher being certified to teach in both panels. They worked in both Public and Catholic Boards of Education in various regions of the Province. LTO positions accounted for the majority of their work experience. Overwhelmingly, the road toward permanent employment for these Ontario teachers consisted of a multitude of LTO positions. The more recent graduates cited that they had held between one and three LTO positions. For those with a few more years of experience, it was most common to have held more than 10 different LTO positions. The teachers with whom we communicated were able to find multiple positions within a small group of schools, and all but one teacher reported having LTO positions located in between one and five schools.

### The Mentors and Supporters

Like the teachers they supported, the majority of the mentors with whom we communicated worked with teachers in the elementary panel. Several had supported teachers in both panels. The predominance of multiple LTO positions as described by the teachers (as above) was echoed by these mentors. Substantially more of their work had been supporting early career teachers in LTO positions than to providing support for NTIP teachers in contract positions. This is not a reflection of mentor/mentee pairs, as those mentors who responded to our questions were neither formally nor informally linked to the mentees. To our knowledge, only one of the mentor respondents had worked with any of the early career teachers with whom we spoke.

The following sections present the voices of early-career teachers, their mentors and their colleagues. Despite the struggles they described, the resounding story is one of hope, strength and continued growth throughout their long journeys from graduation into the teaching position.

## Challenges and Successes

The most common theme among the challenges described by the teachers was their need for security. Cobbling together enough employment to support themselves had been a demanding feat. Several teachers discussed the "balancing act" required as they worked with "multiple Boards to ensure bills can be paid." When pay was sufficient, employment benefits such as extended health care and dental coverage were often just out of reach.

> When in an LTO for more than three months I have received benefits ... the challenge is not having benefits at other times.

The fact that OTs and teachers working LTOs were not paid during school holidays meant that even when they are able to establish a certain standard of living, that standard fluctuated throughout the year. One teacher mentioned that she maintained part-time hours during the school year at the student job she had held since high school, because it provided reliable pro-rated benefits. She returned to that job each summer, just as she had prior to graduation. This teacher also noted that her employment situation contradicted the commonly held view that all French as a Second

Language (FSL) teachers were exempt from graduated entry into the profession. She attributed her status to two factors: 1) she had been unable to take full advantage of networking opportunities afforded during practicum placements, due to the distance between her faculty of education and her home community; 2) local boards had just begun to hire permanent positions "for the first time in seven years."

The overarching theme of their quests for security extended beyond the challenges experienced to include the successes celebrated by the teachers. They told us:

> I have maintained regular employment [despite the fact that] it took ten years before obtaining permanent employment.

> I've also been successful securing contract after contract and ultimately a permanent post at two and half years into my employment with the Board.

> Taking a step back and realizing that three years out of teacher's college I have successfully completed two board interviews, had three LTO's, and am eligible to apply for a permanent position, makes things look a lot brighter.

This discrepancy between the working conditions of early career teachers and their more experienced colleagues was particularly salient for those who had come to teaching as a second career. Several had left jobs in which they had received steady pay and benefits, in order to pursue their passion for teaching and learning. The aspiration for continual growth was shared by all of the teachers who contributed their voices to this chapter. The growth-related successes frequently reflected the teachers' abilities to use challenges, such as ever-changing teaching assignments, as a vehicle for professional learning and career advancement. These successes included:

> Finding a school that matches my goals for career planning,

> Gaining experience in multiple schools/classrooms and becoming confident in my own abilities, and

> Finding a niche that aligns with my philosophy of teaching.

The successful finding of this niche was due, in large part, to the way this teacher embraced the trials posed by the nature of the teaching environments that are frequently assigned to beginning teachers. Rather than fearing or avoiding high-needs classes, this teacher found a calling.

Collectively, this particular group of teachers described more successes than challenges, and were able to recast their challenges as opportunities. This speaks to their optimism and agency.

One of the mentors synthesized the balance between challenges and successes shared by this group of teachers:

> Challenges continue to be the limited number of positions available for the number of teachers entering the profession. It is a long time for someone to start a career and life, keeping that excitement level and willingness to try anything and everything.

The mentors also noted that mentorship was a collaborative process through which both mentors and mentees achieved growth through debriefing, co-planning and co-teaching. This kind of collaboration demanded a significant time investment. One mentor stressed the critical nature of time:

> If we consider time as part of a check box, then it would not be an issue. But, the teaching profession is truly an honourable career choice that requires passionate and authentic discussion with new colleagues ... there must be an honest and open relationship in order to ensure that new colleagues are provided clear expectations of what it takes to be a successful educator in Ontario Public schools.

## Ongoing Professional Learning and Collaboration

The early-career teachers showed overwhelming enthusiasm for professional learning and collaboration. They participated in a wide array of formal and informal learning opportunities, ranging from Additional Qualifications (AQ) courses and Board-organized professional learning sessions, to learning circles and daily informal professional dialogue with colleagues. This teacher's response is typical of the responses we received:

I am constantly looking for ways to continue my professional learning journey. I embrace and seek out professional learning circles; I've taken initiative to lead a collaborative inquiry and 21st Century classroom in my most current position. I've acquired Additional Basic Qualifications to enhance my ability to apply for positions. My eagerness to learn and contribute to positive and progressive school culture aligns well with colleagues and administrative leads who desire to be supported by new and engaging teachers.

With only one exception, the teachers had taken numerous AQ courses, with one completing 14 courses in ten years. All teachers drew attention to the value of informal professional dialogue. Two of the teachers acknowledged the NTIP program for making significant contributions to their professional learning, and they particularly appreciated the job-embedded nature of NTIP learning.

Like the teachers, the mentors emphasized the importance of supportive dialogue. One mentor commented that "when NTIP mentoring, I continue to maintain communication after the NTIP mentoring time concludes." Mentors also highlighted encouragement, provision of reading materials and links to online resources, as well as setting up opportunities for them to collaborate with each other. One principal explained that

> Providing for key teaching assignments and ensuring that their input is valued and welcomed ... part of being an effective principal is to practise distributive leadership, thus connecting new colleagues with experienced colleagues on staff can also serve as a very valuable mentoring relationship.

Mentor-fostered connections extend beyond teacher-to-teacher connections to include teacher-to-school relationships. As one mentor noted:

> Including and providing access to information that may be posted on websites so that when they come in to supply they can see what was handed out to all teachers, whether it be PD opportunities, policy and procedure reminders or updates, special education supports, school memos (i.e., Grade 8 high school visit dates) so that they can feel part of the school and have conversations with students and colleagues ... [this] is very helpful.

## Maintaining Optimism

As conveyed through participants' voices, entering into the teaching profession in Ontario has been a journey that has demanded a tremendous amount of courage, determination and resourcefulness. When asked how they had maintained their optimism, early career teachers highlighted their love of learning, their commitment to collaboration, their connection to family and community and their related drive to make a positive impact. They had maintained their optimism, agency and growth by:

> ... taking stock of the successes in my professional life and by following a path that engages my goals for academic enrichment that I can then invest in my school and my students' lives.

> ... consistently engaging in positive and supportive relations ... I remain grounded and confident in my role by making strong connections with students and colleagues.

> Since graduation, I've grown as a teacher through my experience in various roles at differing schools and by always seeking out professional development opportunities and additional qualifications. The people who have sustained my hope are the students. The people who have sustained my energy are my family, friends, colleagues and ultimately my own self. In terms of sustaining my learning, that driving force has always been at the root of my journey, my own desire to learn.

## Shared Learnings

When responding to a series of questions about their induction journeys, it was hardly surprising that a group of teachers, united by a powerful motivation to learn and to facilitate learning, would find their weightiest answers prompted by a request to share lessons learned.

> We want learners to love learning and if we can get them engaged then we are on the right track.

> In most cases, it will take 4-5 years to obtain a full-time contract - use that time to refine your practice, build your skills and gain a good understanding of your strengths and next steps for growth - use the opportunity to learn with / from your colleagues and build a network to support you.

This can be a time to really find your true teaching personality, and maybe even try a few styles out and see what really fits ... It is as much about you being a fit in a school as it is the school being a good fit for you.

Their mentors emphasized the importance of supportive accompaniment on these learning journeys.

The learning curve from graduating from a pre-service education program and transitioning into professional practice is very steep, and often new teachers do not realize their own learning needs, but do realize that they are overwhelmed. Having a supportive and experienced colleague (and/or administrator) can help new teachers to build professional collaboration skills. Without lines of communication for collaboration, new teachers can gain coping skills that may or may not be conducive to collaborative professional learning. As colleagues, we want to help each other to continually grow as professionals and meet the learning needs of our students.

Finally, the teachers noted that in order to inspire and sustain growth for oneself and others, it is vital to take care of one's own well-being.

Call in sick. No one is going to think less of you and you'll be a better teacher if you take that one day to rest and recuperate. ... Let your body build up an immune system. Give your mental health the rest it needs. Teaching is not an easy profession, and it's one of the few that people demand the same quality of teaching from a first-year teacher as from a 20+ years of experience teacher.

Lastly, **breathe.** You will get through this. You will learn from it. You will be all the better for it. Teaching really is worth it!

## Conclusion

There is much to learn from the voices of the remarkable new teachers showcased in this chapter, as they shared their journeys of growth and progress in challenging and precarious circumstances. There are resonances in the perspectives and learning experiences that were articulated across various locations, differing types of assignments, and changeable conditions. The early career teachers consistently maintained a learning orientation to their practice, finding ways to take meaning from, and seeing success in, circumstances that might be viewed as singularly difficult. These teachers emphasized that students were at the core of their motivation, persistence, and learning. They demonstrated that supportive relationships and collaboration were essential in their work, learning and optimism. They described ways that they had sought, developed and sustained relationships and networks, even in sporadic, short-term assignments, demanding contexts and changing settings. The mentors echoed these observations in their comments, and highlighted the reciprocal learning and growth that they had experienced working with committed and learning-focused new colleagues. They also expressed deep admiration, along with deep concern, for teachers entering the profession.

During a school district visit in 2015, a staff development lead suggested that daily occasional teaching assignments may offer the least powerful models of planning and practice for new colleagues, due to the necessity of making the assignment manageable and the impossibility of co-planning or debriefing. He bemoaned the "unintentional learning" that daily occasional teaching might provide. During a 2016 visit to a faculty of education, one faculty member suggested that we must deliberately and thoughtfully develop strategies to engage in "occasional teaching AS learning." The teachers and mentors featured in this chapter appeared to have found ways to be intentional in their learning. Schools, systems, faculties of education, teacher federations, and governmental bodies concerned with professional growth across the continuum of teacher learning also have roles in response to this new and challenging reality.

How can the broader Ontario educational community address the issues arising from the protracted and uneven entry to the profession of our newest colleagues? It seems that seeking the input and contribution of teachers entering the profession regarding their experiences and areas of concern might be an important first step. In their responses, the early career teachers clearly demonstrated that they have much to offer to colleagues and the broader educational community. Facilitating early-career teachers' involvement in sharing questions and effective practices, designing and shaping professional learning opportunities to address their needs and strengths, developing collaboration and networks with colleagues, and accessing resources builds upon their knowledge and recognizes the particularities of their contexts and journeys. Giving consistent consideration and attention to early career teachers when planning for professional learning, resource sharing, and collaborative work may help to counter the sense of disconnection experienced by those in discontinuous and intermittent assignments. This approach places early career teachers at the centre of learning and development rather than at the margins.

Sharing ideas, strategies, practices, and resources that meaningfully address this challenging entry to practice, across stakeholder groups and institutions, also holds promise. By working collaboratively as teachers, school and district leaders, educational organizations, and as governmental bodies and faculties, we may develop additional measures to support new and experienced colleagues, and build resilience in our profession. While more experienced teachers and early career teachers in other jurisdictions may experience more optimal conditions, the tools and practices developed for and by the resourceful, effective and inspiring early career educators in Ontario may be of benefit. The voices of hope in this chapter have much to teach us. We invite others to join us as we listen to and learn from them; we invite others to heed their calls to action.

## Acknowledgements

*The authors are deeply grateful to the following early career teachers and mentors for their thoughtful and authentic contributions to this chapter: Bob Boal, Linda Carswell, Jenny Gonyou-Brown, Karen H., Lisa Jarvis, Jakub Kasperski, Mackenzie Marshall, Jennifer Mota, Lucio Pavone, Deborah Wilson, and others who preferred to remain anonymous.*

## References

Directions Evidence and Policy Research Group. (2014). *Ontario Regulation 274 final report*. Directions EPRG: Vancouver, BC.

Kane, R. (2009). *NTIP Evaluation Executive Summary: Cycle 1 and 2.* Retrieved from http://www.edu.gov.on.ca/eng/policyfunding/memos/april2009/ExecutiveSummary.pdf

Ministry of Education. (2010). *The new teacher induction elements manual.* Toronto, ON: Queen's Printer for Ontario.

Ministry of Education. (2012). *More opportunities and better supports for young teachers.* Retrieved from https://news.ontario.ca/edu/en/2012/08/more-opportunities-better-supports-for-young-teachers.html

Ontario College of Teachers. (2011) *Transition to teaching 2010: Early career teachers in Ontario schools.* Toronto, ON: Ontario College of Teachers.

Ontario College of Teachers. (2016) *Transition to teaching 2015.* Toronto, ON: Ontario College of Teachers.

Part 2

# Programmatic Support for Early Career Teachers Across Canada

## Chapter 10

# The Pan-Canadian Document Analysis Study of Teacher Induction and Mentoring Programs and Policies (2013-2016)

*Benjamin Kutsyuruba, Keith D. Walker,*
*Ian A. Matheson, Lorraine Godden*

Because education is a provincial/territorial responsibility in Canada, significant variations exist between jurisdictions in terms of their support for early career teachers. Therefore, this multi-year pan-Canadian examination of programs and policies of support for new and beginning teachers was undertaken to provide a comparative perspective of the variances in each region. The initial study (Kutsyuruba, Godden, & Tregunna, 2013) was replicated and updated three years later (Kutsyuruba, Godden, Matheson & Walker, 2016). This chapter details the most recent study findings related to: 1) the organization and mandates of teacher induction programs in each jurisdiction; 2) the role of mentorship as an aspect of teacher induction programs in each jurisdiction; and, 3) the mandated roles, duties, and responsibilities of school administrators in teacher induction and mentorship processes in each jurisdiction. This initiative represents one of the phases of a multi-year pan-Canadian research project centered on exploring the differential impact of teacher induction and mentorship programs on the early-career teachers' retention, as perceived across the provinces and territories.

# Methodology

This study featured document analysis as a qualitative research method of data collection and analysis (Atkinson & Coffey, 1997; Berg, 2001; Bowen, 2009; Hodder, 2000; Miller & Alvarado, 2005; Prior, 2003). Based on classic and recent methodological sources on content analysis of documents (Krippendorff, 1980; Lombard, Snyder-Duch, & Bracken, 2010; Merriam, 1998; Neuendorf, 2002; Salminen, Kauppinen, & Lehtovaara, 1997), a rigorous set of steps (domain definition, category construction, sampling, data collection, data analysis, and interpretation) was developed for conducting this analysis. Documents were sourced and collected from provincial education authorities, teacher associations/federations, teacher unions, and individual district school board websites. These publicly available policy, planning, and curriculum documents were considered external communication, and included government communiqués, websites, program/policy memoranda, newsletters, handbooks, agendas, and minutes of meetings. Documentation from each province and territory was reviewed in its entirety, and no cross-searches were conducted between two provinces. Key search terms employed were: *new teachers, induction, mentoring, new teacher support, professional development for new teachers,* and *entry into the profession*. Documents found on the organization websites related to these topics were noted and selected. Search records with document identification were kept for each province and territory, and documents and relevant information were electronically saved, printed, and allocated an identification code; then they were sequentially organized into files per province and territory.

Considering the methodological advantages and limitations of document analysis (Bowen, 2009; Caulley, 1983), the data analysis was determined by both the research objectives (deductive) and the multiple readings and interpretations of the documents (inductive). The publicly available documents and the informal responses to formal policies by various stakeholders were analyzed in a complementary fashion (McMillan & Schumacher, 2010). Given the multitude and variety of documents, thorough reviews were the first step in this analysis. Although originally selected, given their content, title, or possible link, eventually some documents were not deemed appropriate to this inquiry. The content of the documents in relation to the research objectives was highlighted and recorded into charts. The data were organized according to themes related to the model of provision and level; policy-mandated, government-funded programs; teacher association/federation and/or union programs; hybrid or collaborative programs; and individual school district programs. The 2013 document analysis study was an initial attempt to explore how induction and mentorship programming were provided for new teachers in all provinces and territories in Canada. The researchers analyzed a total of 131 documents to determine the general organization of induction programming, explored whether mentoring was included within such programming, and explored the role of administrators. In 2016, the document analysis was updated to review an additional set of 120 documents that included revised and newly available documents. In addition, the research team undertook a series of consultations with expert panelists from across Canada who were able to provide insight about the organization of induction programming that was not publicly available in the initial stages of document searching.

## Outcomes Across Canada

The findings are reported by individual province and territory. However, it is important to note that a number of general observations were also established. First, there was evidence of mentoring and induction support for beginning teachers at four different levels: 1) provincially mandated/ministry level support; 2) provincial teacher association/federation/union level support; 3) hybrid programs (e.g., universities and teacher associations working collaboratively); and, 4) decentralized programming (school district level support). Second, three types of provision to support beginning teachers were evident: 1) induction and mentoring support; 2) teacher induction support only; and, 3) mentoring support only (although the composition of programs varied even within each provision type). Third, while mentoring was present across all provinces and territories, the role of the school administrator in induction and mentoring support was not consistently evident. Finally, some programs were commonly underpinned by academic theory, including a rationale for their provision of support. Below, we organized the findings gleaned from the documents according to each province and territory.

## Alberta

A 2013 task force put together by the Government of Alberta aimed to determine how the Government attracted, prepared, and inducted new teachers (Alberta Government, 2014). The task force concluded that a mandatory internship would provide valuable support for new teacher development. In particular, recommendations included following teaching preparation programs with a mandatory one-year paid internship/articling program for all new teachers. This would include supervision for teacher-interns with their own classroom by an experienced teacher, and a reduced full-teaching load. The task force also recommended establishing formal processes for the selection and training of mentors, and the inclusion of facilitating approaches for meaningful interactions. The task force called for a province-wide mentorship framework to be developed that would allow for implementation of consistency at the overarching structural level across the province, but also one that would allow for tailoring at local contexts. The Ministry of Education was also conducting a pilot study about supporting new teachers in Northern Alberta school districts, along with their investigation of other induction programs for teachers both within and outside of Canada. The pilot study was focused on identifying and describing practices for induction, including mentorship.

The Alberta Teachers' Association (ATA) offered a beginning teachers' conference and a handbook detailing the mentoring process for new teachers, mentors, and administrators. The ATA also offered a wealth of information on mentorship on their website, including information about how to apply the program within school settings within Alberta. A five-year longitudinal study of beginning teacher retention funded by the ATA led to the production of *A Principals' Guide to Teacher Induction* (Alberta Teachers Association, 2013)—a handbook that describes the perspectives of new teachers on current induction practices, as well as their values.

Thirty of the sixty-three total Alberta school districts have developed administrative procedures for teacher growth, including an annual professional growth plan, wherein teachers could develop a planned program of mentoring a teacher. Many school district websites outlined initiatives at a local level including new teacher orientation, a handbook, a relocation guide, as well as induction or mentorship support programs; however, specific details about orientation, induction, and mentorship programs were often unavailable through the district websites.

**British Columbia**

The Ministry of Education of British Columbia had committed to an additional two years of funding for the *New Teacher Mentoring Project* (NTMP) (British Columbia Teachers' Federation, 2014). The goals of the NTMP included developing sustainable models of mentorship within school districts, building strong peer-mentoring relationships within teaching communities, developing technology supports including a website with resources to support mentoring across the province, building a network/community of mentors, and evaluating the program to better meet the needs of teachers. The first summer institute on mentoring, *Mentors as Learners and Leaders*, was held in July 2014 for mentors across the province.

Initially, the New Teacher Mentoring Project was provincially-mandated through the Ministry of Education, though it had been additionally funded, supported, and administered in collaboration with British Columbia Teachers Federation (BCTF). The ministry-supported project focused on working with school districts, directly building new programs in 10 targeted districts, in addition to providing consultation and support for an additional 18 districts which had requested support to build and improve their existing programs. To accomplish building induction and mentorship programs within the 10 targeted districts, as well as provide support to districts that had requested support, a Provincial Mentorship Research Team (PRMT) was created to visit each district and provide three main services: consulting on how to best build a successful district program, facilitating mentoring workshops, and advocating for quality induction and mentoring programs. The project website may be found at www.mentoringbc.ca. The BCTF provided a number of services for new teachers, including a member's portal to access resources, a conference to support new teachers, and a handbook to support new teacher induction.

Of the 60 district school boards in BC, this study found 23 school districts had produced documents that described some level of support aimed at new and beginning teachers, or at least mentioned support within documents. Although many district websites include information about the existence of a mentorship program and/or a new teacher orientation, specific details about the operation of said programs were not always publicly available.

## Manitoba

The induction support for new and beginning teachers in Manitoba was offered primarily at the teachers' federation level. The Manitoba Teachers' Society (MTS) had a clear policy statement identifying that employers would assist new teachers with orientation, professional development, create supportive working conditions, and provide release time for workshops and professional development (Manitoba Teachers' Society, 2010, p. 51). The MTS also provided new teachers with the *Beginning Teacher's Handbook* (Manitoba Teachers' Society, 2016) that included sections on working with education support staff and building an inclusive classroom. In 2015, the MTS produced a brochure entitled *Becoming a Teacher* that includes useful information to assist transitions for new teachers in Manitoba. Since at least 2014, the MTS had held a conference entitled *The Fab 5 Beginning Teachers' Conference* (Manitoba Teachers' Society, 2015) to support new teachers with sessions and workshops on classroom management, student engagement and teamwork, working with parents and supporting diversity, among other topics. At the school district level, 14 of 38 school district websites included reference to, and information about, orientation sessions and mentorship programs for new teachers.

## New Brunswick

In New Brunswick, new teachers received support through the *Professional Orientation and Induction of New Teachers* (POINT) program—a program introduced by the New Brunswick Teachers Association (NBTA) in 2010/2011. This program replaced a former province-wide *Beginning Teacher Induction Program*, established in 1995, which was very successful and generated interest and replication from additional jurisdictions, both in Canada and in other nations. The new POINT program identified three overarching strands of support for new teachers. First, the target audience for POINT services was defined as new teachers who possess a contract or LTS and who were in their first year of teaching (New Brunswick Teachers' Association, 2010a). Second, any remaining POINT funding from the 2009-2010 budgets was to be used to increase mentor capacity throughout the province. Third, future POINT monies were to be distributed equitably based on FTE, with the suggestion that funds were used to "support an initial contact with teachers near the beginning of the school year, as well as another contact with teachers during the winter that traditionally is a time of struggle for new teachers" (New Brunswick Teachers' Association, 2010b, p. 2).

In addition to POINT, the NBTA held a separate budget line to provide new teachers to the province with a *Welcome to New Teachers* event, which was designed to inform new teachers of the work of their local association (branch of NBTA), federation, legal rights, insurance, pension etc. In addition, the NBTA prepared updates and printed the contents of a handbook, for which the New Brunswick Department of Education donated the binders (New Brunswick Teachers' Association, 2011). These handbooks were distributed to new teachers through the districts during late summer or early fall of the year the new hires commenced their teaching positions.

Education in New Brunswick is governed by the Department of Education and Early Childhood Development (EECD). The EECD provided funding for the Early Career Learning Program (ECTP), which supported early career teachers in their first two years of contract employment. Funding was provided to each District based on their number of new teachers for each year. Each district was then responsible for allocating the funding. All four districts operated a mentorship program for their ECTs either through school based or on multi-school mentors. Funding was also provided to support professional learning for the ECT. Connections were loosely made between the EECD and the New Brunswick Teachers' Association to ensure there was no cross-over in service provided through their POINT Program. There was also an *Early Teacher Handbook* (New Brunswick Teachers' Association, 2015) that was updated in 2015 with contributions from the Newfoundland and Labrador Teachers' Association, the Nova Scotia Teachers Union, Ontario Secondary Schools Teachers' Federation, the Prince Edward Island Teachers' Federation, the Saskatchewan Teachers' Federation, the British Columbia Teachers' Federation, and the Elementary Teachers' Federation of Ontario.

Of the seven public school districts in New Brunswick, two had documents that mentioned support of new and beginning teachers. While the

Anglophone North document referred directly to the POINT program, the Anglophone East School District document described the teacher induction program, involving a variety of professional development opportunities during a new teacher's first year. These included district orientation, classroom management, cooperative discipline, teacher evaluation, finance and payroll, staff, communication, teaching students with exceptionalities, differentiation, and other curriculum related topics (Anglophone East School District, 2012). Teachers were assigned a mentor selected by the school administrator to support them in their first year, and a workshop was provided for new teachers in September of each year.

### Newfoundland and Labrador

The Newfoundland and Labrador Teachers' Association (NLTA) website included a section devoted to the outlining of support for beginning teachers. Detailed information for new teachers on collective agreements, a new teacher handbook, and information regarding benefits, ethics, and professional development opportunities were provided. The 30-page handbook for new teachers offered information on several areas (Newfoundland and Labrador Teachers' Association, 2005). Topics included: classroom management, procedures, student/teacher interactions, preparation for the first day, assigning work, homework, routines, working with other teachers, being prepared for absences, professional well-being, and stress management. A section of the handbook was distinctly preserved for information on a new teacher conference and mentoring opportunities (Newfoundland and Labrador Teachers' Association, 2007).

In conjunction with the handbook for new teachers, the NLTA offered new teachers a mentor (Newfoundland and Labrador Teachers' Association, 2005). The mentorship was intended to provide "on-site support that meets the immediate needs of beginning teachers and helps provide direction for professional choices" (p. 13). However, as highlighted in the handbook for new teachers, the mentoring program was not always offered in particular schools, suggesting that if new teachers wished to participate in such a relationship, they must specifically request to participate with either the NLTA, their local professional development division, or their school principal. The NLTA also offered a handbook on mentoring new teachers specifically for the mentors (Newfoundland and Labrador Teachers' Association, 2007). Of the two school districts within the province of Newfoundland and Labrador, only the English school board offered information regarding new teacher induction practices within their district.

## Northwest Territories

The Northwest Territories (NWT) Induction Program was established in 2001 in order to retain competent teachers in the profession; to promote the personal and professional well-being of the new and beginning teachers; to build a foundation for continued professional growth through structured contact with mentors, administrators and other veteran teachers; and to transmit the culture of the school and teaching profession (Government of the Northwest Territories, 2011). The model of the program consisted of four phases: 1) pre-orientation, 2) orientation, 3) systematic sustained supports, and 4) professional development (Government of the Northwest Territories, 2008). At the pre-orientation phase, beginning and new teachers were provided with a binder of information, access to the NWT Teacher Induction website, and a mentor contact. The orientation phase consisted of regional workshops, community cultural activities, school activities, professional information (resources, curriculum, and school policies), mentorship training with both mentors and protégés, and regional education authority 'meet and greet' activities. During the systematic sustained supports phase, the formal mentor program commenced with trained mentors and built in release time. In addition, the phase included a review of the mentorship plan in November and May, experienced teacher observations, 'First Class' resources and networking, and a program newsletter. In the final professional development phase, beginning and new teachers were provided with in-service and curriculum based workshops, on-line learning, committee participation, and staff meetings.

Despite the challenges of a vast geographic area, a formal mentorship program had become a major component of the NWT induction program. The content of the NWT Mentorship Program was detailed in a publicly available internet-based resource at http://www.newteacher-snwt.ca. Mentorship pairs engaged in regular formal or informal meetings throughout the year, with allowances and release time (half day per month) provided for protégés to learn and grow from interactions with peers (Northwest Territories Teacher Induction, n.d.). Opportunities to attend workshops were also provided. In addition, the mentorship team reflected on the process, reviewed the mentorship plan, and made any needed changes. Several studies had been conducted on the NWT teacher induction and mentorship program, noting overall positive value of the induction program in all its phases and the four areas of support (Abu Rass, 2012; Tolley, 2003).

## Nova Scotia

The Department of Education stated that the current mentoring and coaching program in Nova Scotia would be evaluated in order to support the approach to professional learning based on best practices (Nova Scotia Department of Education, 2009). It appeared to us that there had been significant discussion and interest at the Department of Education level for teacher induction (including the mentoring of teachers); however, an induction program at the provincial level had not yet been implemented.

To support new and beginning teachers within the province, the Nova Scotia Teachers Union (NSTU) produced a number of strategies, including a handbook. The NSTU handbook included a variety of information about contact details, useful telephone numbers, etc., and tips for "surviving and thriving in the classroom" (Section 3.1 to 3.21). In addition, the handbook detailed all of the new teacher initiatives offered by the NSTU including: *Each One Reach One* (mentoring program), benefits of membership sessions, *Teacher Induction Program* (TIP), professional development workshops specifically designed for new teachers, regional conference for new teachers, a handbook entitled *Beginning Teachers: Helping you to Survive and Thrive in the Classroom*, links to local new teacher communities, and a welcome night for new teachers. At the district level, the support for new teachers included orientation and induction programs for new teachers, as well as coaching and mentorship programs; however, details about each program were limited, with information available through six of the eight school boards.

**Nunavut**

In Nunavut, all professional development was left to the Nunavut Professional Improvement Committee (NPIC) and the Nunavut Teachers' Association (NTA). All new teachers were required to register for, and participate in, a two-year mentorship program that involved work with an experienced Nunavut educator, though the program was not yet ready to officially launch, and new teachers were advised to check in with school administrators about any informal mentoring opportunities. A website for the Nunavut Teacher Induction Program provided information for new teachers, including information about orientation and the mentorship program, and may be found at http://ntip.gov.nu.ca. New teachers were also provided with a checklist to be completed in conjunction with use of the New Teacher Induction Program website (New Teacher Induction Program, 2016). The checklist guided new teachers through the website, including sections on essential forms (e.g., pay and coverage), essential information, school profile, community profile, and a section about the program. According to the website, included in the orientation process for new teachers was a residential awareness workshop that was designed to inform inductees about the history of residential schooling.

**Ontario**

The Ministry of Education funds the *New Teacher Induction Program* (NTIP)—a province-wide initiative designed to support the growth and professional development of new teachers (Ontario Ministry of Education, 2010). The program consisted of: 1) orientation for all new teachers to the school and school board, 2) mentoring for new teachers by experienced teachers, and 3) professional development and training in major policies and strategies of the ministry, classroom management, communication skills, and instructional approaches (Ontario Ministry of Education, 2010). In conjunction with the orientation, mentoring, and professional development and training elements of the NTIP, the performance appraisal process for new teachers has been designed to support and promote the continued growth and development of new teachers. The mentor and the new teacher determined the new teacher's needs, and completed the Individual NTIP Strategy Form, which was to be revised throughout the year as needs changed. Some research has been conducted on the effectiveness of the NTIP program; where Kane (2010) found that mentoring was the most significant component of the program, according to teachers. Glassford and Salinitri (2007) argued that high-quality mentoring can lead to improvements in both teaching and student achievement when it is a part of a properly funded and permanent program, and the alignment between the aims of the NTIP program and the actual procedures of the program still requires examination (Barrett, Solomon, Singer, Portelli, & Mujuwamariya, 2009).

In addition to NTIP, the Ministry also produced *Mentoring for All*—an eBook designed to support mentors (Ontario Ministry of Education, 2016). The resource contains sections on creating a mentoring web/framework, building relational trust, facilitating learning focused conversations, providing meaningful and growth oriented feedback, and realizing powerful mentoring designs. The eBook was available on "mentoring moments"—a website that entails an online community of practice for educators across Ontario, supporting teacher professional development (http://mentoringmoments.ning.com). Along with other resources for mentors and educators, the website included a discussion forum, groups for educators interested in various topics, and a place for educators to post blog entries. Longitudinal research from 2012-2015 (Ontario Ministry of Education, 2016) revealed that having a number of mentoring supports (e.g., mentoring; web), differentiated learning, the encouragement of principals, and a collaborative school culture all made a positive difference for new teachers.

### Prince Edward Island

While the school district and Prince Edward Island Teachers' Federation (PEITF) searches did not yield any results, the Prince Edward Island Department of Education and Early Childhood Development website did include a report about the *Beginning Teacher Induction Program,* which was described as being jointly and successfully offered in 2012 by the school boards, the University of PEI, and the PEITF. The report also indicated that a package would be provided to teachers for ongoing help alongside the provision of workshops throughout the year. The report described the inclusion of mentorship in the BTIP; however no detailed information of such a provision could be established from our search and analysis. A handbook (Beginning Teacher Induction Program, n.d.) was available for beginning teachers' induction that included information about beginning a career as a teacher, organization, the first day, planning, PD, classroom management, parents, establishing a positive environment, strategies, personal care, substitute teachers, and the action plan that was to be prepared and developed by the new teacher, with the assistance of their assigned mentor.

## Quebec

Some documentation was found from searching the Department of Education website that was concerned with new teachers, teacher induction and mentoring, though the documents were somewhat dated and therefore it was difficult to conclude whether they remain current practice in the Province. The new teacher induction offered by Commission scolaire des Patriotes, implemented in approximately 2004, promised to "help beginning teachers get off to a good start in their new profession" (Lepine, 2009, p. 1). The program offered eight training workshops that were focused on classroom management, evaluation, differentiation, and parent-teacher relationships. Also offered was a mentoring program, where the aim was to help new teachers achieve autonomy, responsibility, and professional identity, and to encourage them to stay in the profession.

The Quebec Provincial Association of Teachers (QPAT) produced a handbook for new teachers in the province of Quebec (Quebec Provincial Association for Teachers, 2012). The aim of the document was to "help any teacher who is new to the teaching profession in Quebec" (p. 4). The content included an outline of the role of QPAT, teacher's rights and responsibilities (including contract, workload, seniority and recognized experience, and teacher certification, illness, special leaves, parental rights, insurance, and pension), getting started (including knowing your classroom, substitution, professionalism and communication, discipline, communicating with parents, and wellness), and resources for teachers (including the local union directory). In addition to the handbook, as part of the support for new teachers to Quebec, QPAT formed a *New Teachers Committee* (Quebec Provincial Association for Teachers, 2011), with responsibility for producing appropriate information for new teachers, and working with local unions to develop and implement teacher induction programs, including both professional career issues and union involvement. In 2013, the QPAT produced a pamphlet about mentoring (Quebec Provincial Association for Teachers, 2013) that provided information for teachers about the QPAT position on mentoring. Included in the pamphlet were approaches to mentoring and suggestions for the mentor and protégé relationship. Seven District websites included references about mentoring and induction programs in various reports, though details about these programs were unavailable to the public.

## Saskatchewan

The Saskatchewan Teachers Federation (STF) offered a number of resources for new teachers including: a handbook for new teachers, a handbook for administrators, a new teacher conference, targeted resources, professional growth partnerships, and an induction ceremony (Saskatchewan Teachers' Federation, 2009). Examples of typical sessions within the beginning teacher conference included teacher professionalism, classroom management, adaptive dimension and differentiated instruction, assessment and evaluation – Q & A session, developing social justice literacy, financial fitness, getting started, infusion of First Nations, Metis, and Inuit content, perspectives and ways of knowing, multi-graded teaching, Services Disponibles en Français, starting out right, Stewart Resources Centre, and supporting EAL students in your classroom. The STF handbook for beginning teachers included an introduction, what orientation might look like, how to maintain a balance, managing a classroom, establishing professional relationships, examining practice, diversity, home contact, being a professional, reflection, FAQs, and resources.

In addition to the resources provided to new and beginning teachers through the STF, evidence was seen of provision to support teacher induction and mentoring within some school divisions in Saskatchewan. Provisions include mentors/coaches for new teachers, orientation events/retreats, and a new teacher handbook.

## Yukon

The Department for Education had produced a number of resources to support new and beginning teachers to the Territory, including a *Handbook for Yukon Teachers* dated August 2011 (Yukon Education, 2011), which mentioned *New Teacher Orientation and Mentoring* of teachers through collaboration with the Yukon Teachers Association (YTA). The Yukon Teachers Association (YTA) was responsible for implementing the Yukon's mentorship program for beginning teachers in collaboration with the Department for Education (DoE) (Yukon Teachers' Association, 2012). The program participants met 2-3 times per year as a group to share their expertise. In addition, new teacher/experienced teacher pairs met quarterly. The new teacher observed the experienced teacher working in a classroom twice per year for half a day, with the remainder of the day left for meeting collaboratively; the alternate two whole day meetings were for the experienced teacher to observe the new teacher teaching, with the other half of the day for collaborative work (Yukon Education, 2011).

## Summary of the Findings

Overall, and as expected, the pan-Canadian landscape for new and beginning teacher induction practices and mentoring was varied and multilayered. This document analysis revealed policy-mandated government-funded programs, programs offered by provincial teacher associations, federations or unions, hybrid programs which were based upon cooperation between the provincial and territorial governments, teacher associations, universities, First Nations or local communities, and decentralized models maintained at a local level by school boards/divisions or schools. We believe that such a variety of provisions may be attributed to the lack of a federal bureau of education, and the fact that Section 93 of the *Constitution Act* affords the provinces exclusive responsibility for education in Canada.

A summary of our findings, according to the levels of support for teacher induction and mentoring in Canadian provinces, is provided in Table 1. These findings illustrate the support found at the provincially-mandated level, the provincial teacher association level, hybrid support between multiple levels, and decentralized support at the school district level. Table 1 presents the findings by name of the province or territory, and a key outlines the acronyms adopted to portray individual types of support.

**Table 1**
*Pan-Canadian Provision of Teacher Induction and Mentoring Programs*

| Provincially mandated / Ministry level support | Provincial Teacher Association / Federations / Union support level | Hybrid programs | Decentralized programs (school district support level) |
|---|---|---|---|
| Northwest Territories (IM, A) | New Brunswick (IM) | Alberta (IM, A) | Alberta (22/58) |
| Ontario (IM, A) | Nova Scotia (IM) | British Columbia (34/60) | Manitoba (14/38) |
| Nunavut (IM, A) | British Columbia (TI) | Manitoba (TI) | Newfoundland and Labrador (1/2) |
| | Saskatchewan (IM, A) | Newfoundland and Labrador (IM, A) | New Brunswick (2/7) |
| | | Nunavut (TI) | Nova Scotia (6/7) |
| | | Yukon (IM, A) | Prince Edward Island (*1/2) |
| | | Prince Edward Island (IM) | Quebec (7/9) |
| | | Quebec (TI) | Saskatchewan (11/29) |

Key:
(IM) Induction and mentoring support available
(TI) Teacher induction support only
(M) Mentoring program or support only
(A) Administrators' role identified according to support

Table 2 further illustrates the findings of the decentralized pan-Canadian support for teacher induction and mentoring revealed through our search of publicly available documents. Great variance in the support of new teachers through induction and mentoring policies and initiatives was found in the Canadian provinces, with multiple avenues of support existing. The first column on the left indicates the province where decentralized supports were found in the provincial English speaking school divisions. The following columns denote the type of support found to be offered by individual district school boards. The types of support are described as mentoring and induction support, induction only support, mentoring only support, and whether the role of the administrator was identified in the document. The numbers of individual school boards that are in accordance to each category are listed with totals at the bottom of each column. This table does not include information of provincial level support for new and beginning teachers.

**Table 2**
*Decentralized Supports by Number of School Boards*

| Province (Total no. of English speaking SD) | Induction and Mentoring support | Induction only | Mentoring Only | Administrator's role |
|---|---|---|---|---|
| Alberta (22/58) | 13 | 4 | 5 | 8 (3 as evaluator) |
| British Columbia (34/60) | 6 | 5 | 10 | 0 |
| Manitoba (14/38) | 4 | 7 | 2 | 7 (5 as evaluator) |
| New Brunswick (2/7) | 1 | 1 | 0 | 0 |
| Newfoundland and Labrador (1/2) | 2 | 0 | 0 | 1 (as evaluator) |
| Nova Scotia (6/7) | 3 | 3 | 1 | 0 |
| Prince Edward Island (*1/2) | *1 | 0 | 0 | 0 |
| Quebec (7/9) | 5 | 1 | 1 | 2 (undetermined role) |
| Saskatchewan (11/29) | 2 | 4 | 5 | 2 |
| Total | 37 | 25 | 24 | 20 |

* Indicates that the support found in PEI did not contain enough details to denote that induction or mentoring is a component, although the collaborative nature of the online planning forum would suggest that these details might be a consideration.

Conducting the study over several year spans, we were able to observe the evolution and changes in induction and mentorship supports since 2013; thus we obtained an updated picture of the provision of support for new and beginning teachers across Canada. We have learned that in Alberta the establishment of a province-wide mentorship program was being investigated, in addition to a system of easing new teachers into the profession via an internship approach encompassing reduced teaching responsibilities. In British Columbia, additional funding continued to support the *New Teacher Mentoring Program*, and a new mentoring initiative had begun to be developed and implemented at the district level. Manitoba introduced a conference for new teachers that focused on professional development and networking, and Nunavut was preparing to launch the *Nunavut Teacher Induction Program* to support beginning teachers across the territory. Ontario released a second version of the handbook designed to support mentors in 2016, and educators were able to access an online community of practice resource designed to support teacher professional development. At the district level, updates were made to almost every province to include more information or reflect changes in the district organization (e.g., New Brunswick).

## Looking Forward

As indicated, the organization and mandates of teacher induction programs in each jurisdiction in Canada varied. Our findings show that support, in the form of either induction based programs and policies and/or mentoring related support, existed in all Canadian provinces. However, only two of the provinces addressed teacher induction and mentoring at a provincial level; while many of the provinces provided support through a hybrid or more collaborative process. Furthermore, many of the provinces that addressed teacher induction support and mentoring at the teacher federation or hybrid level also offered decentralized support at the localized school district level. In addition, there was also variance within each province regarding the programming offered at the localized school district level. While findings suggest that support and programming may exist, the lack of publicly available documents online makes it difficult to establish the exact nature of provision offered. The documents examined in this study detail a variance between structure and types of support at the localized school district level. Programs that included mentoring as part of an overall teacher induction provision were seen in every province and territory. However, the study also found that in five of the provinces and territories, mentoring programs existed that were not part of an overall induction provision, and in six of the provinces and territories, induction programs existed where mentoring was not part of the induction process. Therefore, the role of mentoring within teacher induction across Canada may be more widespread than this study has revealed, and should be further explored. Due to the study's delimited focus on publicly available documents, we acknowledge this chapter may not be indicative of the full range of mentorship and/or induction programming and support available for novice teachers in Canada. Further research might be undertaken to establish the exact nature, structure, and variance of the provision of all types of support for novice teachers in Canada to provide a comprehensive understanding of teacher inducting and mentoring practices on a pan-Canadian scale.

This study did reveal a sporadic and inconsistent approach to the support of new and beginning teachers in the pan-Canadian context. However, due to the delimitations and the scope of this study, it is likely that there exists a richer and deeper level of provision of support for new and beginning teachers than revealed by our research. Empirically, research has shown that support from high-quality induction and teacher mentorship programs for new and beginning teachers correlates to increased teacher effectiveness, higher satisfaction, commitment, and early-career retention of novice teachers, in addition to improved classroom instruction and student achievement (Glazerman et al., 2010; Henry, Bastian, & Fortner, 2011; Ingersoll & Strong, 2011). Identifying the full extent of how new and beginning teachers are supported across Canada creates an invaluable resource for both pan-Canadian and international school contexts to learn from other jurisdictions, to possibly take initiatives to mitigate the attrition, and provide timely induction and mentorship of early career teachers for the benefit of their students.

# References

Abu Rass, R. (2012). Supporting newly recruited teachers in a unique area, the Northwest Territories in Canada. *Journal of Education for Teaching: International Research and Pedagogy, 38*, 141–161. doi:10.1080/02607476.2012.

Alberta Government. (2014). *Task force for teaching excellence*. Retrieved from http://open.alberta.ca/dataset/0c3c1074-b890-4db0-8424-d5c84676d710/resource/6efd9eaf-e356-4360-9df9- 81eebabe68e6/download/GOAE-TaskForceforTeachingExcellence-Report-WEB-updated.pdf

Alberta Teachers Association. (2013). *Teaching in the early years of practice: A five-year longitudinal study*. Retrieved from https://www.teachers.ab.ca/SiteCollectionDocuments/ATA/Publications/Research/Teaching%20in%20the%20Early%20Years%20of%20Practice%20(PD-86-19b).pdf

Anglophone East School District. (2012). *Beginning teacher induction program*. Retrieved from www.web1.nbed.nb.ca/sites/ASD-E/professional- development/Pages/Beginning-Teacher-Induction-Program.aspx

Atkinson, P., & Coffey, A. (1997). Analyzing documentary realities. In D. Silverman (Ed.), *Qualitative research: Theory, method and practice* (pp. 45-62). Thousand Oaks, CA: Sage.

Barrett, S. J., Solomon, R. P., Singer, J., Portelli, J. P., & Mujuwamariya, D. (2009). The hidden curriculum of a teacher induction program: Ontario teacher educators' perspectives. *Canadian Journal of Education, 32*, 677–702.

Beginning Teacher Induction Program. (n.d.). *Beginning teachers' induction program handbook*. Retrieved from http://www.gov.pe.ca/photos/original/ed_teacherhandb.pdf

Berg, B. L. (2001). *Qualitative research methods for social sciences*. London: Allyn and Bacon.

Bowen, G. A. (2009). Document analysis as a qualitative research method. *Qualitative Research Journal, 9*, 27–40. doi:10.3316/qrj0902027

British Columbia Teachers' Federation. (2014). *The mentor, Issue 4*. Retrieved from: http://bctf.ca/uploadedFiles/Public/NewTeachers/Mentoring/TheMentorOct2014.pdf

Caulley, D. N. (1983). Document analysis in program evaluation. *Evaluation and Program Planning, 6*, 19–29.

Glassford, L. A., & Salinitri, G. (2007). Designing a successful new teacher induction program: An assessment of the Ontario experience, 2003-2006. *Canadian Journal of Educational Administration and Policy, 60*, 1–34.

Glazerman, S., Isenberg, E., Dolfin, S., Bleeker, M., Johnson, A., Grider, M., & Jacobus, M. (2010). *Impacts of comprehensive teacher induction: Final results from a randomized controlled study (NCEE 2010-4027).* Washington, DC: National Center for Education Evaluation and Regional Assistance, Institute of Education Sciences, U.S. Department of Education.

Government of the Northwest Territories. (2008). *NWT Teacher induction manual (7th ed.).* Yellowknife, NT: Department of Education, Culture, and Employment.

Government of the Northwest Territories. (2011). *NWT Teacher induction: A program for beginning teachers.* Retrieved from http://www.newteacher-snwt.ca/index.html

Henry, G. T., Bastian, K. C., & Fortner, C. K. (2011). Stayers and leavers: Early-career teacher effectiveness and attrition. *Educational Researcher, 40,* 271–280.

Hodder, I. (2000). The interpretation of documents and material culture. In N. K. Denzin & Y. S. Lincoln (Eds.), *Handbook of qualitative research* (2nd ed.) (pp. 703–715). Thousand Oaks, CA: Sage.

Ingersoll, R. M., & Strong, M. (2011). The impact of induction and mentoring programs for beginning teachers: A critical review of the research. *Review of Education Research, 81,* 201–233.

Kane, R. G. (2010). *NTIP evaluation final report: Executive summary (Cycle III).* Toronto, ON: Ministry of Education of Ontario. Retrieved from http://cal2.edu.gov.on.ca/may2010/NTIP_Evaluation_Report_2010.pdf.

Krippendorff, K. (1980). *Content analysis: An introduction to its methodology.* Beverly Hills, CA: Sage.

Kutsyuruba, B., Godden, L., Matheson, I., & Walker, K. (2016). *Understanding the role of teacher induction and mentorship programs in teacher attrition and retention.* Kingston, ON: Queen's University.

Kutsyuruba, B., Godden, L., & Tregunna, L. (2013). *A Pan-Canadian Document Analysis Study of Teacher Induction and Mentoring Programs.* Kingston, ON: Queen's University.

Lepine, M. (2009). *Beginning teachers.* Paper presented at the Conference on New Teacher Induction, Quebec, QC. http://www.mels.gouv.qc.ca/sections/virage11/index_en.asp?page=colloqueB

Lombard, M., Snyder-Duch, J., & Bracken, C. C. (2010). *Practical resources for assessing and reporting intercoder reliability in content analysis research projects.* Retrieved from http://matthewlombard.com/reliability/index_print.html

Manitoba Teachers' Society. (2010). *Professional policy of teacher education, licensing, certificates and credentials: Induction of teachers.* Retrieved from http://www.mbteach.org/library/Archives/Handbooks/HB-bylawpolicy.pdf

Manitoba Teachers' Society. (2015). *The fab 5 beginning teachers' conference.* Retrieved from http://www.mbteach.org/pdfs/pd/PD-prgm-FAB5-Winnipeg.pdf

Manitoba Teachers' Society. (2016). *The beginning teacher's handbook.* Retrieved from: http://www.mbteach.org/pdfs/hb/HB-BeginTeachersHbook.pdf

McMillan, J. H., & Schumacher, S. (2010). *Research in education: Evidence-based inquiry (7th ed.).* New York, NY: Pearson.

Merriam, S. B. (1998). *Case study research in education.* San Francisco: Jossey-Bass.

Miller, F. A., & Alvarado, K. (2005). Incorporating documents into qualitative nursing research. *Journal of Nursing Scholarship, 37,* 348–353.

Neuendorf, K. A. (2002). *The content analysis guidebook.* Thousand Oaks, CA: Sage.

New Brunswick Teachers' Association. (2010a). *Professional Orientation and Induction for New Teachers (POINT) Project Outline.* NB: New Brunswick Teachers Association.

New Brunswick Teachers' Association. (2010b). *Proposed POINT plan.* Fredericton, NB: New Brunswick Teachers Association.

New Brunswick Teachers' Association. (2011). *Beginning teachers' handbook.* Retrieved from http://www.nbta.ca/resources/beginning_teachers_binder/BeginningTeachersHandbook.pdf

New Brunswick Teachers' Association. (2015). *Early career teachers' handbook.* Retrieved from: http://www.nbta.ca/early_career_teachers/ecth_handbook.pdf

New Teacher Induction Program (2016). New hires' checklist. Nunavut Teacher Induction Program. Retrieved from http://ntip.gov.nu.ca/new-hires

Newfoundland and Labrador Teachers' Association (2005). *Handbook for beginning teachers (3rd ed.).* Retrieved from https://www.nlta.nl.ca/files/documents/new_tchr_info/new_tchr_hndbk.pdf

Newfoundland and Labrador Teachers' Association (2007). *Mentoring beginning teachers handbook.* Retrieved from https://www.nlta.nl.ca/files/documents/tchrmntr_hdbk.pdf

Northwest Territories Teacher Induction. (n.d.) Retrieved from: http://www.newteachersnwt.ca

Nova Scotia Department of Education (2009). *Department of Education response to Report and Recommendations of the Education Professional Development Committee.* Retrieved from http://www.ednet.ns.ca/files/reports/EPDC-Report-Response_Fall_2009.pdf

Ontario Ministry of Education. (2010). *New teacher induction program: Induction elements manual.* Retrieved from http://www.edu.gov.on.ca/eng/teacher/pdfs/NTIP-English_Elementsseptember2010.pdf.

Ontario Ministry of Education. (2016). *Mentoring for all v2.* Retrieved from: http://api.ning.com/files/6QtNvWPQNL6h2tqeCG*Ievn6kwXaoHJrs-bh*ZXkTCLHi6znVY*WC0FJvYHtEpAmy-WGggwjzzA-dNhbRUY-vaK-OYG7-CDIdR/2016MentoringforAll.pdf

Prior, L. (2003). Using documents in social research. Thousand Oaks, CA: Sage.

Quebec Provincial Association for Teachers. (2011). *New teachers committee.* Committees. Retrieved from Quebec Provincial Association for Teachers website: http://www.qpat-apeq.qc.ca/en/pages/aboutqpat/committees

Quebec Provincial Association for Teachers. (2012). *Handbook for new teachers.* Retrieved from Quebec Provincial Association for Teachers website: http://www.qpat-apeq.qc.ca/documents-qpat/category/1-publications?lang=en

Quebec Provincial Association for Teachers. (2013). *Mentoring.* Retrieved from Quebec Provincial Association for Teachers website: http://www.qpat-apeq.qc.ca/documents-qpat/category/1-publications?lang=en

Salminen, A., Kauppinen, K., & Lehtovaara, M. (1997). Towards a methodology for document analysis. *Journal of the American Society for Information Science, 48,* 644–655.

Saskatchewan Teachers' Federation. (2009). *Taking your place in the professional community: Handbook for beginning teachers.* Retrieved from Saskatchewan Teachers' Federation, Beginning Teachers Documents Advisory Committee website: https://www.stf.sk.ca/portal.jsp?Sy3uQUnbK9L2RmSZs02CjVy0w7ZkI/ks6g2u00g-zAtsk=Fportal.jsp?SaVRU/jbEgyDLe5BSdsr0vZGZJmzTYKNX8t/KNvKOzGw2wgvCZAZSsw==F

Tolley, M. (2003). *The induction experiences of beginning elementary teachers in the Northwest Territories* (Masters Thesis), University of Saskatchewan, Saskatoon, SK.

Yukon Education. (2011). *Handbook for Yukon Teachers.* Retrieved from http://www.education.gov.yk.ca/pdf/Handbook_for_Yukon_Teachers.pdf

Yukon Teachers' Association. (2012). *Mentorship Program Information.* Retrieved from http://www.yta.yk.ca/index.php/component/content/article/27- professionaldevelopment/professional-development-applications/229-mentorship- programinformation.html

# Les premières années d'enseignement : Réalité professionnelle, besoins de soutien et mesures d'insertion offertes au sein des commissions scolaires au Québec

*Joséphine Mukamurera, Sylvie Fontaine*

## Introduction

Ce chapitre donne un aperçu de la situation québécoise en matière de soutien à l'insertion professionnelle des enseignants débutants. Les données analysées sont issues de deux recherches financées par le Conseil de recherche en sciences humaines du Canada. La première, dirigée par la professeure Joséphine Mukamurera (Université de Sherbrooke) avec la collaboration du professeur Stéphane Martineau (Université du Québec à Trois-Rivières – UQTR –), porte sur les besoins de soutien des enseignants débutants et les pratiques d'aide à l'insertion professionnelle au sein des commissions scolaires au Québec. Dans le cadre de cette recherche, une enquête par questionnaire a été réalisée à l'automne 2013 auprès de 250 enseignants débutants identifiés comme ayant cinq ans d'expérience et moins. La deuxième recherche est une enquête pancanadienne conduite à l'hiver 2016 sous la direction de Benjamin Kutsyuruba (Queen's University) et de Keith Walker (University of Saskatchewan) (voir chapitre 2). La recherche avait pour objectif d'explorer l'impact différentiel des programmes d'insertion professionnelle et de mentorat auprès des jeunes enseignants. Les données provenant de ces deux recherches (uniquement la province de Québec pour l'enquête pancanadienne) sont complémentaires et permettent de dresser un état des lieux sur ce qui se fait en matière de soutien à l'insertion au Québec et de voir comment cela est reçu par les enseignants débutants eux-mêmes.

## Problématique

Depuis les quarante dernières années, les compressions budgétaires successives en éducation, la complexification croissante du travail enseignant, et la précarisation persistante de l'emploi (Organisation de Coopération et de Développement Économiques – OCDE –, 2005; Tardif, 2013; Valencic Zuljan et Marentic Pozarnik, 2014), ont modifié en profondeur les conditions d'insertion professionnelle et contribué à accentuer la pénibilité des premières années d'enseignement. La survie du jeune enseignant prend ainsi plusieurs visages : survie à l'embauche, à la précarité professionnelle, absence de continuité dans la carrière, complexité et lourdeur de la tâche, compétences insuffisantes, pratique guidée en permanence par un rapport à l'urgence, etc. (Mukamurera, Bourque et Gingras, 2008; OCDE, 2015; Wentzel, 2011) Par ailleurs, au moment où les enseignants en insertion professionnelle sont dans une phase de leur carrière où leurs compétences sont moins développées, où ils ont moins confiance en leurs capacités que leurs collègues plus expérimentés et où ils ont encore beaucoup à apprendre (Commission européenne, 2005; Conseil supérieur de l'éducation – CSE –, 2014; Feiman-Nemser, 2003; Wentzel, 2011), ils se retrouvent confrontés aux mêmes responsabilités que les enseignants expérimentés dans des environnements de travail plus difficiles (milieu socioéconomique, région, caractéristiques des élèves) et font face aux pires tâches (CSE, 2014; Feiman-Nemser, 2003; Mukamurera, 2011; OCDE, 2015). Il n'est donc pas étonnant que 10% à 50% d'entre eux, selon les pays, remettent leur carrière en question et abandonnent l'enseignement durant les cinq premières années d'insertion (Forseille et Raptis, 2016).

Les enseignants débutants doivent relever un double défi, celui d'enseigner et d'apprendre à enseigner (Feiman-Nemser, 2001), mais aussi organiser un double apprentissage, celui des élèves dont ils ont la responsabilité et celui du métier dans lequel ils entrent (Roustan et Saujat, 2008, cités par Philippot, 2014) et ce, dans des conditions de travail souvent peu favorables. De plus en plus conscients des difficultés que vivent ces enseignants et des conséquences à moyen et long terme sur la persévérance professionnelle et sur la qualité de l'enseignement, nombre de chercheurs et organismes nationaux et internationaux préconisent la mise en place de mesures de soutien et d'accompagnement, voire des programmes exhaustifs d'insertion professionnelle (CSE, 2014; OCDE, 2005). Par conséquent, en Amérique du Nord et ailleurs dans les pays de l'OCDE, certaines mesures d'insertion sont proposées aux enseignants débutants, bien que l'offre et le taux de participation soient encore limités (Ingersoll, 2012; Kutsyuruba, Godden et Tregunna, 2014; OCDE 2015; Valencic Zuljan et Marentic Pozarnik, 2014).

Le Québec n'est pas en reste par rapport à cet enjeu et comme l'observe le CSE (2014, p. 42), « le milieu scolaire s'est mobilisé autour de cet enjeu et un certain nombre d'organismes et d'établissements scolaires ont mis en place des mécanismes de soutien pour leur personnel débutant, mécanismes qui varient en temps et en intensité selon les ressources consacrées. » On observe aussi une volonté politique de soutien financier pour encourager ces initiatives, notamment l'existence d'une mesure spécifique dans le budget du ministère de l'Éducation depuis l'année 2011-2012. Cependant, la seule mise en place d'un dispositif ou d'un programme d'insertion ne garantit pas son efficacité. Il doit reposer notamment sur une meilleure connaissance et une prise en compte de la situation professionnelle ainsi que sur les besoins de soutien des enseignants débutants. Dans le même sens, Perry et Hayes (2011, p. 12) soulignent que, «Understanding the induction period and the particular problems encountered by beginning teachers will help in designing more effective teacher education and induction programs.» Les programmes d'insertion étant un phénomène relativement récent au Québec, des recherches restent encore à faire pour constituer des données empiriques permettant d'éclairer les orientations et les pratiques en matière de mesures de soutien à l'insertion professionnelle. L'objectif de ce chapitre va dans ce sens et vise à analyser les besoins de soutien et de l'offre de mesures d'insertion durant les cinq premières années d'enseignement au Québec. Trois questions spécifiques sont au cœur des analyses dont les résultats seront présentés dans ce chapitre : Quelles sont les réalités professionnelles vécues aujourd'hui par les enseignants au cours de leur période d'insertion professionnelle? Quels sont leurs principaux besoins de soutien? De quelles formes de soutien bénéficient-ils, et quelle est leur appréciation ? Quelles sont les retombées observées?

# Cadre de référence

La toile de fond qui oriente la collecte et l'analyse de données est constituée autour de quatre concepts. Il s'agit du concept principal d'insertion professionnelle qui chapeaute l'ensemble, mais aussi des notions qui lui sont liées telles que celles de soutien, de besoin de soutien et de programme d'insertion professionnelle.

## Le concept d'insertion professionnelle

Selon Weva (1999, p. 194), l'insertion professionnelle est un processus qui débute « dès la sélection des nouveaux enseignants et se termine lorsque ceux-ci ont réalisé l'adaptation nécessaire afin de fonctionner pleinement et efficacement au sein du système scolaire. » L'insertion s'avère être ainsi un processus inscrit dans le temps et ayant une durée plus ou moins longue « selon les conditions d'exercice (ex. : temps plein ou temps partiel, une seule ou plusieurs écoles), le soutien offert par le milieu et la capacité d'adaptation de l'enseignante ou de l'enseignant. » (CSE, 2014, p. 7). On admet généralement qu'elle s'étend sur les cinq premières années d'enseignement (Kidd, Brown et Fitzallen, 2015; Ingersoll, 2012; Comité d'orientation de la formation du personnel enseignant – COFPE –, 2002), mais on sait que certains enseignants débutants peuvent attendre jusqu'à six ans et plus avant de se sentir pleinement insérés, notamment en raison de la précarité professionnelle (Mukamurera, 2005). Mukamurera, Martineau, Bouthiette et Ndoreraho (2013) distinguent cinq dimensions de l'insertion professionnelle qui peuvent être autant de sources de besoins de soutien et pour lesquelles des mesures d'insertion peuvent s'avérer pertinentes.

La première dimension concerne l'intégration en emploi, qui est le point de départ du processus d'insertion. Elle renvoie à l'embauche, aux modalités d'entrée en carrière et aux caractéristiques des emplois occupés. La personne en insertion doit survivre à l'embauche, c'est-à dire à la précarité qui caractérise aujourd'hui le marché du travail et la profession enseignante, avec toute l'insécurité et l'instabilité professionnelles qui l'accompagnent.

La deuxième dimension est relative à l'affectation spécifique et aux conditions particulières de la tâche. Elle a trait à la nature, aux composantes et à l'organisation de la tâche, à la correspondance entre la tâche spécifique et la formation, à la stabilité de la tâche et du milieu, ainsi qu'à la charge de travail.

La troisième dimension est liée à la socialisation organisationnelle. L'enseignant novice n'est pas nouveau seulement dans la profession, il est nouveau aussi dans une organisation scolaire en particulier, qui a ses caractéristiques, sa culture, ses valeurs, ses règles de fonctionnement, ses attentes et sa dynamique interne (Feiman-Nemser, 2003; Lacaze et Fabre, 2005). L'enseignant débutant a alors besoin de se familiariser avec son nouvel environnement, d'acquérir les connaissances sociales et les procédures lui permettant de s'y intégrer et de développer son plein potentiel dans son rôle professionnel. Un environnement scolaire sain (Bickmore et Bickmore, 2010; Feiman-Nemser, 2003) et proposant un soutien, aide le nouvel enseignant à interpréter les situations qu'il vit de manière adéquate et à développer un sentiment d'accomplissement, voire de compétence (Van Mannen, 1978).

La quatrième dimension est celle de la « professionnalité » et renvoie à l'adaptation et la maîtrise de la fonction professionnelle, par le développement et la consolidation des savoirs et des compétences spécifiques à la profession. Dans le cas des enseignants du Québec, la maîtrise de la fonction professionnelle requiert le développement des douze compétences professionnelles identifiées dans le référentiel de compétences qui guide les programmes de formation à l'enseignement au Québec (Gouvernement du Québec, 2001). Le CSE (2014) souligne que la professionnalité continue de se développer en cours d'insertion grâce à l'expérience, mais qu'elle est surtout stimulée par divers moyens, qu'ils soient formels ou informels, isolés ou intégrés dans un programme d'insertion professionnelle, telles que les lectures, la réflexion sur sa pratique, le partage d'expériences et l'entraide entre pairs, l'assistance par les pairs, le soutien administratif et les activités de formation.

Enfin, la cinquième et dernière dimension, la dimension personnelle se réfère aux aspects émotionnels et affectifs de l'insertion et du travail enseignant en tant qu'expériences humaines exigeantes et déstabilisantes. En effet, parallèlement à l'apprentissage du métier proprement dit, l'enseignant débutant doit apprendre à gérer la pression psychologique inhérente à l'entrée en carrière, il doit apprendre à organiser son temps, à gérer la charge de travail et à développer sa capacité de résilience. Il est en développement personnel et cela est essentiel pour s'épanouir dans son travail, pour déployer efficacement les compétences acquises et pour maintenir un engagement sain dans sa pratique et envers son milieu scolaire et sa profession.

### Du concept de soutien à celui de programme d'insertion et de besoin de soutien

À notre connaissance, aucune étude n'a encore défini la notion de soutien ni celui de besoin de soutien. Leur signification est plutôt implicite, relevant quelque peu du sens commun. Pour notre part, nous définissons le soutien comme étant toute forme d'assistance, d'aide, de conseils ou d'appui donnée à quelqu'un afin de l'aider en fonction de ses besoins. Il n'existe pas une typologie consensuelle et exhaustive du soutien apporté aux enseignants débutants et celui-ci peut être de différentes natures (Bickmore et Bickmore, 2010; Gold, 1996; Hudson, 2012; Mitescu Lupu, 2011) telles que : le soutien émotionnel et affectif, le soutien axé sur l'équilibre travail-vie personnelle, le soutien pédagogique, le soutien disciplinaire et curriculaire, le soutien écologique (axé sur la socialisation organisationnelle) et le soutien intégré aux conditions de travail.

Le soutien peut être proposé de manière spontanée et ponctuelle, mais il est de plus en plus question d'organiser des mesures d'insertion institutionnelles, voire des programmes d'insertion plus exhaustifs. Différents auteurs définissent un programme d'insertion comme étant un programme systémique conçu pour fournir une aide planifiée et soutenue aux enseignants débutants durant au moins leur première année d'enseignement (Bickmore et Bickmore, 2010; Broquard, 2010; Ingersoll, 2012), afin de faciliter leur adaptation aux nouvelles responsabilités ainsi que leur épanouissement personnel et professionnel (Perry et Hayes, 2011). Un programme d'insertion efficace est bien plus qu'un seul dispositif ou une mesure en particulier tel que l'accueil administratif ou même le mentorat (Potemski et Matlach, 2014). Il intègre d'autres mesures d'insertion telles que le soutien administratif, le soutien des pairs, le temps de planification en commun avec des collègues, les activités d'accueil et d'orientation, les réseaux d'entraide, les ateliers de formation, l'observation en classe, l'ajustement des conditions de travail dont l'attribution d'une charge de travail réduite, etc. (Bickmore et Bickmore, 2010; Kutsyuruba, Godden et Tregunna, 2014; Ingersoll, 2012; Mukamurera *et al.*, 2013). Enfin de compte, par « programme d'insertion », nous entendons, un ensemble constitué de mesures, d'activités et de dispositifs institutionnels établis dans le but explicite d'aider (accueillir, introduire, orienter, intégrer, initier, accompagner) de manière formelle et systématique les nouveaux enseignants au cours de leurs premières années de carrière. Le caractère formel et systématique d'un programme d'insertion professionnelle (PIP) évoque l'idée que le soutien est proposé dans un cadre officiel et relativement organisé.

Les besoins de soutien des enseignants débutants sont généralement des besoins professionnels et des besoins personnels (Bickmore et Bickmore, 2010; Gold, 1996; Wang et Odell, 2002). Selon ces mêmes auteurs, les besoins professionnels comportent l'apprentissage et la consolidation des connaissances, les compétences, les stratégies et les ressources relatives aux contenus de l'enseignement, à la pédagogie et à la réflexion sur sa pratique. Les besoins personnels concernent les aspects émotionnels et psychologiques tels que le développement de la confiance en soi, d'une image positive de soi, du sentiment d'efficacité et de la capacité à gérer le stress. Outre ces catégories, Feiman-Nemser (2003) reconnait que l'entrée dans un nouveau milieu s'accompagne aussi d'un besoin d'acculturation organisationnelle. Les besoins de soutien relatifs à l'insertion en emploi sont rarement considérés, tant par les écrits que par les responsables scolaires, ce que déplore Wentzel (2011, p. 192) en ces termes : « l'insertion dans l'emploi est encore trop rarement considérée, par les acteurs chargés de l'organiser (autorités scolaires, employeurs, responsables de formation continue, etc.), comme une étape importante du processus de professionnalisation au même titre que la formation initiale. »

## Éléments méthodologiques

Rappelons que ce chapitre a pour objectif principal de décrire et d'analyser les besoins de soutien des enseignants débutants ainsi que la nature du soutien reçu, sa pertinence et ses effets. Les données utilisées proviennent de deux enquêtes par questionnaire réalisées auprès des enseignants débutants.

La première a été conduite au Québec à l'automne 2013 par Joséphine Mukamurera (Université de Sherbrooke) et Stéphane Martineau (UQTR) et avait pour objectif général de donner un aperçu des besoins de soutien des enseignants débutants, d'analyser l'offre de soutien dans le milieu scolaire et de documenter la pertinence et les effets des dispositifs d'insertion professionnelle mis en place. Le questionnaire a été envoyé par la poste à 2 200 enseignants avec cinq ans d'expérience et moins identifiés dans les bases de données des deux fédérations syndicales qui regroupent les enseignants des 60 commissions scolaires francophones du Québec. 250 enseignants débutants ont répondu à ce questionnaire. Ce sont majoritairement des femmes (82%), comme c'est le cas dans l'ensemble de la profession au Québec. L'âge moyen des répondants est de 33 ans. Tous les ordres scolaires (préscolaire-primaire, secondaire, formation générale aux adultes, formation professionnelle) sont représentés. Presque tous les répondants (95%) ont vécu une expérience de précarité dès leur entrée en carrière, et au moment de l'enquête 49% ont encore un statut précaire tandis que 51% ont un poste régulier.

La deuxième enquête relève d'une étude pancanadienne menée par Kutsyuruba et Walker (2016) ayant pour but d'explorer l'impact différentiel des programmes d'insertion professionnelle et de mentorat sur la rétention des enseignants en début de carrière dans les provinces et les territoires canadiens. Dans le cadre de leurs travaux, un questionnaire a été envoyé à plus de 1 000 enseignants, avec cinq années d'expérience ou moins, à travers le Canada. Au Québec, 21 enseignants ont rempli le questionnaire en ligne disponible sur le site web du Carrefour National de l'Insertion Professionnelle en Enseignement (CNIPE). Ce sont les réponses de ces derniers que nous considérons dans ce chapitre. Sur le plan des caractéristiques démographiques, ces 21 enseignants sont majoritairement des femmes (90%), âgées de 24 à 28 ans, formés dans des universités québécoises et qui enseignent, en accord avec leur formation, à l'ordre du primaire. Tous ont vécu des expériences de précarité en occupant des postes occasionnels et, pour plusieurs (67%), pendant trois années ou plus.

Au sujet du traitement des données, nous avons procédé à l'analyse statistique descriptive (fréquences et pourcentages, tableaux croisés) mais aussi, dans le cas de la première enquête, à certains tests statistiques non paramétriques (test du Khi-deux, seuil de signification de p < .05) pour voir s'il y avait une association significative entre les variables. Cependant dans ce chapitre, la présentation détaillée des résultats repose davantage sur des analyses descriptives.

## Les résultats de l'enquête de l'automne 2013

### Les conditions d'entrée en carrière et expérience d'insertion

Les résultats mettent en évidence les conditions périlleuses d'entrée en carrière pour les enseignants débutants, notamment en raison de la précarité d'emploi massive, des tâches difficiles et de l'instabilité professionnelle. En effet, 95% des répondants sont entrés en enseignement par un emploi précaire, dont 46 % d'entre eux par la suppléance occasionnelle, sans contrat. Bien que le taux de précarité parmi les répondants diminue avec le temps (Khi-deux = 25,91, ddl = 5, p < .001), on constate tout de même que pour plusieurs, elle peut durer longtemps. En effet, non seulement en moyenne 49% des répondants avaient encore un statut précaire au moment de l'enquête, mais cette précarité touche aussi 43% des répondants avec entre quatre et sept ans d'expérience en enseignement. Cette précarité s'accompagne généralement d'instabilité de tâche et de milieu d'exercice. À cet égard, 34% des répondants ont enseigné dans plus d'une commission scolaire (CS) et 37% ont enseigné dans plus de cinq écoles différentes, voire dans une dizaine d'écoles pour 22% d'entre eux. Les tâches ne sont pas des plus faciles non plus, car près de deux tiers (64%) des répondants ont déjà enseigné de une à plus de cinq disciplines en dehors de leur champ de formation, les enseignants à statut précaire étant les plus touchés par cette réalité (Khi-deux = 9,086, ddl = 2, p = .011).

Du point de vue de l'expérience personnelle, 38% des répondants affirment avoir vécu une insertion professionnelle difficile ou très difficile, particulièrement parmi les enseignants ayant un statut précaire (Khi-deux = 7,468, ddl = 1, p = .006). De même, 14% des répondants sont insatisfaits voire très insatisfaits au travail et seulement 26% affirment être très satisfaits. En outre, seulement 7% des répondants se sont sentis très compétents durant leur première année d'enseignement tandis que 28% ont eu le sentiment d'être peu ou pas du tout compétents. Quant à l'engagement personnel dans la carrière enseignante, la situation est relativement positive puisque 81,5% des moins de 40 ans souhaitent rester dans l'enseignement au-delà des 15 prochaines années. On remarque cependant que 6% et 5,5% envisagent de quitter la profession à court (0 à 5 ans) et à moyen terme (6 à 10 ans). Il est également préoccupant de voir que 41% des répondants ne choisiraient plus l'enseignement si l'occasion se présentait à nouveau, en particulier parmi ceux dont l'enseignement n'était pas leur premier choix de carrière. Enfin, mentionnons que 31% des répondants affirment n'avoir bénéficié d'aucun soutien durant leurs cinq premières années d'enseignement, ni formel ni informel.

### Les besoins de soutien durant les premières années d'enseignement

D'emblée, soulignons que plusieurs enseignants ressentent le besoin d'être soutenus pour faciliter leur insertion professionnelle durant leurs premières années d'enseignement. Le besoin de soutien est encore plus flagrant durant les deux premières années, où respectivement 70% et 46% ressentent régulièrement le besoin d'être soutenu. Le besoin de soutien est aussi présent mais de manière moins importante durant la troisième (26%), la quatrième (12%) et la cinquième année (7%). En revanche, concernant la nature des besoins de soutien spécifiques (aspects de l'insertion et du travail enseignant), le test du Khi-deux (rapport de vraisemblance) ne révèle aucune différence significative en fonction du nombre d'années d'expérience d'enseignement des répondants. Cela s'explique probablement par le fait que, comme nous l'avons mentionné plus haut, les enseignants débutants sont généralement soumis aux mêmes conditions difficiles d'insertion pendant leurs premières années de carrière, notamment la lourdeur et l'instabilité de la tâche et du milieu scolaire de travail.

Pour identifier les besoins spécifiques de soutien, une liste de 31 éléments a été proposée aux répondants afin qu'ils puissent indiquer les besoins de soutien qu'ils ont ressentis durant leurs cinq premières années d'enseignement, selon une échelle à trois niveaux : peu ou pas besoin de soutien, besoin d'un soutien moyen et besoin d'un soutien important. La description des besoins présentée ci-après est basée sur la fusion des deux dernières catégories, c'est-à-dire le besoin de soutien moyen et important. Les résultats montrent que les besoins spécifiques de soutien sont multiples, qu'ils touchent à différents aspects de l'insertion et du travail enseignant, le plus prédominant (connaissances des rouages administratifs et syndicaux) étant ciblé par 93% des répondants et le moins prépondérant (pratiques assurant le respect et l'équité à l'égard des différences entre les élèves) étant évoqué par un tiers des répondants (35%). Dix-huit besoins de soutien sont en tête de liste et concernent près de trois quarts des répondants et plus, ce qui en dit long sur leur prépondérance. Mais les autres besoins de la liste concernent aussi un nombre non négligeable de répondants, soit de 57% à 69%. Par conséquent, pour avoir un aperçu éclairé de la situation, nous présentons en ordre décroissant d'importance l'ensemble des besoins de soutien, accompagné du pourcentage de répondants qui considèrent ce besoin comme étant moyen et important:

1. connaissance des rouages administratifs et syndicaux (93%)
2. gestion des problèmes de comportement des élèves (91%)
3. réponse aux besoins des élèves à risque ou en difficulté (88%)
4. proposition de tâches et de défis adaptés aux élèves handicapés ou en difficulté (trouble) d'apprentissage ou d'adaptation (EHDAA) (87%)
5. évaluation des apprentissages (87%)
6. besoin d'écoute, d'empathie et d'encouragement dans les moments difficiles (85%)
7. intégration pédagogique et sociale des EHDAA (84%)
8. besoin d'être rassuré dans ce qu'on fait (82%)
9. connaissance et adaptation au fonctionnement et à la culture de l'école (81%)
10. gestion du stress inhérent à l'entrée en carrière et aux conditions d'insertion (79%)
11. gestion des différences et des rythmes d'apprentissage en classe (78%)
12. différenciation pédagogique (78%)
13. motivation des élèves (76%)
14. connaissance des attentes institutionnelles (75%)
15. planification de l'enseignement et des situations d'apprentissage (73%)
16. appropriation et mise en œuvre des orientations du renouveau pédagogique (71%)
17. maintien en classe d'un climat propice à l'apprentissage (71%)

18. développement de la confiance en soi et de l'image positive de soi comme enseignant (70%)
19. familiarisation à l'environnement de travail (69%)
20. proposition de défis appropriés aux élèves particulièrement avancés ou à haut potentiel (65%)
21. rétroaction sur mon enseignement en classe (64%)
22. intégration au sein de l'équipe-école et de l'équipe-cycle (62%)
23. assistance directe (aide) dans ma classe (61%)
24. organisation du quotidien (gérer la multitude de tâches, être guidé dans les choix à faire, gestion du temps, etc.) (61%)
25. utilisation de différentes méthodes d'enseignement (59%)
26. participation des parents dans le cheminement scolaire de leur enfant (59%)
27. exploitation pédagogique des technologies de l'information et des communications (59%)
28. développement d'un sentiment d'appartenance à la profession (57%)
29. persévérance dans la profession enseignante (57%)
30. maintien d'un rapport positif à la profession (57%)
31. mise en place de mesures qui assurent le respect et l'équité à l'égard des différences entre les élèves (35%)

En examinant la nature de ces besoins, il apparait que les besoins de soutien sont de nature variée. Ils reflètent aussi bien les besoins professionnels liés aux compétences (en particulier celles relatives à l'action en classe et l'aide aux élèves en difficulté) que les besoins d'acculturation au système et au milieu d'exercice (règles d'embauche et d'affectation, environnement de travail, attentes, intégration) ainsi que les besoins de nature personnelle (écoute, assurance, sentiment d'efficacité, gestion du stress, gestion du quotidien, rapport à la profession). Par ailleurs, le fait que plus de la moitié des répondants considère qu'une tâche stable dans le temps (90%), l'obtention d'un poste régulier (79%) et l'allègement ou la réduction de la tâche des nouveaux enseignants (60%) faciliteraient leur insertion professionnelle indique qu'il existe aussi des enjeux relatifs à l'insertion en emploi et à la charge de travail.

**La nature du soutien reçu et l'appréciation des enseignants débutants**

Un peu plus de deux tiers des répondants (69 %) affirment avoir bénéficié d'un soutien à un moment ou l'autre de leurs cinq premières années d'enseignement, sur une base informelle (équipe-école, famille et amis) ou dans le cadre d'un programme d'insertion de leur commission scolaire ou de leur école. L'enquête a d'ailleurs révélé que 37 des 60 commissions scolaires francophones du Québec (61,6%) disposent d'un programme d'insertion professionnelle et 41% des répondants auraient vraisemblablement participé à ces programmes. Toutefois, ce sont seulement 29% des répondants qui estiment avoir reçu, dans le cadre de ces PIP, un soutien structuré et systématique.

Les enseignants ayant reçu le soutien en sont généralement satisfaits, mais davantage à l'égard du soutien informel (83%) et surtout si celui-ci provient de l'équipe-école (93%), tandis que le soutien formel recueille un taux de satisfaction de 68%. Soulignons par ailleurs que le soutien ne correspond pas toujours à la nature des besoins réels ressentis par les enseignants débutants, car 57% estiment que le soutien correspondait peu ou pas du tout à leurs principaux besoins, tandis que seulement 10% considèrent que le soutien correspondait tout à fait à leurs besoins.

Concernant les mesures de soutien spécifiques dont les enseignants ont bénéficié, elles apparaissent variées aussi, mais l'accessibilité est inégale d'une mesure à l'autre. Les plus populaires sont les mesures d'accueil, d'orientation et d'information telles que la présentation à l'équipe-école (84%), la trousse d'accueil ou dossier d'entrée en fonction (61%) et la rencontre d'information sur l'école (59%). Mais 68% affirment avoir aussi bénéficié du soutien de leur direction d'école. Aussi, 37% ont bénéficié des sessions de formation et 36% ont bénéficié de l'observation en classe suivie de la rétroaction. Certaines mesures, perçues pourtant comme ayant été très aidantes, ne sont proposées qu'à une minorité d'enseignants. Mentionnons notamment le temps de planification en commun jugée très utile par 70% de ceux qui en ont bénéficié alors que seulement 33% des répondants y ont eu accès. C'est le cas aussi de l'allégement de la tâche, considéré comme très utile par 64% des répondants alors que seul 5% de l'ensemble des répondants y ont eu accès, de l'assignation d'une personne-ressource (62% contre 23% d'accès) et du mentorat (56% contre 32% d'accès).

Enfin, l'enquête révèle la nature des retombées des PIP pour les enseignants débutants. Les répondants devaient donner leur appréciation des effets perçus selon une échelle à trois niveaux : aucun effet perçu, effets peu significatifs et effets significatifs. En considérant le niveau « effets significatifs », il apparaît que l'impact des PIP touche surtout le développement des compétences pédagogiques, notamment les stratégies d'enseignement (46%), la gestion de classe (43%), l'adaptation des interventions aux élèves en difficulté (35%), la qualité générale de l'enseignement (34%), la relation avec les élèves (29%) et l'évaluation des apprentissages (29%). L'impact se fait sentir aussi sur la motivation à rester au sein de la même école ou au sein de la même commission scolaire (37%), le sentiment d'appartenance à l'équipe-école (29%), le sentiment de confort et de bien-être dans l'exercice de sa fonction (26%) et la motivation à persévérer dans la profession (24%). Très peu de répondants estiment que la participation à un PIP a contribué à augmenter leur motivation au travail (21%), à réduire leur détresse professionnelle (21%) et à gérer leur stress et leurs émotions négatives (20%). Pour tous ces effets, le test de Khi-deux (rapport de vraisemblance) indique une association significative entre la correspondance du soutien aux besoins ressentis (pas du tout, un peu, tout à fait) et la perception de l'impact (aucun effet perçu, effets peu significatifs, effets significatifs), avec la valeur de p variant généralement entre .001 et .010, sauf pour la motivation au travail où $p = .037$. Plus précisément, c'est davantage lorsque le soutien reçu correspond assez ou tout à fait aux besoins ressentis par les enseignants débutants que les effets sont considérés significatifs.

## Ce que nous révèle l'enquête de 2016

Bien que l'échantillon de 21 enseignants du Québec participant à l'enquête de Kutsyuruba et Walker (voir le chapitre 2 dans ce livre) soit insuffisant pour tirer des conclusions valides, nous avons identifié quelques éléments-clés qui complètent l'étude québécoise dont il a été question plus haut dans ce chapitre. Rappelons que l'enjeu ici n'est pas tant de comparer les pourcentages des deux études puisque les échantillons sont quantitativement et qualitativement différents, mais de disposer d'informations supplémentaires permettant de compléter, de nuancer et de discuter l'état de la situation de l'offre de soutien aux enseignants débutants au Québec.

### La nature du soutien reçu

La grande majorité des enseignants qui ont répondu à l'enquête (86%) indiquent avoir bénéficié d'un programme d'insertion professionnelle (PIP) sous la responsabilité de la commission scolaire ou de l'école où ils enseignent. Bien que le PIP ne soit pas décrit de manière spécifique, des mesures fréquemment mentionnées par les répondants sont l'évaluation par la direction de l'établissement (81%), le mentorat formel (24%) et informel (76%), le partage de ressources (52%) et les sessions de formation de nature ponctuelle (48%).

### La satisfaction au regard du soutien

Une question ouverte permettait aux enseignants de se prononcer sur l'adéquation entre le soutien reçu et leurs besoins de nouveaux enseignants. Trois constats se dégagent des réponses fournies par les enseignants. Premièrement, il y a ceux qui sont tout à fait satisfaits des mesures de soutien dont ils ont bénéficié (38%). Des commentaires tels que « l'enseignante mentor était extraordinaire » ou encore « … j'ai eu une superbe évaluation de la direction, très détaillée et utile, [ce n'est] pas toutes les directions qui prennent la peine et le temps de le faire. ». Deuxièmement, ceux qui sont tout à fait insatisfaits (33%) comme l'indique le commentaire suivant : « Non. Souvent les formations sont à 90% inutiles. Exemple : Ma première année, nous avons reçu une formation en gestion de classe au mois de mars ! ». Enfin, il y a ceux qui sont plus mitigés (19 %) et qui se disent partiellement satisfaits ou insatisfaits, mais qui comprennent la situation : « Oui et non. La profession est déjà très exigeante alors à un certain point, j'ai arrêté de demander de l'appui puisque mes mentors semblaient déjà débordées avec leur propre travail. Elles m'ont consacré beaucoup de temps et du matériel et m'ont énormément aidé, mais cela n'a pas pu répondre à tous mes besoins. ».

### Les effets perçus

Les enseignants disent avoir particulièrement apprécié le programme d'insertion professionnelle dans sa totalité (40%), le mentorat informel (30%) et le partage de ressources avec d'autres enseignants (15%). Pour plusieurs (72%), le soutien reçu leur a permis de mieux connaitre l'école et la commission scolaire. Ils jugent que ce soutien est exhaustif (62%) et qu'il leur a fourni les outils nécessaires pour persévérer lorsque la situation est plus difficile (57%). En ce sens le soutien qu'ils ont reçu a un impact sur leur enseignement (71%). Toutefois, pour plusieurs d'entre eux (69%), l'expérience de la première année d'enseignement est empreinte d'essais-erreurs.

**Le mentorat**

Au total, 60% des répondants ont pu bénéficier du soutien d'un mentor. L'aide apportée par le mentor se situe dans trois catégories : 1) le soutien professionnel (l'aide à la planification, l'évaluation, le bulletin et le partage de ressources); 2) le soutien moral (aide dans les moments difficiles, grande disponibilité et confidentialité assurée, partage d'expériences de vie) et, 3) l'intégration à l'école (intégration à l'équipe-école). Le mentorat comporte cependant un certain nombre de défis identifiés par les répondants. Outre le manque de temps qui revient à quatre reprises, les répondants ont aussi mentionné parmi les défis, leur peur de déranger le mentor, l'absence de structures formelles pour les rencontres et le fait que le mentor n'enseignait pas au même niveau qu'eux.

**À propos du soutien de la direction d'école**

L'équipe scolaire administrative (directeur ou directeur adjoint) joue aussi un rôle important dans l'insertion professionnelle du nouvel enseignant et c'est pourquoi ce volet a été sondé dans l'enquête. Selon les enseignants (64%), les directions ont le succès de leur insertion professionnelle à cœur. En ce sens, elles communiquent clairement leurs attentes au nouvel enseignant (58%), offrent des conditions de travail appropriées (52%), facilitent l'observation de modèles enseignants (68%) et font la promotion d'une culture de collaboration (73%). Les enseignants se sentent appuyés par la direction (74%) et se sentent à l'aise de discuter de leurs problèmes avec cette dernière (66%). En revanche, le temps consacré aux rencontres avec les mentors est considéré comme satisfaisant par seulement 17% des répondants de même que le temps consacré à la réflexion sur l'apprentissage des élèves (37%). De plus, la moitié des répondants (48%) seulement indiquent que la rétroaction de la part de la direction est suffisante pour les guider dans l'amélioration de leur enseignement. Enfin, 43% des enseignants attribuent une responsabilité à leur direction dans leur décision de poursuivre ou pas leur carrière en enseignement.

**Au final**

Au total, 84% des répondants ne songent pas à quitter leur emploi. La principale raison évoquée par près de la moitié des répondants (48%) dans leur décision de poursuivre leur carrière en enseignement est l'élève : le souci de faire une différence pour l'élève, de contribuer à son apprentissage, de le préparer au monde de demain. Trois enseignants ont aussi mentionné le milieu de travail stimulant alors que deux autres ont dit aimer leur travail et y prendre un réel plaisir.

Les enseignants soulignent l'intensité et le rythme de travail effréné et constatent que leur vie sociale, et parfois familiale, est très limitée en début de carrière. Ils disent recourir à plusieurs stratégies telles que, demander de l'aide aux collègues, discuter avec les collègues, les amis, les conjoints, faire du sport, établir des priorités, pour maintenir un certain bien-être au travail. Fort de leur première expérience, ils suggèrent aux enseignants qui entrent dans la profession d'être patients, de ne pas s'attendre à ce que tout soit parfait dès le début. Ils insistent également sur l'importance de demander de l'aide et de poser des questions si besoin. À la question « Si vous étiez mentor, que feriez-vous sans aucune hésitation? », ils répondent : être disponible et partager mes ressources. L'extrait suivant résume bien l'ensemble des commentaires émis pour cette question : « J'irais à elle au lieu d'attendre qu'elle vienne à moi. Les enseignantes débutantes savent qu'il y a des ressources à leur portée, mais elles n'ont pas le temps d'aller les chercher. Il faut que ce soit le contraire, que les ressources viennent à eux, dans leur classe. »

**Réflexions suscitées par les résultats et conclusion**

Les résultats des deux enquêtes rapportées dans ce chapitre démontrent de manière concrète la pénibilité de l'expérience d'insertion en enseignement: précarité, affectations de tâches hors champ de formation, tâches instables, changements fréquents d'écoles, faible sentiment de compétence et expérience de pratique souvent empreinte d'essais et erreurs. Dans un tel contexte, comment les enseignants débutants peuvent-ils développer leur plein potentiel et devenir rapidement efficaces dans leur exercice professionnel s'ils sont laissés à eux-mêmes? D'ailleurs, ces enseignants indiquent avoir régulièrement ressenti le besoin d'être aidé, en particulier durant les deux premières années de service où le besoin semble flagrant.

Une attention particulière devrait donc être donnée à la période d'insertion professionnelle, phase cruciale et déterminante pour la suite de la carrière et la qualité de l'enseignement (Randall, 2010; Valentic Zuljan et Marsentic Pozarnick, 2014).

Autrement, le choc de la réalité risque de nuire à la mobilisation et au transfert efficace des acquis de la formation initiale (Valencic Zuljan et Marentic Pozarnik, 2014) qui représente un investissement considérable en temps et en argent. Feiman-Nemser (2003, p. 27) reconnait également l'importance du soutien durant cette phase de la carrière en ces termes : « If we leave beginning teachers to sink or swim on their own, they may become overwhelmed and leave the field. Alternatively, they may stay, clinging to practices and attitudes that help them survive but do not serve the education needs of students. »

Par ailleurs le fait que certains enseignants ressentent encore le besoin d'aide au-delà des deux premières années n'est pas un fait négligeable. Il est possible d'envisager le soutien de façon progressive, plus systématique en début de carrière et davantage occasionnel voire à la carte après les deux premières années. Il est important aussi de prendre en considération que l'impact sur les pratiques en classe et sur l'apprentissage des élèves est plus significatif au-delà de deux ans de participation à un PIP (Glazerman *et al.*, 2010). Cela fait penser que le suivi auprès des participants est une voie pertinente pour stimuler et pérenniser le transfert des acquis dans la pratique.

En cette période où les organismes scolaires sont fortement encouragés à mette en place des programmes d'insertion, la tentation, voire la pression d'agir rapidement, peut être forte au risque de manquer plus ou moins la cible au regard des besoins réels des enseignants débutants. Les résultats présentés dans ce chapitre montrent la nature plurielle et multidimensionnelle de leurs besoins : besoins professionnels, personnels, d'acculturation au système et au milieu d'exercice, besoins liés aux conditions de travail. Proposer une mesure d'insertion considérant un seul type de besoin, tel que le soutien à l'enseignement (Gold, 1996), est-il suffisant pour en optimiser les effets et favoriser une insertion aboutie? Cela est peu probable. D'une part, une mesure peut répondre à un besoin en particulier mais ignorer plusieurs autres qui sont peut-être aussi ou plus déterminants pour l'individu. Par exemple, tout en reconnaissant la nécessité du soutien émotionnel en début de carrière, Wang et Odell (2002) rappellent que ce soutien ne contribue pas nécessairement au développement des compétences professionnelles attendues. D'autre part, étant donné la variété des besoins chez un même enseignant, l'efficacité de chaque mesure prise de façon isolée peut s'avérer limitée. C'est la combinaison de mesures qui s'avère fructueuse. À cet égard, Smith et Ingersoll (2004) ont par exemple montré que le mentorat, une mesure pourtant pertinente et très valorisée dans le milieu et par nos répondants, ne réduit pratiquement pas à lui seul le taux d'abandon de la profession ni le taux d'attrition dans une école. L'impact devient significatif lorsque cette mesure est combinée avec d'autres, comme le soutien de la direction, la planification et la collaboration avec les collègues. Parlant du soutien de la direction d'école, rappelons que nos résultats confirment son rôle crucial dans la décision de poursuivre la carrière en enseignement. Les résultats de la recherche de Bickmore et Bickmore (2010) permettent de comprendre que le soutien de la direction agit surtout au niveau des besoins personnels des enseignants débutants en leur permettant de se sentir appuyé et valorisé dans leur travail, de développer l'appréciation de leur compétence, la confiance en soi et le sentiment d'appartenance à l'école.

Il est intéressant de voir qu'actuellement plus de la moitié des commissions scolaires au Québec disposent d'un programme d'insertion professionnelle comprenant différentes mesures. C'est l'une des conditions essentielles (Bickmore et Bickmore, 2010; Leroux et Mukamurera, 2013). L'appréciation des débutants à l'égard de ces mesures est relativement positive pour plusieurs d'entre elles. Les impacts paraissent aussi divers (pratiques en classe, sentiment d'appartenance à l'école et motivation à y rester, motivation à rester dans la profession, réduction de la détresse psychologique, etc.), comme l'ont montré d'autres études ailleurs (Gaikhorst, Beishuizen, Zijlstra et Volman, 2015; Ingrsoll, 2012). On observe toutefois que la participation à ces programmes est encore limitée, ce qui est d'ailleurs le cas un peu partout (OCDE, 2015; Kidd, Brown et Fitzallen, 2015). Par contre, ce qui est plus préoccupant, c'est que les mesures de soutien jugées très utiles par les enseignants débutants qui en ont bénéficié sont les moins proposées, comme celles relatives à l'ajustement des tâches pour les débutants, à la libération pédagogique pour participer à certaines mesures d'insertion, à l'accompagnement personnalisé (assignation d'une personne-ressource, mentorat) et à la planification en commun avec des collègues.

Rappelons que les PIP sont encore récents dans la plupart des commissions scolaires (Mukamurera *et al.*, 2013). On pourrait alors s'attendre à ce que les effets soient encore plus significatifs pour les enseignants débutants et pour les organismes scolaires lorsque les conditions d'efficacité pourront être réunies (Leroux et Mukamurera, 2013) et que certaines améliorations pressenties pourront être apportées, notamment en ce qui concerne l'accessibilité des mesures, la coordination des PIP, l'intensification de l'accompagnement individualisé et la formation des mentors (Mukamurera *et al.*, 2013).

En fin de compte, les résultats présentés dans ce chapitre soulignent l'importance de proposer aux enseignants débutants des mesures ou des programmes d'insertion fondés sur une prise en compte de leurs besoins, de l'étape de carrière et de leurs conditions d'exercice, d'une part, et sur une approche systémique et multidimensionnelle du soutien, d'autre part. Le tout doit être aménagé et coordonné de manière à éviter une surcharge excessive aux enseignants débutants et à créer un environnement de travail positif au sein du milieu d'exercice.

# Bibliographie

Bickmore, S. T. et Bickmore, D. L. (2010). Revealing the principal's role in the induction process: Novice teachers telling their stories. *Journal of School Leadership, 20*(4), 445–469.

Broquard, C. M. (2010). *The juxtaposition of secondary and beginning teacher induction programs.* [Thèse de doctorat en éducation]. University of California, Los Angeles, USA.

Comité d'orientation de la formation du personnel enseignant – COFPE – (2002). *Offrir la profession en héritage.* Avis du COFPE sur l'insertion en enseignement. Québec, Québec : Gouvernement du Québec.

Commission européenne, Direction générale Éducation et Culture (2005). *Projet de principes européens communs concernant les compétences et qualifications des enseignants.* Bruxelles, Belgique : Commission européenne.

Conseil supérieur de l'éducation – CSE (2014). *Le développement professionnel, un enrichissement pour toute la profession enseignante.* Québec, Québec : Gouvernement du Québec.

Feiman-Nemser, S. (2001). From preparation to practice: Designing a continuum to strengthen and sustain teaching. *Teachers College Record, 103*(6), 1013–1055.

Feiman-Nemser, S. (2003). What new teachers need to learn. *Educational leadership, 60*(8), 25–29.

Forseille, A., et Raptis, H. (2016). Future teachers clubs and the socialization of pre-service and early career teachers. *Teaching and Teacher Education, 59*, 239–246.

Gaikhorst, L., Beishuizen, J.J., Zijlstra, B.J.H. et Volman, M.L.L (2015). Contribution of a professional development programme to the quality and retention of teachers in an urban environment. *European Journal of Teacher Education, 38*(1), 41–57.

Glazerman, S., Isenberg, E., Dolfin, S., Bleeker, M., Johnson, A., Grider, M., et Jacobus, M. (2010). *Impacts of comprehensive teacher induction: Final results from a randomized controlled study* (NCEE 2010-4028). Washington, DC : National Center for Education Evaluation and Regional Assistance, Institute of Education Sciences, U.S. Department of Education.

Gold, Y. (1996). Beginning teacher support. Attrition, mentoring and induction. Dans J. Sikula, T.J. Buttery et R. Guyton (dir.), *Handbook of research on teacher education* (p. 548–594). Second Edition. New York, NY : Macmillan Library.

Gouvernement du Québec (2001). *La formation à l'enseignement. Les orientations et les compétences professionnelles.* Québec: Ministère de l'Éducation du Québec.

Hudson, P. (2012). How can schools support beginning teachers? A call for timely induction and mentoring for effective teaching. *Australian Journal of Teacher Education, 37*(7), 70–84.

Ingersoll, R. M. (2012). Beginning teacher induction: What the data tell us. *Phi Delta Kappan, 93*(8), 47–51.

Kidd, L., Brown, N. et Fitzallen, N. (2015). Beginning teachers' perception of their induction into the teaching profession. *Australian Journal of Teacher Education, 40*(3), 154–173.

Kutsyuruba, B., Godden, L. et Tregunna, L. (2014). Curbing early-career teacher attrition: A pan-Canadian document analysis of teacher induction and mentorship programs. *Canadian Journal of Educational Administration and Policy, 161*, 1–42.

Lacaze, D. et Fabre, D. (2005). Présentation du concept de socialisation organisationnelle. Dans N. Delobbe, O. Herrbach, D. Lacaze et K. Mignonac (dir.), *Comportement organisationnel. Volume 1. Contrat psychologique, émotions au travail, socialisation organisationnelle* (p. 273–302). Bruxelles, Belgique : De Boeck.

Leroux, M. et Mukamurera, J. (2013). Bénéfices et conditions d'efficacité des programmes d'insertion professionnelle en enseignement : état des connaissances sur le sujet. *Formation et profession, 21*(1), 13–27.

Mitescu Lupu, M. (2011). What can professional satisfaction and sense of support tell us about teachers' learning at work? *Journal of Educational Sciences and Psychology, 63*(2), 86–93.

Mukamurera, J. (2005). La professionnalisation de l'enseignement et les conditions d'insertion dans le métier. Dans D. Biron, M. Cividini et J.-F. Desbiens (dir.), *La profession enseignante au temps des réformes* (p. 313–336). Sherbrooke, Québec : Éditions du CRP.

Mukamurera, J. (2011). Les multiples dimensions de l'insertion professionnelle : portrait, expériences et significations d'enseignants. Dans B. Wentzel, A. Akkari, P.-F. Coen et N. Changkakoti (dir.). *L'insertion professionnelle des enseignants : regards croisés et perspective internationale* (p. 17–38). Bienne, Suisse : HEP-BEJUNE.

Mukamurera, J., Bourque, J. et Gingras, C. (2008). Portrait de l'insertion dans l'enseignement au Québec pour les nouvelles générations d'enseignants. Dans L. Portelance, J. Mukamurera, S. Martineau et C. Gervais (dir.). *L'insertion dans le milieu scolaire. Une phase cruciale du développement professionnel de l'enseignant* (p. 49–72). Québec, Québec : Presses de l'Université Laval.

Mukamurera, J., Martineau, S., Bouthiette, M. et Ndoreraho, J. P. (2013). Les programmes d'insertion professionnelle des enseignants dans les commissions scolaires du Québec : portrait et appréciation des acteurs. Éducation et formation, e-299, 13–35.

Organisation de coopération et de développement économiques – OCDE (2015). *L'enseignement à la loupe. Nouveaux enseignants : quel soutien ?* Paris, France : OCDE.

Organisation de coopération et de développement économiques – OCDE (2005). *Le rôle crucial des enseignants. Attirer, former et retenir des enseignants de qualité.* Paris, France: OCDE.

Perry, B. et Hayes, K. (2011). The effect of a new teacher induction program on new teachers reported teacher goals for excellence, mobility, and retention rates. *The International Journal of Educational Leadership Preparation, 6*(1), 1–12.

Philippot, T. (2014). L'entrée dans le métier des enseignants débutants à l'école primaire française : préoccupations, tensions et compromis profession-nels. *Formation et profession 22*(2), 13–30.

Potemski, A. et Matlach, L. (2014). *Supporting new teachers: what do we know about effective state induction policies.* Washington, DC : The Center on Great Teachers and Leaders, American Institutes for Research.

Randall, M. (2010). Advice for the first three years. *Teaching Music, 17*(5), 36–41.

Smith, T. et Igersoll, R. (2004). What are the effects of induction and mentoring on beginning teacher turnover? *American Educational Research Journal, 41*(3), 681–714.

Tardif, M. (2013). *La condition enseignante au Québec du XIXe au XXIe siècle. Une histoire cousue de fils rouges : précarité, injustice et déclin de l'école publique.* Québec, Québec : Les Presses de l'Université Laval.

Valencic Zuljan, M. et Marentic Pozarnik, B. (2014). Induction and early-career support of teachers in Europe. *European Journal of Education, 49*(2), 192–205.

Van Mannen, J. (1978). People processing: Strategies of organizational socializa-tion. *Organizational dynamics, 7*(1), 19–36.

Wang, J. et Odell, S. J. (2002). Mentored learning to teach according to stan-dards-based reform: A critical review. *Review of Educational Research, 72*(3), 481–546.

Wentzel, B. (2011). Insertion et développement professionnel : tentions et intensions convergentes. Dans B. Wentzel, A. Akkari, P.-F. Coen et N. Changkakoti (2011), *L'insertion professionnelle des enseignants : regards croisés et perspective internationale* (p. 191–202). Bienne, Suisse : HEP-BEJUNE.

Weva, K. W. (1999). Insertion professionnelle des nouveaux enseignants : responsabilité de l'administration scolaire. Dans J.-C. Hétu, M. Lavoie et S. Baillauquès (dir.), *Jeunes enseignants et insertion professionnelle. Un processus de socialisation ? De professionnalisation ? De transformation ?* (p. 187–208). Bruxelles, Belgique : De Boeck et Larcier.

# Threading the Needle: Examining the Teacher Induction Program (TIP) in the Western Québec School Board

*Trista Hollweck*

**Threading the needle** (Verb, present participle)*:* (idiomatic)
*to find harmony or strike a balance between conflicting forces,*
*interests, etc. Normally used to indicate the difficulty of doing*
*so; also, sarcastically, for a failed attempt.* (**Wiktionary.org**)

International educational research has shown that high quality mentoring and induction for beginning teachers can enhance development and retention of highly effective teachers and increase student success (Darling-Hammond & McLaughlin, 1996; Fletcher, Strong & Villar, 2008; Smith & Ingersoll, 2004; Wang, Odell & Schwille, 2008). Although the terms *mentoring* and *induction* are often used interchangeably in the literature, it is important to note that "conceptually, mentoring is but one component, albeit usually the most important element, of a program of planned induction" (Bullough, 2012, p. 62). Mentoring and induction have grown internationally in popularity as a means to support teachers; yet programs vary greatly in terms of effectiveness (Feiman-Nemser, 2012; Ganser, 2006). Adding to the confusion, coaching is also gaining traction in education as an effective approach to enhance teachers' professional growth. Also often used interchangeably with the term mentoring or viewed as a component of mentoring, coaching remains ill-defined and programs vary greatly. In this chapter, mentoring and coaching are viewed as different, yet complementary, approaches that form a critical part of teacher induction. Specifically, the chapter reports on Western Québec School Board's (WQSB) Teacher Induction Program (TIP), a program that aims to support teachers in their first two years of employment. With no clear pattern guiding the development and implementation of mentoring, coaching and induction programs in Canada or Québec, TIP was developed at the grassroots level and is inextricably linked to its context, a small English school district in Western Québec.

WQSB's Teacher Induction Program is best conceptualized as a patchwork quilt. Quilting is a needlework technique that involves two or more layers of fabric—called the quilt back and top—that sandwich padding of some sort and are stitched together in a decorative pattern (http://www.quilthistory.com). Among the types of quilts, the patchwork quilt is the most utilitarian. Designed to keep its user warm and supported, the quilter uses a variety of pieces of fabric that are already in their possession to form fabric blocks which are then sewn together in a pattern of some kind. Much like a patchwork quilt, WQSB's TIP was developed to support teachers who are new to the district. Whereas the district's context forms the quilt back, the numerous influences, initiatives, commitments, and district partners make up the fabric blocks that need to be sewn together in the quilt top. Without a clear model for induction in the district, feedback from key stakeholders (administrators, union representatives, Mentor-Coaches, consultants, directors and Teaching Fellows) must also be stitched into the quilt to avoid its early unravelling. Now in its seventh year, an emerging and exciting pattern is beginning to take shape in the TIP quilt, which may have important implications for other Canadian districts exploring mentoring, coaching, and induction.

## The Quilt Back

The Western Québec School Board (WQSB) is located in Gatineau, Québec and is a member of the provincial English School Network. It provides English language education to students in the Outaouais, Pontiac and Abitibi-Temiscamingue regions. Although it is a relatively small school board in staff (450) and students (6655), it has the largest geographic catchment in Québec and services a disparate area roughly twice the size of Nova Scotia. The WQSB is comprised of both urban and rural schools and has a unique composition of student population in terms of language and culture, especially in its northern schools. Historically, there has been a problem with teacher attrition, due in part to: 1) the geographical proximity of the school board to Ontario schools where teachers receive a significant pay increase; and, 2) the challenging conditions of teaching in small rural, and often northern, schools. In recent years, there has been an increase in teachers applying for work in the WQSB. This is likely a result of more full-time teaching opportunities being offered in a growing district at a time when there is a shortage in the neighbouring province of Ontario and new regulations imposed from the Ontario Ministry of Education[1]. With many more teachers looking for long-term teaching appointments in the district, the WQSB recognized the need to develop an induction program that would support its new teachers and help retain *highly effective* teachers in all of its schools. Three clear aims frame the development and implementation of WQSB's TIP, previously called the New Teacher Program (NTP). These aims are: 1) to retain effective teachers new to the district; 2) to provide leadership and professional growth opportunities for veteran staff; and, 3) to improve teaching and learning across the district. It is these three aims, along the context of the WQSB, that form the quilt back onto which the TIP pattern is stitched.

## The Quilt Top

No two patchwork quilts are ever alike. Not only is this uniqueness a result of the variety of fabric pieces available to individual quilters, but these pieces or units can also be sewn together in hundreds, if not thousands of different ways to create the quilt top. Like a patchwork quilt, induction programs differ from district to district. Much depends on the creativity and skill of the quilters or the program developers. In the WQSB, the development of TIP began with a small volunteer committee of consultants, administrators, and teachers led by Michel Dubeau, the Director of Education responsible for the new teacher dossier. The committee was tasked with stitching a variety of pieces together into a coherent pattern.

---

1   Regulation 274/12 first introduced in fall 2012 mandated standardized hiring
    procedures and defined a pathway to permanent employment that usually requires
    new teachers to start on daily supply rosters and short-term occasional teaching
    before gaining eligibility to apply for longer-term occasional assignments, and
    eventually to compete for permanent employment opportunities with a school
    board.

Lacking skill and expertise in induction, mentoring and coaching, the committee started by exploring available models in the province, country and even internationally to help guide them with their quilting process.

**Mentoring and Induction in Québec**

Although the Québec Ministry's (MELS, 2016) *Education Act* (Section 22, paragraph 6.1) stipulates clearly that teachers must "collaborate in the training of future teachers and in the mentoring of newly qualified teachers," what this actually looks like in practice is ultimately left to each individual school district. Unlike some other provinces, Québec has no self-regulatory body that licenses and governs the teaching profession, such as Ontario's College of Teachers. Hence, it is the responsibility of individual school boards to develop, deliver and fund ongoing professional learning for its members, which includes new teacher induction. As noted in the pan-Canadian document analysis study of induction and mentorship programs (Kutsyuruba, Godden, & Tregunna, 2013), there have been some attempts by the Ministry of Education (MELS) to provide guidance around these processes to the districts. The authors referred to a document produced in March 2009 that examined the role of mentoring and share its eight recommendations:

> That MELS provide money to be dedicated to organized mentoring activities; that MELS, school boards, and universities collaborate to develop organized mentoring programs based on the available research and tailored to suit local needs; that mentoring should be a required activity for all first year teachers and an option for all second-year teachers; that school boards and schools develop strategies to train mentors; that an administrator or in-school committee assign mentors to new teachers as an initial step, and that new teachers later choose their own mentors; that mentors be given release time to receive training and to meet mentees; that when there are not enough active teachers to serve as mentors, school boards hire local retired teachers on a part-time basis to support new teachers; and that existing projects to train mentors be networked and supported by MELS funding, in order to deliver mentoring programs effectively and efficiently. (pp. 37-38)

To date, there has been little Ministerial funding available and few supported networking opportunities within the English education community. As a result, there is great disparity among the approaches to induction and mentoring across the various school boards. Adding to this, there is no established provincial forum to share best practices, and it is also extremely difficult to navigate district and provincial documentation to better understand the different program offerings (Kutsyuruba et al., 2013). In fact, although the WQSB's TIP is one of the more robust and structured induction and mentoring programs in the province's English sector, it was left out of the report due to a lack of publicly accessible documentation.

In recent years, positive steps are being taken to address some of these challenges. First, Ministerial funding has been earmarked for districts to support the mentoring of new teachers. Second, there have been attempts by various groups to convene English school boards around the issue of mentorship and induction, such as the Leadership Committee for English Education in Québec's (LCEEQ) Mentorship Project for New Teachers (2012-2013), the Québec Provincial Association of Teachers' (QPAT) New Teacher Committee (2011) and the Directors of English Education Network's (DEEN) learning partnerships (2014). Although moving in the right direction, there still remains a large variance in the type and structure of induction and mentoring programs offered throughout Québec, challenges with accessing and sharing best practices, and very little interaction and networking amongst and between the English and French education communities.

## The Development of WQSB's Teacher Induction Program (TIP)

In quilting, there are special techniques used to sew patchwork pieces into blocks and a variety of block patterns (such as four patch, nine patch, and rail fence) to choose from when assembling the quilt top. As noted by Liz Johnson (2013), "the precise execution of these techniques is paramount to a beautifully finished quilt. It's similar to putting together a puzzle; each piece has to fit perfectly in order for the larger picture to come into view." Similarly, for the TIP development team, there were many competing initiatives, visions, and influences that needed to be stitched together skillfully to keep the final TIP quilt from unravelling. As new quilters, the team turned to research and established mentoring and induction programs for guidance. Championing the importance of induction, Feiman-Nemser (2012) outlined several key components for effective programs: individualized professional development focusing on an orientation to school and community, instructional strategies and curricular guidance; reduced workload; serious mentoring for at least two years which includes sanctioned time, initial training, ongoing development and appropriate matches; and administrative support (p. 15). Without any readily available induction programs designed specifically for the Québec context, the WQSB purchased the Virginia-based *Mentoring in the 21st Century* (Rutherford, 2005) resource kit. The kit provided a comprehensive mentor training plan with all the required tools, such as session outlines, learning exercises, mentor handbooks, participant manuals, DVDs and posters. With only a few schools involved in its pilot year (2009), the TIP team strictly followed the kit's training plan. Administrators selected veteran teachers to attend a 2-day training session offered during the summer and each newly minted mentor left with two giant binders full of mentoring resources. Despite the American context, the induction team found the resource kit useful. However, feedback from participating mentors revealed the sheer bulk of resources was overwhelming and often sat unused. It was clear that a more structured and context-specific program was needed. As well, it was evident that relying purely on the good-will of the TIP development committee and veteran teachers as volunteers would ultimately make the induction program unsustainable. In 2010, a part-time (30%) school board consultant position was created to help with program development, coordination and delivery. As the number of teachers new to the district grew, by 2012 a full-time (100%) position was established.

At the same time that the induction and mentoring program was being developed in the WQSB, a long-standing learning partnership with Ravenswood School in Bromley, England and OLEVI, the International Centre for Teaching and Learning, was looking at evaluation and supervision practices. WQSB directors, administrators, and veteran teachers were paired with counterparts from Ravenswood School and OLEVI to explore what 'high quality' teaching looked like in the Western Québec context. From this learning partnership, an influential evaluation document and teaching observation tool (the Professional Rubric for the Observation of Teaching Tool) was produced. Both are foundational documents in the evaluation and supervision of WQSB teachers. Framed around the 12 *Core Professional Competencies for the Teaching Profession* (MELS, 2001), these 'living' documents continue to be updated as new understanding around evaluation and supervision practice occurs. As a result of these learning partnerships, the evaluation and supervision of teachers became a large part of the fabric of the district and would need to be sewn into the TIP quilt. Another important fabric piece that added to the TIP quilt came from an LCEEQ grant for the induction team and a few veteran teachers to examine Ontario's New Teacher Induction Program (NTIP) and meet some of its leaders. The learning from this experience added a renewed focus on professional learning for new teachers, mentor-training and the need to develop context-specific resources.

## An Emerging Pattern

Starting in 2010, in order to be placed on the 'priority of employment' list and be eligible for tenure, all teachers new to the district (regardless of previous teaching experience) must complete the TIP's two-year commitment. Over the years, feedback from key stakeholders had informed the program's development and implementation. Although it remains a living and responsive program, an emerging pattern is taking shape as the program structure and terminology is clarified. First, the program's name was changed from the *New Teacher Program* to the *Teacher Induction Program* (TIP) and 'new teachers' became *Teaching Fellows* in recognition of the important role a mentoring and coaching fellowship plays in teacher induction. Finding the right terminology has been a challenge and these name changes were responses to stakeholder feedback that not all TIP participants were 'new' to the teaching profession and that to be labelled as such could be off-putting and could hinder the program's focus on professional learning through a fellowship approach. As well, mentors became *Mentor-Coaches*, reflecting the district's use of the distinct but complementary approaches. Finally, TIP's structure was defined as having three key pillars: Professional Growth, the Mentoring and Coaching Fellowship (MCF), and Evaluation (see Figure 1). Each of these pillars are described below.

*Figure 1*. The three pillars of WQSB's Teacher Induction Program

## Pillar 1: Professional Growth

Whereas professional learning expands beyond district borders, this pillar recognizes that continued learning on the job with colleagues is essential for the improvement of a school district (Hargreaves & Fullan, 2012). TIP provides one day of orientation for Teaching Fellows in year one and six optional Professional Learning (PL) opportunities in year two. The workshop-style PL is offered by district consultants and veteran teachers (mostly Mentor-Coaches), and focuses on curricular guidance and/or important board initiatives, frameworks or approaches (such as Tribes, Sound Prints, the Daily Five, Visible Learning, Indigenous Pedagogy, Universal Design for Learning). The opportunity to lead the PL workshops offers veteran teachers a shared sense of purpose and direction, new leadership roles, and emphasizes the importance of sharing best practice and 'growing the top,' a key aim of TIP. Mentor-Coaches are also provided with two PL sessions, usually facilitated by the TIP consultants and/or mentoring and coaching specialists. Teaching Fellows and Mentor-Coaches are also encouraged to engage in PL through school, district and ministry initiatives, as well as beyond the provincial borders. Ultimately, the goal of this pillar is to offer current professional learning opportunities and provide a structure for teachers to share their experiences and build relationships.

## Pillar 2: Mentoring and Coaching Fellowship (MCF)

The Mentoring and Coaching Fellowship (MCF) pillar is both the most research-driven and the most expensive component of WQSB's TIP. The MCF emerged from the district's belief that there needed to be opportunities for Teaching Fellows to reflect, collaborate and practice new learning in their own environment with support from their colleagues (Feiman-Nemser, 2012; Hargreaves & Fullan, 2012, Joyce & Showers, 2002). As part of the MCF, every Teaching Fellow is paired with a non-evaluative, administrator-selected Mentor-Coach in their first year of TIP. As highlighted in the literature (Feiman-Nemser, 2012), the most ideal match for the Mentor-Coach would be someone from the same school, same grade and same subject area. However, considering the context of the WQSB, there are often times when only some or even none of these criteria are possible and a distance Mentor-Coach is assigned. Although a large body of literature highlights the importance of self-selection and choice in mentoring and coaching practice (Van Nieuwerburgh, 2012; Moir & Bloom, 2003; Sharpe & Nishimura, 2017), it has also been shown that the practice can be highly diverse and inconsistent (Kyriacou & O'Connor, 2003; Totterdell et al., 2002) and may actually support ineffective practice rather than promote more effective teaching (Feiman-Nemser, 2012). In response, the WQSB chose a mandated and systematic approach to coaching and mentoring, with an aim towards consistency and equal opportunity for all teachers new to the district. As key stakeholders in the induction process, administrators are responsible for selectively recruiting teachers to serve as Mentor-Coaches. Ideally, these veteran teachers are carefully selected for their instructional and leadership skills, as well as for 'fit' in terms of workload, interest, personality and position in the school community. In the last seven years, more than 45 teachers have been trained as Mentor-Coaches, and they have worked with more than 250 Teaching Fellows. Feedback from Teaching Fellows, Mentor-Coaches and administrators consistently note the MCF as the most important component of TIP and credit effective fellowships for professional growth and improved teaching and learning. With nearly half of WQSB's 450 teachers involved in the MCF in some capacity since 2009, it has the potential, if done well, to greatly impact the culture of the district.

In the MCF, each Mentor-Coach and Teaching Fellow pair, or fellowship, is expected to observe each other in practice, meet regularly (weekly or per cycle) to set goals, and reflect on professional growth. Two TIP-funded release *Fellowship Days* for shared professional learning are also provided. These days are based on the fellowship needs and interests and are often used to do observations of other classrooms in the district. Classroom visits are not only rich learning opportunities for the fellowship, but they also help to build relationships within and across schools, celebrate effective teaching and learning, and help to capture the knowledge within the district.

It is evident from the research literature that the type of structure and selection methods, as well as training and support for Mentor-Coaches, are paramount to an effective mentoring and coaching program (Carver & Feiman-Nemser, 2009; Ingersoll & Strong, 2011). Along with two PL sessions, Mentor-Coaches in the WQSB are provided with individual support from the TIP team and multiple resources, such as a TIP handbook. Since 2010, professional learning sessions have provided Mentor-Coaches with a venue to share experiences, and have focused on how to provide meaning feedback through classroom observations (Jackson, 2013), how to have hard conversations (Abrams, 2009), and how to use the GROW model (Whitmore, 2010) in coaching sessions. A recent focus of the MCF has been on defining mentoring and coaching and clarifying what each approach entails. Mentor-Coaches are required to set goals based on the six mentoring and coaching competencies developed in-house through the MCF. Each term, they submit a written reflection to the TIP team around these goals and their own professional learning. In exchange for the heavy workload, Mentor-Coaches are paid a small stipend of one thousand dollars that can be redeemed as income (taxable), days off, or put towards technology.

**Quilting Primer: Learn the Lingo.** Along with the recent and well-received name changes (TIP, Mentor-Coach and Teaching Fellow), work has been done by the TIP team to unpack key terminology such as mentoring and coaching. This has proven to be a challenging task, as the terms have conflicting interpretations and usage within the educational and research communities (CUREE, 2005; Fletcher & Mullen, 2012; Knight, 2007; Moir & Bloom, 2003; Sharpe & Nishmura 2017). Often, the terms mentoring and coaching are used interchangeably, or coaching is described as a component of mentoring or vice versa. Although there have been recent attempts in the United States, Australia and the United Kingdom to clarify the key differences, there remains work to be done for the Canadian context. In the WQSB, mentoring and coaching are viewed as distinct, yet complementary, approaches in an effective induction process. Much depends on the fellowship needs and it requires skill on behalf of the Mentor-Coach to know when to use a mentoring or coaching stance. Understanding the terminology is an important first step to help Mentor-Coaches in their dance along the hyphen.

*Mentoring.* The concept of mentoring can be traced back to Ancient Greece and Homer's "Odyssey" where Mentor was a friend of Odysseus and adviser of Telemachus. This reference conjures up the image of a more knowledgeable and experienced individual taking up a supportive role of overseeing and encouraging reflection and learning within a less experienced individual (Ganser, 2006). Mentoring in this context is an informal and voluntary process where the trusted advisor's role is to facilitate the protégé's career and personal development. Although informal mentoring continues to have a place in education, research indicates that there was a trend in educational reform in the 1980's toward the professionalization of the role, which includes systematic training and increased regulation and accreditation, especially in the UK and USA (Moir & Bloom, 2003; Mullen, 2012).

The structured workplace model has greatly shifted the purposes and uses of mentoring. Depending on the context, the research literature (Feiman-Nemser, 2001; Hargreaves & Fullan, 2012; Mullen, 2012) highlights two main rationales for most mentoring programs. For some programs, the goal of mentoring is to increase teacher retention, and as such, the role of the mentor is to provide emotional guidance and teaching support as new teachers begin to construct a 'professional identity' (Gold, 1996) within a school. Wang and Odell (2002) described this socialization aspect of mentoring as the 'humanistic perspective.' For other programs, mentoring is viewed as a means to transform teaching and learning in a system. This is a more complex role and the mentor is viewed as being critical in the development of a new teacher's professional practice (Feiman-Nemser, 2001; Ganser, 2006; Mullen, 2012). Wang and Odell (2002) called this view of mentoring the 'situated apprenticeship perspective,' for its focus on the improvement of teaching quality. In the WQSB, both views of mentoring are combined under the three TIP aims of retaining effective teachers, providing leadership opportunities to veteran teachers, and ultimately, improving teaching and learning across the district.

Another debate in the mentoring literature revolves around the issue of whether mentoring should be voluntary or mandated. Voluntary mentoring transpires through informal and spontaneous communication, and mentees often select their own mentors. Proponents for the voluntary approach argue that this type of mentoring has been shown to enhance the development of the whole person (Varney, 2009). However, critics raise questions about the quality of the mentoring experience, and whether a mentee-selected mentor is always the best example of high quality teaching (Feiman-Nemser, 2012). On the other hand, mandated mentoring assigns and structures mentoring partnerships, and there is an expectation that mentees will make documented gains through the mentoring experience. Those in favour of mandated mentoring note the transformative potential of mentoring and its potential to "recreate" the teaching profession (Hargreaves & Fullan, 2000). By selecting and training mentors, districts have more control over the type of mentoring that will transpire, ensuring the process is connected to other reform components. Critics of mandated mentoring are concerned that in this approach mentoring is turned into an achievement measure, which jeopardizes the original spirit and integrity of mentoring (Mullen, 2012). They argue that it makes mentoring feel impersonal and evaluative rather than a process for fostering professional collaboration. Although the WQSB has taken a mandated mentoring position by using administrator-selected Mentor-Coaches, the research literature indicates that regardless of the mentoring approach (voluntary or mandated, informal or formal), an effective mentoring process has the potential to improve professional culture by targeting introspection, as well as open and reciprocal dialogue among colleagues around issues of teaching and learning (Feiman-Nemser, 2012; Hargreaves & Fullan, 2012).

*Coaching.* Coaching has long been well established in business and sports. However, it is a relatively recent initiative in the field of education (Fletcher, 2012: Van Nieuwerburgh, 2012). Like mentoring, coaching can be difficult to define and the practice can be multifaceted, ambiguous, and contextually driven (Fletcher, 2012; Knight, 2007; Mullen, 2012; Van Nieuwerburgh, 2012). As a millennial educational phenomenon, it is often perceived in the literature to be nearer to the practical than the theoretical and remains scantly researched (Fletcher, 2012). As coaching gains traction, there have been more studies and work published that aim to clarify the coaching process and its impact on teaching and learning (Knight, 2007; Munro, 2016; Starcevich, 2009; Passmore, 2010; van Nieuwerburgh, 2012). Although mentoring and coaching share some key principles, such as a focus on professional learning in a trust-based and collaborative relationship, there is general agreement in the literature that coaching is a more structured, less directive, and more short-term process than mentoring. Whereas mentors are generally understood as more senior and skilled professionals who provide advice and share their knowledge and expertise with the person being mentored, or mentee, coaches can be generalists who are trained to ask probing questions in order to enhance reflection and guide inquiry based on the agenda set by the person being coached, or coachee. Coaching has also been described as focusing more on the practice of teaching rather than on personal and professional growth; but this remains debated and seems to depend on how coaching is conceptualized in the literature. Ultimately, coaching in education remains an ill-defined and under-theorized field (Fletcher & Mullen, 2012; van Nieuwerburgh, 2012) and like mentoring, more research is needed to determine whether properly organized and supported coaching programs are improving learning and teaching in schools.

I have developed a conceptualization of WQSB's most recent understanding of the two processes and their unique principles (as captured in Figure 2). A Mobius strip is used to show how mentoring and coaching, while distinct approaches, are interconnected and anchored in shared principles in an effective induction program.

# TEACHER INDUCTION

**MENTORING and COACHING**
**are anchored in a collaborative and reflective relationship.**
Both are focused on personal and professional growth based on
trust, empathic listening, safety, mutual respect,
curiosity and confidentiality.

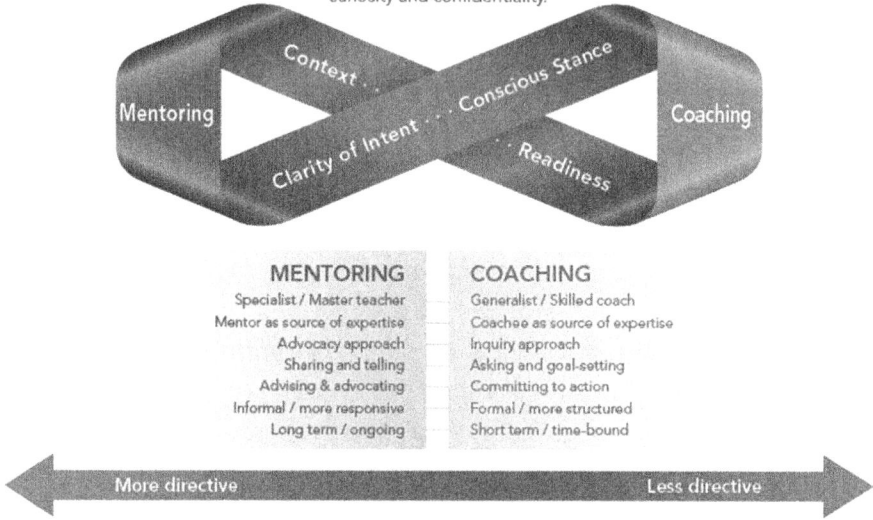

Mentoring     Context . . . Conscious Stance     Coaching
Clarity of Intent . . . Readiness

| MENTORING | COACHING |
|---|---|
| Specialist / Master teacher | Generalist / Skilled coach |
| Mentor as source of expertise | Coachee as source of expertise |
| Advocacy approach | Inquiry approach |
| Sharing and telling | Asking and goal-setting |
| Advising & advocating | Committing to action |
| Informal / more responsive | Formal / more structured |
| Long term / ongoing | Short term / time-bound |

← More directive                    Less directive →

*Figure 2.* Mentoring and coaching during teacher induction

Returning to the quilt metaphor – just as there are many block patterns to choose from when sewing a patchwork quilt, so there are many different approaches to mentoring and coaching in education. Since TIP initially began by using the *Mentoring in the 21st Century* model which defined coaching as a component of mentoring, the MCF continues to evolve, as various coaching approaches such as appreciative coaching (Orem et al., 2011), cognitive coaching (Costa & Garmston, 1994), instructional coaching (Knight, 2007), evocative coaching (Tschannen-Moran & Tschannen-Moran, 2010), and adaptive mentorship (Ralph & Walker, 2011) are explored. Ultimately, as each new piece of learning gets stitched into the MCF, the overall TIP quilt grows.

## Pillar 3: Evaluation

Evaluation is the most controversial of the TIP components in terms of participant feedback and mentoring and coaching research. This pillar refers to a rigorous two-year high-stakes (job or no job) evaluation process for all Teaching Fellows in order to make WQSB's 'priority of employment' list and be eligible for tenure. Up until 2016, this process included three formal observations by school administration, one formal observation by the TIP team (see team composition[2]) and the submission of a Professional Growth Portfolio based on Québec's 12 Professional Competencies (MELS, 2001). Teaching Fellows in their second year of TIP are no longer paired with a Mentor-Coach, but must still complete the same high-stakes formal evaluation process. This rigorous evaluation process grew from the WQSB-Ravenswood partnership and is based on the requirements outlined in the MELS information document (2006) that states:

> The principal or director is responsible for evaluating the educational and professional practices of teachers on proba-tion. However, the MELS favours an approach that fosters the active participation of the teacher in question. In this approach, tools for gathering and recording information make it possible to identify, develop and evaluate the dif-ferent competencies. The teacher concerned, as well as the coordinator for the school board or private or special status institution, must be informed of the results of the evaluation. (p. 16)

Following Québec Ministry guidelines, administrators in the WQSB are responsible for completing an official evaluation document at the end of each year for all Year 1 and 2 Teaching Fellows. In order to inform their final evaluation each term, it is expected that they complete formal classroom observations throughout the year using the WQSB-designed *Professional Rubric for the Observation of Teaching Tool* (PRO Teaching Tool), and pro-vide the Teaching Fellow with meaningful feedback for growth. In one of these term observations, the TIP team and Mentor-Coach (see footnote 2) join the school administration. There are three aims of the TIP team obser-vation approach: 1) to ensure consistency in the evaluation practices across

---

2    The TIP team is currently comprised of three members, the director of Human Resources and two consultants responsible for TIP coordination and implementation. The formal observation team may include two of these members who accompany the administrator(s) and Mentor-Coach (if agreed upon by the Teaching Fellow). It is important to note that the Mentor-Coach is present in a supportive and non-evaluative role.

the district; 2) to provide professional learning opportunities for administrators around classroom observations and meaningful feedback delivery; and ultimately, 3) to provide meaningful feedback to the Teaching Fellow from an outside perspective. In spite of these aims, key stakeholders (Teaching Fellows, Mentor-Coaches and union members) argue that these formal team observations add an unnecessarily stressful high-stakes component to a snapshot (20-30 minute) visit. There is also some confusion around the role of these classroom visits in the final evaluation. To date, the TIP team's role in formal observations remains hotly debated and divisive in the district.

In order to increase transparency and address some stakeholder concerns, since 2015 the Mentor-Coach has been invited to participate in the formal observations along with the TIP team, playing a non-evaluative and advocacy role. Including Mentor-Coaches in the formal evaluation process of their Teaching Fellow has received mixed reviews in the research literature. The traditional concept of mentoring views the relationship between mentor and mentee as one based on confidence and trust (Carver & Katz, 2004; Fransson, 2010; Piggot-Irvine et al, 2009). From this perspective, mentoring and evaluation remain separate functions. However, an increased focus on improving teacher effectiveness as the rationale for mentoring and coaching programs is leading some districts to include mentors and coaches in formal assessment to varying degrees (Carver & Feiman-Nemser, 2009; Fransson, 2010; Rippon & Martin, 2006; Yusko & Feiman-Nemser, 2008). Some researchers (e.g., Hobson et al, 2009; Wang & Odell, 2007) argued that including Mentor-Coaches in the assessment process will jeopardize the supportive and open collaborative partnership that should promote risk-free learning. Others (e.g. Carver & Feiman-Nemser, 2009; Rippon & Martin, 2006; Yusko & Feiman, 2008) showed that Mentor-Coaches are able to support as well as assess their new teachers, once a trust relationship has been formed. In fact, Carver and Feiman-Nemser (2009) found that the dual role of assessor and supporter created a "collective sense of professional accountability" (p. 317) among Mentor-Coaches and Teaching Fellows. After this second year of Mentor-Coaches participating in the formal observation of their Teaching Fellows, stakeholder feedback will make an important contribution to this discussion.

The final component of the two-year evaluation process for Teaching Fellows has been the yearly completion of a Professional Growth Portfolio submitted to their school administration. Using the 12 Professional Competencies (MELS, 2001) as its framework, Teaching Fellows were expected to set term goals, provide evidence of their growth and write reflections. What resulted from WQSB's attempt to make the evaluation process more collaborativeand inclusive and "foster active participation" (MELS, 2006) was perceived by many teachers as an added burden or a 'make-work project' in an already challenging job. Critical feedback from stakeholders spurred the WQSB's recent (2016) move toward a *Reflective Record* rather than the Professional Growth Portfolio. The Reflective Record aims to streamline the evaluation process, retain inclusivity, reduce paperwork and make the evaluation experience more meaningful for both the Teaching Fellow and administration. Each term the Teaching Fellow is expected to: 1) set two goals with their Mentor-Coach and administrator; 2) reflect in writing on the impact of these goals on student learning; and 3) provide at least one piece of evidence. Administration is also expected to provide each Teaching Fellow with written feedback for growth each term, based on classroom observations. Recent district and provincial professional learning for administrators has focused on classroom observation strategies and ways to give teachers meaningful feedback. Undoubtedly, feedback from this year's TIP cohort will inform next steps with regards to having the Reflective Record as part of the evaluation process.

## Threading the Needle

After seven years, the TIP quilt remains unfinished, but a discernible pattern is starting to emerge. Like all sewing projects, there have been many dropped stitches and loose threads along the way. In particular, four key lessons have been learned that may be useful to other Canadian districts interested in developing mentoring, coaching and induction programs. First, TIP cannot be removed from its context. It was discovered early on that no pre-packaged program could simply be sewn onto the WQSB quilt back. Rather, TIP is a homegrown program made up of a variety of patchwork blocks, each representing the different partners, influences, initiatives and competing priorities within the district. Second, TIP is a living process. By clarifying key terminology and putting clear structures into place, TIP has been woven into the fabric of the district. However, stakeholder feedback and ongoing professional learning must continue to guide how the patchwork blocks are arranged and rearranged in the quilting process. Third, the importance of effective selection and training of Mentor-Coaches cannot be understated. With the Mentoring and Coaching Fellowship (MCF) highlighted as the most important component of TIP, the Mentor-Coach has a major influence, either positive or negative, on the experience of a Teaching Fellow. The careful selection and specialized training of Mentor-Coaches increases the likelihood of an effective fellowship, which can lead to improved teaching and learning throughout the district. More work needs to be done in the WQSB to ensure all Mentor-Coaches have equal access to high quality systematic mentoring and coaching training, are regularly supported, and have time and space to collaborate and share best practices. Fourth, trust is foundational to TIP's success. Ultimately, all stakeholders must be aware of, and trust, the district's vision for teacher induction. Over the years, the TIP quilt has evolved and changed based on feedback and new learning however, the program changes are not always clearly communicated and misunderstandings persist throughout the district. Compounding this issue, mistrust and conflicting views regarding the role of evaluation in teacher induction remain. More effort needs to be made at a district level to make TIP transparent, address concerns and ensure that all stakeholders feel included in the feedback process. As a constant work in progress, WQSB's TIP remains an unfinished project. However, as this chapter shows, a definite pattern is starting to emerge that may offer insight for other Canadian districts working on their own mentoring, coaching and induction quilts.

# References

Abrams, J. (2009). *Having hard conversations*. Thousand Oaks, CA: Corwin Press.

Bullough, R. (2012). Mentoring and new teacher induction in the United States: A review and analysis of current practices. *Mentoring & Tutoring: Partnership in Learning, 20*(1), 57–74.

Carver, C. L., & Feiman-Nemser, S. (2009). Using policy to improve teacher induction critical elements and missing pieces. *Educational Policy, 23*(2), 295–328.

Carver, C. L., & Katz, D. S. (2004). Teaching at the Boundary of Acceptable Practice What is a New Teacher Mentor to Do? *Journal of Teacher Education, 55*(5), 449–462.

Costa, A. L., & Garmston, R. J. (1994). *Cognitive coaching: A foundation for renaissance schools*. Norwood, MA: Christopher-Gordon Publishers, Inc.

CUREE (2005). National Framework for mentoring and coaching. Retrieved from http://www.curee.co.uk/files/publication/1219925968/National-framework-for-mentoring-and-coaching.pdf

Darling-Hammond, L., & McLaughlin, M. (1996). Policies that support teacher development in an era of reform. In M. McLaughlin & I. Oberman (Eds.), *Teacher learning: New policies and practices* (pp. 202–218). New York, NY: Teachers College Press.

Feiman-Nemser, S. (2001). From preparation to practice: Designing a continuum to strengthen and sustain teaching. *The Teachers College Record, 103*(6), 1013–1055.

Feiman-Nemser, S. (2012). Beyond solo teaching. *Educational Leadership, 69*(8), 10–16.

Fletcher, S. J. (2012). Coaching: An overview. S. Fletcher & C.A. Mullen (Eds.). *The SAGE Handbook of Mentoring and Coaching in Education* (pp. 24–40). Thousand Oaks, CA: SAGE Publications.

Fletcher, S., & Mullen, C. A. (Eds.). (2012). *The SAGE handbook of mentoring and coaching in education*. Thousand Oaks, CA: SAGE Publications.

Fletcher, S., Strong, M., & Villar, A. (2008). An investigation of the effects of variations in mentor-based induction on performance of students in California. *Teachers College Record, 110*(10), 2271–2289.

Fransson, G. (2010). Mentors assessing mentees? An overview and analyses of the mentorship role concerning newly qualified teachers. *European Journal of Teacher Education, 33*(4), 375–390.

Ganser, T. (2006). A status report on teacher mentoring programmes in the United States. In C. Cullingford (Ed.), *Mentoring in Education: An International Perspective* (pp. 33–55). Burlington, VT: Ashgate.

Gold, Y. (1996). Beginning teacher support: Attrition, mentoring, and induction. In C. B. Courtney (Ed.), *Review of research in education* (Volume 16, pp. 548–594). Washington, DC: American Educational Research Association.

Hargreaves, A., & Fullan, M. (2012). *Professional capital: Transforming teaching in every school*. New York, NY: Teachers College Press.

Hargreaves, A., & Fullan, M. (2000). Mentoring in the new millennium. *Theory Into Practice, 39* (1), 50–56. Retrieved from http://dx.doi.org/10.1207/s15430421tip3901_8.

Hobson, A. J., Ashby, P., Malderez, A., & Tomlinson, P. D. (2009). Mentoring beginning teachers: What we know and what we don't. *Teaching & Teacher Education, 25*(1), 207–216.

Ingersoll, R., & Strong, M. (2011). The impact of induction and mentoring programs for beginning teachers: A critical review of the research. *Review of Education Research, 81*(2), 201–233.

Jackson, R. R. (2013). *Never underestimate your teachers: Instructional leadership for excellence in every classroom*. Alexandria, VA: ASCD.

Johnson, L. (2013). Quilt basics- Piecing quilt blocks by machine part 4A of 5. [website] Retrieved from: http://www.sew4home.com/tips-resources/sewing-tips-tricks/quilting-basics-piecing-quilt-blocks-machine-part-4a-5

Joyce, B. R., & Showers, B. (2002). *Student achievement through staff development*. Alexandria, VA: ASCD.

Knight, J. (2007) Instructional coaching: A partnership approach to improving instruction, Thousand Oaks, CA: Corwin Press.

Kutsyuruba, B., Godden, L., & Tregunna, L. (2013). *Early-career teacher attrition and retention: A pan-Canadian document analysis of teacher induction and mentorship programs* (Final Report). Kingston, ON: Queen's University.

Kyriacou, C., & O'Connor, A. (2003). Primary newly qualified teachers' experience of the induction year in its first year of implementation in England. *Journal of In-Service Education, 29*(2), 185–200.

MELS (2001). Teacher training: Orientations and professional competencies. Retrieved from http://www.education.gouv.qc.ca/fileadmin/site_web/documents/dpse/formation_ens_a.pdf

MELS (2003). Attracting, developing and retaining effective teachers in Québec. Report by the Ministere de l'education du Québec (Canada). Retrieved from http://www.mels.gouv.qc.ca/dftps/interieur/PDF/attirer_a.PDF

MELS (2006). The probationary period for teachers in preschool, elementary or secondary school: Information document. Retrieved from: http://www.education.gouv.qc.ca/fileadmin/site_web/documents/reseau/formation_titularisation/StageProbatoire_a.pdf

MELS (2016), Government of Quebec *Education Act.* Retrieved from http://legisQuébec.gouv.qc.ca/en/ShowDoc/cs/I-13.3

Moir, E., & Bloom, G. (2003). Fostering leadership through mentoring. *Educational Leadership*, 60(8), 58–60.

Mullen, C. A. (2012). Mentoring: An overview. S. Fletcher & C.A. Mullen (Eds.). *The SAGE Handbook of Mentoring and Coaching in Education* (pp. 7–23). Thousand Oaks, CA: SAGE Publications.

Munro, C. (2016, August). Coaching in education: An introduction. *e-Leading: Management Strategies for School Leaders, 2016* (27). Retrieved from http://www.growthcoaching.com.au/PDF/e-leading-chris-munro.pdf

Orem, S. L., Binkert, J., & Clancy, A. L. (2011). *Appreciative coaching: A positive process for change.* New York, NY: John Wiley & Sons.

Passmore, J. (Ed.) (2010). *Excellence in coaching: The industry guide* (2nd Ed.). London: Kogan Page.

Piggott-Irvine, E., Aitken, H., Ritchie, J., Ferguson, P., & McGrath, F. (2009). Induction of newly qualified teachers in New Zealand. *Asia Pacific Journal of Teacher Education*, 37(2), 175–198.

Ralph, E. G., & Walker, K. D. (Eds.). (2011). *Adapting mentorship across the professions: Fresh insights and perspectives.* Calgary, AB: Detselig Enterprises.

Rippon, J. & Martin, M. (2006). What makes a good induction supporter? *Teaching and Teacher Education, 22*(1), 84–99.

Rutherford, P. (2005). *21st century mentor's handbook: Creating a culture for learning.* Alexandria, VA: Just Ask Publication.

Sharpe, K., & Nishimura, J. (2017). *When mentoring meets coaching.* Toronto, ON: Pearson.

Smith, T. M., & Ingersoll, R. M. (2004). What are the effects of induction and mentoring on beginning teacher turnover? *American Educational Research Journal, 41*(3), 681–714.

Starcevich, M. M. (2009). *Coach, mentor: Is there a difference. CEO Center for Coaching and Mentoring, Inc.* Retrieved from http://www.coachingandmentoring.com/Articles/mentoring.html

Totterdell, M., Bubb, S., & Heilbronn, R. (2002). *Evaluation of the effectiveness of the statutory arrangements for the induction of newly qualified teachers.* London: Department for Education and Skills.

Tschannen-Moran, B., & Tschannen-Moran, M. (2010). *Evocative coaching: Transforming schools one conversation at a time.* New York, NY: John Wiley & Sons.

Van Nieuwerburgh, C. (Ed.). (2012). *Coaching in education.* London, UK: Karnac Books.

Varney, J. (2009). Humanistic mentoring: Nurturing the person within. *Kappa Delta Pi Record, 45*(3), 127-131.

Wang, J., & Odell, S. J. (2002). Mentored learning to teach according to standards-based reform: A critical review. *Review of Educational Research, 72*(3), 481–546.

Wang, J., & Odell, S. J. (2007). An alternative conception of mentor–novice relationships: Learning to teach in reform-minded ways as a context. *Teaching and Teacher Education, 23*(4), 473–489.

Wang, J., Odell, S. J., & Schwille, S. A. (2008). Effects of teacher induction on beginning teachers' teaching: A critical review of the literature. *Journal of Teacher Education, 59*(2), 132–152.

Whitmore, J. (2010). *Coaching for performance: growing human potential and purpose: the principles and practice of coaching and leadership* (5th Ed.). London, UK: Nicholas Brealey Publishing.

Yusko, B., & Feiman-Nemser, S. (2008). Embracing contraries: Combining assistance and assessment in new teacher induction. *The Teachers College Record, 110*(5), 923–953.

# The Assessment of Students' Learning: A Major Challenge for Beginning Teachers in Québec and Ontario.

*Sylvie Fontaine, Ruth Kane, Thursica Kovinthan*

## Introduction

All teachers have responsibility for assessing student learning and reporting students' progress to students and their parents. This responsibility is complicated by the changing culture and practice of assessment, which has been motivated by the growing recognition that what classroom teachers do, in terms of assessment, impacts the ways students learn (Rey & Feyfant, 2014). The primary purpose of assessment and evaluation has been reframed as explicitly improving student learning (rather than solely measuring progress), and consequently, the teacher's role in assessment has shifted along with the expectation for assessment to be embedded in instruction. In Canada and elsewhere, education systems are increasingly driven by an accountability paradigm and committed to cross-system assessments that are outside the control of teachers (e.g., provincial and international assessments). DeLuca (2012) argued that the current context of accountability in North America calls upon initial teacher education institutions to ensure that assessment literacy is one of the fundamental goals of their pre-service programs. However, researchers over recent decades suggested that assessment of student learning is consistently identified as a key challenge for beginning teachers, many of whom note a lack of preparedness through their initial teacher education programs. This chapter draws on evidence from longitudinal studies in two Canadian provinces, Quebec and Ontario, to consider ways we might address beginning teachers' limited levels of assessment literacy through initial teacher education and induction.

First, we draw on the international research in general to demonstrate that beginning teachers find their responsibilities for assessment to be a significant challenge. Seeking to better understand the role of the teacher in assessment, we consider the shifting context of assessment literacy. We look at how research on assessment has advanced, what its impacts are on the role of the classroom teacher and at a system level, and how education has embraced an accountability paradigm that locates elements of assessment beyond the reach of the classroom teacher. Using Quebec and Ontario as our sites of focus, we examine how teacher education is taking up assessment in pre-service programs within these jurisdictions. Finally, we illuminate the potential for induction to be a means to enhanced beginning teacher assessment literacy.

## Preservice Teachers' Lack of Preparation in Student Assessment

National and international researchers pointed to a lack of preparation for pre-service teachers with regard to the assessment of student learning (DeLuca & Klinger, 2010; DeLuca, 2012; DeLuca & Bellara, 2013; Fontaine, Kane, Duquette, Savoie-Zajc, 2012; Kane, Jones, Rottmann & Penna, 2013; Stiggins, 1999; Volante & Fazio, 2007). The limited time allocated to prepare pre-service teachers to become assessment literate is often identified as a factor of importance in the lack of preparation (e.g., DeLuca & Klinger, 2010). The time factor becomes important when considering the impact of the knowledge acquired in the assessment course. Indeed, in a recent study, Box, Skoog and Dabbs (2015) came to the conclusion that the knowledge on formative assessment acquired by pre-service teachers does make a difference in their decision to integrate formative assessment within their teaching. Misalignments between assessment policies and assessment courses (DeLuca & Bellara, 2013) or between assessment courses and classroom assessment practices (Ogan-Bekiroglu & Suzuk, 2014; Laurier, 2014) can also account for the gaps identified in pre-service teachers' preparation in student assessment. In addition, it has been reported that despite the education they receive, pre-service teachers maintain a low level of self-efficacy with regard to student assessment and evaluation across the four years of their program (Volante & Fazio, 2007).

These same conclusions were reached in a national mixed methods longitudinal study of beginning secondary teachers' sense of preparedness in New Zealand (NZ) (Anthony & Kane, 2008). In accord with the international studies cited above, the NZ study identified the beginning teachers' perceived lack of preparedness in relation to assessment of student learning to be a key finding. This was confirmed in data from the mentor teachers, over half of whom reported that their new teachers required additional support in their development of appropriate assessment procedures (Anthony & Kane, 2008). A key finding of this national longitudinal study was that initial teacher education must do better in preparing teachers with respect to the purposes and uses of assessment to support learning (Anthony & Kane, 2008).

In the Province of Quebec, Fontaine et al. (2012) conducted a study to identify factors underlying beginning teachers' decisions about their teaching career. They administered a questionnaire to 371 secondary graduating teachers in 11 universities in Québec. Participants had to indicate their perceived level of preparedness for each of the 12 competencies of the program. They also had to elaborate on their career intentions for the next few years. Fontaine and colleagues followed-up with 3 rounds of interviews over an eighteen-month period with a sample of 40 respondents. Although graduating secondary teachers perceived themselves to be generally well-prepared at the end of their program, their first year in teaching was not free of challenges. Indeed, assessment of learning, classroom management, workload and working conditions were perceived as particularly challenging throughout the year. Furthermore, the challenges with the assessment of student learning endured over the eighteen-month period and were found to be linked with the intention to leave teaching as a career. Fontaine et al. (2012) endorsed the misalignment issue, indicating that participants' comments highlighted a lack of synergy between initial teacher education course work and the reality of having responsibility for assessment in the classroom" (p. 393).

Despite the extensive research on the need for assessment courses within teacher education, international researchers suggest that many pre-service programs do not benefit from these findings (Xu & Brown, 2016). Rather, there is growing evidence that pre-service education programs offer limited one-term general introduction to assessment courses

(Greenberg & Walsh, 2010) or in some cases, no courses are offered at all (Popham, 2011). There is ample evidence to suggest that teacher education might be struggling to ensure that beginning teachers graduate with the knowledge and skills to effectively develop and enact appropriate assessment that supports student learning. Indeed, researchers have noted that initial teacher education programs may graduate beginning teachers with an inadequate level of assessment literacy. Given these findings of the aforementioned studies across different jurisdictions it is important to give attention to understanding better the role of the teacher, especially the beginning teacher, in the assessment of student learning.

## The Context of Assessment Literacy

For over 30 years, researchers have examined the role of assessment in supporting student learning (e.g., Allal & Mottier Lopez, 2007; Black & Wiliam, 1998a, 1998b; Bloom, Hastings, & Madaus, 1971; Crooks, 1988; Hadji, 2012; Morrissette, 2009; Scallon, 2004, 2008), with a growing realization that what teachers do in classrooms in terms of assessment impacts the ways that students learn. In the literature, the terms of formative and summative assessment (Scriven, 1967; Bloom, 1969) are used to distinguish the purposes of assessment conducted by teachers. The purpose of assessment is closely linked to the nature of the decision resulting from the assessment (Laurier, 2014). Thus, formative assessment aims to support student learning, is continuous throughout the year, and leads to teachers' pedagogical decisions; whereas summative assessment of student achievement, usually occurring towards the end of a learning period, leads to administrative decisions (Laurier, 2014). More recently, specific terminology categorized what was initially called formative assessment. When teachers assess their students to guide their learning and, concurrently, obtain indications about how they might adjust their teaching to improve students' learning, the term "assessment for learning" is used (Stiggins, 2007). The term "assessment as learning" is used to specifically reflect the integration of assessment within teachers' instruction and as a means to foster students' metacognition in regard to their learning (Earl, 2003). Assessment, then, becomes embedded in the instruction provided by teachers. In both cases, it "is a process in which assessment-elicited evidence is used by teachers to adjust their ongoing instructional activities, or by students to adjust the ways they are trying to learn something" (Popham, 2009, p. 5).

In the last decade, Canadian education systems have embraced a paradigm of accountability that requires educational institutions to provide concrete indications of efficacy (Laveault, 2014). This practice is coherent with increased participation in international exams (e.g., PISA, TIMMS, PIRLS) which provide results on students' achievement for specific subjects (mathematics, reading, etc.), as indications of education systems' levels of efficacy. Along with these international measures, most Canadian provinces impose standardized exams prepared by specialists within the provincial ministry of education. Success in these exams is a condition to certification. Table 1 presents the provincial examinations by level (grade) and subject that are administered in the provinces of Quebec and Ontario.

**Table 1**
*Mandated Provincial Examinations*

| Quebec | Ontario |
| --- | --- |
| **Elementary School** | |
| Grade Four – French Writing & Reading | Grade Three – Reading, Writing, Mathematics |
| Grade Six – French Writing & Reading, Math | Grade Six - Reading, Writing, Mathematics |
| **Secondary School** | |
| Year Two – French Writing | Grade Nine - Mathematics |
| Year Four – History and Citizenship Education, Math, Science and Technology and Applied Science and Technology | Grade Ten - Ontario Secondary School Literacy Test as graduation requirement. |
| Year Five – French Writing, English | |

In addition to official ministry of education examinations, other educational organizations and school boards in the Province of Québec provide schools with common exams across a number of subjects for teachers to administer in their classroom. Therefore a large proportion of the assessment of student learning is not the teacher's responsibility, as was once the case; and thus the teacher's role with regard to assessment of student learning is changing (Laveault, 2014).

The prominence of external examinations within the current accountability era is one factor that contributes to the modification of teachers' responsibility in regard to assessment. Another contributing factor lies in the abundance of research showing the impact of formative assessment on student learning and on improving standardized test scores (Black, Harrison, Lee, Marshall, & Wiliam, 2002; Black & Wiliam, 1998a, 1998b; Ruiz-Primo & Furtak, 2007; Scallon, 2000). This research may explain why educational organizations in the USA have chosen to initiate "reform efforts to promote the use of formative assessment in classrooms" (Box et al., 2015, p. 957). Consequently, formative assessment has been "infused into or adopted for educational assessment and evaluation policies or practices" around the world (Birenbaum, DeLuca, Earl, Heritage, Klenowski, Looney, Smith, Timperley, Volante, Wyatt-Smith & Hung, 2015). The end result is then a shift in the teacher's role and, consequently, a focus on formative assessment in the teacher's assessment practice (Wiliam, 2011). In Canada, this shift is clearly stated in official ministry documents such as: *The Policy of the Evaluation of Learning in Québec* (Ministère de l'Éducation du Québec, 2003) and *Growing Success: Assessment, Evaluation and Reporting in Ontario Schools* (Ontario Ministry of Education, 2010). In both documents, there is recognition that teachers need to integrate assessment *of, for* and *as* learning into their classroom practice. Therefore, it is legitimate to question how this shift in the teacher's role in regard to the assessment of students is taken into account in their pre-service education and in their induction into the profession.

## Teacher Education in the Province of Québec

In a perfect world, educational context, ministry policies on assessment and evidence-based research on assessment, for instance the impact of formative assessment on student learning, would translate into teacher education programs. At the end, beginning teachers would be assessment literate and ready to implement what they have learned in regard to student assessment in their classroom. But is this the case? Teacher education in Québec aims at developing responsible teachers, able to work autonomously within their professional context. The educational program is grounded in a competency-based approach, fostering the development of 12 professional competencies, and a compulsory 700 hours of practicum in school class-rooms over a four-year program (Ministère de l'Éducation du Québec, 2001). Competency number five is concerned with the assessment of students: "To evaluate student progress in learning the subject content and mastering the related competencies" (p. 90). To ensure pre-service teachers are developing this competency, every education program offers at least one distinct course, usually 45 hours, on assessment and evaluation of students. This is a common practice to develop the *scholarship of assessment* (DeLuca, 2012) necessary for pre-service teachers.

In a recent study, Béland, Dionne and Loyle (2014) examined the course outlines of 29 assessment and evaluation courses provided by eight universities in Québec and one university in Ontario. Their analysis shows that course outlines have a lot in common, as they all focus on: 1) competencies number 5 (outlined above) and number 12 (To demonstrate ethical and responsible professional behaviour in the performance of his or her duties); 2) content related to planning, data collection and interpretation, and judgement; 3) ministry documents; 4) projects and final exam to assess students; and 5) lectures, workshops and group discussions as a mean of conveying knowledge and skills. The analysis shows sparse notions on measurement and statistics, ethics of assessment and evaluation, historical development of the discipline of assessment and evaluation or the process of differentiation in assessment. Formative assessment, or assessment *for* and *as* learning, is not specifically mentioned in the list of content identified in course outlines. Because all course outlines indicate the use of ministry documents (including policies on assessment and evaluation), it is possible that formative assessment may be addressed during classes. However, this cannot be derived from the information provided within the course outlines alone (Béland et al., 2014). In order to find out if formative assessment and any other ministry specific orientations in regards to the assessment of students are indeed addressed in the teacher education classroom, one would need to interview professors and students or spend time observing during class time.

According to DeLuca (2012), "Preparing teachers for the world of assessment within the current accountability paradigm of education in the United States and Canada should be a fundamental aim of teacher education programs, given the increased reliance on assessment across educational systems" (p. 588). However, numerous studies show that this preparation is not where it should be (DeLuca & Klinger, 2010; Fontaine et al., 2012; Mertler, 2009; Stiggins, 1999; Volante & Fazio, 2007). Furthermore, it seems that the challenges with the assessment of student learning endure beyond the first year of teaching (Fontaine et al., 2012). It is then necessary to explore what is done to develop this competency for beginning teachers.

## Teacher Induction in Québec

Despite numerous research studies indicating the impact of supporting beginning teachers (Conseil supérieur de l'éducation, 2014; Leroux & Mukamurera, 2013; Mukamurera, 2014; Mukamurera & Balleux, 2013; Organisation de Cooperation et de Développement Économiques (OCDE), 2005), in 2016 there are still no official provincial induction programs in Québec. However, induction programs do exist in some school boards or schools. In a recent study, Mukamurera, Martineau, Bouthiette and Ndoreraho (2013) surveyed 69 Quebec school boards to examine the support offered to beginning teachers. Three types of support were identified within the 29 school boards that answered the survey: 1) formal institutional induction programs (73%); 2) informal "household" induction programs (28%) and, 3) informal support (93%). Aspects addressed as part of the induction of the beginning teacher, in order of frequency, were: 1) integration to the school and the school culture; 2) teaching methods, 3) belonging to the profession, 4) pedagogical differentiation, 5) perseverance in the profession, 6) personal development, 7) assessment of student learning, 8) collaboration school-family-community and, 9) teacher performance evaluation. It is interesting to note that five of nine elements are linked with beginning teacher professional identity (1, 3, 5, 6, 9); whereas, the remaining four focus on specific competencies, and assessment of learning is seventh in the list. With regard to modalities, workshops and mentoring are favoured, but official documentation and an identified contact person are also among the four most popular forms of support. The main difficulties identified by respondents include the lack of time and the lack of financial support to implement the support to its full potential (Mukamurera et al., 2013). Although this research shed light on what has been happening within some school boards and schools in Québec, more work needs to be done in order to get a comprehensive picture of the beginning teacher induction situation across the province. Since the Comité d'orientation sur la formation du personnel enseignant (COFPE) has begun the dialogue about teacher induction, a number of local initiatives have been put in place, as reflected in Mukamurera's study. However, now is the time to ensure that all beginning teachers are entering the profession with the support they are entitled to. This calls for an evaluation of the existing programs and a commitment to build on the evaluation's recommendations to improve, formalize, and generalize the programs across the province.

## Teacher Education in Ontario

Faculties of Education across Ontario must meet specific requirements around the inclusion of courses on assessment in order to have their programs accredited by the Ontario College of Teachers (OCT), the governing body of teachers in Ontario. Section 9 Part III - Accreditation of Program of Professional Education, emphasizes the need for curriculum knowledge related to learning assessment and evaluation as well as knowledge of pedagogical and instructional strategies, which includes using assessment to address students' different learning needs, to drive instruction and the effective use of assessment and evaluation of learning in subject specific domains (Ontario *College of Teachers Act, 1996*).

What teacher candidates need to know and understand about their future responsibilities for assessment is detailed in the *Growing Success: Assessment, Evaluation, and Reporting in Ontario Schools* (Ontario Ministry of Education, 2010) document. Typically referred to as *Growing Success*, this document covers relevant information for grades 1-12 with a recent addendum, *Growing Success, The Kindergarten Addendum* (Ontario Ministry of Education, 2016), which addresses the needs of the early childhood sector. The shift in educational assessment and evaluation research and policy towards formative assessment is reflected in the formal discourse on assessment, evaluation, and reporting within these two documents. A guiding principle for this discourse is the assertion that assessment *as* learning fosters the development of students' autonomy, self-regulation, and general learning skills, which, in turn, contribute to improved summative assessment results and the general goal of lifelong learning (Bierenbaum et al., 2015).

The implementation of this framework in day-to-day teacher practice is not without problems or challenges, given the fundamental shift in approaches to instruction and assessment that are required. In fact, *Growing Success* authors acknowledged this challenge and called on teachers to recognize the interdependence of assessment practices, and encouraged them to approach their professional learning goals through an assessment *for* and *as* learning framework. Given the tight linkage between good assessment, instruction, evaluation, and reporting and its reliance on teachers' professional judgment, there is significant pressure on teachers to develop best practices in the area of assessment early on in their career. Yet, as identified earlier in this chapter, assessment of student learning has been identified frequently as a key challenge for teachers, particularly new teachers. Furthermore, there continue to be gaps in assessment education within Ontario faculties of education, which are responsible for helping new teachers develop these skills in preparation programs (DeLuca & Bellara, 2013; DeLuca & Klinger, 2010).

In spite of the requirements for assessment education within teacher preparation programs, within Ontario there is still limited evidence of mandated, formalized assessment education courses present in initial teacher education (DeLuca & Klinger, 2010). Canadian studies (e.g., DeLuca & Klinger, 2010; Volante & Fazio, 2007) have shown that teacher education programs fall short of providing comprehensive programming in assessment for pre-service teachers, resulting in teachers making assessment-related decisions without sufficient knowledge or training in assessment. While it is often assumed that attention to assessment is present throughout curriculum and methods courses in teacher education programs, most faculties approach the incorporation of assessment and evaluation through offering either a focused course/s on assessment and evaluation; partial courses where assessment is one component; an integration of assessment across a number of courses; or a combination of these approaches (Volante & Fazio, 2007).

In Ontario, as a consequence of instructions from the Ontario Ministry of Education in 2013-2014, universities expanded their current eight-month programs to four semesters (two years, or, where study is continuous, 16 months). One might assume that this 'imposed restructuring' would have given Ontario teacher education institutions an opportunity to reconsider the presence of courses related to assessment. A review of Ontario Faculty of Education websites in November 2016, and a comparison to programs available in 2013, showed that the inclusion of courses specifically focused on assessment (as determined from their course titles only) remains ambiguous, despite the addition of an extra two semesters to teacher education programs. This is further complicated where some institutions need to continue to offer active concurrent programs alongside of the new extended consecutive programs, both of which may share courses. Given the lack of preparation in assessment literacy among teacher education graduates, and the critical importance of beginning teachers developing assessment literacy early in their careers, we turn now to examine the potential of induction programs for beginning teachers as one way to mitigate these challenges.

## The Ontario New Teacher Induction Program (NTIP)

In Ontario, the introduction of the New Teacher Induction Program (NTIP) in 2006-2007 is underpinned by the assumption that participation in induction, mentoring and professional learning opportunities will enhance a beginning teacher's development towards his/her full potential, through complementing and supplementing the work of initial teacher education. Thus, there is an implicit understanding that becoming a teacher is an ongoing process of professional learning, of which initial teacher education is but the first step, and that ongoing learning and guidance are essential to ensure and support effective teaching, learning and assessment practices in Ontario's schools.

It is mandatory for school boards to offer the NTIP and for new teachers to participate in the program. The NTIP applies to all teachers certified by the Ontario College of Teachers (including teachers trained out-of-province) who have been hired into permanent positions – fulltime or part-time – by a publicly-funded school board, school authority, or provincial school to begin teaching for the first time in Ontario. A comprehensive longitudinal evaluation of the NTIP by a team of researchers from the University of Ottawa was conducted from 2007 – 2012 with the key focus of examining the experiences and impact of the NTIP with respect to three key participant groups: new teachers; mentor teachers; and principals (Kane, Jones, Rottmann & Pema, 2013). In this chapter, we re-examine the data from this five year evaluation with a particular focus on the impact of the NTIP on beginning teachers' assessment practices.

The evaluation of the NTIP comprised a five-year mixed-methods study which generated data through on-line questionnaires, specifically designed for each group (new teachers, mentor teachers, principals) that were completed in each of the five years, and school-board based case study interviews with new teachers, mentor teachers and principals in years one and two. Across the five years of the NTIP evaluation, approximately 28,500 new teachers were appointed by Ontario school boards. During the five-year study, online questionnaires were completed by more than 7,000 new teachers, 4,516 mentor teachers and 3,029 school principals. During 2007 and 2008, interviews were conducted with 182 new teachers, 139 mentors and 70 principals in English and French language public and Catholic school boards across Ontario. In the following sections, we re-examine the data from this longitudinal, province-wide evaluation of the NTIP and demonstrate the potential of induction programs such as Ontario's NTIP to mitigate beginning teachers' limited assessment literacy.

### Feelings of Lack of Preparation

Beginning teachers' feelings of a lack of preparation are directly associated with novice and beginning teachers' attrition from the teaching profession (Anthony & Kane, 2008; Fontaine et al., 2012; Kutsyuruba, Godden, Covell, Matheson, & Walker, 2016). Results from the NTIP questionnaires across each of the five years showed that new teachers identified student assessment as one of the key areas that they were least prepared for as they began their teaching careers. This lack of preparation was found to be correlated to intentions to leave the profession, suggesting that teachers who were less prepared in student assessment were more likely to leave the teaching profession.

Interviews with new teachers further confirmed the lack of self-efficacy that new teachers felt around assessment, with new teachers' responses echoing the findings of Volante and Fazio's 2007 study.

> Like I really didn't understand how things worked, especially with the school year and significant events like reporting time. You have anecdotal reports, you have the report cards and then the whole process of putting the report cards together and also managing my time as a teacher and making sure things are marked and given back in a timely matter and ready for report card reporting and then even how to do assessments and evaluation, and especially because I'm in the arts it's different; in math, one plus one equals two and because these things are touched on during your Bachelor of Ed. but it's like night and day the experience of real life teaching. (Secondary)

Teachers attributed the lack of preparation they felt to not having enough time on student assessment during initial teacher education and to concerns that the content of the assessment courses during teacher education were not consistent with the school board practices, thus lacking in practical applications. For new teachers who completed their teacher education somewhere other than Ontario, the challenges were confounded by a lack of familiarity with the policy requirements as detailed in the *Growing Success* policy document.

> ... it's at the assessment level, where I was totally lost. Those who were trained in Ontario already had something, a basis, except that our board customizes things a lot, so they too had to have training ... because I was really lost, so that helped me a lot. If I didn't have that, the year would have been very difficult for me. [Translation] (Elementary)

Kutsyuruba (2016) suggested that because teachers' quality and abilities are directly linked to student achievement, there is an onus on schools and school boards to help new teachers effectively transition into their new professions. This is particularly apparent in the case of assessment practices where new teachers, as above, often found themselves required to conduct, record and report assessment in board-specific ways. While beginning teachers in this study initially identify low levels of efficacy with assessment, the impact of the mentoring and professional learning opportunities were demonstrated to mitigate some of these initial challenges.

## Impact of Mentoring

A key element of the NTIP program is that school boards must ensure that each new teacher who participates in the NTIP is matched with a teacher mentor. The implemented program was based on growing evidence that confirmed the benefit of supporting new teachers through an induction process, and that high quality mentoring helped to mitigate some of the challenges new teachers experienced, and reduced rates of attrition (Kutsyuruba et al., 2016). In particular, mentoring is an effective means of supporting the professional learning of new teachers (Marable & Raimondi, 2007) and has been shown to improve retention (Ingersoll & Smith, 2004).

From each year of the new teacher questionnaires, data identified that working with a mentor was positively correlated with the development of student assessment strategies. New teachers who worked with mentors were more likely to use assessment and evaluation strategies that accommodated the needs of all students and were better able to manage classroom time effectively in support of student learning. Interview data from new teachers identified key areas in assessment and evaluation that were supported by the mentoring relationship. These included becoming familiar with school board specific requirements around assessment, evaluation, and reporting.

> In terms of assessment and evaluation I think that's what I needed the most help with because with ESL we didn't really have that the same way the board does or the Ministry, so I've had a lot of help from the curriculum leader and the two other teachers in terms of giving me resources, checking my lesson plans, checking unit plans, looking at how I design units, like universal design and backward design, or however you want to call it. (Secondary)

Being able to discuss assessment challenges with an experienced mentor during the first year teaching helped to mitigate the anxiety around provincial, school, and classroom level reporting requirements that teachers are expected to have mastered the moment they step into the classroom.

### Impact of Professional Learning Sessions

In addition to mentoring, new teachers identified specific targeted professional learning sessions provided by NTIP that were most useful for their practice. Developing assessment strategies was consistently ranked as very useful, as were sessions on the use of assessment and evaluation strategies that accommodate the needs of all students during these professional learning sessions. Professional development that assisted teachers to provide their students with numerous and varied opportunities to demonstrate the full extent of their abilities was also identified by the new teachers as being highly beneficial. These findings suggest that the NTIP program played a critical role in addressing gaps left by the teacher education programs among new teachers with respect to their assessment literacy.

## Discussion and Conclusions

New teachers have responsibility for ensuring that assessment activities foster and support ongoing student learning and that they are required to provide evidence for students, and their parents/ caregivers. In both Quebec and Ontario, there are explicit requirements for teacher education programs to ensure that their graduating teachers have knowledge and experience of the purposes and approaches to assessment *as, for* and *of* student learning. Yet researchers have demonstrated that new teachers graduate from their teacher education programs feeling unprepared to undertake these responsibilities. In addition, it is apparent that pre-service teacher education programs in Ontario and Quebec are inconsistent in their offerings of courses that focus specifically on assessment education, and/or in their commitment to ensuring that assessment literacy is a core element of methods courses across subject areas. In Ontario, the mandatory NTIP has served to mitigate some of the challenges faced by new teachers. These findings have implications for policy makers, initial teacher education, and the systems and school leaders responsible for implementing induction programs within both Ontario and Quebec.

The evidence cited in the earlier sections of this chapter should cause significant concern for policy makers, teacher educators, and those charged with ensuring effective education within public school systems in Ontario and Quebec. There is sustained evidence that beginning teachers feel unprepared to fulfil their responsibilities in the assessment *for, as* and *of* student learning. Further, there is evidence that initial teacher education must step up and own some of the responsibility for this problem. Those responsible for initial teacher education are called upon to ensure that graduating teacher candidates are knowledgeable of the shifting conceptualizations of assessment. Steps also need to be taken to ensure that attention to developing teacher candidates' assessment literacy is at the forefront of both specific courses on assessment and also embedded within curriculum and pedagogy courses such as teaching elementary social studies or teaching senior history. It is not enough to offer solitary courses on assessment; we need to ensure that teacher candidates engage with assessment across all courses.

We acknowledge the evidence that fundamental change in education (and teacher education) can be achieved only slowly - through programs of professional learning that build on existing good practice (Black & William, 1998b). Thus, it is critical – as demonstrated with findings from the evaluation of the Ontario NTIP – that education systems, policy makers and school boards give due attention to the capacity for induction and mentoring programs to address beginning teachers' challenges in embracing their roles in the assessment of students. The opportunities offered to beginning teachers through a well-designed induction program that includes the support of experienced mentors and ongoing professional learning options are essential for maintaining currency of knowledge in the field. Provision of these opportunities and supports for the beginning teachers is surely entailed in the collective responsibilities of teacher educators (within universities or school board administration), as these functions clearly help to ensure improvements in teaching and ultimately enhance the prospects of student learning and achievement.

# References

Allal, L. K., & Mottier Lopez, L. (2007). Régulation des apprentissages: Orientations conceptuelles pour la recherche et la pratique en éducation. Dans L. K. Allal & L. Mottier Lopez (dir.), *Régulation des apprentissages en situation scolaire et en formation* (pp. 7–23). Bruxelles: de Boeck.

Anthony, G. J., & Kane, R.G. (2008). *The role of initial teacher education and beginning teacher induction in the preparation and retention of New Zealand secondary teachers.* Final Report to the New Zealand Council for Educational Research.

Béland, S., Dionne, É., & Loye, N. (2014). *Comparaison du contenu des plans de cours en évaluation des apprentissages/compétences au premier cycle.* Communication présentée au colloque de l'Association francophone pour le savoir (ACFAS). Montreal : Université Concordia.

Birenbaum, M., DeLuca, C., Earl, L., Heritage, M., Klenowski, V., Looney, A., Smith, K. Timperley, H., Volante, L., Wyatt-Smith, C., & Hung, R. (2015). International trends in the implementation of assessment for learning: Implications for policy and practice. *Policy Futures in Education, 13*(1), 117–40.

Black, P. J., & Wiliam, D. (1998a). Inside the black box: Raising standards through classroom assessment. *Phi Delta Kappan, 80*(2), 139–148.

Black, P. J., & Wiliam, D. (1998b). Assessment and classroom learning. *Assessment in Education: Principles, Policy and Practice, 5*(1), 7–74.

Black, P., Harrison, C., Lee, C., Marshall, B., & Wiliam, D. (2004). Working inside the black box: Assessment for learning in the classroom. *Phi Delta Kappan, 86*(1), 8–21.

Bloom, B. S. (1969). Some theoretical issues relating to educational evaluation. In R. W. Tyler (Ed.), *Educational evaluation: new roles, new means: the 63rd yearbook of the National Society for the Study of Education* (part II) (Vol. 69(2), pp. 26–50). Chicago, IL: University of Chicago Press.

Bloom, B., Hastings, J., & Madaus, G. (1971). *Handbook on the formative and summative evaluation of student learning.* New York, NY: McGraw-Hill.

Box, C., Skoog, G., & Dabbs, J. M. (2015). A case study of teacher personal practice assessment theories and complexities of implementing formative assessment. *American Educational Research Journal, 52*(5), 956–983.

Conseil supérieur de l'éducation. (2014). *Le développement profession-nel, un enrichissement pour toute la profession enseignante.* Québec: Gouvernement du Québec.

Crooks, T. (1988). The impact of classroom evaluation on students. *Review of Educational Research, 58*(4), 438–481.

DeLuca, C. (2012). Preparing teachers for the age of accountability: Toward a framework for assessment education. *Action in Teacher Education, 34*(5-6), 576–591. DOI:10.1080/01626620.2012.730347

DeLuca, C., & Bellara, A. (2013). The current state of assessment education: Aligning policy, standards, and teacher education curriculum. *Journal of Teacher Education, 64*(4), 356–372.

DeLuca, C., & Klinger, D. A. (2010). Assessment literacy development: Identifying gaps in teacher candidates' learning. *Assessment in Education: Principles, Policy & Practice, 17*(4), 419–438.

Earl, L. (2003). *Assessment as learning: Using classroom assessment to maximize student learning.* Thousand Oaks, CA: Corwin Press.

Fontaine, S., Kane, R., Duquette, O., & Savoie-Zajc, L. (2011). New teachers' career intentions: Factors influencing new teachers' decisions to stay or to leave the profession. *Alberta Journal of Educational Research, 57*(4), 379–408.

Greenberg, J., & Walsh, K. (2012). *What teacher preparation programs teach about K-12 assessment: A review.* Washington, DC: National Council on Teacher Quality.

Hadji, C. (2012). *Faut-il avoir peur de l'évaluation ?* Bruxelles: de Boeck.

Ingersoll, R. M., & Smith, T. M. (2004). Do teacher induction and mentoring matter?. *National Association of Secondary School Principals Bulletin, 88*(638), 28–40.

Kane, R. G., Jones, A., Rottmann, J., & Pema, E. (2013). *Evaluation of the new teacher induction program – In practice, phase one, two and three* (Final Report to the Policy Branch). Toronto, ON: Ontario Ministry of Education.

Kutsyuruba, B. (2016). *The role of school administrator in effective teacher induction and mentoring programs* (Report to the New Teacher Centre). Kingston, ON: Queen's University. Available from: https://earlycareer-teachersdotcom.files.wordpress.com/2014/10/ntc-report-july-2016-final-draft.pdf

Kutsyuruba, B., Godden, L., Covell, L., Matheson, I., & Walker, K. (2016). *Understanding the contextual factors within teacher induction and mentoring programs: A international systematic review of research.* Kingston, ON: Queen's University. Available from: http://educ.queensu.ca/sites/web-publish.queensu.ca.educwww/files/files/People/Faculty/Systematic%20Review%20Teacher%20Induction%20and%20Mentoring.pdf

Laurier, M. (2014). La politique québécoise d'évaluation des apprentissages et les pratiques évaluatives. *Éducation et Francophonie, 42*(3), 31–49.

Laveault, D. (2014). Les politiques d'évaluation en éducation. Et après? *Éducation et Francophonie, 42*(3), 1–14.

Leroux, M., & Mukamurera, J. (2013). Bénéfices et conditions d'efficacité des programmes d'insertion professionnelle en enseignement: état des connaissances sur le sujet. *Formation et Profession, 21*(1), 13–27. DOI:10.18162/fp.2013.32

Marable, M., & Raimondi, S. (2007). Teachers' perceptions of what was most (and least) supportive during their first year of teaching. *Mentoring and Tutoring: Partnership in Learning*, 15(1), 25–37.

Mertler, C. A. (2009). Teachers' assessment knowledge and their perceptions of the impact of classroom assessment professional development. *Improving Schools*, *12*(2), 101–113. DOI: 10.1177/1365480209105575

Ministère de l'Éducation du Québec (MEQ) (2003). *Politique d'évaluation des apprentissages.* Québec: Gouvernement du Québec.

Ministère de l'Éducation du Québec (2001). *La formation à l'enseignement. Les orientations et les compétences professionnelles.* Québec: Gouvernement du Québec.

Morrissette, J. (2009). Une resocialisation de l'évaluation des apprentissages. *Revue Canadienne des Jeunes Chercheur(e)s en Éducation*, *1*(2), 1–8.

Mukamurera, J. (2014). Le développement professionnel et la persévérance en enseignement: Éclairage théorique et état des lieux. Dans L. Portelance, S. Martineau et J. Mukamurera (Dir.), *Le développement et persévérance professionnels en enseignement. Oui, mais comment?* (pp. 9–33). Québec: Presses de l'Université du Québec.

Mukamurera, J., & Balleux, A. (2013). Malaise dans la profession enseignante et identité professionnelle en mutation: le cas du Québec. *Recherche et Formation, 74*, 87–100.

Mukamurera, J., Martineau, S., Bouthiette, M., & Ndoreraho, J.-P. (2013). Les programmes d'insertion professionnelle des enseignants dans les commissions scolaires du Québec : Portrait et appréciation des acteurs. *Éducation et formation*, e-299, 13–35.

Ogan-Bekiroglu, F., & Suzuk, E. (2014). Pre-service teachers' assessment literacy and its implementation into practice. *Curriculum Journal*, *25*(3), 344–371. DOI:10.1080/09585176.2014.899916

Ontario College of Teachers Act (1996). Ontario Regulation 347/02 – Accreditation of Teacher Education Programs.

Ontario Ministry of Education (2010). *Growing success: Assessment, evaluation, and reporting in Ontario schools.* Ontario: Queen's Printer for Ontario..

Ontario Ministry of Education (2016). *Growing success: The kindergarten addendum.* Ontario: Queen's Printer for Ontario.

Organisation de coopération et de développement économiques – OCDE (2005). *Le rôle crucial des enseignants. Attirer, former et retenir des enseignants de qualité.* Paris: OCDE.

Popham, W. J. (2009). Assessment literacy for teachers: Faddish or fundamental? *Theory Into Practice*, *48*(1), 4–11.

Popham, W. J. (2011). Assessment literacy overlooked: A teacher educator's confession. *The Teacher Educator, 46*(4), 265–273.

Rey, O., & Feyfant, A. (2014). Évaluer pour (mieux) faire apprendre. *Dossier de veille de l'IFÉ, 94*, 1–44.

Ruiz-Primo, M.A., & Furtak, E.M. (2007). Exploring teachers' informal formative assessment practices and students' understanding in the context of scientific inquiry. *Journal of Research in Science Teaching, 44*(1), 57–84. DOI:10.1002/tea.20163

Scallon, G. (2000). L'évaluation formative. Québec: Éditions du renouveau pédagogique.

Scallon, G. (2004). *L'évaluation des apprentissages dans une approche par compétences.* Saint-Laurent, Québec : Éditions du renouveau pédagogique.

Scallon, G. (2008). Evaluation formative et psychologie cognitive : Mouvances et tendances. Dans J. Grégoire (Dir.), Évaluer les apprentissages : Les apports de la *psychologie cognitive* (pp. 159-173). Bruxelles: de Boeck.

Scriven, M. (1967). The methodology of evaluation. Dans R. W. Tyler, R. M. Gagné et M. Scriven (dir.), *Perspectives of Curriculum Evaluation* (vol. 1, pp. 39–83). Chicago, IL: Rand McNally.

Stiggins, R. J. (1999). Evaluating classroom assessment training in teacher education programs. *Educational Measurement: Issues and Practice, 18*(1), 23–27.

Stiggins, R. (2007). Assessment through the student's eyes. *Educational Leadership, 64*(8), 22–26.

Volante, L., & Fazio, X. (2007). Exploring teacher candidates' assessment literacy: Implications for teacher education reform and professional development. *Canadian Journal of Education, 30*(3), 749–770.

Wiliam, D. (2011). What is assessment for learning? *Studies in Educational Evaluation, 37*(1), 3–14. DOI:10.1016/j.stueduc.2011.03.001

Xu, Y., & Brown, G. (2016). Teacher assessment literacy in practice: A reconceptualization. *Teaching and Teacher Education, 58*, 149–162.

## Chapter 14

# Ontario's New Teacher Induction Program: Our Continuing Learning Journey

*Jim Strachan, Kate Creery, Aggie Nemes*

## Introduction

Established in 2006, Ontario's New Teacher Induction Program (NTIP) supports the growth and professional learning of new teachers. It is the second job-embedded step along a continuum of learning and growth for new teachers, building upon the first step of initial teacher education. In this chapter we will share our findings about the key factors that contribute to the growth of new teachers, along with our emerging understandings of the power of building what we term a "mentoring web", not just for new teachers but for all educators.

## Context: What is the New Teacher Induction Program?

The concept of the NTIP was recommended in 2005 to the Minister's Education Partnership Table by the Working Table on Teacher Development. The Working Table was comprised of key education partners, including faculty of education candidates, new teachers, parent organizations, teacher federations and trustee representatives.

The NTIP consists of the following induction elements:

- Orientation for all new teachers to the school and school board;
- Professional development appropriate to the individual needs of new teachers;
- Mentoring for new teachers by experienced teachers.

As indicated below (see Figure 1), there are the four goals of NTIP explained from the perspective of a new teacher:

- **Confidence:** "I can do it...I have the supports to be a successful teacher."
- **Efficacy:** "My teaching makes a difference in the lives and learning of every single student."
- **Instructional Practice:** "By using evidence based instructional strategies I am able to respond to the diverse learning needs of my students and ensure student success."
- **Commitment to Continuous Learning:** "I want to keep learning and growing as a professional in collaboration with my students, colleagues, administration, parents/guardians, and school community."

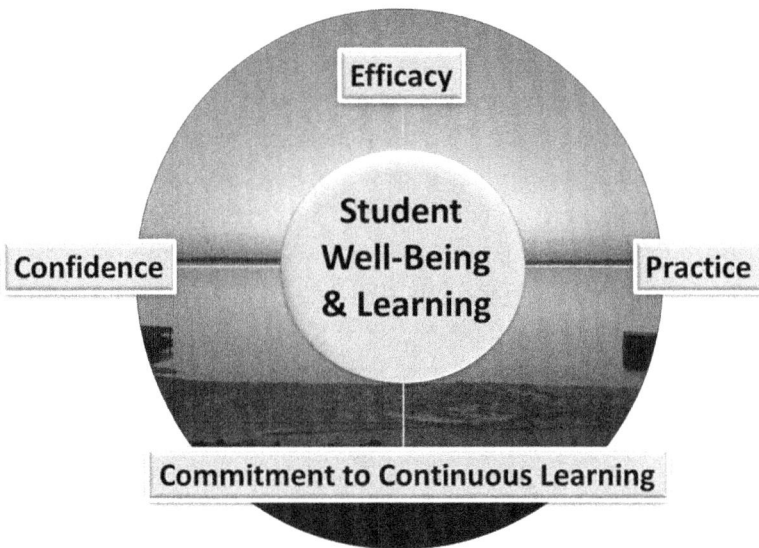

*Figure 1.* New Teacher Induction Program Goals

Improving student well-being and learning is the ultimate outcome of the New Teacher Induction Program. While the NTIP induction elements outline the "what" of the program, the "how" of implementation is determined by each school district, as they best understand the unique learning needs of new teachers in their Board.

## Program Scope

In Ontario, newly hired permanent teachers and new Long Term Occasional (LTO) teachers with assignments of 97 days or longer must be supported in their first year under NTIP. Additionally, boards may extend NTIP supports to teachers in their second year in either category. Each year in Ontario approximately 8,000 new hires access NTIP supports (Table 1). Including 2nd Year teachers and mentors, the total number of teachers participating in NTIP exceeds 18,000 annually.

**Table 1**
*NTIP Hiring by Year*

|  | 2009 / 2010 | 2010 / 2011 | 2011 / 2012 | 2012 / 2013 | 2013 / 2014 | 2014 / 2015 |
|---|---|---|---|---|---|---|
| *1st Year Permanent Hires* | 4600 | 4788 | 4269 | 4836 | 4259 | 4067 |
| *1st Year Long Term Occasional Teachers* | 3306 | 3950 | 3895 | 3487 | 3686 | 3946 |
| *Total New Hires* | 7906 | 8738 | 8164 | 8323 | 7945 | 8013 |

In addition to the NTIP induction elements, new permanent teacher hires are evaluated twice within their first 12 months of employment, through the Teacher Performance Appraisal process. Upon completion of two satisfactory evaluations, a notation reflecting completion of NTIP is placed on the teacher's certificate of qualification and registration that appears on the Ontario College of Teachers public register (Ontario Ministry of Education, 2010, p. 5).

## Funding for NTIP

Annually in Ontario, 13.7 million is allocated to support the NTIP. Each of Ontario's 72 school boards board receives a $50,000 base amount, plus a "per new teacher" amount determined by the number of teachers hired for NTIP implementation. This per teacher amount fluctuates annually based on hiring, but on average the amount provided is approximately $1,200 - $1,500 per new teacher hire. Ontario's school authorities, which are geographically isolated or hospital schools, also receive this "per new teacher" NTIP funding.

### The Role of the Ministry of Education

In addition to funding NTIP, the role at the Ministry of Education is to foster capacity building for mentorship and educator development within school boards via a menu of supports:

- Facilitating professional learning for Mentors and Board Teams;
- Creating and disseminating resources for boards to adopt and adapt in their support of mentorship (e.g., Mentoring for All eBook, Online Mentoring Modules in Adobe Spark, Adobe Connect Learning sessions); and
- Developing tools to monitor implementation of NTIP via triangulation of data, in order to measure impact and inform evolution of the program at both a provincial and district level (e.g., NTIP Longitudinal Research, Board Visits, Board Survey Tool, NTIP Plans/Final Reports).

## Factors that Influence the Growth of NTIP Teachers

At the Ministry of Education level in Ontario, we are learning that NTIP works. Through longitudinal research from 2012- 2015, Christine Frank & Associates (CFA) (2015) found that new teachers had made meaningful and sustained improvements in all four of the core goal areas of NTIP.

The diagram below is a visual summary of the emerging learning from the longitudinal research about the key factors that make a difference in the growth of new teachers.

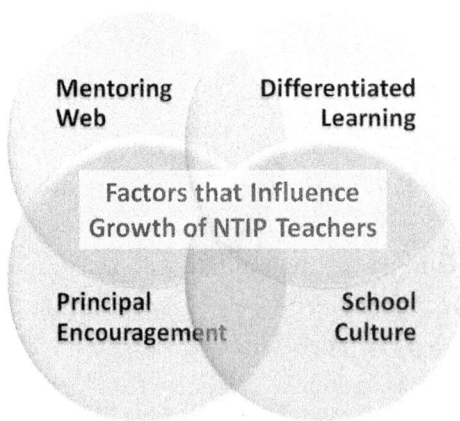

*Figure 2.* Key Factors That Make a Difference in the Growth of New Teachers

The "Venness" of this figure is important because it illustrates the inter-connectedness of these four areas. We know that learning is messy, recursive and iterative. There is no one right way, but these four factors working together can make a solid contribution to the success of our new teachers and ultimately their students.

## Our Learning at a Glance

**Mentoring web.** Having a formally assigned mentor is not linked to growth – being mentored is. High growth new teachers accessed 5 to 7 different mentorship supports (i.e., built a mentoring web; see Figure 3 below).

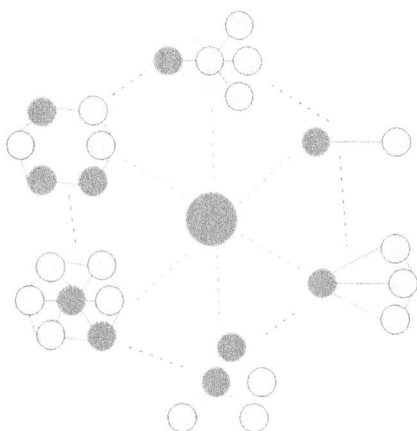

*Figure 3.* Illustrative Example of a Mentoring Web

**Differentiated learning.** High growth new teachers constructed their NTIP via a menu of authentic learning opportunities using joint release days with multiple mentors. Classroom observation and debriefing was the learning design with the strongest correlation to growth in instructional practice.

**Principal encouragement.** Ongoing feedback and encouragement from the Principal was the strongest predictor of growth in NTIP. This speaks to the power of listening, the power of encouragement, and the ability of the principal to provide a meaningful piece of a mentoring web for a new teacher.

**School culture.** A collaborative school culture was an important factor in building a sense of confidence and efficacy for new teachers. When you're new you tend to adapt or adopt the culture you find yourself in ... so again one observes the importance of all mentors, colleagues and supports for all learners in the school.

## The Importance of Mentorship

Mentorship is truly the heart of the NTIP. Multiple models of mentorship provide a "web" of personalized support for beginning teachers and directly align with the key goals of the New Teacher Induction Program. The acrostic below represents our thinking about the fundamental aspects essential to any mentoring relationship.

**Table 2**
*Mentoring Is...*

| | |
|---|---|
| **Mutual** | Mentoring relationships that flourish are reciprocal – all parties learn and grow |
| **Evolving** | Mentors exhibit flexibility of stance and role based on the needs of the person they are supporting |
| **Non-evaluative** | Mentoring supports are not connected to evaluation or judgement of a colleague's performance |
| **Trusting** | Relational trust is built through effective listening and fostered in an environment characterized by emotional safety and mutual respect |
| **Open** | Through powerful learning designs (e.g., observation and debriefing) practice is deprivatized and the intentional sharing of knowledge and practice occurs |
| **Real** | Mentoring activities are personalized, based on each person's authentic learning goals and connected to their "real world" |
| **Supported** | Conditions to foster effective mentoring relationships are supported at both the school and board level (e.g., joint release days, foundational learning for mentors) |
| **Honours strengths** | A deliberate seeking out of the strengths and attributes that each person brings to the mentoring relationship sets the context for meaningful sharing to occur |
| **Invitational** | All parties have voluntarily chosen to engage in mentorship |
| **Personalized** | Each person may choose to engage in multiple models of mentorship as they build a web of mentoring supports |

## Building Mentoring Webs

Often when we adpat or adopt an initiative or program we try to replicate a structure without attending fully to the complexities of relationships which enable the structure to actually be effective. Thinking about our approach to mentorship illumintaes this distinction:

- *Do you have a mentor?* (structure – a one to one match)
- *Are you being mentored?* (relationships – a mentoring web of multiple mentors existing within an environment of relational trust)

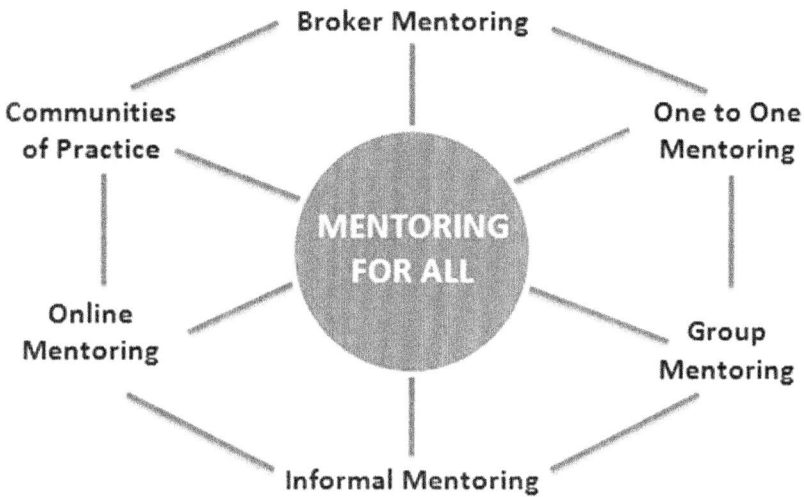

*Figure 4.* A Web of Multiple Models of Mentorship

As depicted in Figure 4 above, mentoring webs are constructed by the learner. Each web is unique, based on authentic learning needs. When we think about building a mentoring web, the idea is that the more strands that are found in the web, the stronger and more resilient the web of relationships will be.

Table 3 reflects a variety of mentoring approaches, which may be incorporated into the web of supports for any new teacher. Regardless of the mentoring model, one of the most powerful things a mentor can do is help their colleague hold up a mirror to their practice, and in this mirror, see all their strengths and attributes, not just the flaws and challenges of what isn't working. Through this de-privatization of practice, the quiet victories and moments of beauty that teaching provides can be surfaced, elevated and celebrated. This is authentic "inside out", learner driven collaborative professionalism.

**Table 3**
*Building a Mentoring Web via Multiple Models of Mentorship*

**Broker Mentoring**

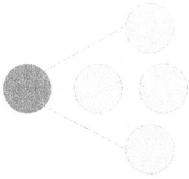

ROLES
- Mentor provides orientation to school or work site logistics and culture
- Mentor brokers involvement of colleagues as needs arise

CONSIDERATIONS
- Consultant type relationship, fewer opportunities for collaboration and coaching
- May be initial support until other mentoring relationships are established or ongoing throughout the year

**One to One Mentor Matching**

ROLES
- Mentor is site-based and is matched on an individual basis to a new colleague
- Mentor adopts consultant, collaboration and coaching stances based on the needs of the person they are working with

CONSIDERATIONS
- Mentoring relationships that flourish are reciprocal – both parties learn and grow
- Greater "ownership" occurs when the mentor has volunteered and the person being mentored has been involved in the choice of mentor

## Group Mentoring

ROLES
- Mentor works with two or more individuals or one individual may have two or more mentors
- Model provide opportunities for collaboration between both new and experienced colleagues

CONSIDERATIONS
- This model provides flexibility if school or work site has large number of new staff (or mentors)
- This model is often embedded in a school or site wide "mentoring culture" where all staff are engaged in ongoing collaboration

## Informal Mentoring

ROLES
- Individuals connect with a variety of colleagues as needs arise
- Mentor/mentee roles are fluid – often referred to as Peer Mentoring as in many cases the informal mentors are relatively new themselves

CONSIDERATIONS
- Spontaneous, informal nature of relationship lends itself to collaboration
- Relying on "accident, geography and friendship" may not work for all, as new staff could feel isolated if not part of any mentoring relationships

## Online Mentoring

ROLES
- Using online conferencing new staff can participate in discussion and sharing with both experienced and other beginning colleagues (e.g., teachontario.ca)

CONSIDERATIONS
- Enables access to a variety of resources and perspectives outside the school or work site
- Not everyone may feel comfortable sharing issues and concerns in a "public" online forum

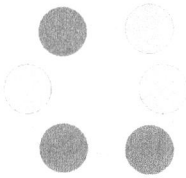

ROLES
- Educators with similar teaching assignments and/or professional interests form learning networks across a region or district
- These networks may meet face to face and/or online

CONSIDERATIONS
- Extends the mentoring web beyond school or work site
- While board level support of these learning networks can be very helpful, it is important that the learning agenda is not externally mandated

Brendan Hyatt, from the Northwest Catholic District School Board, provides this relection on the value of "joint release days" as a tool for new teachers to construct their NTIP with a variety of mentors.

Our NTIP teachers were given a minimum of five days release to support their completion of the NTIP strategy form and address their personal learning needs. They indicated to us that this time had been critical.

In addition to school-based collaboration, new teachers utilized release days to work with other staff members in our system who have different skill-sets and knowledge from their mentors. We encouraged classroom observation and debriefing and reminded principals that being approachable and open to communication was vital for their new teachers.

If we want the students' learning to be authentic then we need to ensure that our new teachers have opportunities to explore, ask questions and reflect on their role. Student success is vital and support for our new teachers is crucial in the development of excellent practitioners in our system.

## Mentoring as Learning

One of the most powerful potential outcomes from this "intentional sharing of knowledge and practice" has been the learning of mentors themselves. Here is a summary of learning themes that NTIP Mentors have expressed as a result of their learning from and with beginning teachers, with some illustrative quotations.

1. *Increases Reflection on Current Practice:*
   Mentoring has opened me up to the possibility of growth and to the potential new ideas.... this has helped me become more reflective about my own practice.
2. *Fosters Inspirational Connections with Colleagues:*
   Mentoring has improved my relationships with other teachers (not just new teachers). I've become more aware of the value of colleagues, and more encouraged to share.
3. *Impacts Teaching Practice and Learning of Students:*
   Learning about the importance of listening and coaching didn't just help me support beginning teachers, it helped me become a better mentor for my students!

## Mentoring for All

As we seek to broaden and deepen our work with mentorship across the province of Ontario, we are increasingly engaged with school boards providing a continuum of mentorship based on the authentic learning needs of the mentors they support.

Figure 5 illustrates this move away from an "initiative driven" and/or "role specific" approach to supporting mentors to what we characterize as mentoring for all. (Ontario Ministry of Education, 2016, p. 4).

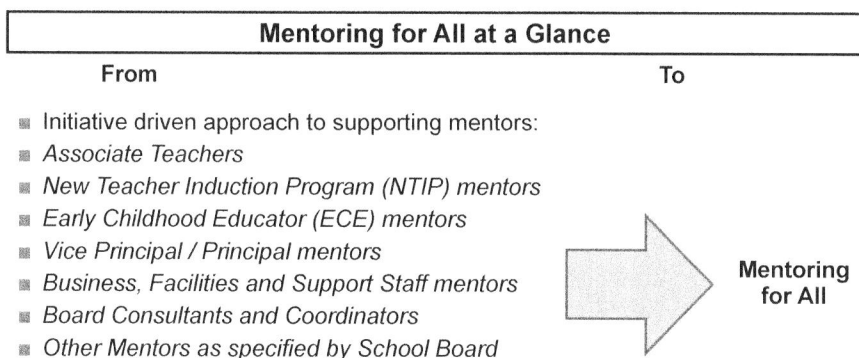

| Mentoring for All at a Glance | |
| --- | --- |
| **From** | **To** |
| ▪ Initiative driven approach to supporting mentors: | |
| ▪ *Associate Teachers* | |
| ▪ *New Teacher Induction Program (NTIP) mentors* | |
| ▪ *Early Childhood Educator (ECE) mentors* | **Mentoring for All** |
| ▪ *Vice Principal / Principal mentors* | |
| ▪ *Business, Facilities and Support Staff mentors* | |
| ▪ *Board Consultants and Coordinators* | |
| ▪ *Other Mentors as specified by School Board* | |

*Figure 5.* Mentoring for All

We have found that effective mentorship skills are highly transferable and include:

- Creating a Mentoring Web
- Building Relational Trust
- Facilitating Learning Focused Conversations
- Providing Meaningful and Growth Oriented Feedback
- Utilizing Powerful Mentoring Designs

Reciprocal learning is a foundational component of all mentoring relationships. One of the most powerful outcomes of mentorship is that it serves as a means for job embedded de-privatization of practice and fosters reflection, learning and growth of the mentorsthemselves. In summary, mentorship is an act of learning.

Many boards are developing a vision wherein every employee has access to a skilled web of mentors who are able to support them in their roles. NTIP sits within this context of mentorship, as described by Kate Creery of the Upper Grand District School Board, who sees the efficacy of building a culture of learning through mentorship.

## Culture of Learning through Mentorship

Building on the informative supports offered by mentoring webs for new and experienced classroom teachers and principals, Mentor training, release time, and opportunities for focused learning conversations have been enthusiastically welcomed by Early Childhood Educators, Finance, Human Resource and Operations professionals, as well as Program Leaders, Superintendents, and Principals.

The quote from an Early Childhood Educator (ECE) illustrates how a true culture of learning with and from each other, regardless of role, has been tangible at each of our Mentoring for All sessions, regardless of professional role.

"We are all focused on what is ... best for children. It was powerful to share with a colleague who had a totally different perspective! Our board will only get better with this Mentoring for All over time." (ECE participant, April 2016).

Our conversations, large and small, continue and as a Board, we are committed to deepening and extending our exploration of models of mentoring in the coming years. We are ensuring that all new and experienced employees have opportunities to build the relational trust and develop "real world," job embedded networks for professional learning conversations.

## Building Mentoring Webs through Faculty / Field Partnerships

In addition to the Mentoring for All work supported by the Ontario Ministry of Education, we have been building Mentoring Webs through Faculty and Field partnerships. We have such partnerships with Laurier University's Faculty of Education's four local partner Boards, : Waterloo DSB, Waterloo Catholic DSB, Wellington Catholic DSB, and the Upper Grand DSB. This group of boards and faculty have joined together to offer an Additional Qualification course to experienced educators.

This course, approved and recognized by the Ontario College of teachers and leading to designation on the Ontario Teachers' Record Card, allows participants to explore models of mentoring and their own mentoring practice intentionally and deeply.

Focused in-class learning, augmented by "in-the-field" mentoring, allows for exploration of learning focused conversations, deep listening, culturally responsive mentoring, as well as personally relevant "Mentoring Inquiry" projects, and leads to a truly meaningful 125 hours of learning and dialogue about the power of mentoring to our shared professional journeys.

Participants report that the mentoring course was one of the most meaningful educational experiences ever attended. While the course continues into a second year, across our four DSB's, we are building an extended "Mentoring Web" of passionate and deeply committed mentors!

## Mentoring as an Authentic Learning Design

Mentorship enables all learners to build a strong web of support that is personal to their unique learning needs and goals. Opportunities for professional learning and growth are collaboratively constructed and reflect the 4R's of authentic learning summarized below.

1. *Relational*

   Relational trust creates an inclusive learning space with all partners in the learning process listening to each other (students, educators, parents and school community). All learners collaboratively construct communities of practice that build upon their strengths, attributes and experiences.

2. *Responsive*

   Learners are listened to, and their individual and collective voices directly inform learning designs. The "how" and "what" of the learning designs employed are based on authentic learning goals identified by the participants. Learning "makes sense" to the learners and involves authentic collaboration, choice and voice and agency.

3. *Recursive*

   Rich learning tasks reflect embedded beliefs that learning itself is a messy, iterative, recursive process. Protocols for application of learning, follow-up, and evaluation of impact are embedded into the learning process.

4. *Real World*

   Learners construct learning together that is relevant and has authentic real-world connections and applications. Learning designs that leverage peer-to-peer networks for deep learning and foster the intentional sharing of knowledge and practice are utilized. A direct connection to student learning and well-being is clearly evident (i.e. students are at the centre of the learning).

Creating a menu of authentic learning opportunities that feature both voice and choice for new teachers begins with knowing our learners. Aggie Nemes, from the Toronto Catholic District School Board, reflects on the challenges of differentiation and the impact that sustained learning has had over time on new teachers.

## Knowing our Learners

While the definition of new teachers may, at first glance, be a simple one (i.e., first LTO assignment longer than 97 days or new permanent hires), in the reality for the individual teacher this is a much more complex issue. Due to increased competition for jobs and Ontario Regulation 274, many "new" teachers have been in a variety of assignments prior to their involvement in the NTIP. Flexibility, timing, choice and differentiation are key factors to consider when constructing a menu of professional learning opportunities. Authentically listening to teacher voice (through surveys and feedback forms) is perhaps the most important consideration in responding to varied needs of new teachers.

When a teacher has an opportunity to participate in a learning community (multiple sessions, trying out new ideas in their classrooms, analyzing successes and challenges), the learning is authentic, rich and long-lasting.

At the Toronto Catholic District School Board (TCDSB), a variety of challenges, in terms of professional development, exist: high numbers of eligible teachers (300 - 1200 in any given year); wide range of assignments (including Music, French Immersion, Construction Technology and Chemistry); and students from diverse backgrounds (both economically and culturally).

In order to meet these varied professional learning needs, the decision was made to offer Kindergarten to Grade 12 sessions focusing on the "who" of teaching, understanding the learner.

## Providing Sustained and Recursive Learning Opportunities for New LTO Teachers

Teachers in their first LTO assignment are invited to participate in a professional learning series (PLS) which focuses on building equitable and safe classrooms. Through collaboration with the Board's Community Relations and Safe Schools departments, the first day is structured to highlight equity strategies (e.g., reflecting the learner in the classroom) as well as mindsets for effective educators (e.g., Ross Greene's Collaborative & Proactive Solutions (CPS), sunshine calls, 13 second retreat). All of this serves to provide sustained and recursive learning opportunities for new LTO Teachers. Subsequent sessions investigate provincial Safe School policies, community partnerships as well as delving deeper into factors ensuring equitable and welcoming classrooms. Guest speakers from organizations such as The Harmony Movement are invited to add to the equity conversation. One teacher who completed the series commented: "Although equity and inclusion seems daunting, it can start to be achieved by simply listening and learning. Simple words can change a child's life forever."

## Deepening Learning for New Permanent Hires

New permanent hires participate in a PLS dedicated to supporting at risk students. The TCDSB's Mental Health Lead facilitates the first session in unpacking the provincial Supporting Minds document (which highlights class-based approaches to support students experiencing anxiety, depression or self harm behaviours). First-hand accounts of survivors are also shared to further raise the awareness of new teachers of how to reach struggling students. This is the first session aimed at deepening the learning for new permanent teacher hires.

The second session takes a look at the academic, social, emotional and physical impact of poverty on students and learning about strategies to support them with an asset-based mindset. Practical ideas about how to start a breakfast program, help students get glasses or subsidies for trips are also shared. In subsequent sessions, guest speakers with real-life connections to at-risk students have included Tim Huff, author of Bent Hope, who works with homeless youth in Toronto. Father Greg Boyle, a Los Angeles-based priest and author of Tattoos on the Heart, is also a guest speaker. He created Homeboy Industries to offer opportunities to gang members wanting to start a new life.

New teachers are encouraged to recognize that, despite the challenges, their students have unlimited potential. As one teacher reflected: "My students have assets that I need to use as leverage."

An additional PLS (facilitated by Kathy Gould Lundy, author of Teaching Fairly in an Unfair World) is offered to second year teachers to investigate the role of drama and literature in building caring classrooms.

Through these professional learning opportunities, new teachers are encouraged to learn the stories and realities of all their students and to create learning environments which meet their needs. In the words of one new teacher: "The most important job we have as teachers is to teach the whole child, spiritually, physically and intellectually. They could be dealing with so many other external factors that we do not know about!"

## What are the "Stones in Our Shoe?"

Learning is complex, messy and iterative; and as we seek to meet the diverse needs of new teachers across the province, NTIP will need to continue to be responsive to our changing educational landscape. Since NTIP began in 2006, there have been many changes in the sector, including blended entry to the profession, Ontario Regulation 274/12, and enhancements to Initial Teacher Education (ITE).

The path to permanent teaching has become longer. Five years of daily and long term occasional teaching is currently the norm in the province of Ontario before a beginning teacher is able to obtain a permanent position. Additionally, school and board teacher surplus procedures may result in multiple assignment changes for many beginning teachers in their first five years.

Ontario Regulation 274/12 has formalized this blended entry process, as it requires a successful interview in order to be hired to a board's Occasional Teacher (OT) Roster, which is ranked by seniority. After 10 months with a minimum of 20 days of occasional teaching, the new teacher would next need to complete a successful interview process in order to access the board Long Term Occasional Teacher (LTO) List. Once hired to an LTO position of four months or longer, the new teacher requires a satisfactory OT evaluation in order to be eligible to apply for a permanent position.

The enhanced Initial Teacher Education program began in September 2015. It has doubled the length of the program to four semesters and has doubled the practicum requirement to a minimum of 80 days. Additionally, the core content of the ITE program has been updated to reflect current areas of knowledge and skills essential for teachers beginning their careers, with recognition that learning in these areas will continue to deepen and grow throughout a teacher's career.

One could view these changes as challenges. but we prefer to think of them as opportunities to continue to grow and evolve the New Teacher Induction Program in partnership with school boards, teacher federations and faculties of education. In that vein, Ontario is about to embark on a new five year longitudinal study where we will be learning from beginning teachers who may not be currently supported by NTIP, or who are experiencing "gaps" in support as they enter the profession.

Study participants will include newly hired LTO and permanent contract teachers currently participating in NTIP, along with new Occasional Teachers hired within the past 5 years and not currently eligible for NTIP supports. This "non NTIP" group will be comprised of Daily and Short Term Occasional Teachers (less than 97 day assignments) as well as Long Term Occasional Teachers no longer eligible for NTIP. Our learning from this work will inform future policy and program directions as we strive to support all new educators on their learning journey.

## What are Our Next Steps? (So What / Now What)

As we think about how NTIP needs to evolve, it is deeply important to listen to the voices of the new teachers, mentors and principals whose work and collaboration is at the heart of the program.

We have been privileged to conduct 60 NTIP Board visits over the past four years. At each visit focus groups of new teacher and mentor participants were asked what aspects of NTIP were most meaningful to their professional growth and how NTIP could be even more effectively implemented. Using "dotmocracy", participants identified the ideas that they felt had the greatest resonance with their lived experiences.

In a sense the dotmocracy recommendations summarized below are like a mirror held up to each school board but also to the Ministry of Education. This mirror reflects both the strengths of the current program and the voices of new and experienced educators as they seek to personalize and construct an authentic and meaningful NTIP that enhances the learning and growth of all.

## Build a Mentoring Web for Every New Teacher

At almost every board visit we heard the idea of building a mentoring web. The core of this idea being that beginning teachers could access multiple models of mentorship both within and beyond their school. The more strands found in the mentoring web, the stronger and more resilient the web is and the more learning there is for the beginning teacher.

## Mentor our Mentors

We know that mentorship is critical to the success of the New Teacher Induction Program. So the question becomes: Who mentors our mentors? During our board visits, mentors expressed a desire to continue to learn, and to refine their craft in order to become even more effective in the support they provide beginning teachers. And of course what we have also heard is how reciprocal the mentoring relationship is and that mentoring itself is an act of learning.

## More Joint Release Days to Support Collaboration

In some form, every board offers joint release days to support collaboration. These days are highly valued, and our beginning teachers and mentors are simply saying "more please." Additionally, beginning teachers would like the flexibility to use these days with multiple mentors.

## Provide Choice from an Authentic Learning Menu

Providing choice from an authentic learning menu acknowledges the vast array of prior experiences many NTIP teachers bring and also allows for differentiation of support based on authentic learning needs.

## The Importance of Relational Trust

We have learned and been reminded that relationships are complex and need continued care. All our relationships (as a Ministry with boards, faculties, and federation partners) require relational trust built through listening with uncertainty and understanding the complexity and messiness of learning. As we continue to learn with and from each other, unique and authentic mentoring webs, constructed by each learner, have tremendous potential to support collaborative professionalism, de-privatization of practice, knowledge construction and ongoing growth for all learners[3].

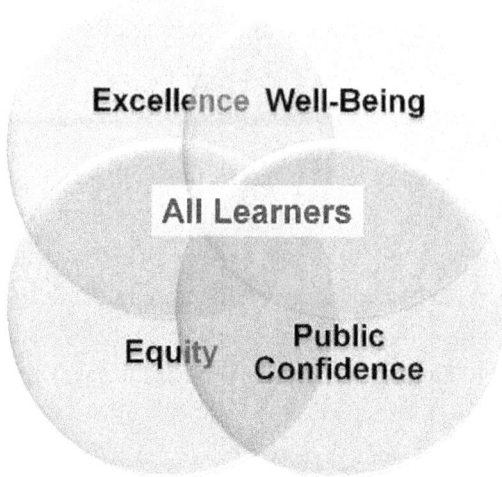

*Figure 6.* Achieving Excellence: A Renewed Vision for Education in Ontario

In conclusion, we look forward to continuing our learning journey in Ontario, as depicted through the purposes of education (Figure 6) that ultimately seek to achieve excellence for all learners.

## References

Frank, C., & Associates (2015). *Longitudinal evaluation of Ontario's New Teacher Induction Program (NTIP): NTIP reflections Year 3 Final Report.* Barrie, ON: CFA.

Ontario Ministry of Education. (2016). *Mentoring for all eBook v2.* Retrieved from: https://www.teachontario.ca/community/explore/mentoring-for-all

Ontario Ministry of Education. (2010). *The New Teacher Induction Program: Induction elements manual.* Toronto, ON: Queen's Printer for Ontario.

---

3   For more information about the program, please see the additional NTIP Information and Mentoring Resources:
 • New Teacher Induction Program Overview: http://www.edu.gov.on.ca/eng/teacher/induction.html
 • Professional Learning Resources for Board NTIP Teams: http://mentoringmoments.ning.com/group/mentoring-mentors/page/ntip
 • Mentoring for All Online Learning: https://www.teachontario.ca/community/explore/mentoring-for-all

# Developing Experienced Teachers to Mentor New Teachers in Ontario: Insights from Israel

*Annette J. Ford*

*"If you are a good teacher... come learn to be a good mentor!"*
- from an Israeli mentor course advertisement

## Introduction

Excellent teachers of children are not automatically excellent mentors to new teachers. To effectively mentor new teachers, experienced teachers need to understand adult learning processes and teachers' needs, and they need skills in mentoring (Leshem, 2014; Moir & Hanson, 2008b; Rajuan, Tuchin, & Zuckermann, 2011). These understandings and skills do not automatically result from a person's proficiency in teaching children; but, rather, require learning, preparation, and support based on clear understandings of the principles and practices of mentoring and teaching (Achinstein & Athanases, 2006; Moir & Hanson, 2008a; Schatz-Oppenheimer, 2014). However, few programs adequately prepare experienced teachers to mentor new teachers (Leshem, 2014; Schatz-Oppenheimer, 2014). Many programs focus on mentor preparation by offering workshops and manuals without developing ongoing, inductive, and collaborative communities of learning for mentoring (Achinstein & Athanases, 2006; Jonson, 2008).

In Canada, the support of new teachers has been "sporadic and inconsistent" (Kutsyuruba, Godden, & Tregunna, 2014, p. 32). Only Ontario and the Northwest Territories have comprehensive induction programs, and not all induction programs in Canada include mentoring (Kutsyuruba et al., 2014). Because there is little research on curriculum and development for mentors of new teachers, there is a need to both study programs that train mentors of new teachers and to develop well-conceptualized curricula for mentor development (Athanases et al., 2008; Helleve, Danielson, & Smith, 2015; Orland-Barak, 2010).

Mentoring is a caring relationship wherein a more experienced person guides someone who is less experienced toward personal and professional growth (Kram, 1988; Newby & Heide, 2013). Mentoring involves not only instruction and guidance, but also a committed, caring, and reciprocal relationship that develops through one-on-one or small group interaction on a regular basis over a period of time. In an educational context, mentoring is often the synergetic process in which someone "further along the path" guides others in discovering new insights, solving critical problems, and collaborating for the purpose of gaining and applying wisdom and knowledge.

This chapter emerged from my PhD thesis research on the curriculum and practice of a country-wide professional development program in Israel that develops the mentors for new teachers through courses that function as communities of learning. For my PhD research, I studied several programs that offered professional development to mentors of new teachers: the New Teacher Center's program in the United States, the Aga Khan University's program in Pakistan, and the Israeli Ministry of Education's program in Israel. Because Israel's program was less represented in the literature than the New Teacher Center's in the United States, and because Pakistan's program had ended due to funding issues, I studied Israel's program for my field research, using case study methodology to investigate how the Israeli program develops experienced teachers to mentor new teachers. My case study research included semi-structured interviews with 20 directors, coordinators, instructors, and mentors in the program, as well as analysis of curriculum documents and observation of the mentor coordinator training and the Israeli culture. In the following sections, I describe a) Israel's mentor development program, b) the importance of context; c) Ontario, Canada's New Teacher Induction Program; and, finally, d) a proposed mentor development program for Ontario. I conclude with a summary of the contribution and significance of the insights presented.

# Israel's Mentor Development Program

In the mid-1990's Israel's Ministry of Education (MoE) determined that every new K-12 teacher should be mentored and that the experienced teachers who served as mentors should have opportunities and incentives to be trained for these mentoring roles (Orland-Barak, 2003; Rajuan et al., 2011). These decisions emerged from research that showed the benefits of mentoring new teachers and the problem that "not all experienced teachers have the supervision and leadership skills necessary to guide the new teachers through their first difficult year" (Rajuan et al., 2011, p. 173). To the date of this writing, the Israeli MoE oversees mentor development courses offered at universities and colleges throughout the country and provides a monthly forum at the Mofet Institute, a center for supporting teacher educators' professional development. This forum serves to guide instructors and coordinators in planning, organizing, and developing the courses (Rajuan et al., 2011; Schatz-Oppenheimer, 2014).

## New Teacher Induction in Israel

The Israeli MoE mandated one year of induction for all new teachers, whom they call "stajers" (*stah-zhairs*). In this induction year, stajers are hired by a school and have full responsibility for their own classes. At the same time, they attend weekly interactive workshops to guide them in connecting theory with practice, and they each receive mentorship from a more experienced teacher (Leshem, 2014; Schatz-Oppenheimer, 2014). The induction year serves as a bridge for the stajers between the worlds of teacher training and professional teaching. A purpose for that year is "to soften the absorption process and perhaps even prevent the 'reality shock' that is often linked to it" (Schatz-Oppenheimer, Mendel, & Zilberstrom, 2014, p. 5). After the first induction year, the MoE offers the teacher optional mentoring with an experienced teacher for the next several years (Schatz-Oppenheimer et al., 2014).

In the induction year, stajers are evaluated through mid-year and end-of-year assessments by their mentor, their principal, and a representative of the MoE. If the stajers are successful, the MoE awards them a teacher license, which is in addition to the teaching certificate they received from their teachers' college or university (Leshem, 2014). If the stajers do not succeed in the first year, they repeat the year (Schatz-Oppenheimer, 2014).

After successful completion of the first year and two further successful years of teaching, a teacher is awarded tenure (Schatz-Oppenheimer, 2014).

**Description of Israeli Mentor Development Program**

The Israeli mentor development program offers two levels of courses for experienced teachers to become trained mentors of new teachers— either 60 hours over one year or 150 hours over two years. Incentives for teachers include free tuition for the courses, a slightly increased monthly salary, and reimbursement for travel to the courses (Rajuan et al., 2011). Mentors are not hired full-time. Instead, they mentor new teachers along-side their regular teaching responsibilities. After completing the two-year program, mentors receive certification of a "mentor teacher," which can lead to greater recognition in the school (Leshem, 2014).

To become a mentor, the teacher should: 1) be certified and licensed; 2) work at the same school as the new teacher; 3) have at least five years of teaching experience; 4) have experience teaching at least one subject that the new teacher teaches; 5) have attended a mentor development course; and, 6) participate in professional development meetings (Schatz-Oppenheimer et al., 2014). The courses are taught in teachers' colleges and universities by instructors who have training in pedagogy or counseling. The teachers' colleges prepare elementary teachers, and the universities prepare secondary teachers for teaching. Most of the instructors are experienced teacher educators.

The mentoring courses emphasize the role of mentors as reflective practitioners and co-constructors of knowledge, and provide opportunities for mentors to "document their experiences through portfolios, cases, and stories of critical incidents in their practices" (Orland-Barak, 2003, p. 195). Six prominent curriculum themes in the mentor development courses are: mentor identity, the new teacher's world, mentor guidance and communication skills, new teacher assessment, mentor course activities, and mentor course assignments. The curriculum reflects Vygotsky's (1978) view of learners growing and developing through the guidance of others. When mentors share with course colleagues the problems they experience with their new teacher mentees, others in the course learn with them, together exploring possible solutions. The mentors learn with and from one another to serve as role models, questioners, and guides for the new teachers. This growth in community is important for mentors' learning (Moir & Hanson, 2008a; Rajuan et al., 2011) and for the development of their professional identities (Kosnik & Beck, 2009).

My research showed that although the Israeli mentor development program has challenges to overcome in terms of teachers' initial perceptions of the mentor development courses and the attitudes held toward them, many teachers grow as mentors through the program and see great value in the program. In the courses, mentors realize that there is much about mentoring new teachers that they had not previously known. They are grateful when they realize that the courses have equipped them to understand and identify with new teachers, to communicate with them, and to guide them more effectively. Course participants leave the courses not only as stronger mentors, but also as stronger teachers. By analyzing their own teaching in light of broader teaching theory and other mentors' practice, those being trained to mentor are able to grow in their own professional skills (Leshem, 2014; Kosnik & Beck, 2009; Moir & Hanson, 2008b). As the course instructors see the benefit of the courses and communicate the courses' importance, mentors grow in trust and respect for the instructors and in co-constructing knowledge (Moir & Hanson, 2008a). The directors, coordinators, and instructors of the Israeli program continue to strengthen as the program evolves.

## The Importance of Context

I believe that educational policy makers and practitioners can learn from programs in other contexts, such as the mentor development program in Israel; but there is a need to understand both the foreign and local contexts before seeking to implement policies or practices from other places. Rather than looking to other educational systems for ultimate answers, educators must understand that the educational techniques and practices of one country cannot simply be grafted into the educational system of another (Sadler, 1900, as cited in Bereday, 1964). When educators look to other systems for "miracle solutions" that offer quick success for their educational problems, they often wonder why success is elusive. Sadler stated,

We cannot wander at pleasure among the educational systems of the world, like a child strolling through a garden, and pick off a flower from one bush and some leaves from another, and then expect that if we stick what we have gathered into the soil at home, we shall have a living plant (as cited in Bereday, 1964, p. 310).

First, there is a need to understand the contexts of the societies in which educational institutions and programs are found; then to consider those contexts in light of one's own; and then to critically evaluate the possible effects of the intended concepts or practices to be borrowed. Only after these considerations can the key aspects of a mentoring initiative be judiciously adapted to enhance a different local context.

This adaptation process involves understanding and interacting with the foreign culture with "a high degree of intellectual and moral humility" (Farrell, 2003, p. 167). Hayhoe and Pan (2001) noted, "Of greatest importance is the readiness to listen to the narrative of the other, and to learn the lessons which can be discovered in distinctive threads of human cultural thought and experience" (p. 20). A humble attitude of listening and learning, combined with openness to adjustment and change, can aid in bridging the gap between cultures and in introducing needed educational development to other contexts. Shared wisdom can enrich all cultures where there is a willingness to listen and learn from one another and to evaluate the possible short and long-term effects of each potential decision.

## New Teacher Induction Program in Ontario

One potential context for the adaptation of Israel's mentor development program is in the Province of Ontario, Canada. Ontario's population is similar to Israel's, and the Ontario Ministry of Education funds and regulates the Ontario education system in a fashion quite similar to Israel. In Ontario, people who desire to be teachers must first complete a bachelor's degree, and then study for two years in a teacher education program. After successfully completing their teacher education program they may apply to the Ontario College of Teachers, Ontario's teacher accreditation board, for a teaching license. Teachers in Ontario participate in professional development workshops and training, and they can choose to take Additional Qualifications (AQ) courses through local universities to expand their subject knowledge, sharpen their classroom skills, or to prepare for career changes within the teaching field (Ontario College of Teachers, 2017).

In response to concern over teacher attrition, especially in the first three years of teaching, and with the desire to provide better induction and professional development to new teachers, Ontario initiated the New Teacher Induction Program (NTIP) in 2006 (Glassford & Salinitri, 2007). The NTIP program includes three mandatory induction elements for new teachers: 1) orientation to the school and school board, 2) mentoring by an experienced teacher throughout the year, and 3) professional development and training (Ontario Ministry of Education, 2010a). In the new teachers' first year of teaching, their principal observes and evaluates them twice, and they must receive two satisfactory evaluations from their principal within their first 24 months of teaching (Ontario Ministry of Education, 2010a). At that time, they receive a notation from the Ontario College of Teachers that they have successfully completed their induction.

Mentoring is perceived to be the most important aspect of the NTIP program, as new teachers experience the presence and continued support of their mentors (Glassford & Salinitri, 2007; Kane, 2010; Kane & Francis, 2013). To prepare the mentors, the Ontario MoE provides optional written resources and training workshops with follow-up sessions. The mentors' resource handbook describes the mentor's role as a non-evaluative consultant, collaborator, and coach (Ontario Ministry of Education, 2010b). The *NTIP Mentoring Handbook* states,

> The relationship between mentor and new teacher is one of trust and confidence. It is important to establish this trust early in the relationship, so that your new teacher is able to engage in open and honest dialogue about his or her successes and challenges in the classroom, without concerns that this may in any way be connected to performance appraisal. (Ontario Ministry of Education, 2010b, p. 3)

The *Handbook* also provides optional guidelines for mentors' interactions with their new teacher mentees for each month of the school year.

The goal of the Ontario Ministry of Education (2010a) is for the NTIP program to offer a mentor training component that includes training in collaboration and coaching, communication, conferencing and feedback, confidentiality, and teacher crises. Although this is the goal, the program lacks adequate mentor development. In her final report on the program, Kane (2010) stated the need to "offer mentor training that introduces mentors to a range of mentoring models and clarifies the opportunities of their roles" and to "provide a range of guidelines for mentors as to key areas of focus for new teacher-mentor engagement" (p. 9). In a study on 47 teacher educators in the NTIP program, Barrett and colleagues (2009) said, "respondents were concerned that clear criteria for mentors' work be established" and that there be more preparation for the mentors (p. 690). Kane and Francis (2013), following a secondary analysis of data from an evaluation of Ontario's NTIP program, noted that it is essential that Ontario provide "programs for mentor teachers that focus on ways to support professional learning," and through mentor development, teacher education programs could be more actively involved in shaping induction (p. 373). Because mentor development is not strongly addressed in Ontario, there is need to grow and learn from other mentor development programs.

## A Mentor Development Program for Ontario

It is my belief that the New Teacher Induction Program in Ontario could derive benefit from other models of mentor development. The outline of a potential program presented below is based on Israel's mentor development program, along with additional insights from another well-known mentor development program offered by the New Teacher Center in Santa Cruz, California. This outline builds on the existing structures within the Ontario's NTIP program.

### Program Objective

Recognizing that experienced teachers are not automatically excellent mentors to new teachers, and that mentoring can lead to greater teacher satisfaction and retention and ultimately to increased student learning, the purpose of this proposed mentor development program is to prepare experienced teachers to mentor new teachers with care and for professional growth. In this program, mentors would be chosen to mentor new teachers only if they have completed or are participating in an AQ course on mentoring and are recognized as exemplary teachers. These could be teachers who have demonstrated strong communication skills, who are respected by their peers, who have had experience with adult learners, and who have current knowledge of professional development (New Teacher Center, 2016a).

Although in the New Teacher Center's model teachers leave their teaching practice for at least two years to become full-time mentors of 13-15 new teachers (Moir & Hanson, 2008b), there is benefit in providing partial release time for classroom teachers to be "mentor teachers" who continue to model best practices of teaching in their classrooms as they mentor one or two new teacher mentees. These mentor teachers, having completed the mentor development program, would receive an increased salary as they accept the responsibility not only of teaching their own students, but also of mentoring new teachers. This would provide opportunity for the new teachers to observe their mentors' classes and learn directly from their teaching practices. For full effectiveness in new teacher mentoring, the new teacher mentee would learn not only from the mentor's coaching, but also from the mentor's role modeling (Anderson & Shannon, 1988; Kram, 1988).

The mentoring period would be aligned with the duration of NTIP program of two years, with a potential extension if requested by both the mentor and the new teacher mentee. This multi-year mentoring could improve teacher practice and student achievement (New Teacher Center, 2016a). Both the mentor and the new teacher would receive release time from teaching for informal, reciprocal classroom observations, follow-up discussions, and professional development opportunities (Ontario Ministry of Education, 2010a).

To qualify as certified mentors of new teachers, two two-semester AQ courses would be offered for active mentors of new teachers. The courses would meet for three hours every two weeks during the school year. The first-year course, *Principles and Practices of New Teacher Mentoring*, would introduce five topics: 1) foundations of mentoring, 2) mentor identity, 3) new teacher challenges, 4) mentor-new teacher communication and guidance, and 5) mentor-new teacher observation and feedback.

## Topic 1: Foundations of Mentoring

The foundations of mentoring topic would begin with an understanding of the nature and purpose of mentoring. This would include examining Anderson's (1988) Mentoring Model for mentors of new teachers and considering Noddings' (1984; 2005) Ethic of Care and how it relates to education. Further, this foundations topic would include a consideration of the history and development of mentoring in education, particularly of new teacher mentoring.

This topic would also include consideration of Orland-Barak's (2010) conceptualization of mentoring new teachers as "Mentor-as-Praxis." After over 10 years of research in the area of mentoring and teacher induction, Orland-Barak (2010) wrote that praxis "constitutes an encounter between participants (in our case mentors and mentees) at the intersection between theory and practice" (pp. 9-10). In a praxis-based curriculum, mentoring should be learned not in the traditional "theory as informing practice" paradigm, but rather in a way that "validates theory and practice as existing in a reciprocal relationship" (p. 10). Mentor-as-praxis involves first seeking to understand a mentoring context in theoretical terms based on prevalent knowledge about mentoring, then evaluating that knowledge in the immediate context of mentoring, and finally allowing the new insights to inform a new theoretical understanding of the situation, which in turn shapes further practice (Orland-Barak, 2010). When studying teacher mentoring through a "mentor-as-praxis" lens, a mentoring course is not simply a "how-to" list of ways to practically succeed in mentoring, but instead is a research-informed study of mentoring practice that then reciprocates to inform further research and practice.

### Topic 2: Mentor Identity

A second topic in the mentor development course would be mentor identity. When thinking about their new identity as mentors, students in the course would reflect on the questions, "Who am I as a mentor?" and "How do I transition from teacher to mentor?"

The first question, "Who am I as a mentor?", brings to light an understanding of the mentors' self-concept and awareness as a mentor. This would take place through reviewing mentors' roles highlighted in the literature and through identifying personal learning and teaching styles (Rajuan et al., 2011), which in turn would include exploring characteristics of mentors, as described in Kram's (1988) career and psychosocial functions of mentoring. Career functions of mentoring include: sponsorship, promoting the mentee for advancement in the organization;

"exposure-and-visibility," introducing the mentee to key people and advo-cating for the mentee; coaching, helping the mentee navigate the profession and grow professionally; protection, shielding the mentee from potentially damaging contact with others; and challenging assignments, guiding the mentee through challenging and profitable work that might not have been accomplished alone (Kram, 1988). Psychosocial functions include: role modeling, setting an example that the mentee desires to follow; "accep-tance-and-confirmation," showing continued non-evaluative support, encouragement, and appreciation to the mentee; counseling, helping the mentee understand and negotiate personal and organizational concerns; and friendship, expressing interest in the mentee's life beyond the work-place (Kram, 1988). Issues of mentor identity emerged from my research on the Israeli mentor development program and identified mentors of new teachers as role models, releasers, reflectors, professional supports, emo-tional supports, and excellent teachers.

The second question would be, "How do I transition from teacher to mentor?" To conceptualize this transition, the mentors would need to realize that mentoring adult teachers is different from teaching children. The transition does not occur naturally and is similar to the process of learning a second language, which can cause feelings of inadequacy and frustration (Orland-Barak, 2005). The mentor would need to embrace the understanding that mentoring differs from teaching, and that andragogy requires a different mindset and skillset from pedagogy. It requires a mind-set of change and process – the willingness to grow and develop as a person, educator, and mentor. It further requires a mindset of new teacher growth , the willingness to pull back one's own influence and personality to make room for each person to grow and develop into a uniquely gifted teacher.

## Topic 3: New Teacher Challenges

To mentor a new teacher, the mentor must understand the new teach-er's inner and outer world and the challenges the new teacher faces. In this section of the course, three challenges facing new teachers would be con-sidered: identity challenges, school system challenges, and teaching and communication challenges. Mentors need to understand these challenges to be able to help their mentees recognize and overcome them.

First, the mentors would need to grasp their mentees' new identity as teachers. This part of the course would begin by helping mentors remember their own experiences as new teachers in order to identify with their new teacher mentees. It would look at the attitudinal stages of a new teacher: "anticipation, survival, disillusionment, rejuvenation, reflection, and anticipation" (Watkins, 2016, p. 1) and would consider the approximate dates in the year that the new teacher might experience these feelings. It also would consider the new teachers' feelings described in the Israeli MoE mentoring handbook – feelings of "dissatisfaction, frustration, helplessness and loneliness," of "overload and difficulties in private and professional time management," of "sensitivity to criticism," and of "concern regarding the professional image as crystalized in the eyes of students, colleagues, parents, and the system as a whole" (Schatz-Oppenheimer et al., 2014, p. 21). The topic would also consider stages of professional development and discuss the strengths and weaknesses of models such as the one suggested by Fuller (1969), which includes: 1) the *pre-teaching phase*, in which student teachers have no concerns because they have no experience in teaching; 2) the *early teaching phase*, in which teachers are concerned primarily with themselves and ask the questions, "Where do I stand?" and "How adequate am I?" and 3) *late concerns*, in which mature, experienced teachers turn their focus toward their students and seek the students' wellbeing rather than focusing on their own needs and insecurities.

Second, the mentors would need to recognize the challenges for new teachers in understanding the unwritten rules or hidden culture of the school. New teachers need assistance in examining the system's expectations of them and their own expectations of the system, and they need "awareness of the system's behavioural norms and work patterns" (Schatz-Oppenheimer et al., 2014, p. 21). The mentors would discuss overt and covert school expectations and consider how to communicate these to their new teacher mentees and, thereby, ease their absorption into the school context.

Third, the mentors would need to understand teaching and communication challenges faced by new teachers, such as preparing and teaching lessons, class management, and communicating with various members of the school community. To understand issues that new teachers face in preparing lessons, the mentors would discuss challenges in teaching pedagogical content, such as "mastering the discipline, combining various teaching methods and tools, short term and long term planning and organizing, teaching a heterogeneous class, incorporating technology, etc." (Schatz-Oppenheimer et al., 2014, p. 20). As knowledge for content-based support in mentoring new teachers is also becoming recognized as an important element to address in mentor development courses (Achinstein & Davis, 2014), the mentors would discuss how new teachers can effectively teach content in lessons. They would discuss class management struggles for new teachers, including "switching between the individual to the learning group, students' discipline and behaviour problems, students' study habits and work routines, learning motivation, [and] the class as a social group" (Schatz-Oppenheimer et al., 2014, p. 20). The mentors would also consider the challenges faced by the new teachers in communicating with students, parents, other teachers, and the principal.

## Topic 4: Mentor-Mentee Communication and Guidance

The mentor course would include the topics of the mentor's communication and guidance skills. The topic of communication would address how the mentor can build a communicative, trusting, caring relationship with the new teacher, and the topic of guidance would address how the mentor guides the new teacher into professional growth.

The course would examine the mentoring relationship as a communicative relationship that involves attentive listening and caring dialogue (Noddings, 2005). The mentor seeks to build trust with the new teacher mentee, assuring and demonstrating that confidentiality is respected (Moir & Hanson 2008a; Ontario Ministry of Education, 2010a). The course would address issues of cross-cultural communication and adaptation (Hayhoe & Pan, 2001; Orland-Barak, 2010), as classrooms are becoming increasingly multi-cultural. Another area of communication in the course would be the logistical planning and communication between the mentor and new teacher. This would include how to develop a plan for when and where the mentor and new teacher should meet and consideration of expectations and working details of the relationship (Rajuan et al., 2011, p. 177). A mentoring dialectic in this area would be aimed at "maintaining a mandatory framework of fixed, consecutive, weekly meetings while meeting demands for flexibility and availability in response to everyday occurrences" (Schatz-Oppenheimer, 2014, p. 116). To achieve balance in this area there is need for clear, ongoing communication.

Within the topic of guidance, the course would consider the dialectic of "understanding the novice's dependence on the mentor as an experienced professional while expecting the novice to exercise professional discretion and autonomy" (Schatz-Oppenheimer, 2014, p. 116). The mentors would explore how to find balance in guiding the mentee "from the side," rather than authoritatively directing the mentee or passively doing nothing. In this part of the course, mentors would consider the image of the mentor as a tree, which a participant in my Israeli research described. In this metaphor, the tree chooses not to spread its branches as widely as it could, because although its shade is protective and comforting, a new sapling needs sunlight to grow. In the same way, mentors choose to pull back their ego and directivity to stand beside their mentees, offering support without overshadowing them. This form of guidance is "active passivity" – choosing neither to exercise control over the mentee nor to be passively disinterested. To mitigate an authoritarian posture of mentoring, the mentor seeks to learn from the new teacher. A posture of reciprocity reminds the mentor that the new teacher also has answers and ideas of worth, so the learning is mutual.

### Topic 5: Mentor-Mentee Observation and Feedback

Observation and feedback skills are crucial to mentors of new teachers because in most induction programs the mentor is required to conduct at least some informal observations of their new teacher mentee's teaching. In this course, like that offered by Rajuan and colleagues (2011), different models of supervision would be addressed, such as how to observe a lesson well and how to give and receive feedback. The dialectic here is aimed at "developing an empathetic approach that is fully attentive to the trainee's needs while providing practical and judgmental advice" (Schatz-Oppenheimer, 2014, p. 116). The mentor development course would address this issue of new teacher observation and feedback because it is one that causes discomfort to mentors. The course would consider examples such as that portrayed by an Israeli participant in my research, who urged mentors to observe the new teachers with the aim of encouraging them – to focus on the instructional objective and highlight the areas of success for the new teachers in teaching the class. In feedback conversations, the mentors would learn to say little and listen much, to encourage the new teachers with the positive aspects of the lessons, and to suggest only one or two changes to work on in the weeks ahead.

The second year AQ course in the proposed mentor development program would be *Current Issues in New Teacher Mentoring*. This course would delve more deeply into the topics of mentoring foundations, mentor identity, new teacher challenges, communication and guidance, and observation and feedback, discussing how to mentor new teachers in specific issues they face. The course could also address issues discussed in the second year of the New Teacher Center's Mentor Academies: "issues of differentiation, equity, inclusion, working with English language learners, as well as training in facilitation skills and designing learning experiences that support professional growth" (Moir & Hanson, 2008a, p. 158). As in the New Teacher Center program, an optional third year course, *Action Research in New Teacher Mentoring*, would provide opportunity for mentors to complete an action research project in their school contexts.

The courses in this proposed mentor development program could provide a safe space to discuss mentoring issues. It is my hope that in these "conversation spaces," participants would be able to "solve prevalent issues, conceptualize differences and similarities across their mentoring contexts, establish links between their work as mentors and their work as teachers, and reflect on their educational agendas as teachers and as mentors" (Orland-Barak, 2005, p. 364).

## Conclusion

Israel's mentor development program cannot be adopted as a whole to the Canadian or other contexts because there are different governmental, educational, and professional development structures in place than those found in the context of Israel. For example, there are varied hierarchical control structures and governmental financial commitments to teacher professional development compared to those in Israel that account for the success of that program. Again, the Israeli program cannot be plucked and transplanted into the soil of another nation, and its practices cannot simply be clipped and grafted into another educational system (Bereday,

1964). However, to listen and learn with care from both the Israeli and American contexts, as well as local stakeholders, beneficial elements of the program, such as curriculum topics, may be adapted to other locales, and thus address the needs of beginning teachers in Canada.

This chapter has offered a course curriculum that is lacking in the literature support on mentoring and teacher induction. Athanases and colleagues (2008) noted that "programmes often lack well-conceptualized curricula to develop new mentors to guide new teachers" (p. 745). Helleve and colleagues (2015) also argued that currently there is not enough knowledge about how to best develop curricula for mentor education. The curriculum proposed in this chapter provides needed insights into curriculum concepts for mentor development. The proposal focuses on the mentor's identity and mindset; the new teacher's needs such as teaching, classroom discipline, and communication with students, other teachers, principals, and parents; and the mentor's skills in communicating with, guiding, observing, and offering feedback to the new teacher. The proposed curriculum provides a framework for a potential mentor development program to be offered in the form of AQ courses in Ontario.

With insights gleaned from Israel's mentor development program and other programmatic considerations of how to adapt programs to other contexts, and building on existing structures of Ontario's NTIP program, the proposed course curriculum may contribute to the formation and continuation of other mentor development programs. These insights may be used to better equip mentors to guide and relate to their new teacher mentees and to enhance new teacher induction, teacher retention and development, and student learning in Ontario, other parts of Canada, and, indeed, in other nations.

## References

Achinstein, B., & Athanases, S. Z. (Eds.). (2006). *Mentors in the making: Developing new leaders for new teachers*. New York, NY: Teachers College Press.

Achinstein, B., & Davis, E. (2014). The subject of mentoring: Towards a knowledge and practice base for content-focused mentoring of new teachers. *Mentoring & Tutoring: Partnership in Learning, 22*(2), 104–126. doi: 10.1080/13611267.2014.902560

Anderson, E. M., & Shannon, A. L. (1988). Toward a conceptualization of mentoring. *Journal of Teacher Education, 39*(1), 38–42.

Athanases, J., Abrams, J., Jack, G., Johnson, V., Kwock, S., McCurdy, J., & Totaro, S. (2008). Curriculum for mentor development: Problems and promise in the work of new teacher induction leaders. *Journal of Curriculum Studies, 40*(6), 743–770. doi:10.1080/00220270701784319

Barrett, S. J., Solomon, R. P., Singer, J., Portelli, J. P., & Mujuwamariya, D. (2009). The hidden curriculum of a teacher induction program: Ontario teacher educators' perspectives, *Canadian Journal of Education, 32*(4), 677–702.

Bereday, G. (1964). Sir Michael Sadler's "Study of foreign systems of education." *Comparative Educational Review, 7*(3), 307–314.

Farrell, J. (2003). Equality of education: A half century of comparative evidence seen from a new millennium. In R. Arnove & C. Torres (Eds.). *Comparative Education: The Dialectic of the Global and the Local* (pp. 146–175). Lanham, MA: Rowman & Littlefield.

Fuller, F. F. (1969). Concerns of teaching: A developmental characterization. *American Educational Research Journal, 6*(2), 207–226.

Glassford, L.A., & Salinitri, G. (2007). Designing a successful new teacher induction program: An assessment of the Ontario experience, 2003-2006. *Canadian Journal of Educational Administration and Policy, 60*(11), 1–34.

Hayhoe, R., & Pan, J. (Eds.). (2001). *Knowledge across culture: A contribution to the dialogue among civilisations.* Hong Kong: Comparative Education Research Centre, The University of Hong Kong.

Helleve, I., Danielson, A. G., & Smith, K. (2015). Does mentor-education make a difference? In H. Tillema, G. J. van der Westhuizen, & K. Smith, (Eds.). *Mentoring for learning: "Climbing the mountain"* (pp. 313-332). Rotterdam, The Netherlands: Sense.

Jonson, K. F. (2008). *Being an effective mentor: How to help beginning teachers succeed.* Thousand Oaks, CA: Corwin.

Kane, R.G. (2010), *NTIP evaluation final report – Executive summary (Cycle III).* Toronto: Ministry of Education of Ontario.

Kane, R. G., & Francis, A. (2013). Preparing teachers for professional learning: Is there a future for teacher education in new teacher induction? *Teacher Development, 17*(3), 362–379. doi: 10.1080/13664530.2013.813763

Kosnik, C., & Beck, C. (2009). *Priorities in teacher education.* New York, NY: Routledge.

Kram, K. E. (1988). *Mentoring at work: Developmental relationships in organizational life.* Lanham, MD: University Press of America.

Kutsyuruba, B., Godden, L., & Tregunna, L. (2014). Curbing early-career teacher attrition: A pan-Canadian document analysis of teacher induction and mentorship programs. *Canadian Journal of Educational Administration and Policy, 161,* 1–42.

Leshem, S. (2014). How do teacher mentors perceive their role, does it matter? *Asia-Pacific Journal of Teacher Education, 42*(3), 261–274. doi: 10.1080/1359866X.2014.896870

Moir, E., & Hanson, S. (2008a). A learning community for teacher induction. In A. P. Samaras, A. R. Freese, C. Kosnik, & C. Beck (Eds.) *Learning Communities in Practice* (pp. 155–163). Dordecht, Netherlands: Springer.

Moir, E., & Hanson, S. (2008b). The new teacher development forum: Developing a community of practice. In A. Lieberman & L. Miller (Eds.) *Teachers in Professional Communities: Improving Teaching and Learning* (pp. 61–72). New York, NY: Teachers College Press.

New Teacher Center. (2016a). *High quality mentoring and induction practices.* Retrieved from https://newteachercenter.org/wp-content/uploads/high-quality-mentoring_induction-resource.pdf

Newby, T. J., & Heide, A. (2013). The value of mentoring. *Performance Improvement Quarterly, 26*(2), 141–158. doi:10.1111/j.1937-8327.1992.tb00562.x

Noddings, N. (1984). *Caring: A feminine approach to ethics and moral education.* Berkeley, CA: University of California.

Noddings, N. (2005). *The challenge to care in schools: An alternative approach to education.* New York, NY: Teachers College Press.

Ontario College of Teachers. (2017). *Additional Qualifications.* Retrieved from http://www.oct.ca/members/additional-qualifications.

Ontario Ministry of Education (2010a). *New teacher induction program: Induction elements manual.* Queen's Printer for Ontario. Retrieved from http://www.edu.gov.on.ca/eng/teacher/pdfs/NTIP-English_Elements-september2010.pdf

Ontario Ministry of Education (2010b). *Partnering for success: A resource handbook for mentors.* Retrieved from http://www.edu.gov.on.ca/eng/teacher/NTIPMentor.pdf

Orland-Barak, L. (2003). In between worlds: The tensions of in-service mentoring in Israel. In F. K. Kochan & J.T. Pascarelli (Eds.), *Global Perspectives on Mentoring: Transforming Contexts, Communities, and Cultures* (pp. 191–210). Greenwich, CT: Information Age.

Orland-Barak, L. (2005). Lost on translation: Mentors learning to participate in competing discourses of practice. *Journal of Teacher Education, 56*(4), 355–367. doi:10.1177/0022487105279566

Orland-Barak, L. (2010). *Learning to mentor-as-praxis: Foundations for a curriculum in teacher education.* New York, NY: Springer.

Rajuan, M., Tuchin, I., & Zuckermann, T. (2011). Mentoring the mentors: First-order descriptions of experience-in-context. *The New Educator, 7*(2), 172–190. doi:10.1080/1547688X.2011.574592

Schatz-Oppenheimer, O. (2014). The dialectics of mentoring for beginning teachers. *Education Practice and Innovation, 1*(2), 112–124.

Schatz-Oppenheimer, O., Mendel, B., & Zilberstrom, S. (2014). החונכות‡והליווי למתמחים‡ולעובדי‡הוראה‡חדשים [*Mentoring and accompanying stajers and new teaching staff*]. (O. Tal, Trans.). State of Israel Ministry of Education.

Vygotsky, L. S. (1978). *Mind in society: The development of higher psychological processes.* Cambridge, MA: Harvard University Press.

Watkins, A. (2016). *Role of the principal in beginning teacher induction.* Santa Cruz, CA: New Teacher Center. Retrieved from https://newteachercenter.org/wp-content/uploads/role-of-the-principal_practice-brief.pdf

# Early Service Teachers' Experiences with a Division-Wide Two Year Teacher Induction and Mentorship Program

*Francine Morin, Kathy Collis, Gail Ruta-Fontaine,*
*Cathy Smith, Jennifer Watt*

## Introduction

Induction and mentoring of beginning teachers is viewed by many scholars as an important and integral part of the continuum of teacher education and development (e.g., Darling-Hammond, 2005; Feiman-Nemser, 2001; Ingersoll & Strong, 2011). There is clear evidence that well-designed induction and mentoring programs have positive impacts on new teacher commitment and retention (e.g., Adams & Woods, 2015; Fresko & Nasser-Abu Alhija, 2015); yet the evidence is not so clear for such impacts on pedagogical practices and student achievement (e.g., Darling-Hammond, Berry, Haselkorn, & Fideler, 1999; Howe, 2006; Ingersoll & Strong, 2011; Strong, 2009). While there is quite a variety of induction and mentoring programs in North America and abroad (e.g., Achinstein & Athanases, 2006; Howe, 2006; Villani, 2002), more research is needed to provide evidence of the impact of specific programs on teaching practice and student learning.

This chapter provides an overview of the initiatives undertaken by professional development leaders in one large urban school division in the province of Manitoba, designed to provide support, guidance, and induction programming for early service teachers (ESTs). Selected findings from a two-year study that examined one of these initiatives are reported. The study is part of a multiphase, longitudinal program evaluation which aims to provide ongoing, reliable information that can be used to make decisions and recommendations regarding the school division's induction programming and its impacts. While the new two-year division-wide program initiatives described next encompass a number of components, teacher sub-groups, and professional development models, the scope of the discussion that follows will be limited to the experiences and perspectives of ESTs working in formal one-on-one mentoring relationships.

## Winnipeg School Division's Teacher Induction and Mentorship Program

The Winnipeg School Division (WSD) Teacher Induction and Mentorship Program for early service teachers (ESTs) expanded from serving 21 schools in 2008 to 77 schools in 2013. The new two-year program has roots in what started in 2008 as a three-year Inner City District mentorship program initiative.1 At that time, the WSD established a Professional Learning and Leadership Centre, housed it within a school, and appointed a Program Director who created and implemented the program. Features of the program included an intensive two-year mentorship training program for advanced skills teachers (ASTs), release time for job–embedded learning (JEL), and opportunities for reflection and networking among ESTs and ASTs. Program goals included, and continue to include, improved student learning and graduation rates, teacher efficacy, teacher retention, and learning engagement for both teachers and students. Principles guiding the program promote: situated learning in school-based contexts; opportunities for sustained, multi-year learning and collaboration; opportunities for professional reflection and action research; external program evaluation; and ongoing dialogue with university colleagues.

As the program evolved over time to accommodate a greater number of teachers, additional models such as group mentoring through communities of practice (CoPs) were incorporated to complement the one-on-one mentoring addressed within the learning partnerships. In WSD's induction program, a CoP consists of one facilitator who oversees and supports two or three mentors working with eight ESTs. This model is flexible, responsive to teacher and student needs, and allows for leadership development of mentors over the course of two years. The CoPs aim to meet the particular needs of two teacher groups, one a group of French immersion teachers with second language learning interests and the other a group of Grade 5-12 teachers with interests in engaging reluctant learn-ers. Professional staff was added to the program in 2010 and again in 2015, and currently two Program Support Teachers work in conjunction with the Program Director to coordinate and implement mentorship training, action research processes, learning partnerships, and CoPs. The profes-sional staff members take on the role of facilitating the CoPs and liaising with teachers and school leaders to ensure that there is momentum, that there is proper implementation of the induction program, and that the integration of school and divisional goals takes place.

The WSD two-year induction and mentorship program is informed by principles of adult learning and current research on effective profes-sional development. Inherent in the program design are elements of choice for teacher participants, as well as opportunities for them to co-construct learning experiences. Program leaders create spaces for teacher participants to collaborate, build trust, and cultivate improvement-focused profes-sional conversations. Participants engage in an individualized professional development process that is supported through intentional mentorship and active inquiry into practice. Learning partnerships are provided with time and resources so that participants can focus on the learning goals of ESTs through job-embedded learning (JEL).

The recruitment of mentors is an open and inclusive process. All teachers who demonstrate mentor attributes, as defined within the related literature, are invited to apply for these voluntary positions by responding to a divisional posting. ESTs are also able to recommend colleagues who they feel may be appropriate mentors for them. Program leaders facilitate these requests as a way of further developing mentor-mentee relationships that may already exist informally. Mentors are selected by program leaders based on their application materials (including a resume and references) and then matched to fit with the professional learning needs of ESTs.

Mentors selected for the two-year program take part in four days of mentorship training informed by the work of Lipton, Wellman, and Humbard (2003), that is designed to help mentors develop relationships with mentees that offer support, pose challenges, and facilitate ESTs' professional visions. By taking a non-judgmental, non-evaluative stance, mentors develop broad and inclusive views of their roles and learn to be flexible and responsive to mentees' learning needs. Core features of the mentorship training curriculum include: the development of knowledge and skills for conducting learning-focused conversations, strategies for offering improvement-focused feedback, developing skills and protocols for classroom observation, and knowledge about and ways to support the teacher action research process. Conditions are created that enable mentors to develop strong professional networks. Program leaders visit mentors at their school sites to create spaces for conversations about mentoring and ongoing relationship building.

ESTs articulate their professional development needs as well as the learning needs of their students through a self-reflection process that takes place during program orientation sessions held at the beginning of the school year. This early reflection is used as a launching point for conversations between learning partners and mentees' goal-setting. Moving forward, mentors support novice teachers in articulating action research questions that address their goals, and then help them design educational interventions and action inquiry processes that aim to address those goals.

Teacher action research is also complemented by other forms of context-specific JEL which is highly valued by program participants, as it provides opportunities for partnerships to design and redesign meaningful paths for improving classroom practice (Croft et al., 2010). Each learning partner is granted two days of release time in both program years to facilitate the professional inquiries of ESTs. Mentors and mentees engage in planning, problem solving, and reflection in a variety of configurations. For example, some mentors and mentees host each other for classroom visits that include reflective conversations, or they visit other classrooms of interest. Others co-plan units or research instructional strategies together, while others investigate curricula or conduct case studies around a particular student or group of students.

Large group sharing sessions among teacher participants is also an important feature of the program. These sessions are scheduled periodically throughout the two years for networking and presenting highlights of professional learning for the collective benefit of participants. Teachers learn together through structured and semi-structured conversations revolving around the outcomes of their diverse classroom-based inquiries and explorations. Another purpose of these sessions is to support teachers with information and resources that can be used to fully develop their ongoing professional learning plans. Furthermore, program leaders participate by engaging in learning conversations with sub-groups of mentees and mentors to help them to reflect, plan, and continue to problem solve around their goals and projects.

At the end of each year in the program there is also a large group closing session. Closing sessions provide opportunities for teacher participants to make their learning public, with the ultimate goal of advancing new knowledge gained about teaching and learning. This final event is a celebration of all the achievements of teachers and students that have occurred throughout the year. As part of the closing session, all teachers are invited to take part in the year end program evaluation process. Annual evaluations are viewed as an essential tool for assessing whether or not the induction and mentorship program has been implemented as planned, gauging the extent to which purposes are being achieved, and improving future iterations of the program.

## Program Evaluation Design and Procedures

Internal program reviews, such as the one detailed in this chapter, belong to a family of methodologies called action research that aims to provide educators with new knowledge and understanding that enables them to improve professional practices or resolve any range of educational problems (Hendricks, 2009; McNiff & Whitehead, 2011; Stringer, 2008). In this work, the researcher is positioned as an outsider working in collaboration with insiders, the school division partner (Herr & Anderson, 2015). Overall, a mixed method approach to data collection and analysis was undertaken to: 1) obtain information on various dimensions of the induction program; 2) allow for the generation of convergent findings (Creswell & Plano Clark, 2007); and, 3) select and align methods to accomplish particular tasks within the evaluation study as a whole (Morgan, 2014; Teddlie & Tashakkori, 2009).

Two primary data sources were used to generate data: focus group interviews and online exit surveys. The survey and interview protocols were designed by the lead university researcher. Qualitative data generated from interviews were analyzed using the interpretative strategies suggested by Hesse-Biber and Leavy (2011) and Stringer (2008). This theming method was undertaken manually by two coders and involved: 1) becoming familiar with data by reading and re-reading; 2) segmenting data into units of meaning; 3) sorting units into categories using descriptive codes; and 4) identifying and reporting themes within data. Quantitative data generated from the surveys conducted with teachers were managed and analyzed using IBM *SPSS Base for Windows*. Descriptive analyses were conducted to reduce data and report results: frequencies, distributions, percentages, and means. Sample size did not allow for comparative statistical analyses to be undertaken.

## Results and Discussion

### Online Exit Surveys

Data presented in Table 1 below provide the responses of ESTs (mentees) to one component of an online exit survey which was completed at the end of their first and second years of participation in the new division-wide induction program. Participation rates among mentees in year one were high at 75.9% (22 of 29), and even higher in year two at 85.7% (18 of 21). Eight mentees dropped out of the program for various reasons (e.g., maternity leaves, relocation). Survey items 1-12 were designed to specifically investigate the formal mentoring component of the program. Participants were asked to rate each of 12 statements by clicking the appropriate box on the rating scale presented: N/A = not applicable; SD=strongly disagree; D=disagree; A=agree; SA=strongly agree. To further analyze the ESTs' responses to items, numerical values were assigned to each response and mean scores were calculated (SD=1; D=2; A=3; SA=4). A higher mean score is associated with a higher level of agreement with the survey item. Mentees' mean scores for the "mentoring" portion of the online survey ranged from 1.95 (item 2) to 3.18 (items 4 and 8) in year one, and from 1.56 (item 2) to 3.72 (item 4) in year two. For each survey item, year two responses are presented in italics below year one responses. Mean scores in bold represent the strongest levels of consensus.

**Table 1**

*Distribution of Mentoring Survey Responses and Mean Scores by Item and Year** $n = 22$ (Year 1) $n=18$ *(Year 2)*

| Item | N/A | SD | D | A | SA | Mean |
|------|-----|-----|-----|-----|-----|------|
| 1. My mentor and I have similar teaching assignments. | 0 | 6 | 4 | 6 | 6 | |
| | (0.0%) | (27.3%) | (18.2%) | (27.3%) | (27.3%) | 2.6 |
| | *0* | *0* | *6* | *6* | *6* | |
| | *(0.0%)* | *(0.0%)* | *(33.3%)* | *(33.3%)* | *(33.3%)* | *3.0* |
| 2. My mentor and I have different teaching assignments which is a problem. | 1 | 8 | 7 | 3 | 3 | |
| | (4.6%) | (36.4%) | (31.8%) | (13.6%) | (13.6%) | **2.0** |
| | *2* | *9* | *5* | *2* | *0* | |
| | *(11.1%)* | *(50.0%)* | *(27.8)* | *11.1%* | *(0.0)* | *1.6* |
| 3. My mentor and I are well matched. | 0 | 3 | 4 | 7 | 8 | |
| | (0.0%) | (13.6%) | (18.2%) | (31.8%) | (36.4%) | 2.9 |
| | *0* | *0* | *1* | *7* | *10* | |
| | *(0.0%)* | *(0.0%)* | *(5.6%)* | *38.9%* | *55.6%* | *3.5* |
| 4. My mentor and I developed an effective working relationship. | 0 | 1 | 2 | 11 | 8 | |
| | (0.0%) | (4.6%) | (9.1%) | (50.0%) | (36.4%) | **3.2** |
| | *0* | *0* | *0* | *5* | *13* | |
| | *(0.0%)* | *(0.0%)* | *(0.0%)* | *(27.8)* | *72.2%* | *3.7* |
| 5. My mentor and I had a sufficient number of learning conversations. | 0 | 2 | 3 | 11 | 6 | |
| | (0.0%) | (9.1%) | (13.6%) | (50.0%) | (27.3%) | 3.0 |
| | *0* | *0* | *0* | *6* | *12* | |
| | *(0.0%)* | *(0.0%)* | *(0.0%)* | *33.3%* | *66.7%* | *3.7* |
| 6. Conversations with my mentor were long enough to be valuable. | 0 | 1 | 1 | 14 | 6 | |
| | (0.0%) | (4.6%) | (4.6%) | (63.6%) | (27.3%) | 3.1 |
| | *0* | *0* | *0* | *6* | *12* | |
| | *(0.0%)* | *(0.0%)* | *(0.0%)* | *33.3%* | *66.7%* | *3.7* |
| 7. Conversations with my mentor were effectively organized. | 0 | 1 | 3 | 14 | 4 | |
| | (0.0%) | (4.6%) | (13.6%) | (63.6%) | (18.2%) | 3.0 |
| | *0* | *0* | *1* | *7* | *10* | |
| | *(0.0%)* | *(0.0%)* | *5.6%* | *38.9%* | *55.6%* | *3.5* |
| 8. Conversations with my mentor were primarily focused on my learning. | 0 | 1 | 2 | 11 | 8 | |
| | (0.0%) | (4.6%) | (9.1%) | (50.0%) | (36.4%) | **3.2** |
| | *0* | *0* | *1* | *8* | *9* | |
| | *(0.0%)* | *(0.0%)* | *5.6%* | *44.4%* | *50.0%* | *3.4* |

| | | | | | | |
|---|---|---|---|---|---|---|
| 9. I was able to discuss challenges with my mentor and develop solutions. | 0 | 2 | 2 | 12 | 6 | |
| | (0.0%) | (9.1%) | (9.1%) | (54.6%) | (27.3%) | 3.0 |
| | 0 | 0 | 2 | 5 | 11 | |
| | (0.0%) | (0.0%) | 11.1% | (27.8%) | 61.1% | 3.5 |
| 10. I implemented new teaching strategies as a result of the mentoring process. | 1 | 2 | 4 | 10 | 5 | |
| | (4.6%) | (9.1%) | (18.2%) | (45.5%) | (22.7%) | 2.7 |
| | 0 | 0 | 2 | 5 | 11 | |
| | (0.0%) | (0.0%) | 11.1% | (27.8%) | 61.1% | 3.5 |
| 11. I improved significantly as a teacher as a result of the mentoring process. | 1 | 4 | 5 | 9 | 3 | |
| | (4.6%) | (18.2%) | (22.7%) | (40.9%) | (13.6%) | 2.4 |
| | 0 | 0 | 2 | 9 | 7 | |
| | (0.0%) | (0.0%) | (11.1%) | (50.0%) | (38.9%) | 3.3 |
| 12. Overall, the mentoring component is a strong feature of the Program. | 0 | 2 | 3 | 9 | 8 | |
| | (0.0%) | (9.1%) | (13.6%) | (40.9%) | (36.4%) | 3.1 |
| | 0 | 0 | 1 | 9 | 8 | |
| | (0.0%) | (0.0%) | 5.6% | (50.0%) | 44.4% | 3.4 |

*First row for each item represents Year 1 responses and second row represents Year 2 responses. Mean scores in bold represent the strongest levels of consensus.

ESTs receiving one-on-one support from experienced teacher mentors agreed (3.1), and even more strongly so (3.4) at the end of their two-year experience, that the mentoring component is a strong feature of the division's induction program. The strongest level of consensus for any survey item targeting mentoring across both years of the program occurred for mentors' abilities to develop effective working relationships with their mentees (item 4). Mean scores for this item increased significantly from 3.2 to 3.7 or +0.5 over the two years. In year one of the new program, mentees agreed as strongly (3.2) with one additional item—that conversations with their mentors stayed well-focused on their learning needs.

In year one of the program, conversations between learning partners were considered to have been long enough to be valuable (3.1) which allowed for the mentees' challenges to be addressed and their pedagogical problems resolved (3.0). The large majority of mentees also agreed that they had a sufficient number (3.0) of effectively organized conversations (3.0) with their mentors, and that they were good matches for their mentors (2.9). About two thirds of the mentees responding reported implementing new teaching strategies (2.7) as a result of their work with a mentor, however about one third disagreed.

Mentees' responses to item 11 were surprising, with just over half reporting significant teaching improvement (2.4), and almost half reporting no improvement. It was interesting to find that these responses paralleled those resulting for item 1, which indicates that just over half of these mentees shared a similar teaching assignment with their mentors (2.6); while the rest did not. If the purpose of the mentoring component, at least in part, is to improve mentees' teaching effectiveness, research suggests that mentees should be paired with mentors who share similar teaching assignments and subject specializations to provide optimal conditions for success (Hobson, Ashby, Malderez & Tomlinson, 2009; Smith & Ingersoll, 2004). Given that we know job-alike matches tend to result in better teaching outcomes for mentees, it is surprising that responses to item 2 at the end of year one suggested that mentees did not perceive their mentors' differing teaching assignments to be problematic (2.0).

By the end of their second year of participation in the induction program, a positive trend can be observed across mentees' responses to all mentoring survey items. Consistently, gains are noted between the itemized mean scores that resulted for year one and two of the program. Equally strong levels of agreement were found for survey items 4, 5, and 6. Mentees continued to build effective working relationships (3.7) with their mentors during year two. They agreed most strongly that the number of learning conversations conducted was sufficient (3.7) and that these were long enough to be helpful (3.7). Four additional survey items (3, 7, 9, 10) yielded high mean scores (3.5). Learning partners were well-matched and mentees felt comfortable sharing challenges and solving problems with their mentors. Furthermore, learning conversations were considered to be well-organized and novice teachers indicated that they were indeed implementing new teaching strategies.

Slightly lower, but still relatively strong levels of agreement resulted at the end of year two for the remaining survey items linked to mentoring (1, 8, 11, 12). The mean score for mentors' abilities to stay focused on mentees' professional learning needs increased from 3.2 to 3.4, representing a gain of +0.2. It was gratifying to note that the highest mean score gain (+0.9) overall occurred for item 11. An increase from 2.4 (year one) to

3.3 (year two) indicates that in their assessment, mentees' teaching practice improved significantly by the end of their second year in the program. Mentees attributed this improvement to their involvement with the mentoring process. Interestingly, mentees agreed more strongly (3.0) in year two that their teaching assignments were similar to those of their mentees than they did in year one (2.6); which could be explained by the drop in the number of early service teachers who continued in the second year of the program. Perhaps some of those eight who did not continue had different teaching assignments. Not all ESTs participated in each year of the program evaluation (7 in year one; 3 in year two), and surveys were anonymous, so it is possible that the respondents were different persons. The year two result for common teaching assignments aligns with results for item 2, in which a much smaller proportion of mentees (11.1%) report to have been assigned to mentors working in different teaching contexts and that the matching was problematic for them. In year one, mentees' reports of problematic matches were much higher (27.3%).

### Focus Group Interviews

**Year One.** In the first year of the program focus groups interviews were conducted with two groups of ESTs (n=18), each session lasting approximately one hour. In each focus group, participants were prompted by a facilitator to respond to prepared questions related to the mentoring component of the induction program. During each focus group, a research assistant took notes and later transcribed the focus group conversation using video and audio-recordings of the dialogue. Responses from the ESTs are presented following a thematic structure which reveals their perspectives about the strengths, challenges, suggestions, and value of the mentoring component of the induction program.

ESTs identified much strength in the mentoring program in which ESTs and ASTs were paired into learning partners. Understandably, for ESTs the matching of mentors with mentees was a significant factor which influenced its effectiveness. ESTs found it valuable to be matched with an AST with whom they shared similar experiences, grade level, program, curricular area, or context. Physical proximity to their mentor was also important; many ESTs found it beneficial to have a mentor in the same school, including someone who was already in a support role such as a

Learning Support Teacher (LST) or Resource Teacher. ESTs with mentors outside of their schools found their different contexts provided an opportunity to engage in collegial dialogue and gain perspective on their own school context:

> It is just nice to have someone outside of the building to chat with too, because sometimes in your own building it can be a little political. You have to watch what you are saying so no rumors [are] spread. [It] can be hard to speak the truth [about] some frustrations that you have or if you are feeling incompetent so don't want to say [anything] to other staff... to say I don't know what I'm doing here. So, it is nice to have someone outside to talk to whose job it is [to talk to me]. (EST FG)

ESTs reported that their mentors were able to assist them with classroom management, organization, resources, teaching strategies, curriculum planning, writing Individual Educational Plans (IEPs), becoming orientated with the division's educational resource centre, grant writing, and clarifying the role of resource teachers. Strong relationships developed between mentors and ESTs who were in frequent communication. Mentors used planned and drop-by visits, scheduled meetings, release time, and email communication to stay in touch with their mentees. Mentors helped their ESTs to see their strengths, meet their personal goals, identify their next steps, be accountable, and grow in their teaching.

There were also some challenges ESTs faced with their mentoring partnerships. ESTs found it problematic when they did not share a common context with their mentor. Some ESTs with same-school mentors found the gain in accessibility was offset by the loss of confidentiality and perspective. Many pairs struggled to find time to meet. Once a time was agreed upon, these dates for short leaves needed to be approved by their school-based administrator. Some mentors only wanted to meet outside of the school day, which was stressful for ESTs. Some ESTs found that the needs and expertise of their mentors was considered more significant than their learning needs. There was some discrepancy in what ESTs were looking for from their mentors; some valued the professional in-depth conversations, while others valued the more practical benefits such as the opportunity to access new resources through their mentor.

ESTs made a number of suggestions to strengthen the mentoring program. They suggested, since many schools were already involved in welcoming and mentoring new staff members, that those natural on-site mentors be invited to participate in the formal program and benefit from the training opportunities provided.

> I have been really lucky as I have an unofficial mentor in the school. We have co-taught. She is literally across the hall. I will text her. She has allowed me to create a unit for her to teach which gives me so much confidence. I think it would be important if the option was there to have invited her to be my official mentor. [It] would have been more beneficial to me. For those who don't have anyone, it provides another mentor ... [It] would have been nice to have had time to spend with the person in my building. (EST FG)

ESTs thought perhaps they could nominate or invite potential mentors to become involved in the PLLC, which would expand the pool of available mentors and build on the organic relationships being developed within schools. A second suggestion was to offer ESTs an opportunity to participate in a CoP, in which a group of ESTs and ASTs could pool their knowledge and share information. ESTs requested more clarification about the purpose of the mentoring conversations, how often they are expected to occur and how they should be scheduled. Finally, they recommended that more training be provided to ASTs about how to identify and respond to the learning needs of ESTs, in particular those with more teaching experience.

Most of the ESTs in the focus groups felt the mentoring process was helpful for teachers newest to the profession: "I think the focus still needs to be on new teachers, not ESTs—that is my point." Another EST remarked on when their need was greatest:

> I liked having a mentor, someone safe I could trust, and I know some of you mentioned about venting, but I am not a new teacher. I wish I had one when I was a new teacher. I wish there was a better mentoring program for new teachers and not just for one year, maybe a year and a half. Looking back as a new teacher I could have used it. I didn't need it so much now. [I] could have used one before, but didn't have one. (EST FG)

Some ESTs thought that a mentor would have been beneficial during their time as a term teacher, since new permanent contract teachers may have varying amounts of experiences. Unfortunately, most school divisions will only invest in mentoring for new teachers offered permanent positions. It was the perspective of some that not all new permanent teachers need a mentor, particularly when specialty-focused mentoring is available in their own schools.

**Year Two.** There were 12 mentees who participated in a focus matrix interview process in year two of the program to gather their perspectives and experiences with the one-on-one mentoring component of the induction program. The thematic discussion that follows illuminates ESTs' thoughts and feelings about: the strengths of the program, challenges confronted, suggestions for program improvement, and the values they attached to it.

ESTs identified multiple strengths in the mentorship relationships they had developed with ASTs. They reported that the partnerships with their mentors gave them knowledge, strategies, and resources that they could use with their own students. Some reported that they had a "trusted relationship" with their mentor and believed they had "wrap-around support." It was particularly important to the ESTs that they had access to someone with more experience to talk about issues or concerns that arose in their teaching contexts.

As the ESTs had identified after their first year in the program, they again reinforced the importance of mentors being either in the same school building or within close proximity. Close proximity increased the opportunity for frequent meetings, especially when the mentor and mentee shared a common timetable. The ESTs who had mentors in the same school context explained that they "could easily get instant feedback (if there was a problem, etc.)" and that the convenience of being in the same place increased the "ability to build strong and ongoing relationships." Beyond their immediate mentorship partnerships, the ESTs also appreciated the opportunities to network with other ESTs and ASTs in the program.

Most of the challenges identified within the mentoring relationships occurred in scheduling of meetings or compatibility issues in partnerships. The ESTs who had mentors in different schools described that it was "difficult and stressful" to set up meetings. In one case, the difficulty to find in-person meeting time meant that the EST only had an email relationship with his mentor. The relationship was described as "very professional" but he felt it could have been "more beneficial if it was a more casual, more of a genuine relationship." In other cases, the compatibility issues extended beyond the shared school context. Some ESTs noted that because their mentors taught in different grade or content areas, it was more difficult to make connections and gain specific feedback related to their own concerns. For example, one EST explained being a Grade 11/12 teacher and having a mentor in close proximity, but who was a Grade 5-8 resource teacher and had taught Kindergarten. In another case, a mentee described being matched with a mentor who taught in a small resource setting and used different teaching skills than those she needed to learn for her large group classroom setting. In another case, the EST believed that there were "unequal ideas of what it meant to be a mentor."

To address some of these challenges, the ESTs made numerous suggestions to improve mentoring relationships. The ESTs suggested implementing a detailed questionnaire for mentors and mentees at the beginning of the program to aid in more beneficial matches. One EST explained, "Take time to match the needs of the mentee with a mentor" who will "strengthen their weaknesses." Another advised that it is important to "question the intention of the mentor; it could be detrimental to a new teacher's self-esteem" if the match is not working well. In particular, ESTs expressed a desire to work with mentors who taught at the same grade level. In order to have a wider pool of potential mentors, the ESTs suggested that they should be able to recruit their own mentors if there seemed to be a suitable candidate in their school. They also suggested that retired teachers might make appropriate mentors. They recommended clarifying the criteria for a mentor and then leading a campaign to highlight the benefits of the program to potential mentors. They suggested that perhaps an incentive, whether monetary or in terms of classroom resources, might help increase the number of ASTs willing to be involved in the program. Several ESTs acknowledged the heavy workload of the mentors and suggested a time limit (a maximum number of years) that a mentor might serve in the program.

ESTs also suggested that the matching of mentors and mentees should occur earlier, prior to the start of a new school year. As one noted, "Start earlier, network over the holiday [summer], so when you start in September, the support is already in place." Another suggested that there should be an in-school mentor and an out-of-school mentor, because "having an outside mentor gives another perspective." Several of the ESTs expressed a desire to have more time with their mentors and/or fellow mentees. One suggested that they would appreciate, "more social get-togethers in more relaxed environments" while another wanted to be informed about more workshops that "both mentor and mentee can go to" together. Another EST suggested potential benefits from more time to meet with other mentees who are teaching at the same grade level, because they might be struggling with similar issues that they could talk through.

For the most part, the ESTs were enthusiastic about the value of the mentorship program. They expressed how the mentorship relationships were "always beneficial" for "growth and ongoing learning," helping with "clarification" and offering "new perspectives." One EST said, "I'm grateful, it has been a wonderful experience." The ESTs who saw less value in the program were those who felt that they were matched with someone who had a different teaching approach, grade level, or held different expectations for the partnership.

## Conclusions

This study targeted the collection of data aimed at gaining insights into ESTs experiences with the mentoring component of a new division-wide induction and mentorship program. Detailed findings were presented that emerged from the analyses of the qualitative and quantitative data sets generated by the mentees. Data triangulation was undertaken to formulate conclusions and answer one core research question: "What are ESTs' experiences with mentoring using a formal learning partnership model?"

1. Formal individual mentoring was perceived to be a strong feature of the new two-year division-wide induction program by mentees. Most mentees found the experience valuable, and even more so by the end of year two.
2. Mentees developed trusting and effective working relationships with their mentors.

3. Mentees indicated that learning conversations with mentors focused mostly upon their professional needs; they were long enough to be valuable and afforded opportunities for challenges to be addressed and problems resolved.

4. Learning conversations were effectively organized and sufficient in number.

5. Dialogue and job-embedded learning allowed mentees to be assisted with: classroom management; gaining general pedagogical knowledge; accessing resources; planning for curriculum, teaching and learning; grant writing, and clarifying roles of support teachers.

6. Generally, mentees considered themselves well-matched with their mentors, but more so in year two. Survey and interview findings regarding pairings did not converge; mentees did not perceive their mentors' differing teaching assignments to be problematic when surveyed, but expression of issues with mismatches did emerge during interviews.

7. Two factors contributing to effective learning partnerships emerged during interviews—similar teaching assignments (e.g., grade level, program, school context, and curricular area) and physical proximity. Internal (same school) mentors offered accessibility and opportunities for spontaneous meetings, while external mentors offered increased confidentiality, safety, learning conversations, and program support.

8. Mentees reported having acquired and implemented new teaching strategies as a result of working formally with their mentors by the end of the program.

9. Mentees reported that they had improved significantly in their teaching practice as a result of working formally with their mentors by the end of the program.

10. Challenges identified by mentees included: meeting time with mentors; staying in close communication; mentors who shared their expertise rather than addressing mentee learning needs; discomfort with classroom observation by mentors; some lack of compatibility and problematic pairings (e.g., different teaching assignments, mentee with more teaching experience than mentor).

11. Mentees' suggestions for improving mentorship included: invite and recruit informal mentors or retired teachers into the program; promote the program to mentors and provide incentives, augment mentoring with job-alike CoPs; train mentors to focus on mentee needs, particularly those with more teaching experience; implement a questionnaire for optimal mentee-mentor matching; launch the program in the spring/summer; provide more meeting time, social gatherings, and shared workshop experiences; and, provide each mentee with an internal and external mentor.

## Recommendations

The important factors to consider when making mentoring matches are: subject or grade area expertise, proximity/accessibility, and shared context or circumstance. ESTs reported that there were informal mentors within division schools who could, and perhaps should, have been recruited into the program so they might have accessed mentorship training and support through the program. These more naturally emerging mentors were thought to have been well positioned to mentor ESTs and, in some cases, were already doing so. Both ESTs and these informal mentors would have benefited from having release time to meet together. Interestingly, Charles Coble (cited in Bouffard, 2013), an expert on teacher education and development, cautioned that, "There is growing recognition that general mentoring - the old approach of having a 'buddy down the hall'- isn't actually that effective" (p. 4). In contrast, Hallam and others (2012) found that in-school mentors were more effective than off-site coaches in supporting beginning teachers. Desimone and her colleagues (2013) took a more middle ground position and recommended that formal and informal mentors complement one another and so it was desirable to have both types within an induction program.

Research indicates that it is important to have subject-specific mentoring at the middle and senior years to provide optimal conditions for success (Desimone et al., 2014; Hallam et al., 2012; Harrison, Dymoke & Pell, 2006; Hobson, Ashby, Malderez & Tomlinson, 2009; Ingersoll & Smith, 2004; Smith & Ingersoll, 2004). Same subject partners were found to spend more time together and to focus more on professional pedagogical issues, which was an idea recommended for further examination in the next cycle of evaluation research for this program. In the new induction program, more mentees shared similar teaching assignments with their mentors in the second year of the program, but not all did. Mentees did not perceive different teaching assignments to be problematic, but this perspective was not supported by the research. Working towards subject-specific learning partners is recommended. Perhaps divisional meetings with school leaders could be targeted to recruit subject specific mentors. When subject specific mentors are not available, Desimone and her colleagues (2014) recommended connecting novice teachers informally with subject area specialists in schools or through the university.

In this induction program, a high number of mentor-mentee partners had different teaching assignments in the first year, which may have accounted for the substantive number of mentees who reportedly did not make significant improvements in their teaching practice. The mentoring component in this division-wide program is in place, at least in part, for the purpose of improving mentees' teaching effectiveness. Efforts to resolve matching issues in year two resulted in more mentees reporting improved teaching effectiveness, which was gratifying. It is recommended that the nature of the mentor-mentee pairings for which significant teaching improvements are observed, and the similarity of the pairs' teaching assignments, be monitored and examined further in future program evaluations. If teaching assignments are found to be similar where improved teaching effectiveness continues to be observed, these findings would lend even more support to the extant literature which suggests that if the goal of impacting mentees' teaching effectiveness is to be achieved, teaching assignments must be similar. It is important to take into consideration that some permanent teachers new to the division with access to this induction program were not first-year teachers and, therefore, they may not have experienced the same type of gains in teaching effectiveness as those with less experience may have reported. Research suggests that there is a steady rate of improvement among novice teachers, and after this period the rate of improvement slows (Hattie & Yates, 2013). The more experienced mentees in the program may have plateaued and not shown growth until the second year of the program. Reports of lower levels of improvement in inductees' teaching effectiveness could also have been due to not spending enough time together with advanced skills teachers, supported by evidence of mentees requesting more time with their mentors.

Leaders of the division-wide induction program should continue to make participation in the program optional for new permanent teachers with two or more years of teaching experience. More experienced teachers should be provided with a different kind of mentoring experience that recognizes their stage along a classroom practice developmental continuum (Australian Institute for Teaching and School Leadership, 2014). If funding is limited, inclusion for participation in the program should also be based upon newness to the profession.

In a recent large-scale study (Richter et al., 2013), constructivist approaches to mentoring facilitated by the program leaders were found to decrease teacher burnout while increasing teacher efficacy, job satisfaction, and enthusiasm of the program participants. Richter and others also found that mentoring based on critical reflection and collaboration, also used in constructivist approaches, increased teacher motivation and well-being. However, time for contact between mentors and mentees is recommended, as the same researchers found that those who receive constructivist mentoring need frequent guidance and contact.

In year two of this induction program, mentors were given clearer guidelines around the expected amount of contact time they were to have with their ESTs, and efforts will continue to keep requirements clear and provide more time for mentoring, as better results occurred. These changes are supported by a systematic literature review on induction (Totterdell et al., 2004) in which researchers found that the goals, participant roles, and purposes of the induction program must always be clear to participants. In addition, they found that it was critical for the program leaders to provide specific terms of engagement for those participating in induction programs (e.g., requirements for scheduled meetings, expectations for communication, codes of conduct, use of release time). We also recommend that the induction program begin earlier in the year to allow ample time for professional learning and improvement to occur.

Mentors should help new teachers to discover principles that guide practice and not just learn specific approaches (Wang & Odell, 2002). Other researchers characterized effective mentors as having the ability to provide reasonable challenges for mentees and supporting their ESTs' critical interrogation of practice (Smith & Ingersoll, 2004; Harrison et al., 2006; Hobson, et al., 2009). Based upon mentees' interview comments, mentors in the new induction program were focused on providing resources, teaching strategies, and materials, and so mentors should be encouraged to broaden the scope of their work with mentees.

Case study research completed by Piggot-Irvine and colleagues (2009) emphasized the importance of access to a "community" or "family" of professional support for inductees. Mentees in the learning partnerships did express this desire. The re-grouping of learning partners into job or interest-alike CoPs could be advantageous and add another layer of support for professional learning and development. Within CoPs, ESTs could also be taught how to mentor each other through peer conversations or peer coaching techniques (Kennedy, 2005; Rhodes & Beneicke, 2002). Recent research indicates the structure and purpose of the conversation seem to be more important than having an expert facilitating the conversation (Smith, 2014). In essence, the suggestion from these inductees was that involvement in a CoP would be "value added" to their experience with a learning partner.

In summary, evidence suggests that the WSD's new two-year induction and mentoring program is effective and valued by mentees. However, the conclusions are limited by the methods used, being based solely upon mentees' self-reported survey data and comments describing their experiences. Like other studies on teacher induction, these findings would be more convincing if coupled with student improvement achievement data and observational data showing improved teacher practice, which we recommend in future study designs, as do other scholars (Strong, 2009). Despite the limitations, there are several positive indicators that the new two-year induction program employing the learning partnership mentoring model does make a positive difference in the professional lives of early service teachers.

# References

Achinstein, B., & Athanases, S. Z. (Eds.). (2006). *Mentors in the making: Developing new leaders for new teachers*. New York, NY: Teachers College Press.

Adams, B., & Woods, A. (2015). A model for recruiting and retaining teachers in Alaska's K-12 schools. *Peabody Journal of Education, 90*(2), 250–262.

Australian Institute for Teaching and School Leadership. (2014). Retrieved from: http://www.aitsl.edu.au/docs/default-source/default-document-library/classrooom_practice_continuum

Bouffard, S. (2013, September/October). Getting serious about induction. *Harvard Education Letter, 29*(5), 1-3. Retrieved from http://mdk12.msde.maryland.gov/instruction/teacher_induction/pdf/Harvard_Education_Letter_Induction.pdf

Creswell, J. W., & Plano Clark, V. L. (2007). Designing and conducting mixed methods research. Thousand Oaks, CA: SAGE.

Croft, A., Coggshall, J. G., Dolan, M., Powers, E., & Killion, J. (2010). *Job-embedded professional development: What is it, who is responsible, and how to get it done well.* Washington, DC: National Comprehensive Center for Teacher Quality. Retrieved from: http://learningforward.org/docs/pdf/jobembeddedpdbrief.pdf?sfvrsn=0

Darling-Hammond, L. (2005). Developing professional development schools: Early lessons, challenge, and promise. In L. Darling-Hammond (Ed.), *Professional development schools: Schools for developing a profession* (2nd ed., pp. 1–27). New York, NY: Teachers College Press.

Darling-Hammond, L., Berry, B. T., Haselkorn, D., & Fideler, E. (1999). Teacher recruitment, selection, and induction. In L. Darling-Hammond & G. Sykes (Eds.), *Teaching as the learning profession: Handbook of policy and practice* (pp. 183–232). San Francisco, CA: Jossey-Bass.

Desimone, L. M., Hochberg, E. D., Porter, A. C., Polikoff, M. S., Schwartz, R., & Johnson, L. J. (2013). Formal and informal mentoring: Complementary, compensatory, or consistent? *Journal of Teacher Education, 65,* 88–110. doi: 10.1177/0022487113511643

Education Services Australia. (2014). *Looking at classroom practice.*

Feiman-Nemser, S. (2001). From preparation to practice: Designing a continuum to strengthen and sustain teaching. *Teachers College Record, 103*(6), 1013–1055.

Fresko, B., & Nasser-Abu Alhija, F. (2015). Induction seminars as professional learning communities for beginning teachers. *Asia-Pacific Journal of Teacher Education, 43*(1), 36–48.

Hallam, P. R., Chou, P. N., Hite, J., M., & Hite, S. J. (2012). Two contrasting models for mentoring as they affect retention of beginning teachers. *NASSP Bulletin, 96*(3), 243–287.

Harrison, J., Dymoke, S., & Pell, T. (2006) Mentoring beginning teachers in secondary schools: An analysis of practice. *Teaching and Teacher Education, 22*(8), 1055–1067.

Hattie, J., & Yates, G. (2013). *Visible learning and the science of how we learn.* New York, NY: Routledge.

Hendricks, C. (2009). *Improving schools through action research: A comprehensive guide for educators* (2nd ed.). Upper Saddle River, NJ: Pearson.

Herr, K., & Anderson, G. L. (2015). *The action research dissertation: A guide for students and faculty* (2nd ed.). Los Angeles, CA: SAGE.

Hesse-Biber, S. N., & Leavy, P. (2011). *The practice of qualitative research* (2nd ed.). Thousand Oaks, CA: SAGE.

Hobson, A. J., Ashby, P., Malderez, A., & Tomlinson, P. D. (2009). Mentoring beginning teachers: What we know and we don't. *Teaching and Teacher Education, 25,* 207–216.

Howe, E. R. (2006). Exemplary teacher induction: An international review. *Educational Philosophy and Theory, 38*(3), 287–297.

Ingersoll, R. M., & Smith, T. M. (2004). *Do teacher induction and mentoring matter? NASSP Bulletin, 88*(638), 28–40.

Ingersoll, R. M., & Strong, T. M. (2011). The impact of induction and mentoring programs for beginning teachers: A critical review of the research. *Review of Educational Research, 81*(2), 201–233. DOI: 10.3102/0034654311403323

Kennedy, A. (2005). Models of continuing professional development: A framework for analysis. *Journal of In-Service Education*, 31(2), 235–250.

Lipton, L., Wellman, B., & Humbard, C. (2003). *Mentoring matters: A practical guide to learning-focused relationships* (2nd ed.). Sherman, CT: Mira Via.

Morgan, D. L. (2014). *Integrating qualitative and quantitative methods: A pragmatic approach.* Thousand Oaks, CA: SAGE.

McNiff, J., & Whitehead, J. (2011). *All you need to know about action research* (2nd ed.). Los Angeles, CA: SAGE.

Piggot-Irvine, E., Aitken, H., Ritchie, J., Ferguson, P. B., & McGrath, F. (2009) Induction of newly qualified teachers in New Zealand. *Asia-Pacific Journal of Teacher Education, 37*(2), 175–198.

Rhodes, C., & Beneicke, S. (2002). Coaching, mentoring and peer-networking: Challenges for the management of teacher professional development in schools. *Journal of In-Service Education, 28*(2), 297–310.

Richter, D., Kunter, M., Ludtke, O. Klusman, U., Anders, V., & Baumert, J. (2013). How different mentoring approaches affect beginning teachers' development in the first years of practice. *Teaching and Teacher Education, 36,* 166–177.

Smith, C. (2014). *Developing teacher leaders for social justice: Building agency through community, critical reflection and action research.* Doctoral Dissertation, University of Manitoba.

Smith, T. M., & Ingersoll, R. M. (2004). What are the effects of induction and mentoring on beginning teacher turnover? *American Educational Research Journal, 41*(3), 681–714. doi: 10.1016/j.tate.2008.09.001

Stringer, E. (2008). *Action research in education* (2nd ed.). Upper Saddle River, NJ: Pearson/Merrill Prentice Hall.

Strong, M. (2009). *Effective teacher induction and mentoring: Assessing the evidence.* New York, NY: Teachers College Press.

Teddlie, C., & Tashakkori, A. (2009). *Foundations of mixed methods research: Integrating quantitative and qualitative approaches in the social and behavioral sciences.* Thousand Oaks, CA: SAGE.

Totterdell M., Woodroffe L., Bubb S., & Hanrahan K. (2004). *The impact of NQT induction programmes on the enhancement of teacher expertise, professional development, job satisfaction or retention rates: A systematic review of research on induction.*. London, UK: EPPI-Centre, Social Science Research Unit, Institute of Education. Retrieved from http://www.eppi.ioe.ac.uk/cms/Default.aspx?tabid=307

Villani, S. (2002). *Mentoring programs for new teachers: Models of induction and support.* Thousand Oaks, CA: Corwin Press.

Wang, J., & Odell, S.J. (2002). Mentored learning to teaching according to standards-based reform: A critical review. *Review of Educational Research, 72*(3), 481–546.

## Endnotes

1    The Induction and Mentorship Program in Winnipeg School Division became a reality through the vision and leadership of Pauline Clarke, (former Inner City District Superintendent), the current Chief Superintendent. Funding for the three-year pilot phase of the program (2008-2011) came from the school division, The Winnipeg Foundation and Manitoba Education and Advanced Learning. Currently, the program is administered through the Human Resources Department of the school division. Induction is a first step of an employee's learning pathway and career in Winnipeg School Division.

## Chapter 17

# Positive Impacts of an Induction-Through-Mentoring Model of New Teacher Mentorship: Perceptions of Beginning Teachers in Saskatchewan Rural Schools

*Laurie-Ann M. Hellsten, Lynn Lemisko, Carol L. Demchuk-Kosolofski, Tracy D. Dollansky*

## Introduction

Retention of beginning teachers is of particular concern (Ingersoll, 2001) because the teaching profession tends to have a higher turnover rate than that of most other professions (Carroll & Fulton, 2004; Ferriter & Norton, 2004). Although most beginning teachers are optimistic, idealistic (Martin, Chiodo, & Chang, 2001) and feel prepared for their first year of teaching (McPherseon, 2000), the majority are surprised by their initiation into the profession (Simurda, 2004) and are at increased risk for dropping out of the teaching profession within their first three to seven years (Karsenti & Collin, 2013). Estimated rates of beginning teacher resignation range between 20 and 50% during the first three to five years (Villani, 2002; Voke, 2002). Early experiences shape beginning teachers for the rest of their careers (Moir & Gless, 2001), and have implications for teacher effectiveness and career length (McCormack & Thomas, 2003).

As teachers typically require five to eight years of experience to master the profession (Scherer, 2001), classrooms have the potential to become recurrent training grounds, as teachers leave before becoming experts only to be replaced by novices. In addition to leaving the profession entirely, significant numbers of beginning teachers move away from rural schools to suburban schools upon obtaining relevant teaching experience (Ingersoll

& Merrill, 2010). This cyclical turnover has been demonstrated to have a significant negative impact on student achievement that stretches beyond individual teachers and classrooms (Ronfelddt, Loeb, & Wyckoff, 2013), with students ultimately bearing the true cost of teacher attrition (Karsenti & Collin, 2013). In order to ensure that beginning teachers succeed, we need to induct beginning teachers into a system of support, mentorship, collaboration (Howe, 2008) and continued growth and learning (Carroll, 2005).

With these experiences in mind, approaches to beginning teacher induction have become an issue of special concern in rural school divisions in Saskatchewan, where new teacher migration and teacher wellness are continuing challenges. The purpose of this study was to examine the impact of an induction-through-mentoring model of beginning teacher mentorship on novice teachers working in the Saskatchewan rural context. More specifically, this study focused on the *bliss*, or the positive impacts, resulting from an induction-through-mentorship model that paired master teacher mentors and beginning teacher mentees, with a focus on collaboration in the beginning teachers' schools and classrooms. We focused our investigation by addressing the following overarching question: *What impact does a model of providing release time for mentor teachers to work one-to-one with beginning teachers in their classrooms have on beginning teachers?* We posited that the induction-through-mentorship model would create collaborative relationships that, in turn, would provide co-learning and supportive professional development for both the beginning teachers and their mentors.

## Review of Related Literature

Induction involves the processes through which the teaching community acculturates beginning teachers, and usually refers to structured programs (Wong, 2004; Wong, Britton, & Ganser, 2005) that vary across schools or divisions (Luft, Roehrig, & Patterson, 2003). Induction programs are usually designed to counteract beginning teacher attrition and to positively impact new teacher experiences by increasing commitment to the profession, enhancing teacher effectiveness and satisfaction and by improving classroom instruction and student achievement (Glazerman et al., 2010). Although most beginning teacher induction programs include some aspect of mentorship (Ingersoll & Smith, 2003), a recent international review suggested that mentoring was only one component of a comprehensive induction program (Kutsyuruba, Godden, Covell, Matheson, & Walker, 2016).

Mentorship is typically thought of as a formal assigned relationship involving "one-to-one support of a novice or less experienced practitioner (mentee) by a more experienced practitioner (mentor)" (Hobson, Ashby, Malderez, & Tomlinson, 2009, p. 207). However, the composition of mentorship programs varies widely (Ingersoll & Smith, 2003), and many models of mentorship exist, including the apprenticeship model (Hargreaves, 1988), the nurturing process model (Anderson & Shannon, 1988), educative mentoring (Feiman-Nemser, 2001), peer mentorship (Cornu, 2005), mentorship via professional learning communities (Glazer & Hannafin, 2006; Prytula et al., 2010), and the Adaptive Mentorship (AM) model (Ralph & Walker, 2014).

Regardless of which mentorship model is employed, research has demonstrated the effectiveness of mentorship programs (Algozzine, Gretes, Queen, & Cowan-Hathcock, 2007; Carter & Francis, 2001; Darling-Hammond, 2003; Serpell, 2000), and the ability of these to improve teacher quality, which, in turn, has been considered to be one of the best predictors of student success (Davis & Higdon, 2008). However, the effectiveness of induction programs involving beginning teacher mentorship has been found to vary across settings (e.g., urban-rural; Ingersoll & Strong, 2011). Beginning teachers in rural or remote communities face different challenges than do beginning teachers in urban or suburban schools (McCracken & Miller, 1988). For example, "because of the small size of rural districts and schools, teachers often need to teach multiple subjects and possibly multiple grades, sometimes in multi-grade, mixed-age classrooms" (Barley, 2009, p. 10). The need for beginning teacher mentoring may be "even more critical for teachers beginning their careers in rural schools and communities, especially for individuals with limited experiences in these settings" (Fry & Anderson, 2011, p. 12).

Mentorship programs may also be limited by lack of funds (Carver & Feiman-Nemser, 2009) and may frequently be challenged by issues such as how to best match mentors to mentees, the lack of willing or able mentors, the lack of mentor training (Johnson & Kardos, 2005), and increased mentor workloads (Lee & Feng, 2007; Simpson, Hastings, & Hill, 2007). Despite knowing much about the benefits of mentorship for new teachers, much less is known about the impact of mentorship specifically for beginning teachers employed in rural locations.

## Context of the Study

Two important specific challenges exist with respect to implementing induction programs and beginning teacher mentorship in the Province of Saskatchewan. First, unlike other Canadian provinces, Saskatchewan does not currently have a provincially-mandated beginning teacher induction program, nor does the Province have targeted government funding for beginning teacher induction programs. The Saskatchewan Teachers' Federation does provide beginning Saskatchewan teachers with resources, an orientation, and a handbook that is designed to provide suggestions about how components, such as mentoring, should be delivered (Saskatchewan Teachers' Federation). However, no ongoing and direct assistance has been offered to all individual beginning teachers in the Province. This means that beginning teacher mentorship programs, when they do indeed exist, vary widely between school divisions in Saskatchewan (Hellsten, Prytula, Ebanks, & Lai, 2009).

Second, the Saskatchewan context includes a significant proportion of rural or remote schools. Of the 721 provincially funded schools located across the 28 school divisions in Saskatchewan, just over half ($n$=371) are considered rural schools, another 23 are considered northern schools, and the remaining 327 are considered urban schools. According to Fry and Anderson (2011, p. 12), "barriers to providing quality mentoring are compounded in rural areas."

## Methodology

### Induction-Through-Mentoring Model

Although different mentorship models have been proposed for use with beginning teachers, none of the existing models focused on the beginning teacher's classroom. Hence, we decided to develop our own induction-through-mentorship model of beginning teacher mentorship, which evolved over time and in response to the specific requests of our rural school division partners.

For example, our school division partners agreed that both the mentees and the mentors would need to volunteer to participate in our program. It was also particularly important that the focus of the model was the beginning teachers' classroom because of our partners' belief that beginning teachers needed to remain in their classrooms as much as possible. In addition, we were asked to work within a context of rurality and potentially considerable distances between schools, as well as small schools with multigrade classrooms and "departments of one" in secondary schools. Lastly, we needed a model flexible enough to accommodate and augment existing new teacher induction programs that were underway in each school division. Such induction programs mainly consisted of workshop and orientation meetings conducted on topics deemed important to each school division. In developing our model, we also tried to follow recommendations put forward in the literature as well as recommendations stemming from a review of existing mentorship programs in Saskatchewan, including: making formal mentorship programs a priority in education, providing release time for regularly scheduled meetings, providing opportunities for classroom visits, and providing training to the mentors (Olafson, Elaschuk & Owens, 2002).

Our induction-through-mentorship model provided beginning teachers with the support of volunteer experienced master teacher mentors. Mentor training and mentee-mentor orientations were made possible via partnerships between the College of Education at the University of Saskatchewan and the school divisions. Release time for mentors to visit mentee classrooms and for training and orientation were made possible through external funding from the McDowell Foundation.

## Participants

This study involved year-long case studies of our induction-by-mentoring model over a three year period, conducted in two different rural school divisions in Saskatchewan. Altogether, there were thirteen beginning-teacher/mentor-teacher pairings (four pairings in year one, four in year two, and five in year three). Pairs in years one and two worked in elementary, middle years and secondary classrooms in a rural school division located near a larger urban centre in Saskatchewan. To reduce travel costs and increase time in classrooms, every effort was made to select pairings based on proximity. Because the divisional definition of 'beginning teachers' not only included those who were in their first or second years of their careers, but also those who were new to the school division and those in new roles within the division, several beginning teacher participants in the first year of the project actually had several years of teaching experience.

In contrast, the five pairs participating in the year three study worked in elementary classrooms in a large rural school division where most schools were located at great distances from one another and where divisional offices were located in a town over an hour away from any large urban centre in Saskatchewan. All year three participants were female. In all but one of the pairs, mentees and mentors taught at the same grade or grade cluster level. In two of the pairings, both mentee and mentor taught in the same school. The matching of the remaining mentees/mentors resulted in two pairings where the time to drive between locations was approximately thirty to forty-five minutes one way, and one pairing where the mentor and mentee were at a substantial distance from each other - at least a ninety minute drive, one way. Most mentors were mid-career teachers; while one mentor was retiring at the end of the project year. All of the mentees participating in the third year of our project were in their first or second year of their careers (those in their second year indicated that they were on their first full year contract); none of the mentees possessed multiple years of teaching experience.

## Data Collection and Analysis

Following ethical clearance from both the institution and the partner school divisions, recruitment of potential mentors, mentees and the matching of the pairs were conducted in conjunction with the school division partners. In each year of the project, mentorship training was offered in early fall for the master teachers. In addition, a retreat for both the mentors and mentees was organized, where the mentors and mentees met in person and began to build their collegial relationships. From October through May, the mentors spent at least two half-days per month in their mentee's school/classroom. On occasion, depending on the pair, the mentee visited the mentor's classroom. Classroom experiences took a variety of forms including observations, co-teaching, and coaching.

Focus groups of about an hour, and individual interviews between thirty and forty-five minutes in length, were conducted with all participants in the spring, with the aid of a digital recording device. Focus groups and interviews were scripted with questions co-constructed by members of the research team and the school divisions involved. Transcription of the focus groups and interviews were conducted by a neutral third party, and thematic analysis was used to identify repeated patterns of meaning (Braun & Clarke, 2006). We attempted to ensure that the coding of the transcripts and the interpretations made from the codes were constructed from the raw data contained in the transcribed responses to the interview questions (Boyatzis, 1998).

# Findings

As related to the benefits of an induction-through-mentoring model for beginning teachers in rural Saskatchewan, our analysis of the transcriptions revealed one overarching repeated pattern, The Mentor-Mentee Relationship, and the connected themes, Teaching and Learning, and Mental Health and Wellness (see Figure 1). The theme Teaching and Learning consisted of three sub-themes: Learning Routines and Logistics, Honing Practice, and Collaboration and Co-Learning. The theme Mental Health and Wellness was also comprised of two sub-themes: Developing Perspective and Obtaining Emotional Support.

These themes are discussed below and are supported by illustrative quotes from the interviews and focus groups, each one typical of the majority of participants. Care was taken that the quotes represented both positive and negative views of the beginning teachers' experience. However, other than being referred to as 'mentor' or 'mentee', participant quotes are not individually identified in order to protect the identity of the participants.

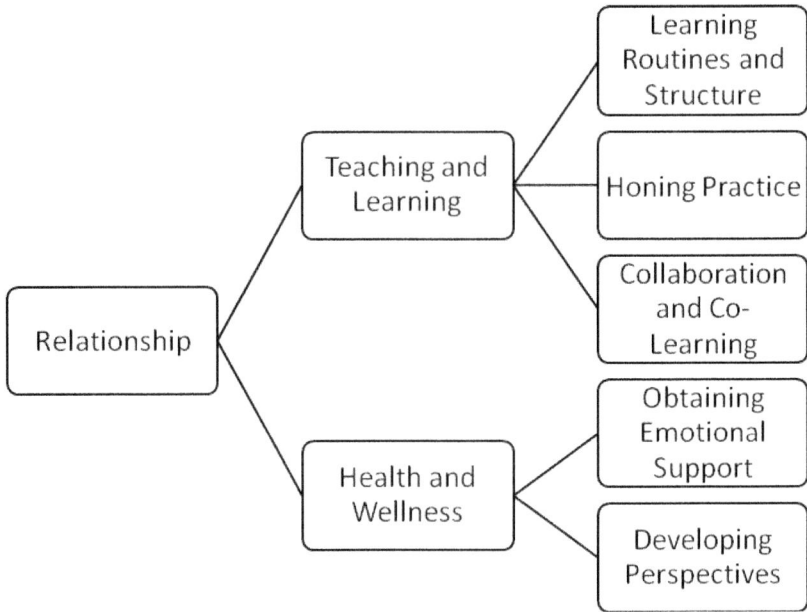

*Figure 1.* Results of Thematic Analysis. Positive Impacts of an Induction-Through-Mentoring Model of New Teacher Mentorship as Perceived by Beginning Teachers and Mentors in Saskatchewan Rural Schools.

**The Mentor-Mentee Relationship**

The mentorship program provided each mentee with a designated mentor or a professional 'friend' who could be relied on and who was available to provide advice via email, phone, or in-person. As one beginning teacher stated:

> My first year of teaching I was petrified. I felt very much alone in my staff ... everybody's busy in a school. You don't really want to be asking too much of somebody else in the school. Everybody's already kind of got a full plate. So having that person [mentor] there that was- I knew that was part of her job was to support me- And to help me, so I knew I could go to her.

Another mentee noted that,

> it's nice to be able to bounce those ideas off each other. It's been great just to have someone with so much more experience to chat with ...

... like she helps me so much in so many different ways. It's crazy to think how I would have gotten through this first year without her. Just having that face-to-face contact and really building that relationship and being able to go out after school with [mentor], both professionally and personally ... I just think that this program was really beneficial to me and I gained a really great colleague and a great friend outside of school.

Mentors also stated the importance of the mentor-mentee relationship: "I think for us, like our relationship building was the greatest thing for ourselves."

Mentorship as a way to network and build relationships with colleagues teaching similar grades or content areas was identified as particularly important for beginning teachers who worked in small rural schools. One mentee described her school and teaching context: "I'm teaching in a very small school with three multi-grades and there's only two and a half teachers at our school."

One mentor observed:

[The mentorship program] gives you that extra contact... Someone that's working in a similar field, in a similar maybe size of school or whatever it happens to be because in schools like this as a math department or a science department you're fairly isolated in your work. I mean I am the math department from grade nine to twelve, right? There's a bio teacher so like the two of us together are the science department. For some [schools], there's not a whole lot of people that you can actually talk to or ask questions, content-specific questions.

One of the mentees also spoke to the positive impact mentors can have in a rural division.

[The program] connected me to somebody who I could talk to other than, you know, if I was in a bigger school where there were other [grade alike] teachers then it wouldn't be as hard. But I didn't have that person to turn to within my school. But I found it to be beneficial in the fact that I was able to connect with people that had knowledge in my grade level because I think that's really important.

Both mentors and mentees indicated their appreciation of technologies that helped them to keep in touch and, in particular, for the face-to-face collaboration opportunities. The importance of the use of email to consult became very evident for both mentors and mentees. As one mentee suggested:

> I just email whenever something comes up. I email her and say, "Hey this is the story. What do you suggest or what do I do from here?" And that's probably been the most helpful for me is that she's just really fast at getting back to me.

Although both mentors and mentees used technology to keep in touch, in-person relationships were very important.

> I like the face-to-face. Actually sitting with somebody and talking. I guess if relationships are the most important factor, which I think they probably are, I don't think you can develop that over Skype or over the internet or even emails. It's not the same.

Based on participant voices, it was evident that the mentor-mentee relationships were valued by both mentors and mentees. Having a designated mentor or a person to whom the mentee felt comfortable to seek out and ask questions (whether in-person or online) was of great importance to mentees.

## Learning Routines and Logistics

Given that beginning teachers are recent graduates of teacher education programs, they were generally familiar with the processes and big ideas related to teaching and learning (e.g., subject area curriculum and lesson and unit planning). However they may not have been familiar with particular 'little things' like daily routines, classroom management and expectations in their schools. For example, one mentee alluded to ways in which she had learned about routines and logistics when she commented:

> .... we're having an assembly tomorrow. That means we wait to get called down or you line up and you sit here; [its] all those little things that you don't really think about until you've hopped into the teaching profession and are on your own, you

can really go to your mentor and just ask them, "How do you do this? And what kind of ideas do you have?"

Mentees also commented on how mentors helped them to be more organized. For example, "she's helped me make my classroom a little bit more efficient and organized." Another mentee noted that the mentor provided "classroom management ideas, just how to organize that crazy cupboard [and] some ideas on how to keep it simple."

One mentee indicated that she had knowledge about a particular instructional strategy, but that her mentor assisted her in understanding how to actually implement the approach. This beginning teacher stated:

> ... it really wasn't about the ability level or the skill level, it was more about the structure of the activity and how to keep it flowing in that classroom management side.

Mentees were not all at the same place or stage. Mentees spoke of learning about the culture of the school – the basic but necessary routines.

> I think that I never really realized how much teachers did behind the scenes coming out of my internship. So, I guess that was maybe an assumption that I had was that 'I did my internship, I'm almost there' kind of thing. But then what I found difficult was the paper work or the meetings and the outside-of-school stuff. And then she was kind of there to help me through ...

In addition, beginning teachers may not have experienced living and working in rural communities and may not have grown up in the rural community where they are teaching. Even when beginning teachers have experience living in rural communities, such experiences did not always generalize to new communities. As one mentor in our study reflected:

> I've always understood that different schools are different. Spending a day out at [name of school] was interesting because it is a very different style of school than any other school that I've been in before.

One mentee elaborated on one of the cultural differences between urban/suburban schools and their rural school:

> It's very different from here [rural school] in the sense that you need to connect with your students. You need to have a bond with them. I was totally surprised when I was at an awards night and I saw a kid hug a teacher. And I was like, "That's not allowed."

Mentees commented on ways they learned about the daily routines and logistics of school life through their relationships with their mentors.

### Honing Practice

Several mentees indicated they had not needed support regarding policies, classroom management, or in establishing of day-to-day routines and seemed to be strong with respect to the 'craft' of teaching (lesson planning, etc.). However, these mentees wanted assistance in honing their practice, including fine-tuning their instructional approaches, feeling secure in risk-taking and enhancing their ability to attend to individual learners.

> This basically was an opportunity for me to have some planning time with a master teacher just to sit down and ask the questions and how do we achieve those goals of the division in the most effective way? And being given the time to have someone to work with and plan with and bounce ideas off of and get ideas from ... When he came to me and said, "You know just take something that you're interested in and make it work within the curricular objectives." - that completely switched in my mind.

One of our mentors spoke to the impact the induction-through-mentoring project had had on his mentee:

> The biggest thing was just for him [mentee] to - I guess for me to re-affirm that what he was doing was good, was strong. He wasn't sure how things were going. But he's very strong for this stage in his career so I think he just needed a confidence booster. With [mentee's name] it was like he already had the building blocks in place. He wanted refinement. He just wanted to polish things up.

In contrast, one of our mentors who had started the project working with a mentee with three years of teaching experience was asked to take on a second mentee late in the project year - a first year teacher who had obtained a contract in February of the year. The mentor reported that experiences with the two mentees were hugely different and thought that the biggest impact of the mentoring would be felt by first-year mentees.

> With [mentee's name] it's been very different because she's treading water. It's a terrible situation. You know you're dropped in this new school, new curricula ... You really need an experienced teacher to walk in and share a tool box. So, with [mentee's name], it's not about student engagement. It's not about big picture stuff. You know this is survival. This is just keep your mouth and nose above water.

Regardless of the years of experience our mentees possessed, mentees in our study unanimously indicated that participation in the mentoring study had a positive impact on their teaching experiences.

## Collaboration and Co-Learning

Collaboration and co-learning was one sub-theme that had positive impact for both the mentors and mentees because co-learning for both mentors and mentees meant professional growth for both. One mentor commented:

> I would say it [mentorship] was beneficial. I think any time you talk to another teacher about teaching and learning it's a two-way street, even if one is more experienced than the other.

A mentee concurred:

> I just feel like this [mentorship] is more of a - there's that colleagueto colleague type vibe. Like maybe more of a mutual respect.

Mentees and mentors who participated in our study were clear that they were able to learn and grow together within their collaborative relationship. This was also highlighted by both the beginning teachers and their mentors in their comments about how they worked together to implement a new divisional initiative. For instance, mentors observed:

> We started working on blended math because we're in the same grade ... it was more collaborative.

We were able to actually just create it [blended math] together because she wasn't sure of what it was too. So we kind of learned together.

... it's still good to have those conversations and see what struggles she's run into, what struggles I have run into and then just have conversations about how we can improve it.

Beginning teacher mentees made similar comments regarding the benefits of collaborative co-learning as they worked toward implementation of the divisional initiative:

... it's been nice to work with [mentor's name] to create a course or to start creating a course that's specifically grade blended ...

It's nice that they're also learning it with us so it's not like we're just new to the thing. ... To have those conversations really about what's working, what isn't.

It was evident that both beginning teachers and mentors benefited from the opportunities for co-learning that arose through engagement in the mentorship program. Both groups experienced enhanced professional growth through collaborative co-learning and both mentors and mentees experienced enhanced feelings of connectedness.

## Obtaining Emotional Support

Participants highlighted the idea that their mentoring relationship proved to be as important in its offering of personal support as it was for offering professional assistance. Mentors were clear in their understandings of this, explicitly noting: "Mental health is just as important as the academics. And you cannot deliver those academics properly if you're not mentally healthy."

Another mentor elaborated:

[As a mentor] I feel for the success of a beginning teacher – it's the emotional as opposed to the actual content. Because so many of them [beginning teachers], they're perfectly competent to plan a lesson, to plan units. But it's the emotional, they can't handle the stressors, they can't handle the frustrations, the disappointments that can come.

A third mentor confirmed the need for mentors to provide support and nurturing:

> It's all about being able to look in their eyes and know they've just had a run in with a parent and they need that venting time. I think where new teachers struggle a little bit is in more of the social... more of the hearing 'it's okay.'

The mentees also spoke of the emotional support mentors provided them. From the perspective of the mentee:

> ... we were able to talk more about professional things but it was nice having that, I guess I felt comfortable going to her about those issues and she would follow up you know – 'I hope you're having a better day today, don't worry things will get better.'

The beginning teacher mentees clearly benefited from the fact that their mentors understood their need for personal support. Based on the comments, it was obvious that mentees received the needed emotional support from their mentors.

## Developing Perspective

Beginning teachers often engaged so intensely in their work that they experienced negative effects to their well-being. Participating mentees noted that the advice offered by their mentors had helped to develop perspective and set realistic expectations; which, in turn, reduced stress and enhanced wellness. In addition, some mentors provided mentees with a sense of protection from the demands put on them by self, other teachers and the community. To illustrate, one beginning teacher commented on how she followed the advice of her mentor who had suggested:

> ... basically set your work hours and don't work beyond them... never be at the school past five; focus on what's important. If it's not going to make or break your day then don't worry about it; make sure you're home by five o'clock so that you have that time to yourself.

Mentees also noted that they had derived benefit from mentors who had advised them that, 'It's okay to fail and try again', that teaching does not require 'perfection' (nor can we expect everything to go perfectly) and that there was no need to feel guilty when things didn't turn out as planned. For example, one beginning teacher ruminated on her reaction to the support she received through conversation with her mentor:

> ... to be able to reflect and just say, you know what I just am not there yet and I just need to calmly work my way in. I think just that whole calmness and ability to just say, like [she] said – it's okay if I didn't get that done, or it's okay if that lesson bombed ... I just have to calmly figure out how I'm going to do it.

Another mentee commented: "I can see for my first-year teaching, okay this is normal, this is what happens and I don't have to stress so much about that."

Mentors can also stand between the beginning teacher mentee and the pressures for performance applied by self, other teachers and the community. Beginning teachers often faced unrealistic expectations regarding extracurricular commitments, and took on more than their fair share to demonstrate their professional commitment. These pressures may have been particularly intense in rural communities where new teachers, without the experience of small town life, felt vulnerable and exposed to the intensity and persistence of local scrutiny. For example, a participating mentee observed:

> ... when you are moving from maybe the city to the small town, you've never lived in a small town, you never had had 800 sets of eyes looking at everything you're doing all the time. That's where I think so much of the uncertainty comes from, and therefore the feeling of burning out or the feeling of unsureness comes.

Mentors were quick to point out that they believed they should protect mentees from the pressure of such expectations, noting: "Help as much as you can, but, oh boy, staffs are terrible for going, "oh let's let the new one without kids do it." Similarly, another mentor commented:

> ... as a mentor, to give that strength and confidence to the mentees to say no, don't overwhelm yourself ... You have to be a community member in your school, but first and

foremost these first couple years you need to figure out your classroom, who you are as a teacher.

It was apparent that mentees had benefited from the mentoring relationship because mentors stood as a protective barrier between mentees and the pressures to perform exerted by the beginning teachers themselves, as well as by teacher colleagues and the wider community.

## Discussion

Our study found that the induction-through-mentorship model created collaborative relationships between beginning teachers and experienced mentor teachers working in rural contexts in Saskatchewan. These relationships provided opportunities for beginning teachers to learn the routines and logistics of their schools and divisions and to hone their practice. We also found that our collaborative model did provide co-learning opportunities for both the beginning teachers and their mentors. The mentors provided beginning teachers with a sense of perspective and emotional support which increased beginning teacher wellness.

The results of our study are not unique. Findings from other studies have suggested that mentoring may be the most effective form of supporting the professional development of beginning teachers (e.g., Carter & Francis, 2001; Marable & Raimondi, 2007). Many benefits of beginning teacher mentorship have been documented, including reduced feelings of isolation, increased confidence and self-esteem, professional growth, and improved self-reflection and problem solving capacities (McIntyre & Hagger, 1996). Beginning teachers tend to perceive induction and mentoring programs positively when they have felt supported from their mentors (Kutsyuruba et al., 2016).

Mentors have also been implicated in helping beginning teachers to adapt to the expectations associated with teaching and with the cultural norms of specific school communities (Bullough & Draper, 2004; Wang & Odell, 2002). This may be a particularly important mentor contribution for beginning teachers working in unfamiliar rural communities. Research has demonstrated the importance of taking into account the geographic remoteness and the established existing faculty social networks of rural school communities (Barley, 2009).

Thus, "mentoring appears to be a preferred support mechanism [for beginning teachers] as it draws upon the expertise of existing school staff" (Hudson, 2012, p. 71). However, in rural divisions, appropriate mentors may not be available from existing school staff. Future research needs to continue to examine how induction-through-mentoring can be efficacious, sustainable, and practical despite the lengthy distances that can exist between mentors and mentees in rural locations.

Teachers often struggle with finding a healthy balance in their lives (Naylor, 2001) and need support in enhancing their personal wellness to enhance energy levels, resiliency and job satisfaction (Pelletier, 1994). We originally posited that mentorship could enhance beginning teachers' wellness by helping to provide a positive, supportive community where teachers feel noticed, valued, challenged, and cherished (Cherkowski & Walker, 2014). Similar to the findings of Hudson (2012), beginning teachers and mentors in our study recognized the need for better personal-work balance. The emotional and psychological support provided by mentors to beginning teachers has been demonstrated to boost beginning teacher self-confidence, provide perspective, and increase morale and job satisfaction (Bullough, 2005; Johnson, Berg, & Donaldson, 2005; Lindgren, 2005; Marable & Raimondi, 2007). As noted above, while we were particularly interested in the issue of the positive impacts of mentors on mentees working in a rural context, teacher retention was insufficient as an end goal. We think new teacher induction programs and processes need to look beyond retention and toward support for flourishing. The notion of 'flourishing', as it relates to teachers and teaching, has only recently been under study (Cherkowski & Walker, 2014).

However, despite these findings, there were limitations to our study. First, our study findings were limited to thirteen mentor-mentee pairings from two rural school divisions in one province. The findings and recommendations we identified may not be generalizable to other school divisions, other rural contexts, or other provinces. Although we know that context matters with respect to the effectiveness of induction programs (Ingersoll & Strong, 2011), and that rural conditions themselves can vary greatly between communities (Barley, 2009), our study highlights the continuing need to examine what works and what will be sustainable with respect to mentoring and induction in rural contexts.

In addition, our study was limited to examining the mentor-mentee experiences across one school year, and longer follow-up of the same mentor-mentee pairings would be helpful in determining the efficacy of the beginning teacher mentorship program for sustaining and retaining beginning teachers in the long-term. Lastly, our study focused on one particular method of beginning teacher mentorship - that of the mentor being embedded in the beginning teachers' classroom. Other methods of mentorship may be as efficacious or even more efficacious for particular mentor-mentee pairings.

To address these limitations, we have planned ongoing research which will expand the study of beginning teacher mentorship in Saskatchewan to multiple and diverse First Nations schools and provincial school divisions, methods of mentoring, and a diverse range of teachers.

This research arose out of our partnership work within the broader teaching community. Together with these partners, we arranged the Saskatchewan New Teacher Mentorship Forum, which has been meeting since April 2015. During those meetings we were able to 1) engage in collaborative discussions among partners aimed at creating common understandings about mentorship; 2) draft a set of principle-driven beliefs regarding beginning teacher induction workshops and mentorship; and, 3) create an induction-through-mentorship conceptual framework based on these beliefs. We have also launched an additional research project that will provide extensive data for evidence-based decision-making and capacity-building in support of beginning teachers throughout the province. Together, with a network of supports from multiple stakeholders, we can develop and advance a province-wide teacher mentoring program in Saskatchewan with the goal of discussing our findings with the Saskatchewan Ministry of Education in hopes that they will consider partnering with school divisions, First Nations and universities in a larger New Teacher Mentorship Program.

# Acknowledgements

*We thank the McDowell Foundation for Research into Teaching for the support of this research. The time this funding provided for us to network and explore possibilities with mentors and mentees and for mentors and mentees to work with each other was extremely valuable. We especially thank the classroom teachers who volunteered to enter into their mentor/mentee relationships, and for their willingness to share their thinking about their experiences.*

# References

Algozzine, B., Gretes, J., Queen, A.J., & Cowan-Hathcock. M. (2007). Beginning teachers' perceptions of their induction program experiences. A Journal of Educational Strategies: Issues and Ideas, 80, 137–143.

Anderson, E.M., & Shannon, A.L. (1988). Toward a conceptualization of mentoring. *Journal of Teacher Education, 39*(1), 38–42.

Barley, Z.A. (2009). Preparing teachers for rural appointments: Lessons from the mid-continent. *The Rural Educator, 30*(3), 10–15.

Boyatzis, R.E. (1998). *Transforming qualitative information: Thematic analysis and code development.* Thousand Oaks, CA: Sage.

Braun, V., & Clarke, V. (2006). Using thematic analysis in psychology. *Qualitative Research in Psychology, 3*(2), 77–101.

Bullough, R.V. (2005). Being and becoming a mentor: School-based teacher educators and teacher educator identity. *Teaching and Teacher Education, 21,* 143–155.

Bullough, R.V., & Draper, R.J. (2004). Mentoring and the emotions. *Journal of Education for Teaching: International Research and Pedagogy, 30*(3), 271–288.

Carroll, D. (2005). Learning through interactive talk: A school-based mentor teacher study group as a context for professional learning. *Teaching and Teacher Education, 21,* 457–473.

Carroll, T., & Fulton, K. (2004). The true cost of teacher turnover. *Threshold, Spring,* 16-17.

Carter, M., & Francis, R. (2001). Mentoring and beginning teachers' workplace learning. *Asia-Pacific Journal of Teacher Education, 29,* 249–262.

Carver, C.L., & Feiman-Nemser, S. (2009). Using policy to improve teacher induction: Critical elements and missing pieces. *Educational Policy, 23*(2), 295–328. doi:10.1177/0895904807310036.

Cherkowski, S., & Walker, K. (2014). Flourishing communities: Re-storying educational leadership using positive research lens. *International Journal of Leadership in Education: Theory and Practice, 17*(2), 200–216.

Cornu, R.L. (2005) Peer mentoring: engaging pre-service teachers in mentoring one another, *Mentoring & Tutoring: Partnership in Learning, 13*(3), 355–366.

Darling-Hammond, L. (2003). Keeping good teachers: Why it matters, what leaders can do. *Educational Leadership, 60*, 6–13.

Davis, B., & Higdon, K. (2008). The effects of mentoring/induction support on beginning teachers' practices in early elementary classrooms (K-3). *Journal of Research In Childhood Education, 2*(3), 261–274.

Feiman-Nemser, S. (2001). Helping novices learn to teach: Lessons from an exemplary support teacher. *Journal of Teacher Education, 52*(1), 17–30.

Ferriter, W., & Norton, J. (2004). Creating a culture of excellence. Listening to the experts: Experienced teachers describe the school working conditions that most affect their decisions to stay or leave. *Threshold, Spring,* 18–21.

Fry, S.W., & Anderson, H. (2011). Career changers as first-year teachers in rural schools. *Journal of Research in Rural Education, 26*(12), 1–15. Retrieved from http://jrre.psu.edu/articles/26-12.pdf

Glazer, E., & Hannafin, M. (2006). The collaborative apprenticeship model: Situated professional development within school settings. *Teaching and Teacher Education, 22*(2), 179–193.

Glazerman, S., Isenberg, E., Dolfin, S., Bleeker, M., Johnson, A., Grider, M., & Jacobus, M. (2010). *Impacts of comprehensive teacher induction: Final results from a randomized controlled study (NCEE 2010-4027).* Washington, DC: National Center for Education Evaluation and Regional Assistance, Institute of Education Sciences, U.S. Department of Education.

Hargreaves, A. (1988). Teaching quality: A sociological analysis. *Journal of Curriculum Studies, 20*(3), 211–231.

Hellsten, L.M., Prytula, M.P., Ebanks, A., & Lai, H. (2009). Teacher induction: Exploring beginning teacher mentorship. *Canadian Journal of Education, 32*(4), 703–733.

Hobson, A., Ashby, P., Malderez, A., & Tomlinson, P.D. (2009). Mentoring beginning teachers: What we know and what we don't. *Teaching and Teacher Education, 25,* 207–216.

Howe, E.R. (2008). Teacher induction across the Pacific: A comparative study of Canada and Japan. *Journal of Education for Teaching, 34*(4), 333–346.

Hudson, P. (2012). How can schools support beginning teachers? A call for timely induction and mentoring for effective teaching. *Australian Journal of Teacher Education, 37*(7), 70–84.

Ingersoll, R.M. (2001). *Teacher turnover, teacher shortages and the organization of schools.* Seattle, WA: Center for the Study of Teaching and Policy, University of Washington.

Ingersoll, R. M., & Merrill, L. (2010). Who's teaching our children? *Educational Leadership, 67,* 14–20.

Ingersoll, R., & Smith, T. (2003, January 1). The wrong solution to the teacher shortage. *Educational Leadership, 60*(8), 30–33.

Ingersoll, R.M., & Strong, M. (2011). The impact of induction and mentoring programs for beginning teachers: A critical review of the research. *Review of Educational Research, 81*(2), 201–233. doi:10.3102/0034654311403323

Johnson, S., Berg, J., & Donaldson, M. (2005). Who stays in teaching and why: A review of the literature on teacher retention. *The Project on the Next Generation of Teachers: Harvard Graduate School of Education.*

Johnson, S.M., & Kardos, S.M. (2005). Bridging the generation gap. *Educational Leadership, 62*(8), 8–14.

Karsenti, T., & Collin, S. (2013). Why are new teachers leaving the profession? Results of a Canada-wide survey. *Education, 3,* 141–149.

Kutsyuruba, B., Godden, L., Covell, L., Matheson, I., & Walker, K. (2016). *Understanding the contextual factors within teacher induction and mentoring programs: An international systematic review of research* (Final report). Kingston, Ontario: Queen's University.

Lee, J.C.K., & Feng, S. (2007). Mentoring support and the professional development of beginning teachers: A Chinese perspective. *Mentoring & Tutoring: Partnership in Learning, 15*(3), 243–363.

Lindgren, U. (2005). Experiences of beginning teachers in a school-based mentoring programme in Sweden. *Educational Studies, 31*(3), 251–263.

Luft, J.A., Roehrig, G.H., & Patterson, N.C. (2003). Contrasting landscapes: A comparison of the impact of different induction programs on beginning secondary science teachers' practices, beliefs, and experiences. *Journal of Research in Science Teaching, 40*(1), 77–97.

Marable, M., & Raimondi, S. (2007). Teachers' perceptions of what was most (and least) supportive during their first year of teaching. *Mentoring and Tutoring: Partnership in Learning, 15*(1), 25–37.

Martin, L.A., Chiodo, J.J., & Chang, L. (2001). First year teachers: Looking back after three years. *Action in Teacher Education, 23*(1), 55–61.

McCormack, A., & Thomas, K. (2003). Is surviving enough? Induction experiences of beginning teachers within a New South Wales context. *Asia-Pacific Journal of Teacher Education, 31*(2), 124–138.

McCracken, J. D., & Miller, C. (1988). Rural teachers' perceptions of their schools and communities. *Journal of Research in Rural Education, 5*(2), 23–26.

McIntyre, D., & Hagger, H. (1996). Mentors in schools: Developing the profession of teaching. London: David Fulton.

McPherson, S. (2000). *From practicum to practice: Two beginning teachers' perceptions of the quality of their preservice preparation.* Unpublished master's thesis. Faculty of Education, Queen's University, Kingston, Ontario.

Moir, E., & Gless, J. (2001). Quality induction: An investment in teachers. *Teacher Education Quarterly, 28*(1), 109–114.

Naylor, C. (2001). *What do British Columbia's teachers consider to be most significant aspects of workload and stress in their work?* BCTF Research Report Section III 2001-WLC-03, October. BCTF Research. Retrieved from http://www.eric.ed.gov/PDFS/ED464030.pdf

Olafson, M., Elaschuk, D., & Owens, E. (2002). Is surviving enough? A study on mentoring programs. Project #85. *McDowell Teaching and Learning Research Exchange*, Eston, SK. Retrieved from: http://www.mcdowellfoundation.ca/main_mcdowell/projects/research_rep/85_is_surviving_enough.pdf

Pelletier, K.R. (1994). *Sound mind, sound body: a new model for lifelong health.* New York: Simon & Schuster.

Prytula, M., Makahonuk, C., Syrota, N., Pesenti, M., Archibald, C., Benson, J., Froelich, L., Gauthier, K., Goodman, L., Hellsten, L., Mihalicz, B., & Vangool, J. (2010). Sustainable successful teacher induction: From praxis to practice. Project #194. *McDowell Teaching and Learning Research Exchange*, Saskatoon, SK.

Ralph, E.G., & Walker, K.D. (2014). Is *adaptive mentorship* a viable mentoring model? *International Journal for Cross-Disciplinary Subjects in Education (IJCDSE), 4*(3), 2005-2008.

Ronfeldt, M., Loeb, S., & Wyckoff, J. (2013). How teacher turnover harms student achievement. *American Educational Research Journal, 50*(1), 4–36.

Scherer, M. (2001). Improving the quality of the teaching force: A conversation with David C. Berliner. *Educational Leadership, 58*(8), 6–10.

Serpell, Z. (2000). *Beginning teacher induction: A review of the literature.* American Association of Colleges for Teacher Education, Washington, DC.

Simpson, T., Hastings, W., & Hill, B. (2007). 'I knew that she was watching me:' The professional benefits of mentoring. *Teachers and Teaching: Theory and Practice, 13*(5), 481–498.

Simurda, S.J. (2004). The urban/rural challenge: Overcoming teacher recruitment and retention obstacles faced by urban and rural school districts. *Threshold, Spring,* 22–25.

Villani, S. (2002). *Mentoring programs for new teachers: Models of induction and support.* Thousand Oaks, California: Corwin Press Inc.

Voke, H. (2002). Understanding the teacher shortage. *ACSD InfoBrief, 29,* 1–17.

Wang, J., & Odell, S.J. (2002). Mentored learning to teach according to standards based reform: A critical review. *Review of Educational Research, 72*(3), 481–546.

Wong, H.K. (2004). Induction programs that keep new teachers teaching and improving. *National Association of Secondary School Principals NASSP Bulletin, 68,* 41–58.

Wong, H.K., Britton, T., & Ganser, T. (2005). What the world can teach us about new teacher induction. *Phi Delta Kappan, 86*(5), 379–384.

# Foundations for professional growth: A longitudinal look at induction practices in Alberta

*Laura Servage, Jaime Beck, Jean-Claude Couture*

## Introduction

In the context of ample literature on beginning teachers' experiences and the need for well-designed and universally accessible induction programs, the Alberta Teachers' Association, and others, have documented the realities of the early years of practice in Alberta schools (Alberta Teachers' Association 2013; Clandinin, et al., 2013; Schaefer, 2013). The message is consistent and clear: no matter how high the standards for entry into teacher preparation programs, and no matter how robust preparation programs may be, teachers will not reach their potential under sub-optimal conditions of early practice. Therefore, educational policy makers must make a priority of creating induction experiences that position teachers for professional growth over the full course of their careers.

This chapter presents some key conclusions drawn from a five-year longitudinal study of beginning teachers (Alberta Teachers' Association, 2013). Funded by the Alberta Teachers' Association, the study examined the impacts of school cultures and induction supports on novice teachers over the first years of their practices. The study was conducted in the Province of Alberta, Canada, and included the experiences of an initial cohort of over one hundred teachers. The study began in 2008, and was completed in 2013.

Although the study generated many insights, in this work we focus on what we feel to be the two most significant themes, both of which explore a developmental perspective on early career growth. First, we learned a great deal about how the needs of early career teachers change during their induction years. Our central observation was that while teachers move quite rapidly from the uncertainty of "praxis shock" in their first year (Goddard & Foster, 2001) to greater confidence, this shift does not necessarily nor solely reflect teacher growth (Day & Gu, 2007). While our study participants wished to grow in their practices, many of their responses were better characterized as adaptations to greater or lesser supports they experienced in their school environments. Second, we recognized by Year Five that we were speaking with teachers who were in a unique liminal space in their careers. They could still viscerally remember their earliest experiences; yet they also had enough experience that they could understand the profession from a more veteran perspective. Their perspectives and retrospectives gave us insights into the ways in which induction experiences are reproduced – for better or for worse – for the next generation of early career teachers.

After sharing related literature regarding the developmental approach to teacher growth and detailing the methodological details of our longitudinal study design, this paper will present a discussion of these two themes. In reflecting on the qualities of effective teacher induction and on the consequences of induction experiences, this paper explores the ways in which the quality of professional growth in established teachers is contingent upon the quality of their professional learning experiences early in their career.

## Thinking Developmentally About Teacher Growth

The longitudinal nature of this study fits well with a developmental approach to thinking about teacher professional growth. Numerous models have been proposed to make sense of the ways that teachers progress through their careers, building on their past experiences to form beliefs, attitudes, and habits of practice (Day & Gu, 2007; Fessler, 1985; Huberman, 1989). These models are variations on a basic trajectory: teachers begin their professional lives with great uncertainty and anxiety, gradually achieve stability and a coherent identity, and in later years may either evolve or stagnate in their practices. If there is a core aim to empirical studies of career learning patterns and the models that explicate them, it is to identify the personal qualities and organizational conditions most likely to sustain well-being and positive professional growth over the full course of teachers' working lives.

A developmental approach comes with both promises and perils. Identifying the professional development needs of teachers at distinct stages in their career can help schools, districts, and professional development providers to better understand teachers' evolving learning needs. In this study, the teachers just entering the profession did have distinct, and often "survival level", needs (Cherubini, 2009; Huberman, 1989). Over time, as we followed these teachers, we were also able to glimpse some of the ways that teacher professional growth might have been adversely impacted if these basic "survival needs" had not been met. However, we were also cognitive of the limitations of relying solely on a developmental approach to meeting teacher needs. As Huberman (1989) noted, "the identification of phases and sequences must be handled gingerly, as an analytic heuristic, a descriptive rather than a normative construct" (p. 32). Similarly, Day and Gu's (2007) study highlighted the non-linear nature of many career paths. In keeping with past research drawing on developmental accounts of teacher learning, we saw general patterns in the experiences of the beginning teachers, but we also noted many variations as well.

## Study Design and Methods

The study was longitudinal, and used mixed methods. We randomly selected participants from a contact list of novice teachers who had attended the 2007/2008 Beginning Teachers' Conference, offered annually by the Alberta Teachers' Association. In Year One (2008) we contacted 135 teachers by phone, and completed surveys with these teachers. The surveys consisted of open and closed-response questions. Although there was some attrition, we were still able to track a total of 90 teachers over the full five years of the study. We established mobility and career paths, and, most importantly, observed teachers' evolving professional self-concepts, beliefs, and practices.

## Study Sample

The majority of the participants were first-year teachers. A small number were either teachers who had some previous experience and were returning to the profession after a long absence, or early-career teachers who had moved to Alberta from another province. The sample was a good representation of the general Alberta teaching population: 83% were female; 53% were elementary specialists; 4% were kindergarten or ECS teachers; and 43% were either secondary teachers or were teaching a combination of grades. In year one of the study, 32% of the teachers (n=135) described their school setting as "rural" and 52% as "urban." The remaining participants came from settings described variously as "satellite communities," "towns," or "commuter communities." Mapping this demographic data against running ATA demographic data, we were satisfied that the sample was a good representation of the Alberta teachers from across the Province.

## Data Collection

Surveys and telephone interviews lasting 15-30 minutes in length were conducted annually with all participants. Every summer, each of the study participants was contacted by telephone and asked a series of open and closed-response questions. The interviewers recorded participant responses in a standardized survey form. The conversations were not recorded. Some questions asked in the telephone interviews were repeated each year to facilitate the identification of trends over time, while other questions were added or revised to elicit information about emerging themes.

As the study progressed, we began to seek deeper insights into these emerging themes. In Years Four and Five of the study, we supplemented annual telephone surveys with ten individual 60-90 minute interviews. We chose interview participants purposively, on the basis of their interest in the study, and based on our desire to capture a rich variety of career trajectories, school settings, and professional experiences. We also held six focus group sessions in different provincial regions (total n=18), targeting rural, "rurban," and urban centers across Alberta. The focus groups explored such topics as career paths, early-career learning, professional identity and the kind of support that participants had received from colleagues, administrators, school districts and the Alberta Teachers' Association.

## Data Analysis

The answers to the closed-response questions asked during the telephone interviews were compiled into basic descriptive statistics. NVivo data-analysis software was used to code responses to the open-response questions and to organize the codes into themes. Some themes were implicit in the questions asked; others emerged as participants gained experience and were able to look back on their first years. During the course of the study, the researchers conducted an ongoing review of the literature on new teachers' experiences in schools, induction practices, school leadership, the attrition of new teachers from the profession and labour dynamics in the K-12 education sector. The researchers reviewed the research literature to determine how the findings of the study to date compared with those of others in the field of new-teacher induction. The focus group conversations and the extended interviews were transcribed and analyzed thematically using NVivo.

# Research Findings

Teacher induction has been widely studied, and there is a considerable volume of existing literature documenting novice teacher identity (Day & Gu, 2010; Hong, 2010; Wang, Odell, & Schwille, 2008), novice teachers' needs (Jones, 2012; Melnick & Meister 2008), and best practices for teacher induction (Glassford & Salinitri, 2007; Howe, 2006; Ingersoll & Strong, 2011; Kardos & Johnson, 2007). Our ultimate findings thus focussed less on reiterating these established discussions, and more on the ways in which induction experiences of varying qualities affected teachers' practices and perspectives in the longer run. First, we found that the degree to which beginning teachers' more immediate, survival-level needs were met impacted their later professional growth. Second, we found that near the end of the study, teachers were likely to offer their newer colleagues the kinds of supports that they themselves had received, for better or worse. Both of these themes highlight the importance of creating conditions in which teachers can have positive induction experiences.

## The Immediate and Longer Term Needs of Beginning Teachers

Induction supports are offered to novice teachers with the understanding that they have support needs distinct from those of their more veteran colleagues (Melnick & Meister 2008). In trying to meet these needs, often with limited resources, we believe that induction programs may miss the important step of determining and focussing on the most critical of these needs. If the net is cast too wide and the induction goals are not clearly stated, then supports may be too fragmented and diffuse to have their desired effects.

Based on our research findings, we assert that the induction programs need to prioritize and provide very practical supports that meet new teachers' basic "survival" needs if the foundations for good practice are to be put in place for later years. Induction and mentorship strategies may place a philosophical emphasis on valuable long-term objectives like reflective practice, lifelong learning, and collaboration skills, but do so without recognizing that these professional habits of mind are built, perhaps paradoxically, on comparably concrete foundations.

What, then are these basic or "survival" needs? Participants identified needs for both practical and affective supports. In their first year of practice, and with respect to practical concerns, teachers reported spending the preponderance of their time locating resources, planning lessons and becoming oriented to the school environment and school community. Teachers needed ready advice and strategies for classroom management and communication with families. Mundane tasks such as completing administrative paperwork and learning school-related reporting systems were both essential and time-consuming. All of these activities were undertaken within the context of efforts to develop global, effective time-management and work strategies – learning to work "smarter not harder."

Thus, study respondents highly valued practical, "just-in-time" information and resources that could be readily applied to solve urgent problems, and otherwise quickly incorporated into practice. Ideally these supports came from formal mentorship relationships; however, if these were not available or not effective, teachers sought them out informally. This did not mean that they had no interest in longer term planning, learning goals and reflection; rather, they could not even consider these things until they had the resources they needed, and had achieved some sense of security in their environment and their emerging professional identities. In summary, the support desired, regardless of its source, was for solutions to urgent, immediate problems that had to be resolved for teachers to make it through their days.

The novice teachers in our study also had strong needs in their first years of practice to achieve a sense of belonging and legitimacy in their school communities (cf. Anthony, Bell, Haigh & Kane, 2007; Day & Gu, 2010; Kardos & Johnson, 2007; Long, et al., 2012). Schools can help address these needs by ensuring that new teachers have support when they are experiencing bouts of uncertainty or self-doubt, and that they have opportunities to participate in creative, higher-order work. Although the majority of participants entered positive and welcoming schools, others felt very isolated, especially during their first year or two of practice. Thus, practical support requirements included effective school orientations, an accessible colleague who could be available to respond to questions quickly, lesson plans that new teachers could quickly grasp and implement, and the resources required to implement those plans.

**Foundations for advancing practice.** These findings, in and of themselves, are not novel; they corroborate what many other studies have found concerning the learning and belonging needs of novice teachers (Feiman- Nemser 2001; Grossman & Thompson 2004; Melnick & Meister 2008). We believe we can add to these existing understandings by emphasizing the concrete and experiential nature of these early learning needs. In the latter years of our study, when we asked these teachers where supports could be more helpful, many respondents surprised us with their emphasis that aspects of their learning could only be arrived at through trial-and-error, practice, missteps, and the passing of time. "Over-planning" was a distinctive example of this. In retrospect, teachers could see that they had over-planned and over-thought many aspects of their work in their earlier years, but they also believed that this was inevitable: direct experience of over-planning was needed to gain judgement of the "right amount" of planning. Study participants, both in situ and retrospectively, stated that they had developed foundational skills like time management, classroom management, and planning only by doing the work, and that this work was challenging regardless of the supports provided. The foundations of practice, then, if acquired through concrete and experiential learning, require an induction pedagogy that similarly theoretically grounded.

This perspective contrasts somewhat with those that prioritize reflection, both in pre-service teaching and throughout the cycle of a teacher's career (Finlay, 2008). While the importance of reflection should not be discounted within the context of an overall program of induction, its over-emphasis very early in practice may lead program designers to downplay the significance of "learning by doing" for beginners, and thus neglect the significance of concrete, practical supports, resources, and skill development. It should also be made clear, from our study, that while effective induction practices did not appear to mitigate the need for experiential learning, they were nonetheless important determinants of how this learning would be integrated into practice in subsequent years. As a final caveat, in an ideal world induction practices would afford ample opportunities for both experiential learning and reflection. However, in practice, and certainly in the case of this study, novices described themselves, their colleagues, and their administrators as "too busy" to create what would have been the optimal conditions for support: experience combined with opportunities to dialogue with skilled and experienced colleagues. As one study participant summarized, "The first year is always going to be overwhelming. But I think if you have someone there that's kind of more realistic telling you how to approach things, you can focus on what's important."

**Becoming lifelong learners.** Although we have emphasized the importance of "basic" supports in the first year of practice, the study findings also indicate that teachers can become trapped in this unreflective mode of practice if their induction experiences do not structure transitions to more advanced professional learning practices. Even teachers who had mentors or other forms of induction supports in their first year were almost universally left to their own devices in subsequent years to refine lessons, improve teaching techniques, and create professional growth plans. Induction programs that are too short and lack a long-term focus can fail to plan and make an intentional transition from offering first-year "survival strategies" to focusing on professional development that helps teachers build and sustain good practice.

From participants' evaluations of their induction supports in their early years, and reflections back on these supports toward the end of the study, we determined that much more conceptual work could go into multi-year, staged induction programs that move novice teachers intentionally, and gradually, from "the basics" to more advanced forms of professional learning. The immediate induction needs of study participants, drawn from their accounts in our study, included:

- A secure and stable work placement;
- Timely access to teaching resources, including lesson and unit plans, which can be put to use in short order;
- A thorough orientation to the school and welcome to the school community;
- Trustworthy and immediately available advice on classroom organization, classroom management and relationships with parents;
- Affectivesupport from colleagues; and
- Accessible "just in time" support at key points during the school year, including year planning and reporting periods.
- These strategies should be offered alongside efforts to reduce the complexity of teachers' assignments in the first year by explicitly limiting extra-curricular expectations and limiting the number of classes that the teacher must prepare for. The most important role for colleagues and mentors at this stage is to be available on a daily basis to provide practical tools and strategies, offer reassurance, and, importantly, to reduce minutiae – the "noise in the system" that new teachers experience – by helping them to discern their daily priorities.

Once teachers' basic needs have been met, they can begin engaging in longer-term professional growth, which results in the development of higher-order skills including:

- Honing pedagogical, assessment and classroom-management skills, using evidence-based practices;
- Becoming lifelong learners by setting personal learning goals and creating professional growth plans;
- Practicing collaboration and teamwork skills by helping peers to learn and by contributing to the school culture;
- Enhancing communication strategies and skills with students, parents and the community; and
- Reflecting on and refining teaching practice.

These activities should occur in collaborative contexts; ideally with trained mentors who can help early career teachers to develop meta-cognition and intentionality toward professional growth. We further assert that when these more advanced skills are offered at a time when teachers' "basic needs" are not being met, they are less likely to "stick," and will not help novice teachers to develop the desired habits of practice.

### Teachers Who Stay: The Impacts of Induction Experience on Practice

Although many induction efforts, and studies of these efforts, have been motivated by concerns that teachers are leaving the profession (Carver & Feiman-Nemser, 2008; Hong, 2010), we propose that school leaders should be equally focussed on the impacts of early career experiences on teachers who choose to stay (Beck, 2016). The beginning teachers in this study entered the profession with good and positive intentions; intentions that were likely shared by the teachers who preceded them and who are now veterans. Yet, participants reported that many of the veteran teachers they encountered had adopted what appeared to be permanently negative attitudes. What experiences might have dampened these teachers' initial enthusiasm?

Some scholars suggest that difficult induction experiences can inhibit the future professional growth of teachers (Feiman-Nemser, 2003; Glassford & Salinitri, 2007), and our findings support these assertions. We can claim no absolute correlation between ineffective induction practices and less-than-optimal professional growth in subsequent years. Nevertheless, we observed patterns in the latter years of this study suggesting that induction experiences do have some long-term effects on career development. Induction experiences themselves varied widely. At the most positive end of the spectrum, we found teachers in innovative schools with supportive school communities and colleagues. These teachers benefited from a school culture and colleagues who modelled positive and continuous professional learning. However, we also met novice teachers in professionally impoverished settings where, for example, there was a lack of mentors in their fields or where, due to stagnant or parochial school cultures, there was no semblance of welcome to novice teachers' ideas, questions, or learning needs. Some remote schools experienced high staff turnover, so, consequently, new teachers' induction experiences in these environments were shaped by weak organizational capacity (Kardos & Johnson, 2007).

In years Four and Five of the study, participants reached defining moments in their careers: points at which they could still remember what it felt like to be a new teacher, but they had also begun to identify with veteran teachers. They had come to the realization that the pace of their job and their sense of being overwhelmed were not going to diminish. Observing their veteran colleagues, many participants recognized that staying positive in such a climate would be a career-long struggle. At these points, they began to make more-or-less conscious choices about the kinds of colleagues they would be in the future.

**Reproducing induction environments.** One question that emerged as our study progressed, then, was the extent to which new teachers re-create, for subsequent generations of teachers, the conditions that they themselves experienced as beginning teachers. In other words, do teachers who experienced isolation as early-career teachers then contribute to cultures of isolation for the teachers who come after them? Turning the question a third way, are teachers who had positive experiences more inclined to ensure that their successors experience positive conditions? Participants' accounts of their own induction experiences and those of newer colleagues provide evidence of both patterns. For example, one teacher who had enjoyed positive collaborative relationships observed that these experiences had encouraged her to take the initiative in reaching out to a teacher who had been transferred from another school. Another participant, whose school culture was characterized by collegiality, said that she considered it a "given" that she would help a beginning teacher: "That's just the way that the staff is. When I was new to the school, people would be helpful; they'd volunteer information. In my school, teachers swap stuff back and forth."

On the opposite end of the spectrum, we heard from teachers who, after being inducted into cultures of scarcity and self-interest, had taken on some of these qualities themselves. Examples included their reluctance to share those "hard-earned" resources with newer colleagues, indifference to novice colleagues, and, most often cited, withdrawal from extra-curricular activities. "As beginning teachers, we're 'yes' people [but] eventually you get tired," reflected one participant. Another said, "You get resentful of the people who aren't doing things." In this case, it is not difficult to see the emergence of a pattern: high engagement in the early years followed by a diminishing willingness to "go the extra mile," especially when the teacher perceives that some staff are expected to carry heavier loads than others.

By the time they had gained seniority, some teachers believed that they were justified in cutting back on their involvement in extracurricular activities, having "paid their dues." The higher burden of labour falls to the up-and-coming novice teachers, and the norm of placing the most difficult workloads on the most vulnerable of teachers is reproduced. Perceptions of unfair burdens placed on novice teachers were prevalent in this study, and the notion that new teachers must "pay their dues" is, according to the literature, detrimental to the professional growth of new teachers (Cherubini, 2009; Ingersoll & Smith, 2004). Yet the very teachers who were on the receiving end of such negative attitudes and practices may have ended up perpetuating these ways as more veteran colleagues.

On a more positive note, while some participants reproduced, perhaps unconsciously, the unsupportive school culture that they had experienced, many others expressed empathy for their junior colleagues and stated that they were determined to offer new teachers better support than they, themselves, had received. For example, one participant noted that he "took a little extra time" to explain the resources he was sharing with a novice: "I didn't want to just say, 'Here, copy this and deal with it,' because I know what it's like to be on the other end and to just be given a pile [of resources]." This participant, and several others, took great pleasure in approaching their newer colleagues with offers of help, support and resources. These gestures may have been acts of healing and compensation for injuries that they, themselves, had experienced as novice teachers.

Such attempts by early-career teachers to give in ways better than they had received, however encouraging, are unlikely to reverse the prevailing "sink or swim" mentality unless these individual efforts are broadly supported at multiple levels. Our study demonstrated that leadership and staff members at individual sites set the school culture and prevailing norms of practice (Kardos & Johnson, 2007). Great variations in these settings suggest that the policies and resources that constitute new teacher induction, themselves unstable, yield predictably unpredictable results. In other words, at least in the Alberta context, there are no systemic conditions that will assure that new generations of teachers will receive the intentional workplace training and supports that lay the foundations for subsequent years of professional learning and practice.

## Implications of the Study

The Alberta Teachers' Association is familiar with the political history of the Province of Alberta, and has consistently emphasized that the success of beginning teachers is contingent upon systemic conditions; conditions that must be carefully considered if an induction program is to yield successful, consistent results (Alberta Teachers' Association, 2012; Campbell, 2012; Fullan, 2010). In the series of reports on this study, we developed an ecological model which highlighted systemic conditions that impact teacher induction, and that function at levels well beyond the school sites and the individual teachers who were the focus of our study. Critically, these conditions included unstable and insufficient funding of the system as a whole, such that induction programs are *ad hoc*, unsustainable, or otherwise unevenly delivered. Ample tools and research are available to inform the design of an excellent induction program; but in our study we saw how conditions of overwork, faced by veterans and novices alike, can undermine the best of designs and intentions upon implementation.

Systemic conditions also include managerial models of school governance and inappropriate performance measures that do little to build capacity or trust in teachers and their professional autonomy. This view of teachers as "professional employees," (Smaller, et al., 2005) is deeply at odds with the ideal of the thoughtful and intrinsically-motivated lifelong learning that is so core to the aims and designs of new teacher induction. The professionalism aspired to in teacher growth at all stages of practice, from pre-service right through the later years, depends on the well-being and autonomy of teachers to pursue growth. This professionalism, as argued by Smaller et al. (2005), "is continually in jeopardy because of organizational decisions made outside the influence of classroom teachers," including "excessively prescribed curricula, testing and reporting, unsustainable class sizes, and increased non-instructional duties" (p. 42).

The systemic conditions described also help to explain why negative or dysfunctional cycles of new teacher induction may exist, and why it is so difficult for well-intentioned teachers to disrupt these cycles on their own.

Conversely, some of the positive cycles of learning and growth we found will remain as pockets of positive innovation that cannot be extended beyond particular site levels to influence the cultures and practices of teaching in other schools.

Systems thinking also helps us to understand why new teachers can fail to thrive. Resources do matter. In particular, the resource of time is important. Over-work, imposed exogenously, creates cultures and norms of scarcity in schools that leave many novice teachers feeling isolated and unsupported. Beck (2016) found that teachers who remain in the profession can be surprised by the recurrence of these kinds of feelings when faced with a new teaching assignment, a new administrator, or another new context. Beyond the basic and fundamental needs of a teacher just entering the profession, then, our study encouraged us to think about how, regardless of career stage, the circumstances in which one teaches may impact how teachers feel about their work and the "passion, commitment, and resilience" that they are able to use to meet the challenges of their profession (Day, 2012). Those contexts where the teachers in our study were having positive induction experiences were those where all teachers were able to thrive.

# References

Alberta Teachers' Association. (2013). *Teaching in the early years of practice: A five-year longitudinal study.* Edmonton, AB: Author.

Anthony, G., Bell, B., Haigh, M., & Kane, R. (2007). *Induction into the profession: Findings from New Zealand beginning teachers.* Paper presented at the Annual Conference of the American Educational Research Association, Chicago, IL.

Beck, J. L. (2016). *Teachers' experiences of negotiating stories to stay by: A narrative inquiry.* (Doctoral Dissertation). Retrieved from Education and Research Archive, University of Alberta. doi:10.7939/R3BV7B138 https://era.library.ualberta.ca/files/cmg74qm452#.WEdvQpJOFRk

Fullan, M. (2010). The big idea behind whole system reform. *Education Canada, 50*(3), 24–27.

Carver, C. L., & Feiman-Nemser, S. (2008). Using policy to improve teacher Induction: Critical elements and missing pieces. *Educational Policy, 23*(2), 295–328. http://doi.org/10.1177/0895904807310036

Cherubini, L. (2009). Reconciling the tensions of new teachers' socialisation into school culture: A review of the research. *Issues in Educational Research, 19*(2), 83–100.

Clandinin, D.J., Schaefer, L., Long, J., Steeves, P., Downey, A., McKenzie, S., Pinnegar, E., & Wnuk, S. (2013). Teacher education: A question of sustaining teachers. In Xudong, Z., & Zeichner, K. (Eds.), *Preparing teachers for the 21st century* (pp. 251–262). New York: Springer.

Day, C., & Gu, Q. (2010). *The new lives of teachers*. New York, NY: Routledge.

Day, C., & Gu, Q. (2007). Variations in the conditions for teachers' professional learning and development: Sustaining commitment and effectiveness over a career. *Oxford Review of Education, 33*(4), 423–443. http://doi.org/10.1080/03054980701450746

Feiman-Nemser, S. (2003). What new teachers need to learn: Addressing the learning needs of new teachers can improve both the rate of teacher retention and the quality of the teaching profession. *Educational Leadership, 60*(8), 25–29.

Feiman-Nemser, S. (2001). Helping novices learn to teach: Lessons from an exemplary support teacher. *Journal of Teacher Education, 52*(1), 17–30. http://doi.org/10.1177/0022487101052001003

Fessler, R. (1985). A model for teacher professional growth and development, In P. Burke & R. Heideman (Eds) *Career-long teacher education* (pp. 181–193). Springfield, IL: Charles C Thomas

Finlay, L (2008). *Reflecting on 'reflective practice'. The Open University. Practice-based professional learning centre.* Retrieved from http://www.open.ac.uk/opencetl/sites/www.open.ac.uk.opencetl/files/files/ecms/web-content/Finlay-(2008)-Reflecting-on-reflective-practice-PBPL-paper-52.pdffrom

Fullan, M. (2010). The big idea behind whole system reform. *Education Canada, 50*(3), 24–27.

Glassford, L. A., & Salinitri, G. (2007). Designing a successful new teacher induction program: An assessment of the Ontario experience, 2003-2006. *Journal of Educational Administration, 60*, 1–34.

Goddard, J. T., & Foster, R. Y. (2001). The experiences of neophyte teachers: A critical constructivist assessment. *Teaching and Teacher Education, 17*(3), 349–365.

Grossman, P., & Thompson, C. (2004). District policy and beginning teachers: A lens on teacher learning. *Educational Evaluation and Policy Analysis, 26*(4), 281–301. https://doi.org/10.3102/01623737026004281

Hong, J. Y. (2010). Pre-service and beginning teachers' professional identity and its relation to dropping out of the profession. *Teaching and Teacher Education, 26*(8), 1530–1543. http://doi.org/10.1016/j.tate.2010.06.003

Howe, E. R. (2006). Exemplary teacher induction: An international review. *Educational Philosophy and Theory, 38*(3), 287–297. http://doi.org/10.1111/j.1469-5812.2006.00195.x

Huberman, M. (1989). The professional life cycle of teachers. *Teachers College Record, 91*(1), 31–57.

Ingersoll, R. M., & Smith, T. M. (2004). Do teacher induction and mentoring matter? *NASSP Bulletin, 88*, 28–40.

Ingersoll, R. M., & Strong, M. (2011). The impact of induction and mentoring programs for beginning teachers: A critical review of the research. *Review of Educational Research, 81*(2), 201–233. http://doi.org/10.3102/0034654311403323

Jones, B. K. (2012). A new teacher's plea. *Educational Leadership, 69*(8), 74–77.

Kardos, S. M., & Johnson, S. M. (2007). On their own and presumed expert: New teachers' experience with their colleagues. *Teachers College Record, 109*(9), 2083–2106.

Long, J. S., McKenzie-Robblee, S., Schaefer, L., Steeves, P., Wnuk, S., Pinnegar, E., & Clandinin, D. J. (2012). Literature review on induction and mentorship related to early career attrition and retention. *Mentorship and Tutoring: Partnership in Learning, 20*(1), 7–26.

Melnick, S., & Meister, D. G. (2008). A comparison of beginning and experienced teachers' concerns. *Educational Research Quarterly, 31*(3), 39–56.

Schaefer, L. (2013) Beginning teacher attrition: A question of identity making and identity shifting. *Teachers and Teaching: Theory and Practice, 19*(3), 260–274.

Smaller, H., Tarc, F., Antonelli, R., Clark, D., Hart, D., & Livingstone, D. (2005). Canadian teachers' learning practices and workload issues: Results from a national teacher survey and follow-up focus groups. Toronto, ON: OISE. Retrieved from http://wall.oise.utoronto.ca/resources/Smaller_Clark_Teachers_Survey_Jun2005.pdf

Wang, J., Odell, S. J., & Clift, R. T. (Eds.). (2010). *Past, present, and future research on teacher induction: An anthology for researchers, policy makers, and practitioners.* Lanham, MD: Rowman & Littlefield.

## Chapter 19

# Teacher Mentorship as Generative Space in British Columbia

*Alison Davies, Anne Hales*

*There are songs and sayings that belong to this place,*
*By which it speaks for itself and no other.*
*Find your hope, then, on the ground under your feet.*
*(Wendell Berry, A Poem on Hope, 2011)*

## Introduction

The Canadian anthropologist Wade Davis described the sacred headwaters of the Stikine, Nass and Skeena rivers in Northern British Columbia as "the most stunningly wild place I have ever been" (Davis, 2013, 1:03). These rivers provide "the very sources of water that gave rise to and cradled the great civilizations of the Northwest Coast" (0:56). Roughly one hundred nautical miles off the western coast of British Columbia lies an archipelago of islands called Haida Gwaii that has been the homeland of the Haida Nation for thousands of years. Further south, Highway 3 winds its way through the canyons and passes of two massive mountain ranges, across the forests and grasslands of the Interior Plateau to the density of human habitation in the Lower Mainland region.

Into this ancient and varied geographical space, British Columbia's newest teachers journey to take up teaching—neither a profession nor a landscape for the faint of heart. Sarah[4] is one recent graduate from Vancouver Island, who accepted the offer of a full time teaching position 1600 kilometres north of her university in a classroom within the Stikine

---

4   'Sarah' is a pseudonym for a new teacher who participated in the New Teacher Mentorship Project.

School District—which encompasses 188,034 square kilometres, and employs 19 full time teachers. Sarah tells of a long lonely drive, in the dead of winter, to pick up the key to the teacherage at a local gas station. On the first day at the school, she watched nervously as the students arrived on their 'sleds' and threw aside their snowmobile helmets and suits. One student sidled up to Sarah to share a "picture of my rabbits," and presented a photo of herself holding out two dead rabbits she had snared on the weekend. "I am a long way from Victoria," Sarah mused. Her life as teacher had begun.

Worthwhile beginnings take us into unchartered territory—a liminal space in which there is room for asking such essential questions as "Where am I?" and "Who am I becoming?" The liminal space new teachers enter is highly charged; they are at once confronted with an awareness of the full responsibilities of being a teacher, and their particular limitations in meeting the public and professional accountability inherent to the profession. In that moment of "praxis shock" (Goddard & Foster, 2001, p. 360), mentorship can serve as a crucible, a relational container within which new teachers can absorb risk, negotiate performativity, and dwell with vulnerability—producing a necessary confrontation with one's potentiality and limitations. Mentoring relationships attend to teachers as they come to the edge of their knowledge, and forge the integration of externally described constructions of teaching with the experiences that shape their emerging practical wisdom.

This chapter's central question is: "In what ways can a provincial mentorship framework create and hold generative space for 'new' teachers to become themselves as ethical educators and decision-makers within diverse contexts?" We narrate how an evolving mentorship project within the Province of British Columbia—the New Teacher Mentorship Project (NTMP)— attempts to conserve spaces that encourage new teachers to become themselves as educators while honouring the diversity and significance of the places they inhabit, and to build collaborative opportunities for organizational leadership. In doing so, we wish to contribute to the characterization and examination of mentorship in Canadian research by re-visiting what and whose needs mentoring programs and activities actually serve— as well as the aims and effects of beginning teacher mentorship. As Jope (2014, p. 181) wondered:

What if, rather than a strict focus on the development of prospective teachers' knowledge and technical skills, teacher educators aspired to cultivate... a kind of openness to the world, a trust in uncertain things, and a willingness to be exposed – what if, beyond specialized propositional knowledge and technical proficiency, we focused on nothing less than the cultivation of *wisdom* in the preparation of new teachers?

This chapter is our attempt to describe a mentorship initiative in the process of discovering the 'ground beneath its feet,' as Wendell Berry encouraged.

## BC's Mentorship Landscape

Historically, induction and mentorship support for new teachers such as Sarah has been as varied and precarious as BC's geographical landscape. New teacher induction and mentorship policies, aims and approaches vary tremendously across British Columbia—as throughout Canada—due in part to the diverse geographical and organizational contexts within which educational policies and practices are created and implemented. Unlike Ontario's New Teacher Induction Program (NTIP), for example, British Columbia does not possess a systemic, government-funded provincial framework for early career teacher mentorship (Ontario Ministry of Education, 2016). A 2012 survey, *Mentoring: The BC Picture,* conducted by the British Columbia Teachers' Federation (BCTF), indicated that just under half of the province's sixty public school districts provided some form of mentorship ranging across a patchwork of informal and structured programs with regionally diverse methods of funding, administration, delivery and accessibility (British Columbia Teachers' Federation, 2012). The lack of an overarching provincial framework means that consistent funding, systemic vision, and program sustainability and availability all remain primary issues. The survey also revealed a slate of differing intentions underlying mentorship, ranging from assisting teachers to adjust to the norms and procedures of schools, to providing workshops identified by school district leaders on relevant topics for beginners.

In 2012, as a response to this systemic gap, the New Teacher Mentorship Project (NTMP) pilot program was launched to explore potential provincial models. Guided through the partnership of the British Columbia Teachers' Federation (BCTF), the University of British Columbia (UBC) and the BC Superintendents' Association (BCSSA), and funded by the BC Ministry of Education (MOE), the NTMP evolved within a context characterized by limited provincial policies, disparate legislative and contractual language defining beginning teachers' status, and unpredictable local funding and staffing provisions. In its first five years, this project took a multi-dimensional approach to working with school districts in urban, suburban and rural contexts in order to explore how educational stakeholders can engage productively in cross-organizational visioning, design, research and enactment, and to provide meaningful and relevant professional learning opportunities for BC's newest teachers and their mentors. Since its inception, NTMP participation has expanded from three to over forty school districts, including the creation of ten new district programs implementing differentiated mentorship models. These various models include one-to-one partnerships, cohorts of mentoring groups defined by new teachers' professional learning foci, and technology-enhanced peer collaboration models that enable teachers to connect across geographically remote communities (Mentoring BC, 2016a).

### Charting the Journey

The NTMP's distributed leadership and multi-organizational governance model provides advocacy and collaborative consultation so that school districts can develop a path towards self-sustaining mentorship programs. The NTMP's program principles emphasize collaboration and place-based adaptability. The NTMP advocates that mentorship models "be responsive to the diversity and distinctiveness of district cultures and practices in all regions of BC," "ensure that mentorship is non-evaluative, non-remedial, and that participation is voluntary," and emphasize "learning through inquiry and critical reflection on practice" (Mentoring BC, 2016b).

The NTMP's provincial advisory committee consists of two representatives from the BCTF (the President and the Director of the Professional and Social Issues Division), two UBC representatives (currently the

Assistant Dean of Teacher Education and a faculty member), and one representative from the BCSSA (a school district superintendent). The BCTF provides various forms of "support in kind," including an office for the project coordinator, IT services, accounting and administrative support for coordinating release time, graphics, research, and communications. UBC administers the operating grant fund and the secondment of the program's Technology Integration Coordinator, and hosts the NTMP's annual Summer Institute—a three-day program to explore mentorship philosophy, pedagogy and facilitation, and sustainable program design. A UBC faculty member conducts ongoing evaluation of the project through surveys and focus groups, providing evidence to inform project effectiveness and guide ongoing project goals. The NTMP has also established connections with scholars within and beyond Canada, as well as provincial professional learning networks (e.g., Growing Innovation in Rural Sites of Learning Network, 2017; Networks of Innovation and Inquiry, 2017; BCECTA: The B.C. Early Career Teachers' Association, 2017).

**Branching Out: The Provincial Mentorship Resource Team**

To bring the resources of the NTMP to their 'particular' place, school districts request consultative and leadership support from the NTMP co-ordinator and a 15-member Provincial Mentorship Resource Team (PMRT). The PMRT team works to carry forward and interpret NTMP aims within regional contexts and cultures. This team was formed through an application process in 2014, intentionally drawing upon professional learning leaders from unions, curriculum and human resources departments, school administration, and teacher mentor communities across the province. The 15 members are regionally organized into five teams of three, and provided with release time, travel allowances and collaborative learning opportunities by the NTMP. The PMRT teams provide consultation and workshop facilitation in their designated regions (Mentoring BC, 2016c).

When a PMRT regional team engages with a new district initiative, their first goal is to establish a cross-role advisory group, including members from the local union, senior administration, school administration, and teachers. Together, the local advisory group and PMRT ensure that program development is designed to encourage sustainability and stimulate leadership capacity, enabling projects to become self-reliant and adaptive to systemic shifts.

Achieving the goal of sustainability working together with district-based advisory groups has not always been successful, and the NTMP has learned the importance of shaping the ways and means for stakeholders to share and inhabit productive leadership space. Striking an advisory group as a functionary committee of 'representatives' implementing a central model has shown limitations when representatives are replaced and roles change. The PMRT currently works with this cross-role group as a 'design team' with responsibility for defining principles, purposes, context and process, building ownership to guide and grow an effective program within a district.

### Researching Mentorship

Concurrent with the field work of the NTMP is a longitudinal research initiative, carried out by the UBC Faculty of Education and funded by a three-year Social Sciences and Humanities Research Council (SSHRC) Partnership Development Grant: *Pedagogical Assemblage: Building and sustaining teacher capacity through mentoring programs in British Columbia* (Mentoring BC, 2016d). The *Pedagogical Assemblage* project explores "the efficacy of mentorship programs and the ways teacher mentorship can enhance teacher effectiveness, grow leadership capacity, and mobilize teacher knowledge" (Mentorship BC, 2016d). The research aims "to provide a greater understanding of how to effectively build and sustain teacher capacity through mentoring programs, and subsequently inform the development of a province-wide teacher mentoring program in British Columbia" (Mentoring BC, 2016d).

Among the preliminary findings emerging from the three-year research inquiry is the necessity of respecting the diverse and particular "place based" needs of BC's beginning teachers—whose geographical circumstances range from inner city urban to rural settings, and encompass the complex needs and demographic characteristics of the students they serve. Effective and sustainable mentorship programs also take into account: "reciprocal professional learning communities, the complexity of teachers' needs, the variety of inquiry foci, increasing cultures of collaboration among schools, teachers, and students, and effective leadership" (New Teacher Mentoring Project, 2016, p. 7).

## A Sense of Place

*What kind of place is this? A place where there is room for words like humour, human, humus, humility to live together. In such a place, to be humiliated is to be reminded that we are communally ecologic, that the rhythmic measures of living on Earth come forth polyphonically in humour and human and humus and humility (Aoki, 1993, p. 293).*

A sense of place—where teachers geographically find themselves as they begin their new careers—has wound its way into stories as NTMP coordinators listened to teachers in northern resource towns, First Nation communities, ski towns, rural two room schools and ocean-edge villages. Teachers shared stories of long drives along snowy highways and logging roads engaged with colleagues in powerful conversations about teaching. They spoke of community elders sharing traditional ways of carving cedar and tanning moose hides. Sitting around campfires, young teachers spoke of how the relationships they formed with colleagues and community members guided them through struggles with isolation and the worry of 'failing' the kids they were teaching. From these conversations, beginning teachers reveal they are not inducted so much into a profession as into a place that belongs to a community and its children–and that the role of 'teacher' can evoke both hope and resistance. Initially, new teachers may encounter resistance within a new community, as they are perceived as strangers authorized to shape and judge children's pedagogical experiences without 'knowing' who those children are. For example, Sarah described how difficult it was to build trust with aboriginal students in the Stikine until they and their parents were convinced she would stay on for a second year.

## Kaitlyn[5]

In her first year of teaching middle school in a Northern resource town, Kaitlyn handed in a resignation letter in October. "I felt so isolated, and didn't feel supported in my new role and living in a new community away from home. I was ready to walk out..." (Mentoring BC, 2016e, 0:26). The local union president visited to convince her she did not need to end her career in that moment. Engaging an experienced local teacher as mentor, a mentoring relationship was established and, with additional classroom supports in place, Kaitlyn continued to work through a difficult year. Over that year, a team of three mentors and four beginning teachers at the same high school formed a group to discuss and problem-solve relevant issues as they arose for the new teachers. Kaitlyn and her mentor also worked one-to-one to co-plan and co-teach in her classroom, which provided opportunities to model, explore and debrief the lessons. At the end of her second year of teaching, Kaitlyn was asked what she had learned from her mentor. She replied:

> [T]he sense of place. Because my mentor has worked in this District for his whole career ... and seeing how proud he was to have been a teacher in this district, how he has affected a small community ... inspires me as a young teacher to get to that point as well and to still love my job at the end of it which is what he continually not only says but he shows. That he still is invested in the profession and sees the importance of it—so that is the deepest message I got ... (Mentoring BC, 2016e, 1:36)

Kaitlyn's story reveals how mentoring can maintain connection with the meaningfulness and impact of teaching within the unnerving uncertainty of daily misalignments. Phelan (2005) describes the necessary "fall from (someone else's) certainty" (p. 339) as teachers sort out how to "think and act well in the presence of children and to dwell alongside, rather than contain, the questions that teaching evokes" (p. 345). The meaningfulness is generated as teachers develop adaptive understanding of who their

---

5   Kaitlyn and Keith's real names are used in these narratives, which have been published through the research work of the Pedagogical Assemblage project and are accessible in a public video gallery at http://mentoringbc.edcp.educ.ubc.ca/research/videos/

students are, how they think, their beliefs and attachments, and how to open new territories of learning. This understanding is entangled in the history and relationships that shape the complex ways of being within any community. While Kaitlyn was immersed in the maelstrom of "the concrete particulars" (p. 355) of daily teaching in an unfamiliar environment, her mentor preserved a space to ask "Why am I becoming a teacher?" Importantly, Kaitlyn's mentor assisted with her development of a range of responses to these 'particulars' allowing her to perceive and articulate for herself a developing sense of efficacy and understanding of 'where' she was.

## Keith

Keith was an art student educated in Britain, who had emigrated to Vancouver where he completed an education degree at UBC. Keith applied for his first teaching position as an art teacher in a high school on Haida Gwaii. The students entering his art room were comprised of island settlers and Haida—a culture with its own ancient and living artistic practice.

As with Kaitlyn's experience, a dilemma arose for Keith, entering into a community as an outsider who was expected to perform as an educational leader, defining and assessing what and how students learn. Drawing on his own cultural and personal practices and understandings, Keith was challenged to teach art within an environment influenced by artistic traditions different that his own – a culture that had produced the magnificent poles, masks and canoes evident in the community. As a participant in a newly established peer mentorship program within the Haida Gwaii School District, Keith benefited from the wisdom of mentors situated within the school (a teacher and a First Nations youth worker) and within the community (a respected Haida artist). The Haida youth worker within the school connected Keith to a Haida carver with whom Keith consulted for advice on the 'appropriateness' of his lessons. Keith also began to study carving with the guidance of the Haida artist. Keith's two mentors within the school assisted him as he constructed his art experiences in a fashion responsive to the particular knowledge and language of his students. This constellation of mentorship supports engendered reciprocal respect, as these educators and artists became known to one another, and to the students Keith was teaching. Keith reflected:

Those students have seen me collaborate with local Haida educators both in the language and the art form. So, the students therefore have a better relationship with me because their level of trust has increased. So, I've collaborated with people that effectively helped me to get to know the students better because the students now trust me and see me as more part of their community than they did in the past. Plus, I can help and advise them about the artwork they are creating in my subject. (Mentoring BC, 2015, 2:28)

In Keith's experience, mentoring conversations created the necessary space for intersubjective exchange of what was known and what is new—a generative exchange of traditional and contemporary epistemologies—and how community and school mentors collectively broker relationships between educator and students.

## Emerging Views

*Miskâsowin: going to the centre of yourself to find your own belonging.* —(*Kovach, 2009, p. 179*)

By narrating beginning teachers' experiences, and describing the NTMP's evolving structure and activities, we attempt to grasp the place of mentorship programs and practices in the teaching lives of early career practitioners. These narratives show how the journey of building a provincial framework for mentorship in British Columbia has been deeply informed by the province's geography, climate, cultures, politics, and the professional dispositions and values of its 40,000 teachers. What has emerged is a conceptualization of mentorship as a crucible—a space where teachers can become *who* they desire to be, as they shape, and are shaped by—*where* they are.

Research literature has characterized mentorship as "an important and effective, perhaps the most effective, form of supporting the professional development of beginning teachers" (Hobson, 2009, p. 209). The broad range of benefits derived from mentoring experiences include "reduced feelings of isolation, increased confidence and self-esteem, professional growth, and improved self-reflection and problem-solving capacities" (p. 209). However, despite research that has suggested "beginner teacher mentoring has great potential to produce a range of benefits" (p.

209), Hobson *et al.* acknowledged that "it is also clear not only that this potential is often unrealised" but "that on occasion, mentoring may even have the potential to do harm" (p. 213). When mentoring programs, or mentors, serve as governance mechanisms within the first years of newly-certified teachers' practice—as channels for promoting particular conceptions of competence and conduct aligned with state education and economic imperatives—beginning teachers may lose the opportunity to establish themselves as professionals and practitioners in their own right by cultivating such qualities as "autonomy in decision-making" and "self-governance" (Grimmett & Young, 2012, p. ix).

One challenge for Canadian public education systems is to develop mentorship models that provide space for new teachers to ask worthwhile questions and shape their professional identities in the midst of demanding, complex work and a culture of public accountability (Clandinin et al., 2015; Ingersoll & Strong, 2011; Sachs, 2000). Such a challenge requires that system leaders simultaneously stimulate, facilitate and protect learning opportunities for new teachers that foster ethical judgment, and allow time and means for individual exploration and integration of emerging understandings into practice. At this point in our conceptual journey, we ponder how a pan-Canadian community of researchers and practitioners might guide centralized policy making bodies, such as provincial or territorial governments, to maintain governance authority over mentorship initiatives while still enabling diverse practices, adaptive responses and even a bit of disruptive pedagogical 'wildness' to flourish. A centralized framework that grounds its intentions and activities on the new teacher's desires and needs, and on local practices and customs, may be "vulnerable to charges of vagueness and toothlessness" (Moore & Clarke, 2016, p. 672) in a policy culture that demands system-wide 'alignment' and measurable indicators linking mentorship initiatives with improvements in both student achievement and teacher performance. Another concern with a decentralized model is that in return for a degree of local autonomy, responsibility for the sustainability of such mentorship initiatives (e.g., funding, staffing) falls to local authorities (p. 667), who may create systemic inequities in program access and efficacy. Without central government policies that incorporate sustained systemic funding along with decentralized governance structures, 'going local' will remain a precarious undertaking. The stories and outcomes emerging from the NTMP offer an opportunity to challenge prevailing conceptions of what mentorship programs can be, and how they might be inhabited. Perhaps this affords an opportunity to envision a provincial mentorship framework that invites teachers to come to themselves as practitioners and professionals, wherever they are beginning.

# References

Aoki, T. (1993). Humiliating the Cartesian ego. In W. Pinar & R. Irwin (Eds.), *Curriculum in a new key: The collected works of Ted. T. Aoki* (pp. 291–301). New York, NY: Routledge.

BCECTA: The B.C. Early Career Teachers' Association. (2017). Retrieved from https://bcecta.wordpress.com

Berry, W. (2011). *Leavings: Poems.* Berkeley, CA: Counterpoint Press.

British Columbia Teachers' Federation. (2012). *Mentoring: The BC picture.* Retrieved from https://bctf.ca/uploadedFiles/Public/NewTeachers/Mentoring/Mentoring2012.pdf.

Clandinin, D.J., Long, J., Schaefer, L., Aiden Downey, C., Steeves, P., Pinnegar, E., McKenzie Robblee, S., & Wnuk, S. (2015). Early career attrition and intentions of teachers beginning. *Teaching Education, 26*(1), 1–16. doi:10.1080/10476210.2014.996746.

Colley, H. (2002). A 'rough guide' to the history of mentoring from a Marxist feminist perspective. *Journal of Education for Teaching: International Research and Pedagogy, 28*(3), 257–273.

Davis, W. (2013, March 1). *Sacred headwaters TED talk.* [Video file]. Retrieved from https://vimeo.com/60841585

Goddard, J.T., & Foster, R. (2001). The experiences of neophyte teachers: a critical constructivist assessment. *Teaching and Teacher Education, 17*(3), 349–365.

Grimmett, P.P., & Young, J.C. (2012). *Teacher certification and the professional status of teaching in North America: The new battleground for public education.* Charlotte, NC: Information Age Publishing.

Growing Innovation in Rural Sites of Learning. (2017). Retrieved from http://ce.educ.ubc.ca/rural-schools-and-community-revitalization/

Hobson, A. J., Ashby, P., Malderez, A., & Tomlinson, P. D. (2009). Mentoring beginning teachers: What we know and what we don't. *Teaching and Teacher Education, 25*(1), 207–216. doi:10.1016/j.tate.2008.09.001.

Ingersoll, R., & Strong, M. (2011). The impact of induction and mentoring programs for beginning teachers: A critical review of the research. *Review of Educational Research, 81*(2), 201–33.

Jope, G. (2014). *Grasping phronesis: The fabric of discernment in becoming an ethical teacher.* [Doctoral Dissertation]. Vancouver, Canada: University of British Columbia.

Kovach, M. (2009). *Indigenous methodologies: characteristics, conversations and contexts.* Toronto: University of Toronto Press.

Mentoring BC. (2016a). *District models.* Retrieved from http://mentoringbc.edcp.educ.ubc.ca/services-and-supports__trashed/district-models/

Mentoring BC. (2016b). *About the New Teacher Mentoring Project.* Retrieved from http://mentoringbc.edcp.educ.ubc.ca/about__trashed/project/

Mentoring BC. (2016c). *Provincial Mentorship Resource Team.* Retrieved from http://mentoringbc.edcp.educ.ubc.ca/provincial-mentorship-resource-team-pmrt/

Mentoring BC. (2016d). *About the SSHRC partnership development grant.* Retrieved from http://mentoringbc.edcp.educ.ubc.ca/research/about/

Mentoring BC. (2016e, June 28). *Kaitlyn Freer.* [Video file]. Retrieved from https://www.youtube.com/watch?v=NP5FW8LTwxA&feature=youtu.be&list=PLFwG05AWu25Cd8DFdU0Y6F1UhVQcyqVWZ

Mentoring BC. (2015, December 5). *Together4Learning.* [Video file]. Retrieved from https://www.youtube.com/watch?v=NqUrzwtUaAY&feature=youtu.be&list=PLFwG05Wu25Cd8DFdU0Y6F1UhVQcyqVWZ

Moore, A., & Clarke, M. (2016). Cruel optimism: Teacher attachment to professionalism in an era of performativity. *Journal of Education Policy, 31*(5), 666–677.

Networks of Inquiry and Innovation. (2017). Retrieved from http://noii.ca

New Teacher Mentoring Project. (2016). *2012-16 report and 2016-19 proposal to the B.C. Ministry of Education.* [Unpublished report.] Vancouver, Canada: New Teacher Mentorship Project.

Ontario Ministry of Education. (2016). The New Teacher Induction Program. Retrieved from http://www.edu.gov.on.ca/eng/teacher/induction.html.

Phelan, A. (2005). A fall from (someone else's) certainty: Recovering practical wisdom in teacher education. *Canadian Journal of Education, 28*(3), 339–358.

Sachs, J. (2000). The activist professional. *Journal of Educational Change, 1*(1), 77–95.

## Chapter 20

# Delta's Story:
## Supporting Innovative Teaching and Learner Success through Mentorship

*Tashi Kirincic*

"A seed holds an incredible life force. When conditions are right, the seed bursts, sending forth an embryo root and stem. Each time, the same thing happens with mind-boggling regularity. *But the key to the process is to give the right seed the right conditions - which is the gardener's job." Gerald Knox* (in Brownlie & King, 2011, p. 19)

## Introduction

Metaphors of organic growth and nature are often used in discussions about mentorship and the role it plays in the professional learning and development of teachers. Just as different seeds require different conditions to sprout and flourish, so do different teachers have different needs. Some require a great deal of attention and care; while others seem to adapt and flourish despite the conditions in which they find themselves. If we think of teacher professional learning as a seed, teacher-mentors as gardeners and a formal mentorship program as the act of gardening then it becomes clear that mentorship must be flexible and adaptive enough to meet the needs of the boundless variety of seeds one might find in a garden. While a one-size-fits-all approach might work for some seeds, it will leave others undeveloped.

The Delta School District's mentorship program described in this chapter was designed with this in mind. However, it is not the intention of this chapter to share a description of a complete and polished mentorship program that can be implemented anywhere, but to share stories of what has and has not worked in Delta's mentorship program and to reveal insights gained from these experiences. Many of these stories are still very much in progress and may raise more questions than they provide answers. The objective in sharing Delta's story of mentorship is to spark authentic conversation about mentorship and uncover possibilities for how a program might be designed to meet the needs of mentorship participants and simultaneously achieve the goals of a district.

## Delta's Model of Mentorship

This is the story of mentorship in Delta...

Delta School District is located outside of Vancouver, British Columbia and is situated on the traditional territory of the Tsawwassen and Musqueam First Nations. The district is spread out over a large geographical area and includes three distinct communities: North Delta, Ladner, and Tsawwassen. Delta School District's twenty-four elementary and seven secondary schools provide safe, culturally diverse and nurturing learning environments. Delta School District's graduation rates are among the highest in British Columbia, and our students consistently rate near the top of the annual Foundation Skills Assessment tests. The district has identified a vision that we are committed to achieving. By 2020, the Delta School District will be a leading district for innovative teaching and learner success. The mentorship program was founded to support the realization of this vision.

Delta's mentorship program strives to:
Increase learner success through innovative teaching,

1. Foster a culture of collaboration and professional learning both within schools and across the district,
2. Positively impact the efficacy and teaching of both protégés and mentors, and
3. Increase retention of skilled teachers.

The Delta School District Mentorship Program is coordinated and supported by a teacher-coordinator with a .5 FTE (full-time teaching equivalent). The program relies on a team-based approach to mentorship, with 2-3 teacher mentors leading and facilitating a team of teacher protégés.

The number of protégés varies depending on the number of participants and their needs, but typically each of these teams operate with 8-12 protégés (Figure 1). Protégés are placed in teams based on the location of their school within the district, the grade level and/or subject area they teach, their interests, and any prior or existing relationships they might have with the mentors.

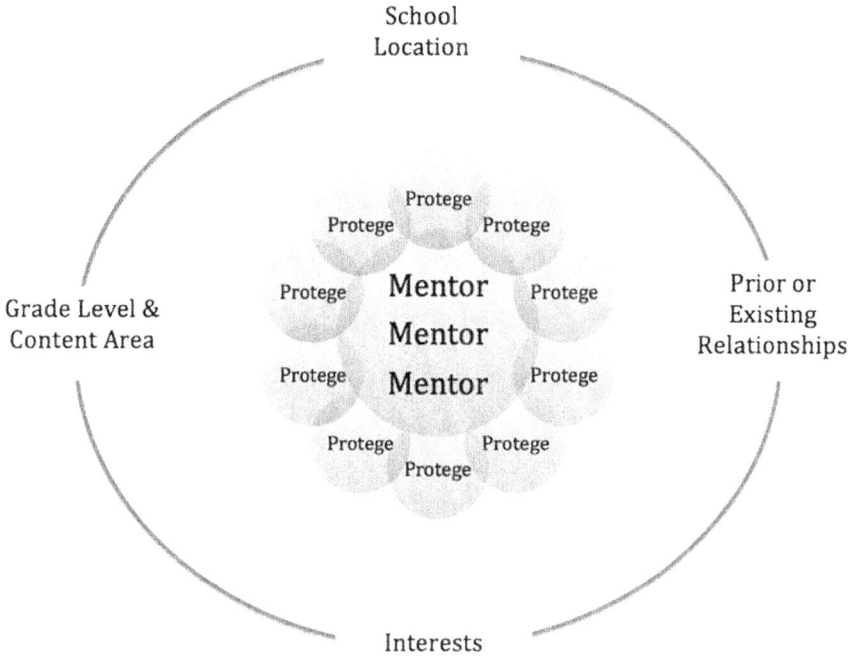

*Figure 1.* Mentorship Team Structure of Delta Mentorship Program

To effectively support the learning of the protégés, the mentors meet with the Coordinator of Teacher Mentorship approximately five times a year for mentor learning sessions. Mentors are provided with release time to attend these sessions. Usually these learning sessions are half-day events, although the first session of the year is a full day. Learning sessions focus on both mentoring skills and teaching practice.

With the support of the Coordinator of Teacher Mentorship, mentors then arrange, plan and facilitate team meetings with a group of protégés. Teams meet four times a year for half-day meetings and all participants are released to attend these meetings. Protégés and mentors also have opportunities to participate in a lesson study, and meet and connect with each other as needed throughout the year (Figure 2).

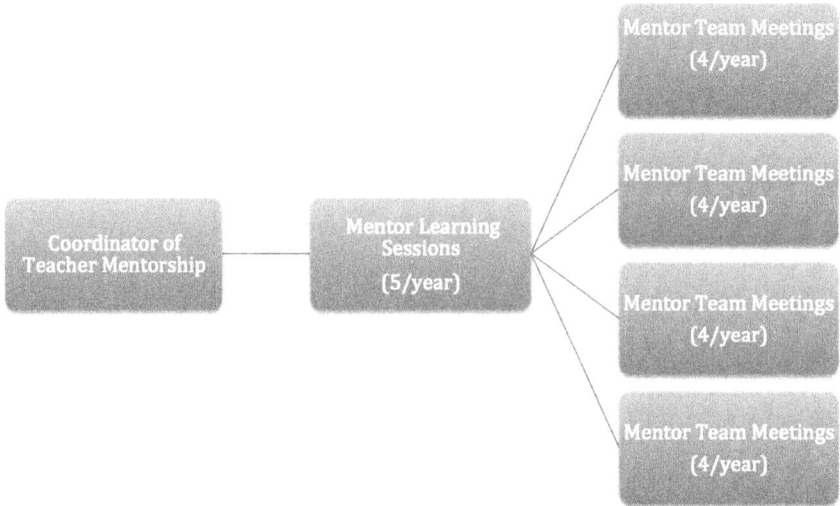

*Figure 2.* Delta Mentorship Program Structure

Participation in the mentorship program is voluntary and non-evaluative. A teacher can join mentorship at any time during the school year. The program targets early career teachers who work at least a .5 FTE and who are in their first two years of a teaching contract with Delta. These are teachers who are new to the district and/or who have had a significant change in their teaching assignment. However, any Delta teacher can self-refer and participate in the program.

Delta's mentorship program is firmly grounded in a 'teacher-to-teacher' mentoring relationship. Although principals, vice-principals and district leaders play an important role in supporting teachers by helping them connect to the program and acting as educational leaders, they do not refer teachers to the program.

All teachers who participate in mentorship are encouraged to push the bounds of their teaching practice by taking risks and trying new things. There is an emphasis on learning for all participants, and the recognition that mentoring is primarily a reciprocal learning relationship which situates mentors as skilled learning partners, rather than as experts who merely dispense knowledge to novice teachers.

# Origins of Delta's Mentorship Program

Delta's mentorship program grew out of the school district's 2010-2011 visioning process and discussions between district and union leadership.

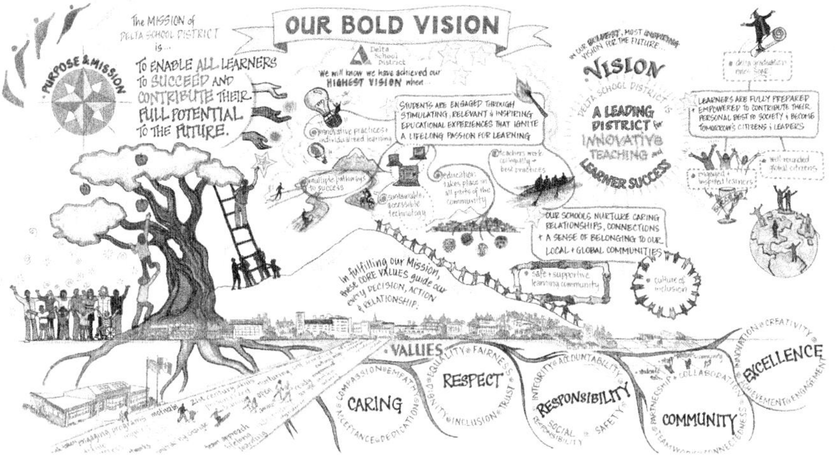

*Figure 3.* Our Bold Vision (Delta School District, 2016)

Once the school district had identified the bold vision to be a leading district in innovative teaching and learner success, both the district and union leadership recognized the absence of a mentorship program as an obstacle to achieving that vision. Consequently, the decision was made to invest in a formal mentorship program.

Delta's mentorship program was designed to be both flexible and responsive. Like the teachers it was intended to support, the program needed to adapt to the changing needs of Delta's learners. Because it was an important part of the plan to achieve the District's bold vision, the mentorship program could not be insulated, but, rather, it needed to be connected to and aligned with other district initiatives. This required a model that could flex and grow with the district's shifting direction. Delta's team-based approach to mentoring supported this by fostering connections both within and across schools.

Another design decision supporting this shift to a learning culture was to invest in the growth and development of the program's mentors. Mentors are more than just vehicles for delivering support to early career teachers. Ideally they are agents of change, who will use the skills they develop as mentors to help build a learning culture across the district. Typically, Delta School District mentors are mid-career teachers, many of whom hold or have plans to adopt formal and informal teacher-leader positions. In order to ensure quality mentoring experiences for early career teachers and to advance the development of teacher-leaders, Delta actually devotes more resources to the learning of mentors than it does to the learning of protégés. It makes sense to invest time, energy and money into teachers who are positioned and have the skills and potential to influence school district culture.

Although the basic structures of Delta's mentorship program have remained stable since its establishment in 2011-2012, the program is not static. The program was designed to allow for change and growth, and every year configurations, approaches and procedures are adapted to better achieve the goals of the program and the district. In its fourth year, Delta's mentorship program is evolving and improving, just as it was designed to do. Examples of these adaptations will be explored in detail in the remainder of the chapter.

## What Can be Learned from Delta's Story of Mentorship?

Delta's mentorship program is firmly grounded in the belief that "place matters," and therefore it is important to note that what is appropriate and has worked in one particular context may not be appropriate or work in other contexts. Despite this, examining Delta's story of mentorship may provide some insights for educators designing or redesigning a mentorship program.

The four core beliefs upon which Delta's mentorship program is structured are as follows:

1. An effective mentorship program is aligned with the vision and goals of the district,
2. An effective mentorship program is a means to build the leadership capacity of teachers,
3. An effective mentorship program is responsive to learner needs, and
4. An effective mentorship program promotes and develops innovative teaching practice.

To provide a comprehensive picture of mentorship in Delta, three questions will be addressed for each of these core beliefs:

1. Where are we now?
2. Where are we going?
3. How will we get there?

Each section below will also conclude with a series of key questions that can be used to help guide the design or redesign of a mentorship program.

## An Effective Mentorship Program is Aligned with the Vision and Goals of the District

### Where Are We Now?

The learning and work of mentors and protégés is closely aligned with the district's vision and with the professional development direction of the district through our inquiry focus: How can we best support our peers so they embrace and model wise practice?

This question was developed during the second year of the mentorship program with the intention of deliberately aligning mentorship with the district's use of inquiry as a learning framework for students, teachers, administrators and leaders. Being aligned in such a way not only helped ground mentorship in the direction of the district, but also helped promote the district's focus on inquiry. The addition of the inquiry question to the framework of mentorship helped to hone the mentorship program's focus on cultivating both the wise teaching practice and leadership capacity of the teachers involved in the program.

Another way that mentorship has been intentionally aligned with the school district is through the use of the values outlined in the bold vision as norms for all mentorship learning sessions and meetings (Figure 4). These values have become central to the mentorship program and provide a common language for participants as they talk about their own learning and the learning of their students.

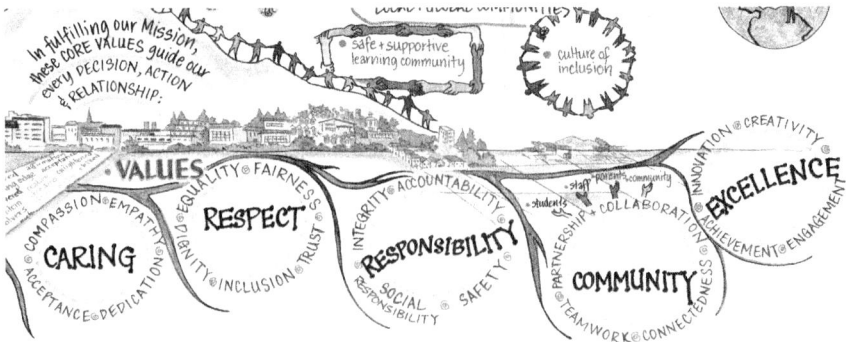

*Figure 4.* District Values that are used as Mentorship Norms (Delta School District website, 2016)

The ways in which Delta School District values have been interpreted as norms for mentoring are as follows:

- Caring: We treat each other with compassion and seek to understand each other. We embrace and celebrate our diversity.
- Respect: We believe there is a space for everyone to participate. We speak, listen and work together with consideration.
- Responsibility: We are committed to working together and agree to honour that commitment to the best of our ability.
- Community: We believe our learning is richer as a result of our connection and collaboration.
- Excellence: We strive for excellence in our teaching as a means to achieve success for all learners. We recognize that everyone is learning and working to improve their teaching practice.

The collective understanding of these values as norms that guide learning interactions helps to connect the mentor teams to each other. Presumably, a mentor or protégé could move from one team to another and find similar expectations and agreements for how the members of the team will interact. A central commitment to these values also ensures that the way mentors and protégés work together is in harmony with the values of the district.

It is also worth noting that mentorship achieves alignment by leading the way in the approaches used in professional learning across the district. For example, the mentorship program was an early adopter of a lesson study model as a framework for collaborative learning. As the district has concentrated on promoting job-embedded professional learning, lesson study is becoming more common across the district. The mentorship program's incorporation of lesson study was an early step in this shift.

## Where Are We Going?

Although the mentorship program is clearly aligned with the broad goals and direction of the school district, there is more work to be done in aligning mentor and protégé learning with school goals and direction. Ideally, teachers should be considering school goals in their instructional design and mentorship can play a role in helping teachers do just that.

## How Will We Get There?

In an attempt to align mentorship with the learning being done at the school level, the structures for lesson study have recently been adapted. For the first time lesson study will be funded through learner grants, which are district-funded school-based grants that groups of teachers can apply for in order to support collaborative inquiry aimed at improving student learning. All learner grant initiatives must address at least one of the four key areas identified by the district: student inquiry, assessment for learning, inclusive learning and/or learner engagement.

Lesson study groups will emerge from mentorship teams, and will be supported in applying for a learner grant to provide release time in order to conduct a lesson study that is connected to both a school goal and learner grant key area. In order to further connect mentorship to schools, lesson study groups will include staff not already involved in mentorship, from the school where the lesson study is situated. The goal of this new process is to create an opportunity for mentorship participants to directly connect their learning in their mentoring context to their learning as part of their school staff.

## Key Questions:
1. Does the school district have a vision or mission with which mentorship can be aligned?
2. How can mentorship support the achievement of that vision or mission?

3. What processes and communities does mentorship need to embrace and align with?

## An Effective Mentorship Program Is a Means to Build Leadership Capacity of Teachers

The emphasis of most mentorship programs is on building the teaching capacity of the teachers being mentored. In Delta, the focus is on developing the innovative teaching practices of *all* teachers involved in mentorship, including the mentors. In addition, Delta's mentorship program has a supplementary focus on building the capacity of mentors to act as teacher-leaders and to facilitate learning-focused conversations in other learning communities. For the purpose of this chapter, these skills are referred to as leadership capacity and skills. In building teaching capacity, we examine promoting and developing innovative teaching practice.

Delta's focus on building the leadership capacity of mentors emerged from the understanding that in order to achieve the district's bold vision, the culture of the district needed to be one of learning and growth. Strong teacher-leaders, equipped with a toolkit of leadership skills, would help move the culture of the district in that direction.

### Where Are We Now?

The mentors in Delta have been well supported in the development of mentoring and leadership skills. The cornerstone of mentor learning in Delta has been Wellman and Lipton's work, *Mentoring Matters,* with their emphasis on the stances and functions of mentorship and learning-focused conversation verbal tools such as pausing, paraphrasing and questioning. Mentor learning has extended beyond these foundations to include topics such as the language of leadership, how to have difficult conversations, facilitating groups, growth and fixed mindset, inquiry as a method of professional learning, and facilitating adult learning. All these skills prepare Delta's teacher mentors to be highly effective teacher-leaders in their schools and learning communities.

Mentors transfer the skills they develop in mentoring to other areas where they may be taking a leadership role or working with other teachers. Spheres in which these skills are useful include leading and working in collaboration or inquiry groups at school, in formal teacher-leader roles such as department-head or school-based professional development chairs, and in any informal learning situations.

Generally, Delta mentors have the reputation of skilled facilitators and leaders, in addition to being master teachers. Although this combination of attributes makes mentors potentially powerful agents of change, they are not yet leveraged to their full potential.

## Where Are We Going?

The goal, moving forward, is that eventually *all* mentors will be seen as teacher leaders in *all* schools and that, as such, they will play a key role in establishing and promoting a growth-oriented culture of learning in schools across the district. When this goal has been achieved all mentors will:

- use their skills to support the learning of their colleagues beyond the confines of the mentorship program,
- be teachers who both lead and teach such that colleagues turn to them when they are looking for direction or support,
- act as educational leaders, and
- share their learning, publicly, both within their schools and across the district.

Furthermore, the mentorship program will:

- be viewed broadly as a positive learning experience and an exciting leadership opportunity,
- attract even more teachers to participate in the mentorship program, as both protégés and mentors, and
- continue to evolve and become even richer and more diverse.

## How Will We Get There?

The mentorship program will continue to build the leadership capacity and skills of the mentors and expand the public profile of mentorship skills as an important part of leadership. Obviously, continuing to offer engaging, rich and responsive learning sessions for mentors is vital to the continued growth of the leadership capacity of mentors. It is also important to broaden the impact of mentorship by involving more teachers. A natural turnover in mentors will help to accomplish this. When mentors leave the program and pursue other leadership opportunities, then space opens for new mentors to join the program and expand their leadership capacity. This natural turnover has the added benefit of new mentors bringing fresh perspectives and diverse skills to the program. Furthermore, as former protégés become experienced teachers, they may take on the role of mentor and use their experiences as protégés to further enrich the learning of new mentors and protégés by sharing their experiences of mentorship.

Another opportunity to broaden the impact of mentorship and build teacher-leader capacity is when the Coordinator of Teacher Mentorship works with other groups of teacher-leaders. There are various groups of teachers with whom the Coordinator of Teacher Mentorship can work, including the Coordinators of Inquiry, Facilitators of Professional Literacy Communities, and school-based collaboration groups. This approach to building the capacity of teacher-leaders, through roles they already occupy, will help to build a strong culture of learning across the district.

### Key Questions

1. How can we support the development of teachers' leadership capacity through mentor learning sessions?
2. How can mentors act as teacher-leaders within their schools and other learning communities?
3. How can we publicly share the learning and work of mentorship participants?

## An Effective Mentorship Program Is Responsive to Learner Needs

Just as effective teachers design their instruction around the needs of their learners, a mentorship program, mentor learning sessions and mentor team meetings must be designed with the learners at the centre. Because the fundamental goal of mentorship in Delta is to provide students with quality learning experiences that lead to learner success, mentorship must ultimately be designed with the needs of students in mind. The result of this attention to learner need is an obligation to seek, analyze and respond to feedback from all stakeholders about the effectiveness of the program. Additionally, this requires that the teachers, at every level of the mentorship program, be committed to improving student learning.

## Where Are We Now?

Since the inception of the mentorship program, structures have been in place for participants to provide feedback in the form of

- formal surveys,
- needs assessments,
- exit slips,
- pre-learning questionnaires,
- self-assessments, and
- meeting reflection forms.

The resulting feedback is used to adapt and alter the program. In fact, two of the core structures of the mentorship program were developed in response to feedback.

The first is the inclusion of lesson study as a formal part of the mentorship program. After the first year of the mentorship program's existence, teachers identified a desire to co-plan, co-teach, and co-reflect as part of their mentorship experience. In response to this feedback, the Coordinator of Teacher Mentorship researched models for this type of learning and added lesson study as an optional mentorship activity. Although the goal of all protégés participating in a lesson study has yet to be realized, those teachers who have participated identify it as a rich and worthwhile learning experience.

The second example of the feedback-response cycle changing the structure of the mentorship program is the evolution of the process for creating mentor teams. In the first year of mentorship, the Coordinator organized the teams by placing teachers with similar teaching loads who were teaching in proximity to each other together on teams. It was a time consuming and frustrating task. The feedback at the end of the first year indicated that the makeup of these teams was not effective. In response, the Coordinator tried a different approach, grouping mentors together and inviting them to identify which protégés fit best with their team. Upon further reflection, and through discussions with several mentors, it has become clear that to build the most coherent and effective teams it is necessary to keep the protégés and their needs at the heart of the decision-making around team composition. In the third year, mentors grouped protégés together and then assigned themselves to teams with the needs of the protégés in mind. The feedback from the mentors was that the teams functioned better as a result of the process used to create them. These stories exemplify the power of adapting an approach based on feedback.

In addition to the use of feedback in the ongoing design of the mentorship program, the Coordinator of Teacher Mentorship and the mentors themselves practice and model responsiveness using the concept of backward design when planning mentor learning session and team meetings. For both mentor learning sessions and team meetings, design starts with the needs of the teacher learners. In addition to creating rich learning opportunities, this planning process also models strong instructional design for the protégés to use in their own year-long, unit and lesson planning.

### Where Are We Going?

An area of growth for the mentorship program is to create and sustain structures that will seek and gather feedback from all levels and stakeholders, particularly school-based administrators. Until recently, there has been very little space for the voices of administrators in the design of the mentorship program. During the 2015-2016 school year, the Coordinator of Teacher Mentorship engaged in an inquiry process as a means of assessing the effectiveness and impact of the mentorship program. The initial stages of checking and scanning involved interviewing the principals of schools where mentors were teaching in order to get a clear picture of how mentorship was impacting school culture. These interviews proved to be a valuable source of information, and several new areas of growth were identified, including the recognition that learning at all levels of the mentorship program needed to be grounded in the needs of students.

### How Will We Get There?

Moving forward, it is important to create and sustain procedures and structures for actively seeking feedback from school-based administrators. Plans to increase feedback include providing administrators with bi-monthly email updates about the mentorship program, and having the Coordinator of Teacher Mentorship make regular visits to schools to speak with principals and vice-principals. Additionally, the Coordinator of Teacher Mentorship will expand the formal interview process with school-based administrators beyond schools with mentors to schools with mentors and protégés.

A formal process (Figure 5) for identifying learning goals has been established to ground mentorship directly in responding to student need. Protégés scan their learners and identify a learning goal based on the needs they have identified. Mentors collectively scan the protégés with whom they work and identify learning goals that will help them support their protégés. Individual mentors may adopt different learning goals so that collectively they can meet the needs of all protégés. Finally the Coordinator of Teacher Mentorship will scan the mentors and identify a learning goal that will best meet the collective needs of the protégés. This connects the work of every level of mentorship to the needs of Delta students. It also allows for flexibility from year to year in determining and adjusting the direction of the program.

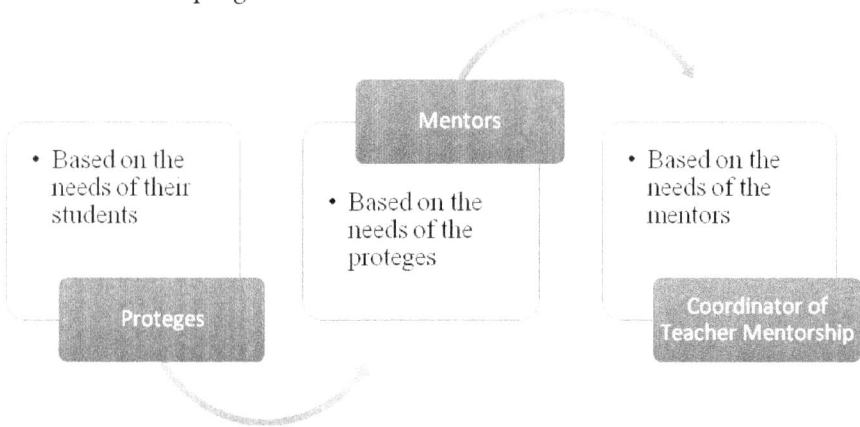

**Mentors**
- Based on the needs of the proteges

- Based on their needs of their students

**Proteges**

- Based on the needs of the mentors

**Coordinator of Teacher Mentorship**

*Figure 5.* Nesting Process for Setting Professional Learning Goals

**Key Questions:**
1. How do you seek feedback about the mentorship program?
2. From whom have you sought feedback? Are there any groups whose voices have not been heard? How will you access feedback from those groups?
3. What do you do with the feedback once you have it? How do you respond to what you learned?
4. What structures or processes do you have in place to identify learner needs?

# An Effective Mentorship Program Promotes and Develops Innovative Teaching Practice

Given that the fundamental goal of a mentorship program is to support student learners in finding success by providing rich learning experiences, the focus of the participants must be on improving teaching practice. To ensure that mentorship participants are being exposed to and developing effective teaching practice, it is important that the program be designed with a clear picture of what teaching practices it will promote.

### Where Are We Now?

Since the first year of the program, the concentration of Delta's mentorship program has been on developing innovative teaching practice. This is reflected in the program's inquiry question (How can we best support our peers so they embrace and model wise practice?) and the design of mentor learning sessions and team meetings. Despite this focus, a limitation of the program was the lack of a comprehensive definition of what exactly was meant by innovative teaching practice. There was a general sense of what innovative teaching looked, sounded and felt like, and a loose shared understanding that it included frameworks such as inquiry, assessment for learning, backward design and inclusive approaches.

In the fall of 2016, the OECD's Seven Principles of Learning (Dumont, Istance, & Benavides, 2010) and the First Peoples' Principles of Learning (First Nations Education Steering Committee, "First Peoples Principles of Learning - British Columbia") were introduced as a framework for describing and understanding innovative teaching practice in the context of the mentorship program. All mentor learning sessions and mentor team meetings are designed using this framework. The use of the framework provides mentors and protégés with a vibrant common language to frame their conversations about teaching.

**Weaving the 7 Principles of Learning & First Peoples Principles of Learning into our Mentoring Relationships**

| The 7 Principles of Learning OECD | First Peoples Principles of Learning FNESC | Examples from my own teaching practice | What does this LOOK like/SOUND like/FEEL like in a mentoring relationship? |
|---|---|---|---|
| Learners at the centre | ✓ Learning ultimately supports the well-being of the self, the family, the community, the land, the spirits, and the ancestors. <br> ✓ Learning requires exploration of one's identity. <br> ✓ Learning is embedded in memory, history, and story. <br> ✓ Learning recognizes the role of Indigenous knowledge | | |
| The social nature of learning | ✓ Learning is holistic, reflexive, reflective, experiential, and relational (focused on connectedness, on reciprocal relationships, and a sense of place). <br> ✓ Learning involves generational roles and responsibilities. | | |
| Emotions are integral to learning | ✓ Learning involves patience and time. <br> ✓ Learning ultimately supports the well-being of the self, the family, the community, the land, the spirits, and the ancestors. <br> ✓ Learning involves recognizing the consequences of one's actions. <br> ✓ Learning requires exploration of one's identity. | | |
| Recognizing individual differences | ✓ Learning recognizes the role of Indigenous knowledge. <br> ✓ Learning is embedded in memory, history, and story. <br> ✓ Learning requires exploration of one's identity. | | |
| Stretching all students | ✓ Learning involves recognizing the consequences of one's actions. <br> ✓ Learning requires exploration of one's identity <br> ✓ Learning is holistic, reflexive, reflective, experiential, and relational (focused on connectedness, on reciprocal relationships, and a sense of place). | | |
| Assessment for learning | ✓ Learning is holistic, reflexive, reflective, experiential, and relational (focused on connectedness, on reciprocal relationships, and a sense of place). Learning involves patience and time. <br> ✓ Learning involves recognizing the consequences of one's actions. | | |
| Building horizontal connections | ✓ Learning involves generational roles and responsibilities. <br> ✓ Learning is holistic, reflexive, reflective, experiential, and relational (focused on connectedness, on reciprocal relationships, and a sense of place). <br> ✓ Learning involves recognizing that some knowledge is sacred and only shared with the permission and/or in certain situations. | | |

*ADAPTED from Aboriginal Education Department 2016

SD37 (Delta)

*Figure 6.* Principles of Learning Framework for Mentorship

## Where Are We Going?

Recently, the senior leadership team and school-based administrators have been working to create definitions of innovative teaching practice and learner success. The goal behind crafting these definitions is to provide a road map for professional learning. The working definitions are:

> Innovative teaching involves continuous reflection and evolution in classroom practice in order to increase the intellectual engagement of students. Through the creation of deep learning tasks that foster curiosity, creativity and inquiry-mindedness, innovative educators take risks in order to positively impact the learning experience and outcomes for all students.

> Learner Success is built upon an intrinsic, deep desire to learn and a feeling of confidence in knowing how to learn. Successful learners develop the mindset and competencies needed to engage deeply in their learning. Educators create the conditions for learner success by ensuring students know where they are with their learning, where they are going with their learning, and how they can get there. Learner success is enhanced when students feel a deep sense of connectedness and the adults supporting them express their belief that the students will contribute positively to society and be successful in life. The result is all students graduating with dignity, purpose, curiosity and options.

The next step for the mentorship program will be to investigate these definitions in the context of mentorship and to integrate mentorship's current definition of innovative teaching with the district's definition. The Principles of Learning Framework that mentors are using to structure mentorship is closely aligned and effectively supplements the district's definitions.

## How Will We Get There?

One immediate change that can be made to integrate the district's understanding of innovative teaching is to change the mentorship program's inquiry question from "How can we best support our peers to embrace and model *wise* teaching practice?" to "How can we best support our peers to embrace and model *innovative* teaching practice?" This simple change helps to narrow and refine the focus of mentor and protégé learning. Additionally, the definitions of innovative teaching and learner success will provide structure to further ground mentoring in actual teaching practice. For example, these definitions can be used in conjunction with an understanding of student needs, school goals, the learner grant key areas and mentorship's Principles of Learning Framework to set appropriate and impactful professional learning goals.

**Key Questions:**
1. Is there agreement in your district on what wise teaching practice is?
2. How can you model those wise practices in mentor learning sessions?
3. How can mentors model those wise practices in their interactions with protégés?
4. Are you using those wise practices in the design of any learning sessions or workshops offered as part of your mentorship program?

## Concluding Thoughts on the Delta Story

If there is a lesson to be learned from Delta's story, it is that mentorship, just like gardening, is messy business. It requires patience and time and necessitates getting down in the dirt to understand the conditions of the garden. Gardeners constantly adapt and adjust their approach to gardening, and continuously tend to their plants. Sometimes their actions do not promote the growth and blooming that was expected and they must try again with a different approach. The work of a gardener is never done; even in the dormant winter months, the bulbs must be removed and the soil prepared to endure the cold.

Delta's story of mentorship is not complete and just as a garden looks different from season to season and year to year, so will the mentorship program. Mentorship structures, framework and procedures will change. What will remain constant is a commitment to supporting early career teachers, growing teacher leadership capacity and promoting innovative teaching with the ultimate goal of providing Delta students with engaging and transformative learning experiences.

# References

Brownlie, F., & King, J. (2011). *Learning in safe schools: Creating classrooms where all students belong* (2nd ed.). Markham, ON: Pembroke.

Delta School District. (2016). *Our vision.* Retrieved from: http://www.deltasd. bc.ca/content/about/ourvision

Dumont, H., Istance, D., & Benavides, F. (2010). *The nature of learning: Using research to inspire practice.* Paris: OECD.

First Nations Education Steering Committee. (n.d.). *First Peoples principles of learning* [Pamphlet]. Retrieved from: http://www.fnesc.ca/ learningfirstpeoples/

Learning Services. (2016). *Principles of learning framework for mentorship.* Delta, BC: Delta School District.

Lipton, L., & Wellman, B. (2003). *Mentoring matters: A practical guide to learning-focused relationships* (2 ed.). Sherman, CT: Mira Via.

# Part 3

# School and School System Support for Early Career Teachers

## Chapter 21

# What Contextual Factors Affect Early Career Teachers? Findings from the International Systematic Review of Research Literature

*Keith D. Walker, Benjamin Kutsyuruba,*
*Lorraine Godden, Ian A. Matheson*

## Introduction

Beginning teachers around the world are situated in a dynamic instructional landscape that influences their development and practice and includes the expectation that they will prepare students to enter increasingly demanding post-secondary situations. Teachers need to be able to respond to local, provincial or state, and national policies within widely different contextual milieux, as they seek to achieve excellence in their practice. Internationally, it has been argued that the first three to four years after initial training are the most crucial for teachers' decisions related to whether or not they will remain in the profession (Jones, 2003). There is a growing consensus in the literature regarding the value of support for beginning teachers (Feiman-Nemser, Schwille, Carver, & Yusko, 1999): support that will help mitigate early career issues. As an overarching support mechanism teacher induction (Serpell, 2000), with effective mentorship functions, is seen as one of the most crucial means for the support of beginning teachers (Doerger, 2003). Consequently, the rationale for this extensive international systematic review (Kutsyuruba, Godden, Covell, Matheson, & Walker, 2016) stemmed from our research team's desire to explore the implementation of induction programs in different contexts and to identify how successful induction programs have responded to the contextual challenges affecting early career teachers worldwide. This chapter provides a snapshot of our review findings.

# The Nature of the Review

In undertaking this international systematic review, we achieved a number of objectives. First we created an international geographic mapping of empirical research (written in English) that detailed the varied and diverse contextual challenges faced by beginning teachers. Second, we generated a representation of the formal programmatic responses of support provided to beginning teachers. Third, we synthesized the known evidence for the effects of the roles of mentors or induction programs for beginning teachers on their professional practice, with attention to attrition and retention rates. Finally, we sought to contribute valuable information to support policy makers and educational leaders on the role of school administrators in supporting beginning teachers.

## Our Literature Review Questions

To meet these objectives, we used the following review questions:

1. Which nations and regions are represented in research literature (written in English) that details formal or programmatic support of beginning teachers in their first five years of teaching?

2. What international research evidence is there to describe various contextual factors that affect experiences of beginning teachers?

3. How do teacher induction and mentorship programs respond to the various contextual factors affecting beginning teachers?

4. What is the role of school administration in supporting beginning teachers?

## Literature Review Methodology

This systematic review was undertaken using the EPPI-Reviewer software (EPPI Centre, Institute of Education, London) to analyze and interrogate research literature entries. Our research group initially defined the terms of reference, and identified the critical focus of the review based upon the research questions. The search strategy for the review involved rigorous electronic and hand-searching of key electronic databases and relevant journals for titles and abstracts relevant to the research questions, as defined by our inclusion criteria. Databases searched included ERIC, Academic Search Complete, ProQuest, and Education Source. Citations uncovered by the search strategies were stored on appropriate document referencing software, and titles and abstracts were screened against the criteria. Full texts that appeared to meet the inclusion criteria were obtained for further screening. All items that satisfied the final stage of screening were then key-worded and included in the systematic map.

Our initial electronic database searches revealed 16479 sources, and our hand-searching the journals uncovered a further 24 entries for potential inclusion. Duplications of electronic searches were removed, which reduced the total number of entries to 6538. Our second step was to screen titles and abstracts of the citations found by electronic means against the following inclusion criteria: article was published between 2004-2014; must have relevance to our research questions; must have included empirical data; must have been focused on early years, primary, secondary or compulsory education (K-12), and the study must have been presented in English. A total of 4768 were excluded: 1696 were not focused on the study context; 2775 were not relevant to our research questions, 315 were not empirically-based; 44 were not in English; and 29 fell outside our date parameters. Following further exclusions of reports that proved to be unobtainable (N=11), the full texts of 734 studies were further screened against the inclusion criteria.

Our third step was to undertake full screening of the 734 articles in our sample. The research group applied the same exclusion criteria as used in the first screening, this time to the full-text articles that had not already been excluded (n=734). Of these, 113 were selected for inclusion in our systematic map. For the full in-depth review, only those studies key-worded as focusing on social, cultural, political, and organizational contexts, with a population focus of compulsory education in the K-12 sector (students aged four to twelve), and featuring new and beginning teacher induction and mentorship programs, were included. The geographic location of the included studies' contexts was also noted.

## The Scope of the Review

The geographic representation of the articles featured in our review was taken from the *location* of the studies were conducted. The largest number of studies were conducted in the United States: a total of 64 out of 113 articles. Articles were also found in the United Kingdom (15), Canada (12), Europe (8), Australia and New Zealand (6), the Middle East (6), combined nations (more than one nation examined in one study) (2), and the Far East (1). In addition to highlighting the geographic regions we also identified the locales within the regions where studies were conducted; these will be included in our presentation.

## The Significance of the Review

Our systematic review highlighted a significant number of research studies that have been carried out on the effects of mentorship and induction on beginning and new teachers' learning, performance, attrition, and retention. First, our review indicated that there are some commonalities involved in the successful induction and mentorship of beginning teachers, in spite of their geographic variance. Second, the literature search employed in this review identified relevant research published in English, whether or not it originated in non-English speaking countries; the bibliographic information on these was extensive and included a variety of different nations. Finally, our search confirmed that research on induction and mentorship of beginning teachers has been conducted for several decades, and that research from 10 years ago remains relevant to the current research agenda.

## The Limitations of the Review

Our review was limited to searching for articles written in English; this approach excluded research conducted in a variety of other nations from being represented. It must be noted that our original inclusion criteria had to be modified, as there was a lack of valid, recent, and robust research on the effects of induction and mentorship that explicitly related to retention and attrition of beginning teachers. In addition, our search strategies concentrated on terminology familiar to us as Canadian and European researchers. We acknowledge that other nations might employ various other terms when discussing support for beginning teachers.

# Contextual Factors Affecting the Experiences of Beginning Teachers

A number of contextual factors emerged from our review that had an impact on the experiences of new teachers during the induction and mentoring process. This chapter selectively discusses the following contextual factors: *social* (e.g., interpersonal interactions with peers and external community relationships), *political* (e.g., initiatives at the national/federal, state/provincial, district, and school levels), *cultural* (e.g., localized and school cultures, issues of diversity), and, *personal/individual* (e.g., personal and individual concerns, self-efficacy, and emotional intelligence). In the following sections, we reflect upon our findings within these four overarching sets of contextual factors and discuss how each of these were found to affect the experiences of beginning teachers in an international context. In addition, we offer findings on the ways in which induction and mentoring programs were found to address these contextual factors within organizational contexts and administrative supports for beginning teachers.

## Social Contextual Factors

Our systematic review found many of the studies identified varying ways that beginning teachers were socialized through professional peer support, including structured interactions (e.g., team-teaching), the establishment of planning partners, sharing of teaching-related information, examination of subject-specific issues, and assistance with marking. In particular, there were many examples citing the importance of conversations with peers, colleagues, mentors, and administrators, including informal chats about teaching. We also found that a number of programs featured opportunities for beginning teachers to make observations of their peers' teaching. In many programs that we examined, professional peer support was described as a valuable social factor for building skills and sharing ideas.

Our examination found many programs that emphasized the importance of different types of relationships in helping with the induction process for beginning teachers. Peer relationships involving professional, social, and emotional types of peer support existed in different capacities across a range of programs internationally, and an absence of peer support was identified as a challenge for new teachers regardless of their geographic jurisdiction. Relationships with the broader community outside their school were also of value to beginning teachers, and were comprised of formal professional, non-formal professional, and non-professional structures.

It was evident from the studies examined in our review that new teachers need and receive a great deal of peer support to aid their social integration into the teaching community. Mentors often supported new teachers by being a source of information, in addition to guiding and helping beginning teachers with navigating the school and broader teaching community. Studies reported that in helping new teachers with the socialization process, mentors acted as guides for social interactions, assisting with social functioning in the school community, and role modeling both as a teacher and staff member. A further notable feature of many programs was that supportive peers were a key form of emotional support. Among all features of strong peer relationships, trust and respect were most frequently cited. Trust helped beginning teachers to feel confident in asking their peers anything, without fearing the repercussions, though building trust takes time. Mutual feelings of respect between teacher and colleagues were essential for emotional support to occur. Where beginning teachers did not experience formal peer support, they emphasized powerful feelings of isolation. Additionally, similar feelings of isolation were felt when beginning teachers perceived a complete lack of relationships with their formal peers. Where the relationship between mentor and mentee lacked effectiveness, the lack of trust, respect, and any effective balance between support and feedback were all reported as important issues.

In many of the studies, beginning teachers received support through external relationships with broader teaching and non-teaching community sources, including individuals working in education settings that were formally connected to the beginning teachers. School psychologists, curriculum facilitators, and induction coaches all provided support, which facilitated the socialization process. Non-formal professionals included individuals who worked in education but were not formally affiliated with new teachers in professional working relationships. Using online learning communities and social networking, Wiki pages, and engaging with former faculty members from universities where they had received training in teacher education programs were also of significance. Beginning teachers also identified community members, including parents of their students, as important non-professional relationships.

The concept of induction continues to be understood as a "helping mechanism" (Serpell, 2000, p. 3) to achieve socialization into school culture. Peers within the school were seen as a natural part of the socialization process, whether in formal and non-formal capacities. Individuals outside of the school can play a key role in helping to sustain teachers in their careers—a need identified by Long et al.(2012). Our investigation found many studies where peers provided beginning teachers with varied types of support that helped them grow as teachers, become active members of the teaching community, and feel emotionally comfortable in their new roles. We also established that individuals outside of the school could assist beginning teachers with the socialization process into the broader teaching profession.

## Political Contextual Factors

A wide body of empirical studies has examined teacher attrition, mentorship, and induction in order to better understand issues faced by beginning teachers. Our systematic review built upon these understandings though examination of the complexities of creating and maintaining supportive school culture—something not previously considered (Long et al., 2012). School culture and support within schools are both influenced by political factors at different levels, including national or federal initiatives, state or provincial initiatives, and initiatives at the district, school, and community levels.

We found that political factors at the national or federal level determined structural elements of mentoring and induction programs, such as the identification of a specific practice and/or frequency of that practice (e.g., Parkinson & Pritchard, 2005). In contrast, we highlight other situations, where national or federal initiatives resulted in seemingly robust guidelines for induction programming but in actuality, great variation was found to exist at the school-level phase of implementation (Anthony, Haigh, & Kane, 2011), in order to meet the individualized needs of schools and teachers. Beginning teachers were seen to favour mandated support that maintained flexibility toward an individualized school culture through encouraging adaptable or flexible programming. School-level induction programs also allowed new teachers to develop their localized knowledge and understanding of national or federal policies and procedures related to teaching and education (Perry & Hayes, 2011) — an opportunity that was valued by some beginning teachers (Grammatikopoulos, Tsigilis, Gregoriadis, & Bikos, 2013).

Within our review, we found many examples of state or provincial initiatives that influenced, guided, and mandated the induction process of beginning teachers. These initiatives were identified in North America, Asia, and Oceania, and were mandated and implemented by governments to include formal mentoring, release time for both new teachers and mentors, professional development, creation of a teaching portfolio, teaching observation, and networking, amongst other facets.

At the district, school, and community levels, our review brought to description factors that were cited for their direct impact upon the induction processes for new teachers. District level programming affected the induction process through the handling and management of mentors, the implementation of professional development, and by virtue of their size, with smaller districts being perceived as more flexible and supportive than larger districts. At the school level, the need for micropolitical literacy was identified (e.g., Castro Kelly, & Shih, 2010): developing knowledge of the micropolitics of individual schools, in addition to developing pedagogical practice, was essential for beginning teachers' successful integration into school culture. At the community level, beginning teachers' integration into the community was noted as an important factor, especially given that support and collaboration were often sourced from the local community.

## Cultural Contextual Factors

Our review revealed that a number of cultural contextual factors impacted the beginning teacher. First, there were several challenges reported regarding teaching philosophies held by beginning teachers, and their school ethos or culture. Where there was a lack of alignment between the teaching philosophy held by a beginning teacher and the ethos of their school, this was particularly problematic, with levels of conflict with school culture being reported as one consequence. Moreover, in some cultural contexts social interaction between beginning teachers and the other teachers in school was not facilitated. This hindered the formation of collaborative, supportive, and collegial ways of working, and prevented trustful relationships from forming; thus the support rendered to beginning teachers was less effectual.

Mentorship and the role of individual mentors were seen as strong mitigation factors related to these challenges. However, complex mentor knowledge was required to support ongoing career development and professional development of beginning teachers. In addition, positive climates for learning and development for all school staff member were seen as essential. Our systematic review found value in moving away from *expert and novice* models of mentorship to the creation of an overarching culture of training and support. Many of the articles in our review reported that mentorship and induction had influence upon the professional and ongoing career development of teachers. This has implications for the type of mentorship adopted and enacted for supporting beginning teachers; and we suggest that mentorship models such as Adaptive Mentorship (Ralph & Walker, 2010; 2011) have a potential role here.

Exposure to diversity within schools was largely seen as a challenge rather than a problem, when there is adequate support for the beginning teacher. Exposure to diversity was reported by some articles to have the potential for the ongoing development of teaching practice, in addition to a lasting impact upon students when beginning teachers were able to confidently engage in meaningful exploration of multi-cultural issues through their teaching practice. School demographics were seen to be important, but not vital, in helping beginning teachers to adjust to cultural difference. Our review found some evidence that the demographics of a school do not necessarily have a direct impact on the overarching institutional culture. For example, a diverse student demographic does not always equate to a culture of diversity within a school. Mentorship and the roles of mentors can have a crucial role in helping beginning teachers to navigate such situations.

Finally, the culture of a school and school district was seen as instrumental in helping beginning teachers decide to remain in the teaching profession. One study argued that the entire school community bears a broad responsibility to support beginning teachers in staying with the teaching profession as a career. There was a significant positive correlation between school culture and climate and a teacher's decision to remain in the school district, with one study suggesting that improvement of working conditions impacts directly upon a teacher's urge to remain in either the specific school or the school district (Wynn, Carboni, & Patall, 2007).

## Personal and Individual Contextual Factors

Our review highlighted a number of personal and individual contextual factors of significant relevance in providing effective support for beginning teachers. Feeling a sense of professional competence was linked to the level of emotional support received by a beginning teacher, both from their peers and from administration in their school. Beginning teacher participants from many of the studies examined in our review, reported feeling significant pressure to achieve professional competence. Such achievement was facilitated for beginning teachers who were in a school culture where engaging in self-reflection was valued and encouraged.

Many studies reported that links between self-reflection and professional development should be established for beginning teachers, ideally through induction, mentorship, and involvement from the broader school community. Levels of peer collaboration, and strength and effectiveness of professional relationships with the entire school community, were valuable in facilitating the individual beginning teacher's ongoing professional and career development. In addition, the empathy of the school community plays a distinct role in helping beginning teachers to develop their emotional intelligence in a manner that supports their developing practice.

A beginning teacher's prior skills and experience were seen to be relevant in several of the studies examined in our review, with one large-scale study reporting that prior experience in a field other than teaching resulted in a new teacher being more likely to stay in the profession (Kapadia, Coca, & Easton, 2007). This finding suggests implications for the structure of initial teacher training and subsequent hiring practices of new teachers. Circumstances, either planned or unplanned, may result in the beginning teacher taking some level of personal initiative in meeting challenges, which in turn impacts upon their development of self-efficacy. This may result in a negative "sink or swim" type of effect upon the beginning teacher. However, where teachers were facilitated through mentorship and induction activities that enhanced their ability to creatively problem solve within an overarching developmentally supportive culture, positive individual outcomes were achieved. The opportunity to experiment with creative problem solving further enhanced the possibility of positive outcomes for the beginning teacher.

Personal and individual concerns and anxieties felt by beginning teachers could be mitigated by the quality and structure of mentorship. Many studies described discrepancies between the levels of support provided through induction and mentorship programing and the levels and type of support required by the beginning teacher. There is potential value in using specific mentorship models to help overcome this challenge.

Finally, the interaction between school context, culture, and beginning teacher expectations was seen to be instrumental in helping beginning teachers form a strong sense of professional identity. Of benefit to facilitating professional identity formation is the ability to tailor induction and mentorship programing in a way that recognizes individual learning dispositions, and that is responsive to learning opportunities.

## Programmatic Response to Contextual Factors Affecting Beginning Teachers

The systematic review sought to describe and synthesize how induction and mentoring programs responded to contextual factors affecting new and beginning teachers; we also examined the organizational contexts of the schools providing support for beginning teachers. Our review revealed organizational and administrative venues through which induction and mentoring programs addressed the above contextual factors.

### Organizational Structures

Strategies used by organizations often include some form of mentorship programming. Components of quality mentoring were identified as: being multi-year developmental processes, requiring supportive and understanding administrators (with associated implications for training, recruitment and ongoing professional development of administrators), training of mentors, evaluations linked appropriately to state and district standards, provision of technology to facilitate effective communication, educated mentors, reflective enquiry and teaching processes, systematic and structured observations of teaching practice, formative teacher assessment, meaningful administrative involvement, and school culture supports.

Our review established that many induction and mentoring programs were comprised of more than one mode of support for beginning teachers. A combination of support types was understood as being representative of how beginning teachers must navigate varied, complex, and dynamic demands when teaching within different school contexts. Often, evaluation of programs through research studies and/or formal evaluation was difficult if programmatic details were absent. Similarly, one study featured the finding that for multiple supports for beginning teachers to be adopted, there needed to be definition of, and rationale for, such supports; these needed to be clearly and appropriately communicated to all relevant stakeholders. In other words, it mattered how specifically and clearly the information was conveyed, as this affected the perceived value of the mentorship and induction supports.

Moreover, our systematic review highlighted the importance of carefully selecting program elements to match new teacher needs. Programs that were flexible in their structure provided opportunities for unique contextual needs to be addressed. Critical to this process was the creation of informal and formal mentoring relationships that were personal, timely and well resourced. Just-in-time support responds to the fluid and dynamic social needs of beginning teachers as they become familiarized with their school, pedagogy, and profession. Commonly, mentoring was equated with induction (Clandinin et al., 2012; Hobson, Ashby, Malderez, & Tomlinson, 2009); however, our review further highlighted that it was but one facet of comprehensive induction. Nevertheless, mentoring was the most widely discussed program element featured in the studies, with successful structures reported as being based on levels of mentor involvement, reliability and accessibility. Furthermore, a high level of trust between all parties involved in the mentoring process was essential for this support to be successful.

Our review established that beginning teachers often feel pressured organizationally to make a good impression in their schools, and consequently they were unlikely to want to reveal any problems and concerns that might be seen as a weakness. Our review identified that beginning teachers held a positive regard for induction and mentoring programs when they experienced strong feelings of support. Likewise, a sense of belonging achieved through effective induction and mentoring support was a common mitigating factor against the anxiety expressed in many other induction and mentorship for beginning teachers' literature reviews.

## Administrative Support

Our review acknowledged the relevance and importance of the administrator's role in the induction and mentoring process. As in other reviews of the literature (e.g., Long et al., 2012), our analysis uncovered strands in the literature that pertained to school administrators' duties and responsibilities, types and formats of support for beginning teachers, the overall impact and outcomes of principal engagement, and the importance of principals' leadership and commitment for the success of teacher induction and mentoring programs.

Various duties of school administrators were revealed through examination of the studies included in our review, varying from informal interactions with the beginning teachers and mentors to development and implementation of programs, mentor assignment, scheduled formal meetings, observations, and teacher supervision and performance evaluation. Likewise, our review pointed to the importance of school administrators' active and positive support for their induction programs, and the negative effects that lack of support and assistance from administrators may have had on beginning teachers' development. In some studies, the principals' commitment to and recognition of the program, as well as active engagement and collaborative culture orientation, were described as having the potential to positively or negatively influence the beginning teachers' commitment to and understanding of the need for the program. The success of new teachers seemed to have been related to the school culture in which their first experiences as beginning teachers took place, and to the principal's pivotal role in building and maintenance of collaborative school culture (Long et al., 2012).

Studies examined in our review indicated that initiatives to lessen the bureaucratic organization of schools and school systems allowed strategies to promote more genuine administrative support from school leaders and collegiality among teachers, which could in turn improve retention. Of significance were administrators' engagement with and support for the work of mentors; their careful and thoughtful approaches to mentor assignment and training were deemed important and well considered The extent to which school administrators were able to support mentors' work and new teaching approaches substantially affected the quality of novice teachers' learning to teach with mentors. In one study, Ingersoll and Strong (2011) found that programs should focus on selection and training of mentors to ensure high levels of support, and that teacher collaboration and principal assistance were the most influential factors for novices. The principal was deemed the instructional leader who actively supports and participates in professional development for beginning teachers (Correa & Wagner, 2011), and a part of this responsibility was directly linked to their work with mentors.

We found empirical data on the direct and indirect impact of school administrators on the effective outcomes of teacher induction and mentoring programs that pointed to the ultimate outcome of teacher development and potential for retention. Direct impact of principal engagement was demonstrated through findings that pointed to the greater importance of relational aspects (including with administrators) than of activities. These highlighted the higher levels of efficacy, satisfaction with teaching, and intention to remain in the profession when beginning teachers experienced encouragement, support, and assistance from their school administrators. Our review found that principals' specific actions and trust orientation positively impacted new teachers' perceptions of having their need for respect, belonging, self-esteem, confidence, and autonomy met. Conversely, the failure of school administrators to satisfy beginning teachers' needs, including provision of support, resources, and clear communication, negatively affected the overall teacher experience and may have been instrumental in novice teachers' intentions to leave the profession.

Besides the supportive role of school administrators, our review highlighted the expectation that school principals would supervise and evaluate the work of the new teachers. This may stem from the expectation for administrators to supervise induction programs for beginning teachers, providing counsel for best instructional practices and classroom management skills (Correa & Wagner, 2011). The supportive role of school administrators in teacher induction may be counteracted by these requirements for supervision and evaluation of the new teachers (Abu Rass, 2010; Chatlain & Noonan, 2005; Cherubini, 2010). The role of evaluation of beginning teachers in induction programs has been fervently debated, with such debates focusing on whether or not beginning teachers should receive both support and evaluation from the same individuals, as part of their induction experience. While evaluation has typically been associated with effectiveness, adequacy, value and appropriateness of a certain action, process, or product, assessment offers feedback and is formative in nature, to guide the professional growth of teachers so they are able to make appropriate adjustments in their teaching or program. This point also raises an important issue, that of beginning teachers' accountability for their progress. Achinstein (2006) highlighted the importance of beginning teachers developing an understanding and awareness of the overall role of a school principal in teacher development, as well as his/her position in relation to beginning teachers' support within the broader context of schooling. Stemming from this position, principals can provide high-quality management through administrative leadership and a climate of trust if they want to support their teachers in terms of autonomy and appraisal (Blömeke & Klein, 2013)

## Discussion and Implications

The findings of our systematic review suggest there were many commonalities shared by beginning teachers across different geographic locations. A heuristic model emerged from our review that offers a visual representation of the findings and their implications for policy, practice, and future research in the area of early career teacher development.

### A Heuristic Model of Contextual Factors that Impact the Beginning Teachers

Based on the key findings revealed through our systematic review, we adapted Bronfenbrenner's (1994) ecological systems theory to create a heuristic visualization (see Figure 1, below) of the complex and multi-layered contextual factors that influence and impact upon mentorship and induction programing for beginning teachers. When employed in this framework, Bronfenbrenner's theory directs attention toward the interaction between the personal/individual, the social, political and cultural, the organizational contextual and environmental variances and nuances, and the potential sources of influence and impact upon induction and mentorship programing.

Within our framework, beginning teachers' personal factors are situated at the core, being both distinctive, and dependent on, and shaped by, organizational, social, political, and cultural contextual factors. Personal factors comprise the social identity of an individual beginning teacher. These includes the beginning teacher's sense of professional competence, emotional intelligence, ability and opportunity to take initiative, prior skills and experience, professional identity, and the quality and structure of mentorship they perceive as an individual. The beginning teacher's personal factors are constantly shaped by both the individual environment and by encounters with other individuals situated within the immediate microsystem environment. The microsystem consists of interpersonal features at the school organizational level. These factors include the school culture, and the ethical values and practices that are embedded into that culture. In addition, they include individual groups of factors relating to the entire school staff, that are unique to that school. Mezosystem refers to the school administration and their management of duties and responsibilities towards beginning teacher support, the types and format of such support, the leadership roles and commitment towards supporting beginning teachers within the school, and the impact and outcomes of school administration involvement in supporting beginning teachers. Exosystem refers to organizational or institutional factors at school district level that shape or structure the environment within which the beginning teacher's experiences of mentorship and induction programming occur. These factors include the policies, procedures, community relationships, organizational structure, and overarching institutional culture of the school district. Macrosystem includes federal/national/provincial and state politics and initiatives, national ideologies and identities, and demographical diversity, including religion, ethnicity, and socioeconomic status.

This heuristic framework is designed to help conceptualize the sources and relationships between the contextual factors that affect mentorship and induction programming. This allows for purposeful, intentional recognition of the full richness of formal, facilitated, and spontaneous avenues of mentorship and induction programing that support early career development of beginning teachers.

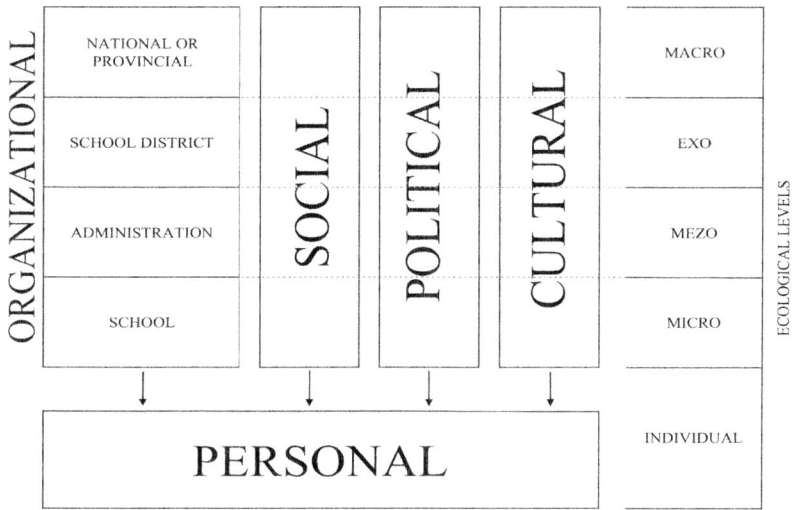

*Figure 1.* A Heuristic Framework of Contextual Factors that Impact Mentorship and Induction Programs for the Beginning Teacher

## Implications for Policy, Practice, and Further Research

We believe that this heuristic framework will be helpful for policy makers and educational leaders in the process of designing, implementing, and maintaining the teacher induction and mentoring programs. Application of the framework allows for the planning, analysis, and evaluation of the entire policy cycle (inasmuch as possible, recognizing the complex and non-linear nature of policy development processes) by offering a broad picture of the gamut and nature of factors that have an impact on effective programming, and successful induction and mentoring experiences of beginning teachers. We contend that the policy environment surrounding the induction and mentoring processes matters, and that this heuristic brings it into focus. Furthermore, it is important to further examine the implications of the increasingly diverse contexts of schooling and the ever-increasing policy requirements for an administrator's role.

In terms of practice, the heuristic is helpful for situating and assessing the existing or planned programs. Given the instrumental role of school administrators in the induction and mentoring processes, it may offer an assistive lens to principals and other administrators by identifying the areas where novice teachers' needs are being or not being met by the programs. The heuristic also provides school leaders with a better understanding of the source and type of challenges faced by a beginning teacher, so that they can then measure the respective alignment or misalignment of the program supports necessary to mitigate those challenges.

Given the empirical support for the significance of mentoring within the induction programs, we see the need to further explore the role of mentorship frameworks as mitigating contextual challenges (especially through forming effective mentoring relationships). While it is evident that school administrators have an important role in terms of involvement within induction and mentoring program provision, further examination of the specific role of administration in mitigating contextual challenges is warranted. Further studies would do well to examine the mechanisms and structures that can help school administrators develop trusting and collaborative relationships with mentors and beginning teachers. Stemming from this point is the need to explore the effect of mentoring and supporting structures available for new administrators and their links with subsequent involvement in induction programs for beginning teachers. In other words, we suggest further research on the connection between the mentoring support experienced by beginning administrators and the subsequent shaping of their role as supportive figure for beginning teachers in their schools. Finally, this review warrants continuing research into the multifaceted nature of organizational and contextual factors that that shape the roles and responsibilities of all stakeholders' participation in induction and mentoring programs.

# References

Abu Rass, R. (2010). The new teacher induction programme in Bedouin schools in the Negev, Israel. *Journal of Education for Teaching, 36*(1), 35–55.

Achinstein, B. (2006). New teacher and mentor political literacy: reading, navigating and transforming induction contexts. *Teachers and Teaching: Theory and Practice, 12*(2), 123–138.

Anthony, G., Haigh, M., & Kane, R. (2011). The power of the 'object' to influence teacher induction outcomes. *Teaching and Teacher Education, 27*(5), 861–870.

Blömeke, S., & Klein, P. (2013). When is a school environment perceived as supportive by beginning mathematics teachers? Effects of leadership, trust, autonomy and appraisal on teaching quality. *International Journal of Science and Mathematics Education, 22*, 1029–1048.

Bronfenbrenner, U. (1994). Ecological models of human development. In T. Husen & T. N. Postlethwaite (Eds.), *International Encyclopedia of Education* (2nd ed., Vol. 3) (pp. 1643– 1647). Oxford, England: Pergamon Press.

Castro, A. J., Kelly, J., & Shih, M. (2010). Resilience strategies for new teachers in high-needs areas. *Teaching and Teacher Education, 26*(3), 622–629. doi:10.1016/j.tate.2009.09.010

Chatlain, G., & Noonan, B. (2005). Teacher induction in Catholic schools. *Journal of Catholic Education, 8*(4), 499–512.

Cherubini, L. (2010). An analysis of the implications between the theoretical framework and the policy context of Provincial education policy in Ontario. *Journal of Contemporary Issues in Education, 5*(1), 20–33.

Clandinin, D. J., Schaefer, L., Long, J. S., Steeves, P., McKenzie-Robblee, S., Pinnegar, E., & Downey, C. A. (2012). *Early career teacher attrition: Problems, possibilities, potentials.* Edmonton, AB: Centre for Research for Teacher Education and Development, University of Alberta.

Correa, V. I., & Wagner, J. Y. (2011). Principals' roles in supporting the induction of special education teachers. *Journal of Special Education Leadership, 24*(1), 17–25.

Doerger, D. W. (2003). The importance of beginning teacher induction in your school. *International Electronic Journal for Leadership in Learning, 7*(21), 1–13.

Grammatikopoulos, V., Tsigilis, N., Gregoriadis, A., & Bikos, K. (2013). Evaluating an induction training program for Greek teachers using an adjusted level model approach. *Studies in Educational Evaluation, 39*(4), 225–231.

Hobson, A. J., Ashby, P., Malderez, A., & Tomlinson, P. D. (2009). Mentoring beginning teachers: What we know and what we don't. *Teaching and Teacher Education, 25*(1), 207–216.

Feiman-Nemser, S., Schwille, S., Carver, C., & Yusko, B. (1999). *A conceptual review of literature on new teacher induction.* Washington, DC: National Partnership for Excellence and Accountability in Teaching.

Ingersoll, R. M., & Strong, M. (2011). The impact of induction and mentoring programs for beginning teachers: A critical review of the research. *Review of Education Research, 81*(2), 201–233.

Jones, M. (2003). Reconciling personal and professional values and beliefs with the reality of teaching: findings from an evaluative study of ten newly qualified teachers during their year of induction. *Teacher Development, 7*(3), 385–402.

Kapadia, K., Coca, V., & Easton, J. Q. (2007). *Keeping new teachers: A first look at the influences of induction in the Chicago public schools.* Chicago, IL: Consortium on Chicago School Research, University of Chicago.

Kutsyuruba, B., Godden, L., Covell, L., Matheson, I., & Walker, K. (2016). *Understanding the contextual factors within teacher induction and mentoring programs: An international systematic review of research.* Kingston, ON: Queen's University.

Long, J. S., McKenzie-Robblee, S., Schaefer, L., Steeves, P., Wnuk, S., Pinnegar, E., & Clandinin, D. J. (2012). Literature review on induction and mentoring related to early career teacher attrition and retention. *Mentoring & Tutoring: Partnership in Learning, 20*(1), 7–26.

Parkinson, J., & Pritchard, J. (2005). The induction experiences of newly qualified secondary teachers in England and Wales. *Journal of In-service Education, 31*(1), 63–81.

Perry, B., & Hayes, K. (2011). The effect of a new teacher induction program on new teachers reported teacher goals for excellence, mobility, and retention rates. *The International Journal of Educational Leadership Preparation, 6*(1), 1–12.

Ralph, E. G., & Walker, K. D. (2010). Enhancing mentors' effectiveness: The promise of the Adaptive Mentorship© model. *McGill Journal of Education, 45*(2), 205–218.

Ralph, E. G., & Walker, K. D. (Eds.). (2011). *Adapting mentorship across the professions: Fresh insights and perspectives.* Calgary, AB: Detselig.

Serpell, Z. (2000). *Beginning teacher induction: A review of the literature.* Washington, DC: American Association of Colleges for Teacher Education.

Wynn, S. R., Carboni, L. W., & Patall, E. A. (2007). Beginning teachers' perceptions of mentoring, climate, and leadership: Promoting retention through a learning communities perspective. *Leadership and Policy in Schools, 6*(3), 209–229.

## Chapter 22

# What Motivates Novice and Experienced Teachers to Engage in Self-Directed Professional Development?

*Carmine Minutillo*

## Introduction

In my lifelong learning journey as an elementary school classroom teacher and, subsequently, as an elementary school principal, self-directed professional development has played an integral role. As a new teacher, I naively assumed that all teachers, regardless of the duration of employment within a school board, participated in some form of self-directed professional development, as part of the self-improvement efforts of a professional teacher. As I gained more experience in a variety of educational settings and became more acquainted with other teachers within my school board, it became increasingly apparent that there was a vast discrepancy in terms of how much and what kind of professional development individual teachers chose to complete.

Early in my teaching career, I approached my principal to seek some guidance regarding what sorts of professional development opportunities I should pursue; I was confident that my principal would be more informed than I in terms of current educational trends and school board emphases. I took my principal's advice to heart and pursued as many self-directed professional development opportunities as my time outside of school-based work would permit. The additional knowledge and experiences that I gained proved to be of great benefit to my teaching practice and, ultimately, to the students whom I taught. The self-directed professional development enabled me to establish professional relationships and to use critical insights in my own practice.

Despite the benefits that this engagement in self-directed professional development had for my own teaching practice, some of my teaching colleagues did not share the same level of enthusiasm. While some other teachers also chose to engage in self-directed professional opportunities, others chose not to participate at all. This discrepancy had led to some teachers' eager seizing of self-directed professional development opportunities; while others choose to shun any suggestion that personal time should be spent on school-related-activity, has been of great interest to me as an elementary school principal. As a leader, I became interested in gaining a better understanding of the leader's role in novice teachers' engagement in self-directed professional development when considering the best interests of students in our school. My inquiry into the importance of school culture and leadership in relation to motivating teachers to participate in self-directed professional development led me to conduct the study I will describe in this chapter. I considered it necessary to investigate the influence of leadership within the culture of the school – whether by teacher colleagues, principals, or others in the school community. Who these persons were and how they may have had an impact on individual teachers' decisions to participate in self-directed professional development pursuits became a focus of inquiry for me.

## The Research Study and Context

This chapter is based on the research study that explored the elementary teachers' motivation for, and the school principal's influence on, their engagement in self-directed professional development. The following research questions guided this study: a) What motivates teachers to engage in self-directed professional development? b) What are the conditions necessary for promoting teachers' engagement in self-directed professional development? and, c) What are teachers' perceptions of the principal's role in supporting, fostering, encouraging, and sustaining the professional development of teachers?

The context for this investigation of the leader's role in teachers' engagement in self-directed professional development was one school board in the south-eastern part of the Province of Ontario. The School Board is geographically large, but hosts a relatively small student population when compared to other school boards in Ontario. The School Board consists of both rural and urban school settings, though primarily in small towns and cities. In recent years, this School Board has placed considerable emphasis on the importance of transformational leadership. Both explicitly and implicitly, there has been much in-servicing and conversations amongst principals and between in-school and central office administration, with respect to transformational leadership.

To address the research questions, qualitative methods of data collection were used in order to gain authentic information and insight into why teachers choose to engage in self-directed professional development. Interviews were conducted with a sample of six teachers (three experienced and three novice teachers) working in different school settings in the School Board. Each of the qualified participants had participated in self-directed professional development over the past two years. As much as possible, in this chapter I compare and contrast the responses from the experienced teachers and novices in the early career phase.

## Theoretical Underpinnings

Several theoretical concepts were important to this study: professional development (including self-directed professional development efforts), motivation, school culture, transformational leadership, and trust. Each of these constructs is discussed below.

### Professional Development (PD)

As a whole, professional development can consist of, but is not limited to, course work, conferences, professional dialogue, teacher collaboration, inquiry-based learning, workshops, and professional reading. The Ontario Ministry of Education (2007) defined PD as "self-chosen learning activities that teachers investigate individually or as part of a professional learning community (e.g., action research, lesson study, graduate work, additional qualification courses, writing)" (p. 3). PD is undertaken to improve practice, to remain current in the profession, and for personal reasons, such as salary improvement and self-interest. PD can be highly varied and diverse, incorporating courses, workshops, professional reading, informal dialogue and collaboration, as well as many other formats. PD may be instigated by the individual teacher, the principal, the school board, the Ministry of Education, or other parties.

For the purposes of this research, the focus was on PD that was self-selected and motivated primarily by each individual teacher, with their wants or needs paramount. In this sense, self-directed professional development mirrors PD in every way with the exception of whose decision it is to partake in such activities. Within the confines of self-directed professional development, PD is solely the teacher's decision with respect to whether or not they will participate. In addition to the decision to participate or not in PD, the individual teacher decides with whom they will participate and the timelines around their participation.

Gall and Renchler (1985) described PD as "efforts to improve teachers' capacity to function as effective professionals by having them learn new knowledge, attitudes and skills" (p. 6). Some scholars have located it within a "professional growth" paradigm that characterizes development as more self-directed, arising from the learner's interests and needs (Feiman-Nemser, 2001). Others have situated it within an "educational change" paradigm that views development as focused upon bringing about change. Guskey (2002), for example, defined teacher PD as "systematic efforts to bring about change in the classroom practices of teachers, in their attitude and beliefs, and in the learning outcomes of students" (p. 381). More recently, scholars have positioned it within the "professional learning" paradigm (Day, 1999).

## Motivation

Although motivation can be physical or mental (Schunk, Pintrich, & Meece, 2008), Weiner (1992) described motivation as an individual's desire to act in a particular way. In order for motivation to take hold, there is a requirement for some form of action or motion (Criss, 2011). More specific to an educational setting, motivation occurs when individuals feel a sense of autonomy, feel a connection to the school, and when they feel that they have the requisite competence to be successful in a school site (Ryan & Deci, 2003).

A framework that is instrumental for this research was Self-Determination Theory (SDT). It served as the lens through which the motivation behind why teachers choose to partake in self-directed professional development can be understood. Within the scope of SDT, three principal needs must be satisfied for well-being and growth to occur: (a) competence, (b) relatedness, and (c) autonomy (Orsini, Evans, Binnie, Ledezma, & Fuentes, 2016). Jansen in de Wal and colleagues (2014) provided an extensive overview of how these three concepts related to teachers' engagement in professional learning. Competence refers to individuals' feeling that they are capable of fulfilling their professional obligations within the school setting and that there is opportunity to exercise this competence. Relatedness entails a feeling of being a relevant part of the social fabric of the school, where there is a connection to others, a sense of caring for one another is mutual, and there is a sense of belonging between colleagues and the greater school community. Autonomy encompasses the notion that individual teachers have control over the decisions that need to be made in their own teaching practice. When the threshold for these three basic needs is met, motivation can flourish. When the threshold for these three basic needs is not met, motivation is stalled (Ryan & Deci, 2000).

## School Culture

Northouse (2010) defined culture as "the learned beliefs, values, rules, norms, symbols, and traditions that are common to a group of people... culture is dynamic and transmitted to others" (p. 336). Similarly, Smith and Stolp (1995) postulated that school culture can be defined as the historically-transmitted patterns of meaning that include the norms, values, beliefs, ceremonies, rituals, traditions, and myths understood, maybe in varying degrees, by members of the school community. Peterson and Deal (1998) elaborated further on culture, maintaining that "culture is the underground stream of norms, values, beliefs, traditions, and rituals that has built up over time as people work together, solve problems, and confront challenges" (p. 28). Developing and maintaining a positive school culture is paramount in helping to coordinate and develop the vision for the school in conjunction with input from teachers (Yin, 1993). As Petersen and Deal (1998) stated, the positive culture of schools entails having staff that share a collective purpose and having the school norms of collegiality, improvement, and hard work pervade all that is done. They continued, "Strong positive cultures are places with a shared sense of what is important, a shared ethos of caring and concern, and a shared commitment to helping students learn" (p. 29).

## Transformational Leadership

Leadership entails promoting a certain cause or vision and taking steps to guide others in the school to follow (DeSpain, 2000). The overall competence of the leader is an important factor for teachers who are considering professional development (Wagner & French, 2010). Teachers were more apt to internalize feedback from their supervisor when they felt that the supervisor was aware of what was happening in the classroom and provided feedback that was specific about teaching practices and classroom activities. Leadership style also appears to have some significance in terms of teacher motivation and professional development. Thoonen, Sleegers, Oort, Peetsma, and Geijsel (2011) indicated that transformational leadership practices stimulate teachers' professional learning by inspiring them to improve personal practice via professional development. Bass and Riggio (2006) defined transformational leaders as: "those who stimulate and inspire followers to both achieve extraordinary outcomes and, in the process, develop their own leadership capacity. Transformational leaders help followers grow and develop into leaders by responding to individual followers' needs by empowering them and by aligning the objectives and goals of the individual followers, the leader, the group, and the larger organization" (p. 4).

In addition to the importance of having teacher colleague support in creating satisfying workplace conditions for professional development to occur, Clement and Vandenberghe (2001) advocated that school leaders must share a healthy collegial relationship with teachers. Vaughan and McLaughlin (2011) found that support from the principal fosters a culture of professional development while allowing individual teachers the autonomy to have some input into improving personal practice. Transformational leadership behaviours in schools set direction, help people, redesign the organization, and manage the teaching and learning program (Leithwood, Harris, & Hopkins, 2008; Leithwood & Jantzi, 2005).

## Trust

Trust is defined as "the extent to which one engages in reciprocal interactive relationships such that there is willingness to be vulnerable to another and to assume risk with the confidence the other party will possess some semblance of benevolence, competence, honesty, openness, reliability, respect, wisdom, and care" (Kutsyuruba, Walker, & Noonan, 2010, p. 24). Adams (2008) emphasized that trust "operates within the cognitive and psychological domain as a motive for behaviour, at the interpersonal level to shape social exchanges, and within organizations to influence collective performance" (pp. 29-30). Kutsyuruba et al. (2010) noted that establishing, maintaining, and sustaining trust in schools between principals and teachers is a complex undertaking. Handford and Leithwood (2012) concluded that there are several indicators for trust: competence, consistency and reliability, openness, respect, and integrity. The notion of trust plays an important part when considering principals' influence on teachers to take on self-directed PD. Wahlstrom and Louis (2008) argued that schools with a high level of trust between teachers and principals exhibit more collective decision-making. Collective decision-making is more likely to occur when all staff members share in the collective goals of the school.

# Research Findings

### Teacher Individual Motivation

Teacher individual motivation deals with the incentives and inspirations behind why each teacher might make a decision to take on particular PD opportunities. As all participants were active in their PD pursuits at some point in their teaching career, there was a wide array of reasons regarding what motivated each of these teachers to take steps to improve their practice. These reasons can be broadly categorized into two main classifications: autonomous and controlled (Jansen in de Wal et al., 2014).

Autonomous motivation refers to motivation that is interest/enjoyment-based (intrinsic) or personal value-based (extrinsic-integrated or extrinsic-identified) where individuals have control over the motivation. In such a landscape, PD is done more to satisfy personal inclinations rather than to satisfy others or to obtain some sort of external award. As such, autonomous motivation is internal in its self-directed nature. In contrast, controlled motivation is largely outside the individual, inclining itself more to a rewards- or judgment-based proclivity. Within the parameters of controlled motivation, extrinsic-external motivation deals mostly with incentives that offer a reward for participation in PD, whereas extrinsic-introjected motivation deals mostly with incentives that provide positive judgment by others upon an individual who engages in PD.

A clear and consistent finding within the conducted research was that, initially, controlled, external motivation was key in motivating participants to engage in self-directed PD. All participants chose to take on PD pursuits as new teachers to gain an extrinsic reward, namely financial gain. For these novice teachers, and from a financial perspective, it was important to move up the teacher pay grid to the highest possible level. In their school board, the highest pay scale on the grid was referred to as A4. The jump from A3, the second highest pay scale on the grid, to A4 entailed an annual pay increase of two to five thousand dollars, depending on years of teaching experience. Over the course of a full teaching career, the monetary incentive at play was enormous. For this reason, it was important for newer teachers to move up to category A4 as quickly as possible, so that they could take full advantage of the salary increases that accompanied this movement. Taking Additional Qualification and Additional Basic Qualification courses was the most logical way to achieve the upward movement to A4. For the more experienced teachers who participated in the study, partaking in PD happened for different reasons later in their careers; however, all veteran teacher participants also described taking on PD pursuits initially to satisfy the financial importance of being at the top of the teacher pay scale, namely A4.

Once the financial incentives of taking on PD were satisfied, other motivational factors tended to take over. Once A4 was achieved, there simply was no further monetary gain to be had in terms of moving up the teaching pay grid and therefore no further external incentive to take on PD. The motivation to engage in self-directed PD shifted from a rewards-based incentive to a judgment-based incentive where PD was sought to gain positive judgments from others. The controlled, introjected motivation at play following the rewards-based external motivation aimed for a positive outlook by colleagues upon participants. For the three novice teachers involved in this research, being seen positively by their colleagues was particularly important. At the forefront of the novice teachers' motivation to engage in PD was the impression that others within their respective schools would look upon them favourably, seeing them as being competent, capable, and self-sufficient. These teachers did not wish to be perceived as being a burden or pest to the more experienced and established teachers who were also busy with their own daily teaching practice. PD was the vehicle through which these novice teachers could take steps to ensure self-sufficiency, thereby gaining a positive outlook from colleagues. While financial incentives entailed primarily taking courses with respect to PD, individual PD undertakings were far broader, incorporating courses in addition to workshops, professional reading, and informal dialogue with colleagues.

Much like novice teachers, the three more experienced teachers shared similar motivations to take on PD when they moved to a new school or to a new teaching position within the same school. For much the same reasons as the novice participants, ensuring their new colleagues at their receiving school or their existing colleagues perceived them as capable teachers was important.

Once financial gain was established and participants were feeling comfortable in their position within a school in terms of collegial relations, the motivation for taking on self-directed professional development shifted once again. From here, the motivation to take on PD took on a more autonomous format, whereby more internal factors came into play. In such a dynamic, the motivation to pursue PD opportunities at hand was founded more on the value that the PD had to the participants' teaching knowledge base or for personal interest and enjoyment.

While all participants in the study explicitly stated that they took on PD initiatives because it was beneficial to their students, the depth of participant responses was greater with the three more experienced teachers. Regarding the obligatory feeling of needing to do one's best for students, participants expressed a strong motivation to continue with much the same PD pursuits as in their introjected, judgment-based scenario of moving to a new school or a new position within the same school. Although the types of PD that were undertaken remained much the same, the motivation for engagement became more student-oriented and more suited to fulfilling the professional obligations of a good teacher to remain current and relevant in terms of pedagogy. PD was again the vehicle through which participants pursued learning that would best meet their needs within the scope of helping their students, as well as helping to ensure they remained on the front end of what was happening in schools, such as confirming their mathematics instruction was current.

When linking the findings of the study to those in extant literature, there was a strong parallel with regard to integrated motivation. In both instances, teachers who believed that they had the ability to better their professional practice and competence were more likely to engage in training opportunities (Dysvik & Kuvaas, 2008). Participants chose to pursue PD for the betterment of their personal teaching practice, which allowed them to remain current within the profession. Better professional practice incorporated improving lessons for students (Kwakman, 2003). Improving lessons for students was aligned with doing one's best for them. By ensuring that the lessons prepared on students' behalf were constructive, participants in the current study and in previous studies were ensured that they were meeting their integrated motivation to be excellent teachers.

## School Culture

In addition to the impetus behind individual teacher motivation with regard to engagement in self-directed PD, there were school culture factors that were important. On a positive note, trust among colleagues, teacher autonomy, and staff collaboration were key elements in encouraging teachers to take on PD pursuits. Elements that discouraged teachers from engaging in PD included the negative mindset of colleagues, unbuilt relationships, and lacking a sense of belonging. Trust, as it relates to autonomy, was an overarching concept in the decision-making process regarding the choice about whether or not to participate in PD.

As supported by Tschannen-Moran (2014), trust among colleagues played an integral role in the choice about whether or not to partake in self-directed PD. Where there was an atmosphere of trust, there was an increased likelihood that steps would be taken together to try and improve personal practice in conjunction with others. The reasoning behind the relationship of trust varied from sharing ideas, to remaining current and relevant, to feeling comfortable in approaching others to ask questions or seek advice about teaching practice. The link to autonomy when addressing trust among colleagues rested with the essential dynamic that these teachers were able to work with whomever they felt most comfortable. As anticipated by Tschannen-Moran (2001), all the participants expressed that predetermined pairings or groupings served to inhibit PD when a relationship of trust had not yet been developed or one particular teacher simply did not trust one of his or her group members.

Specifically in regards to autonomy, moving beyond the ability to select pairings or groupings or to choose a colleague with whom to dialogue informally allowed the imperative of teachers' capacity to select what type of PD to take on and the timelines surrounding PD pursuits. In such settings, teacher autonomy was set in contrast to PD that had been directed by a principal, school board, or Ministry of Education; where PD topics, timelines, and groupings were often predetermined. It was clear that teachers were more apt to take on PD when their autonomy was taken into consideration within the school culture. It was important for principals and school boards, who are in more direct contact with teachers, to allow for such autonomy to take place when introducing new curricular initiatives or facilitating school-based PD. Allowing for teacher autonomy in these circumstances endorsed motivational intentions for taking on PD.

Staff collaboration organically brought together trust among colleagues and teacher autonomy. Collaboration was most likely to take place when there was cooperation and a supportive environment among staff with ongoing PD held as an expectation. To support each other, PD resources were shared, encouragement and advice were forthcoming, and teachers took the initiative to address PD needs, such as starting a Math Club. For any of these PD initiatives to flourish, trust among colleagues and teacher autonomy was of paramount importance.

The connections between the findings of the study and those of the research were plentiful. Adams (2008), Handford and Leithwood (2012), and Louis and Wahlstrom (2011) established that trust among colleagues was essential for positively influencing collective performance. Healthy school cultures, which included a framework of trust, promoted hard work, which often took the form of PD engagements in the work of Petersen and Deal (1998), thus supporting this study's finding that trust was a central precondition to catalyze and support active engagement in PD. In terms of autonomy, Vaughan and McLaughlin (2011) found that autonomy was the key component for teachers to participate in PD, which is the same central finding derived from this study. Regarding collaboration, Tschannen-Moran (2001) identified that trust is an essential component; where trust was present, collaboration was more likely and where trust was deficient, collaboration was problematic, with either scenario having a positive and negative impact on students and staff.

### Principal's Role

Building on the importance of individual teacher motivation and school culture, the principal's role was the third main impetus found to be involved in teachers' engagement with self-directed PD. The principal's role was divided into four core themes: (a) relational disposition, which was subdivided into direct support and interpersonal connection; (b) leadership style; (c) impact on school climate, which was subdivided into role model for PD and shared vision, and (d) trust. All four themes relate to motivating teachers to engage in PD, as seen through the lens of transformational leadership.

Transformational leadership was the overarching concept when considering what influence the principal played in terms of mobilizing teachers to take part in PD. The reason for using the overarching concept of transformational leadership was because of the value encompassed. As noted in the research (Leithwood, Harris, & Hopkins, 2008; Leithwood & Jantzi, 2005), transformational leadership entails setting goals, helping people, redesigning the organization, and managing the teaching and learning program. These four tenets lend themselves to the same criteria that build trust within principal-teacher relationships, while allowing for a certain level of autonomy within a school setting and mobilizing teachers to engage in PD.

As related to personal characteristics, setting up the conditions necessary for participants to take on PD interests, as well as establishing healthy interpersonal relationships between the principal and teachers, was crucial to promoting the four main tenets of transformational leadership. Dysvik and Kuvaas (2008) and Kwakman (2003) concluded that teachers were more motivated and willing to participate in PD when the PD integrated a sharing of their ideas. Thoonen et al. (2011) advocated that transformational leadership practices stimulated teachers' professional learning. Finally, Clement and Vandenberghe (2001) explained that PD occurs most often when principals share a collegial and healthy relationship with teachers. All of this research coincides with the findings of this study in terms of establishing the need for a constructive relationship between the principal and teacher if an optimum level of PD is to become part of the school routine. Setting up the curricular goals for the school and helping colleagues to become more proficient in their teaching practice are collective undertakings; autonomy is built into such endeavours. It is not possible to apply the tenets of transformational leadership to the PD journeys in schools if individual teacher autonomy is prevented from coming to the fore through ongoing input from all stakeholders.

School climate, with its requisite for building a shared vision, is another area of focus that surfaced in this research, as related to transformational leadership. Yu, Leithwood, and Jantzi (2002), Harvey (2013), Barnett and McCormick (2004), and Finnigan (2010) suggested that allowing teachers to share in the vision-building process via transformational leadership served to motivate teachers. Within this study, there was a clear appreciation for principals who learned alongside teachers, as opposed to principals who chose to impart their knowledge to teachers. Learning alongside teachers helped to build trust within principal-teacher relationships, which, in turn, was critical in building and sustaining a healthy school culture. Inherent in a relationship of trust was the need for principals to allow for autonomy through teacher input as school goals were developed and as high expectations were co-developed to set the direction for the school. When a shared vision was able to come to fruition in a school through an exercise in teamwork, where principal and teacher involvement were intertwined, the outcome was increased buy-in from teachers, thereby increasing motivation, encouraging PD, building trust, allowing for autonomy, and solidifying the foundational aspects of creating a healthy school culture.

Regarding trust, the research advocates the view that trust is fostered when a principal embraces a transformational leadership approach (Wahlstrom & Louis, 2008; Handford & Leithwood, 2012). Benevolence, competence, honesty, openness, reliability, respect, wisdom, and care are the characteristics that Kutsyuruba et al. (2010) cited as being necessary for a relationship of trust to flourish between the principal and teachers. As these characteristics are solidified over time, the relationship of trust also further solidifies. Tschannen-Moran (2014) maintained that integrity and competence are critical elements of trust that lead to authenticity within a school leader. Bryk and Schneider (2003) complemented the above research by positing that relational trust is supported by respect, personal regard, competence, and integrity. Lastly, Tschannen-Moran and Gareis (2015) supplemented the characteristics of trust by discussing the notion that in schools where there is reciprocal trust between the staff and the principal a shared focus is more likely, thereby promoting the likelihood of sharing expertise and learning from one another. If such an environment is the case, the probability of teachers choosing to take on self-directed PD increases.

## Conclusions and Implications

In regard to the study implications for policy, there are many ways in which various educational initiatives are carried out in schools. It is not uncommon for such initiatives to be implemented with specific guidelines and/ or criteria that need to be met. With respect to Ministry and School Board policy makers, it is important to embed the opportunity for flexibility and autonomy in the roll-out of any initiatives. The findings of this study demonstrate that PD is more likely if teachers are able to exercise autonomy as a new idea or initiative moves forward. If the Ministry or School Board allows for individual autonomy to better reflect the culture within individual schools, then there is likely to be a greater chance that teachers will be apt to take on the cause. Additionally, it is imperative that any new policy that arrives on the doorstep of teachers comes with a sound rationale as to the benefits for both teachers and students.

Similarly, at the school level, the research findings suggested that principals may have an easier time successfully implementing new policy if teachers have a voice in what is proposed, so that the vision of the new policy can be shared and cultivated together as a team. Cultivation ensures trust, allowing for teacher input, hence autonomy. Being mindful of this dynamic will bring principals to the realization that it is important for teachers to be aware of and understand the directives and underpinnings of a new policy in order to encourage buy-in. For example, if a school chooses to focus PD resources on mathematics instruction, it is imperative that the teachers involved in teaching mathematics are aware of the reasoning behind the decision to focus on math, how it is to be implemented, and what benefit it is likely to have on student achievement. If teacher colleagues are informed of the reasoning behind policy implementation, they are more likely to have an easier time exercising autonomy within the implementation process, thereby taking up the new policy or initiative. Referencing new teachers specifically, ensuring that a colleague or mentor is in place at the school level to assist in navigating the implementation of new policies is essential. In light of the benefits of collegial dialogue when discussing best practices and teaching strategies, new teachers working alongside more experienced colleagues would assist in directing energies and ideas into meaningful practice that benefits students.

In regards to the study implications for the system and school leaders, three practice-oriented themes emerged: a) individual practice that support autonomy, b) developing a school culture that promotes autonomy, and c) the principal's role in support of autonomy. The results from this study provide insights for the district school board, school principals, and teachers who are interested in their self-pursuit of PD.

In this study, teachers were more likely to engage in self-directed PD when they were able to exercise autonomy over the PD options that were available to them. At an individual teacher level, regardless of the motivation that enticed teachers to pursue PD opportunities, participants wanted personal influence over PD choices. These motivations shifted from controlled to autonomous as the participants shifted across career stages. With the individual time and cost factors of self-directed PD, it is essential that teachers be provided support to pursue PD that is career-appropriate, especially once financial rewards for PD disappear. For more novice teachers who find the cost of PD to be a barrier, providing financial incentives, such as schools paying for a supply teacher to allow for release time with a colleague or the school covering all or part of PD expenses such as course or conference costs, encourages participation in PD.

All participants were more motivated to undertake PD opportunities when a positive school culture was present at their respective schools. Implications regarding school culture relates to all members of a school community working together to fashion a positive workspace that promotes PD. There are many players within a school who contribute to creating a positive atmosphere. Individual teachers must be willing to share resources with others and to have collegial relations. Active participation by individual teachers in self-directed PD promotes a positive school culture as well. Furthermore, a critical mass of teachers must be willing to work together for the betterment of the school. Most important for any school looking to maintain a healthy school culture is trust. PD includes asking questions of colleagues and allowing oneself to be vulnerable by attaining new knowledge or applying new learnings in the classroom in front of students. Such vulnerability requires a community of colleagues to be open to changing their practice, incorporating new learnings, and refining personal practice on an ongoing basis. Likely the most vulnerable are novice teachers who are still making their way in a school or the profession. For these new teachers, regular check-ins by the principal to ensure they are feeling comfortable with colleagues and not feeling overwhelmed with workload and other day-to-day issues will catalyze dialogue with colleagues.

Principals can support autonomy by providing the conditions necessary for PD to take place, by creating and maintaining a trusting relationship with teachers, by being a co-learner, and by ensuring a shared vision is in place. Within the structure of the school day and within the budget of the school, principals have the ability to take action to facilitate PD. Space and scheduling may be manipulated to offer time to teachers, which can be one of the main barriers to teachers taking on PD. Likewise, there is sometimes an opportunity for parts of a school budget to be allocated towards teacher PD. In doing so, a second major barrier, expense, may be offset by the school, thereby increasing the possibility of teachers taking on PD. In particular, PD that is specifically beneficial to novice teachers is important in ensuring new teachers' motivation and participation.

# References

Adams, C. M. (2008). Building trust in schools: A review of empirical evidence. In W. Hoy & M. DiPaola (Eds.), *Improving schools: Studies in leadership and culture* (pp. 29–54). Charlotte, NC: Information Age Publishing.

Barnett, K., & McCormick, J. (2004). Leadership and individual principal-teacher relationships in schools. *Educational Administration Quarterly, 40*, 406–434.

Bass, B.M., & Riggio, R.E (2006). *Transformational leadership*. Mahwah, NJ: Lawrence Erlbaum.

Bryk, A. S., & Schneider, B. (2003). Trust in schools: A core resource for school reform. *Educational Leadership, 60(6)*, 40–44.

Clement, M., & Vandenberghe, R. (2001). How school leaders can promote teachers' professional development. an account from the field. *School Leadership & Management, 21*(1), 43–57.

Criss, E., (2011). Dance all night: Motivation in education. Place of Publication: *The National Association for Music Education*.

Day, C. (1999). *Developing teachers: The challenges of lifelong learning*. London, UK: Falmer Press.

DeSpain, B. C. (2000). *The leader is the servant: The 21ˢᵗ century leadership model*. Mexico City: Grupo Editorial Iberoamerica.

Dysvik, A., & Kuvaas, B. (2008). The relationship between perceived training opportunities, work motivation and employee outcomes. *International Journal of Training & Development, 12*, 138–157.

Feiman-Nemser, S. (2001). From preparation to practice: Designing a continuum to strengthen and sustain teaching. *Teachers' College Record, 103*, 1013–1055.

Finnigan, K. S. (2010). Principal leadership and teacher motivation under high-stakes accountability policies. *Leadership & Policy in Schools, 9*, 161–189.

Gall, M. D., & Renchler, R. S. (1985). *Effective staff development for teachers: A research based model*. Eugene, OR: ERIC Clearinghouse on Educational Management, University of Oregon.

Guskey, T. R. (2002). Professional development and teacher change. *Teachers and Teaching: Theory and Practice, 8*, 381–391.

Handford, V., & Leithwood, K. (2012). Why teachers trust school leaders. *Journal of Educational Administration, 51*, 194–212.

Harvey, J. (2013). *The school principal as leader: Guiding schools to better teaching and learning*. New York, NY: The Wallace Foundation.

Jansen in de Wal, J., den Brok, P. J., Hooijer, J. G., Martens, R, L., & van den Beemt, A. (2014). Teachers' engagement in professional learning: exploring motivational profiles. *Learning & Individual Differences, 36*, 27–36.

Kutsyuruba, B., Walker, K., & Noonan, B. (2010). The ecology of trust in the principalship. *Journal of Educational Administration and Foundations, 21*(1), 23–47.

Kwakman, K. (2003). Factors affecting teachers' participation in professional learning activities. *Teaching and Teacher Education, 19*, 149–170.

Leithwood, K., Harris, A., & Hopkins, D. (2008). Seven strong claims about successful school leadership. *School Leadership & Management, 28,* 27–42.

Leithwood, K., & Jantzi, D. (2005). A review of transformational school leadership research 1996–2005. *Leadership & Policy in Schools, 4,* 177–199.

Louis, K. S., & Wahlstrom, K. (2011). Principals as cultural leaders. *Phi Delta Kappan, 92*(5), 52–56.

Northouse, P. G., (2010). *Leadership; theory and practice* (5th ed.). Thousand Oaks, CA: SAGE.

Ontario Ministry of Education. (2007). *Report to the Partnership Table on teacher professional learning: Recommendations of the Working Table on Teacher Development.* Retrieved January 23, 2013 from: http://www.edu.gov.on.ca/eng/teacher/pdfs/partnerreport.pdf

Orsini, C., Evans, P., Binnie, V., Ledezma. P., & Fuentes. F. (2016). Encouraging intrinsic motivation in the clinical setting: Teachers' perspectives from the self-determination theory. *European Journal of Dental Education, 20,* 102–111.

Peterson, K. D., & Deal, T. E. (1998). How leaders influence the culture of schools. *Educational Leadership, 56*(1), 28.

Ryan, R. M., & Deci, E. L. (2000). Self-determination theory and the facilitation of intrinsic motivation, social development, and well-being. *American Psychologist, 55,* 68–78.

Ryan, R. M., & Deci, E. L. (2003). Intrinsic and extrinsic motivations: Classic definitions and new directions. *Contemporary Educational Psychology, 25,* 54–67.

Schunk, D. H., Pintrich, P. R., & Meece, J. L. (2008). *Motivation in education: Theory, research, and applications.* Upper Saddle River, NJ: Pearson Education.

Smith, S. C., & Stolp, S. W. (1995). *Transforming school culture: Stories, symbols, values & the leader's role.* Ann Arbor, MI: ERIC Clearinghouse on Educational Management.

Thoonen, E. E. J., Sleegers, P. J. C., Oort, F. J., Peetsma, T. T. D., & Geijsel, F. P. (2011). How to improve teaching practices: The role of teacher motivation, organizational factors, and leadership practices. *Educational Administration Quarterly, 47,* 496–536.

Tschannen-Moran, M. (2014). *Trust matters: Leadership for successful schools* (2nd ed.). San Francisco, CA: Jossey-Bass.

Tschannen-Moran, M. (2001). Collaboration and the need for trust. *Journal of Educational Administration, 39,* 308–331.

Tschannen-Moran, M., & Gareis, C. R. (2015). Principals, trust, and cultivating vibrant schools. *Educational Policy, Planning, and Leadership, 5,* 256–276.

Vaughan, M., & McLaughlin, J. (2011). What can motivate teachers to learn? Ask them. *JSD: The Learning Forward Journal, 32*(5), 50–54.

Wagner, B. D., & French, L. (2010). Motivation, work satisfaction, and teacher change among early childhood teachers. *Journal of Research in Childhood Education, 24,* 152–171.

Wahlstrom, K. L., & Louis, K. S. (2008). How teachers experience principal leadership: The roles of professional community, trust, efficacy, and shared responsibility. *Educational Administration Quarterly, 44,* 458–495.

Weiner, B. (1992). *Human motivation: Metaphors, theories, and research.* Newbury Park, CA: SAGE.

Yin, C. C. (1993). Profiles of organizational culture and effective schools. *School Effectiveness & School Improvement, 4,* 85–110.

Yu, H., Leithwood, K., & Jantzi, D. (2002). The effects of transformational leadership on teachers' commitment to change in Hong Kong. *Journal of Educational Administration, 40* (4), 368–389. doi: 10.1108/09578230210433436.

# Phantom Power: My Experiences as a School Administrator Related to the Induction and Mentoring of Early Career Teachers

*Terry Kharyati*

## Introduction

New teachers are added to schools every month in many different contexts. Many of their perceived and experienced successes and failures are, in part, beyond their control. Principals have a duty to ensure quality experiences for their students, and therefore would be neglectful in that duty if they did not systematically address the quality of the teaching and learning in the classroom. Such responsibility and duty can be fulfilled by ensuring that all teachers, including new or novice teachers, are truly supported pedagogically, socially, emotionally, and individually. Understanding this fundamental truth was a learning journey for me. This chapter is an attempt to convey my thoughts and notes jotted down during that journey, as perceived through the music and lyrics of The Tragically Hip, and especially through the notion of *phantom power*. My reflection has led me to believe that, ironically, to be effective in supporting new teachers, a principal requires no phantom power at all.

## Context

*"phantom power"*

Music has always been at the forefront of the self-reflection process for me. Certainly, music has always been both muse and grenade; inciting reflection and emotion. When asked to consider the impact of my experiences in the induction of new teachers, I had no choice but to refer to work written by The Tragically Hip. They are a strong voice in my head. I owe a debt to Gordon Downie, Gordon Sinclair, Johnny Fay, Paul Langlois, and Robert Baker for helping me articulate how I have been feeling and thinking as a principal in the Quebec education system for almost 27 years now. On a more formal level, I am writing in response to my participation in a panel discussion on the role of school administrators in teacher induction and mentoring programs held as part of the Pan-Canadian Forum in Kingston, Ontario. My perspectives were not originally shaped by the music, but while preparing for the panel discussion, I immersed myself in the literature produced by The Tragically Hip and found a common language which allowed me to not only better articulate my thoughts, but to also see how their language has impacted those thoughts with a deeper understanding of my own experiences.

## We Are Products of Our Own Lived Experiences

*"the lonely end of the rink"*

I was a teacher for six years. As a first year teacher, I was given two bits of advice: 1) "don't smile until Christmas;" and, 2) "if you have any major issues, see your principal." I was a school administrator for 18 years and was guilty of offering those same bits of wisdom to new teachers and experienced teachers alike. I am sure this was seen by some as archaic and one-dimensional, as the advice is.

During my first year as a teacher I realized that, for the most part, this advice was useless to me because I had nothing to smile about, as that year was a crazy and depressing time for me. And secondly, I never saw my principal if I needed anything because he was much busier than anyone I knew, and I feared that if I did approach him, he would see that clearly he had made a mistake in hiring me as I was so out of my depth (you cannot hide the kind of desperation I felt those first few years). This was what I understood to be a normal induction into the educational fraternity of staff. I survived, but I am certain now that I did not improve, other than to learn how to better survive. Upon reflection, it was the loneliest time of my life, and I could have not been more proud to call myself a teacher. Scholars (Gold, 1996; Wang & Odell, 2008) found that principal behaviours that affect school climate and positive interaction with new teachers also positively improve new teachers' practice and even contribute to improved retention. Similarly, Bickmore and Bickmore (2010) noted that the major conclusion from their investigation was "the importance of including the school principal as an element of a multifaceted induction program. The stories revealed the principal's key role in meeting the perceived personal needs of novice teachers and establishing a healthy school climate in which the novice teacher can flourish" (p. 465). For the record, I loved my principal in those years, as he was a kind and hardworking leader whom I truly tried to impress but whom I never got to really know.

Later, as a new principal, I was also given two bits of advice: 1) "don't smile at staff meetings;" and 2) "if you have any issues, let the Board know before the issue gets to the press." Interestingly, I reverted to my days as a new teacher, feeling alone, targeted, tired, and filled with self-doubt. My level of efficacy was so low that I was sure someone would find me out to be the fraud that I was: undeserving of a job that someone had seen fit to give me, and that "I was squandering that chance." Upon further reflection, I note that it was the loneliest time of my life, and I could have not been more proud to call myself a principal.

I had been a principal for 10 years before a new program was created and implemented in what seemed to me to be an almost overnight fashion. There was not too much talk about it outside of the board office and certainly I was never consulted before its implementation. As an upstart and somewhat seasoned principal with a criticism for everything that I, myself, did not invent or implement, I couldn't believe we were spending $30,000 out of a $95,000,000 budget on what was being called New Teacher Induction. There was no question in my mind; I wanted no part of this initiative. Although I considered myself a data-driven school leader, I did not inform myself of research like McCann and Johannessen (2004) who identified five major areas of concern (relationships, workload and time management, knowledge of the curriculum, evaluation, and issues of autonomy and control) for new teachers as they progress through their first years. And by not involving myself in the process earlier, because of my own "do it my way" desire to be excellent at my job, I neglected what I believe now to be a fundamental truth echoed in Roberson and Roberson (2008): "Through the efforts of the principal, novice teachers can grow to be the teachers they and their colleagues envisioned" (p. 118). Ten years later, here's what I think and what I learned from growing up in the process. Each section has a title for what I think are ingenious and obvious reasons.

## Ego-driven Is the Opposite of Data-driven

*"nothing uglier than a man hitting his stride"*

For the first 10 years of my principalship, I gave first year teachers 'the speech.' I'd say "I hired you, you must be great, see you in June, come see me if you need anything, and remember, don't smile until January after mid-year exams." If they came to me with problems, issues they should "already know how to deal with", or if they sent down students to the office, and/or if they did not follow policy I would greet them with mixed reactions depending on my mood and my unsubstantiated personal belief in their overall effectiveness. To be honest, based on those factors I had already likely decided if they were going to be kept past their first year. Nothing uglier...

In my defense, much of what I was experiencing was a frustration with: "Why, after graduating from very good universities, were these new teachers not sufficiently prepared for the work ahead?" We basically told them through our language and our actions, "survive your first year or two, then you'll know whether this is the right spot for you." Looking back, I realize now what a disappointing support system I had developed. And, sadly, after my first introduction of the New Teacher Induction Program, I believed I did not have anything to learn from it. I was a successful principal in some senses of the profession, but certainly needed to be confident in my ability to hire the right people. I thought, and I am ashamed to state this, that if I had hired someone[6], they would not need pep talks, training, induction, and/or tons of support, short of the two "go-to expressions" of support that I have already shared.

---

6   A note to non-Western Quebec School Board principals: hiring is one of the main tasks of a principal within our board as most hiring for a school is a de-centralized process. Therefore, principals can recruit staff, interview them with support from the board, and recommend the board hire the candidate.

After voluntarily (I recall feeling smug about volunteering to go) attending the sessions of the second year of the program, which were held at the Board Office to explain and unpack the New Teacher Induction Program, I came to the unambiguous realization that I did not have a clear set of defined expectations, nor did I have any real pedagogical plan or processes focussed on staff development for any staff member, new or experienced. I had considered myself an informed and data-driven school leader, and I was embarrassed that a fundamental truth about my primary role seemed to have eluded me: principals need to give informed relevant constructive feedback to all staff about their professional performance.

At the same time, we were working on time management for principals. These were professional development sessions, because one of our main issues was the perceived lack of time to work on pedagogical tasks at the school level. I began to question what I was doing every day to improve the lives of students, other than manage detentions, suspensions, phone calls, emails, and meetings. I was beginning to realize, through the introduction to research and dialogue about that research, that my primary function should be 'to challenge and support students and teachers' and that this work was being neglected. I now firmly believe that this primary function was neglected because I considered myself to be an expert at hiring excellent teachers. I also believed that by their sheer presence in "my" school these new staff members would, through osmosis I suppose, inherit and implement the shared wisdom of the history of the school. With this, I expected that new staff would readily comprehend and embrace the pedagogical plans, rules, processes, procedures, and expectations, and would understand the character of the school, all of which, for the most part, were unwritten. Of my many flaws as a school administrator, my greatest one (I would say "the greatest flaw" because it was rooted in hubris and ignorance) was now publicly exposed. I felt like a fraud, again. But I knew that I wanted to improve, and that I wanted to provide support where needed: support which I knew would enrich the lives of new teachers and, of course, their students. With this I needed help, and I was humbled by the truth about my negligence in this area for such a long time. Nothing uglier than an educator who thinks he or she has learned it all...

# The Need to Build Trust in All Relationships

*"If you can make me scared, if that's what you do*
*If I'm unclear, can I get out of this thing with me and you*
*If you feel scared, and a bit confused*
*I got to say, this sounds a little beyond anything I'm used to".*

After experiencing this training, I started to gain some expertise, but I also came to a realization about how little I was doing to improve instruction in our school, while still expecting everyone to improve with experience. My level of efficacy in supporting teachers was increasing at a very slow rate because in my school, early career teachers were on their own.

Okay, fair enough, to some extent, we all are expected to walk on our own. I know I did. But I realized that I was still expecting them to flourish. And I was judging them if they did not flourish fast enough.

Teachers were feeling the pressure of the job while also feeling the pressure of a boss who said one thing: "I have an open-door policy", but acted in another way when I communicated that "they had better do a more effective job if they wanted another contract." Literally, we were trying to scare teachers into becoming better, yet we were acting in a way that excluded them when we implied "you need to work harder to be a better teacher" (as if just working harder would make you a better pedagogue). In fact, we recognized that we were looking critically at those teachers who treated their own students with the same flawed perspective. At that point, we considered only one factor in the success of a new teacher – their skills and attitude – and we acted accordingly. Although a new teacher's skill and will are obviously factors that contribute to success, we had neglected to consider other factors. Ganser (2002) added two other factors that contribute to new teacher success: 1) workplace conditions, and, 2) elements of induction support.

As the principal, I neither planned for nor achieved success in supporting new teachers effectively. We wanted our new teachers to be strong and confident educators, yet we placed them in classrooms without job security, without experience or the wisdom and perspective that comes with experience, and without the security of knowing I cared about them or their careers. I did not create a relationship conducive to supporting my most vulnerable staff.

# Implementing the Program

*"an inch an hour, two feet a day"*

We knew we had not made gains in making our new teachers better. But, to our credit, we decided to faithfully implement the New Teacher Induction Program. We may have privately criticized that process but we vowed to publically champion it. We decided that we needed to be better at supporting staff and students. And we needed results immediately. We were seeing significant gains and were gaining a deeper understanding of what we needed to do to be a more effective learning organization. We began to develop the expertise, while also beginning to garner "buy-in" with the staff. Our focus was on support, and we energetically embraced our work with our teachers.

In the third year of the New Teacher Induction Program, we formally decided and publicly communicated that, as a school, we were going to support our staff using the concept of Induction programming. We believed that we could all benefit from an Induction program, and that this was not just for new staff members and students. We believed that this mindset and a strong and comprehensive pedagogical collective mindset would give us the tools to support and retain the right teachers for our school, whether they were new or not. We decided to commit to our staff members (and, by doing so, to our students) that we would work to create an environment where all expectations, processes, procedures, and elements of support were to be clearly defined and explained to all members of our staff and students. We said that over the next five years, we would create a self-propelling, self-reflective dynamic in our school that focused on Induction as the primary thought process. We conveyed that these aspirations would be implemented continuously throughout the school year. The New Teacher Induction Program in the board provided our model for implementation. Buy-in was not easy because our professional lives were born from this system of trial-by-fire and what-doesn't-kill-you-makes-you-stronger. And to make progress we had to change our own mindsets about what supporting teachers meant, and we needed to devote thought and time to create the environment where all staff could grow and flourish.

# We Needed to be the Change We Wanted to See

*"the death of inevitability"*

The first years of teaching do not have to be an impossible experience. These first years can be fulfilling and even exhilarating. The New Teacher Induction Program provided us with a common language, which then led to a common vision of support for new teachers. But the Program also opened the pedagogical premise that we are all benefitting from the proper induction of staff members, students and administrators to the culture and expectations of our school. There was no need for preventable problems with copier codes, field-trip forms, expected norms and how "we" communicate. In fact, we came to realize that many of the stressors in a school were caused by variables we knew about and could control. We believed that a well-rounded whole-school community approach that was focused on the induction program would reduce stress, promote health and bring us together. Inevitable and predicted failures were not created by our lack of attention to detail, but rather by our lack of proper pedagogical whole-school planning and development thereof. We wanted to break that traditionally-accepted cycle that existed in our school, that saw new teachers struggle with a very difficult job with little support. We knew that it did not have to be a de facto 'survivor series'. It was not inevitable that life had to be that hard for new teachers. We knew we could change the present experiences of new teachers, and we did. This process led us to believe we could break that traditionally-accepted cycle that existed in our school, that saw students struggle with the most difficult job with little or no relevant support. And we did break that cycle.

# Embracing the Change

*"fully completely"*

"Induction" became the lens through which we would see our primary role as administrators, and we noted that our school bought into this completely. As a result, the New Teacher Induction Program led to the development of a number of related initiatives: induction PD days for staff, induction days for students and parents, development of clear expectations for all aspects of school life, and the supports that must be in place to promote growth and health. Adults began to focus on the knowledge about our adult behaviours and the knowledge about the impact of all our pedagogical plans and pedagogical practices. We developed a culture of self-propulsion, of self-reflection, and of self-improvement ... and it began with our induction programming. Darling-Hammond's (2003) point is relevant here: "Great school leaders create nurturing school environments in which accomplished teaching can flourish and grow" (p. 13). We needed buy-in from teachers and we were rewarded with buy-in from everyone. The driving force in the teaching and learning process was that it was inevitable that students were going to learn, since all teachers were going to do their best. Learning, for everyone, became a welcomed experience and something to be nurtured. The school embraced new teachers just as the school embraced new and younger students with an outlook that 'if I somehow made you better, I was making myself better'.

## Dedication to Doing What is Right

*"all songs are one song"*

We endeavoured to be the best school we could be for our staff members and students. As in-school administrators, we believed that all the people we came in contact with needed to be treated in a manner appropriate to their individual levels of development. In other words, we had to create learning paths for growth for everyone based on a set of standard expectations we would eventually develop for all staff (but had already thoroughly developed for the students). For example, we began to understand that if we viewed teachers as people who had the potential to grow if they were given clear learning intentions and explained success criteria, they would grow. They might not grow as fast as we would like them to, in terms of their effectiveness or efficiency, but they would move forward in their development as more effective and efficient educators. Therefore we would, presumably, need to have more patience and more of an open mindset to help them through their states of development and their states of concern as we encouraged and guided them to move forward confidently and together. We would commit to seeing them as they were and are, appreciating all of them for their diversity in skillset, willset and mindset (we in fact discussed our approach as the role-modelling for how we wanted all teachers to treat their own students). We also stated clearly that we were engaged in this process regardless of whether we were busy, or tired, or whether we thought their concerns or issues were large or small. We had to show to everyone that we were sold on the belief that all people in the system deserved the opportunity to be challenged to do their best, had to be supported to be their best selves, and had to be given the opportunities to develop their positive impact on student achievement.

If we could see all our teachers the way we wanted them to view our students – as people, worthy of being listened to, planned for, and loved, even when they were at their most unlovable – then we would become a wonderful community and a terrific place to learn. I now see how this coincides with Csikszentmihalyi (2003), who cited three types of feedback needed to nurture new teachers professionally and personally: "feedback from others," "feedback from work," and "feedback from personal standards." These concepts reminded me of what I was missing in my career as a teacher, and foremost in my career as a principal – the feedback that was owed to all staff. This, I understood best, was the essence of what we owed to our students. Therefore, the concept of "induction" was not a one-time process or a "program," but rather a way of seeing and better understanding our roles as educators. We developed the mindset that we were the 'parental figures' of all the teachers, support staff and students in the school while they were under our care. The idea that we were the 'parental authority of our school family' imbued us with a great responsibility, which was to ensure that all our teachers were going to be treated with a certain care and that, as in any family, the youngest of the fold deserved extra attention, care, patience, and direction. It all began to make sense, and our defining roles came together into one concept – we had to be caring leaders. We had to care about the right things and we had to care rightly about everyone.

# Implications and Moving Forward

*"...There's no swimming past the drop off*
*Or feeling sorry for ourselves*
*You don't go swimming past the drop off*
*Or else*
*Personal stakes*
*Will get raised and get raised*
*Till your story gets compelling*
*If you lacked the sense*
*Or were wilfully dense*
*Is forever in the telling*
*The surface is green*
*And the dark interweaves*
*In a lonely iridescence*
*It's terribly deep*
*And the cold is complete*
*And it only lacks your presence*
*And nothing else*
*Nothing else*
*Nothing else*
*And no one else"*

In looking back, I realize now that two things needed to happen for me to become a principal who saw that his main role was to be a lead teacher. I needed to have the confidence to invest myself in a formal process of setting and expecting a certain professional standard. I also needed to be able to commit to teaching this professional standard to all staff members and students. I needed to be fully invested and present in the formation of staff guidebooks, parent handbooks, student agendas, and then I needed to be explicit in my explanations and clarification of expectations for all the constituents of our school community. This was the only way to ensure that our vision was "shared" (in terms of being communicated effectively) and maybe even would become "shared" (in terms of the level of buy-in). I had to be the change ... and I did change; I am a changed principal. Hope (1999) described the necessary support from the principal of a school for the improved health of new teachers as involving "...systemic contact with the intention of assisting the new teacher's professional growth and development and of engaging in collegial conversation about the work of teaching" (p. 54).

The following are the supports gleaned from my experiences with "induction" programming (and especially, from my mistakes). I would contend that these are needed for success in schooling overall, too. I see that we need to:

- Ensure that induction programming is well designed and is of high quality; quality assurance is centralized; integrity of programming is assured; and the processes are standardized.

- Ensure buy-in from principals. Challenge and support principals' learning needs.

- Clearly define what an outstanding mentor/coach looks like and what the expectations and potential opportunities are for this function. Professional development and training requires that everyone is involved. Need to make sure that the principals and mentors/coaches know what they are doing.

- Ensure that the pedagogical plans and processes are clearly communicated to the school community.

- Spend money and commit to the long term sustainability of this programming.

- Decentralize pedagogical adaptability by having extra patience with mentors/coaches/mentees/fellows. Provide new teachers with school guidebooks and a pre-school year preparation plan. Listen to teachers and adapt programming accordingly.

- Respect a teacher's time and workload. Processes must have as little negative impact as possible on classroom.

- Consider that school climate and organizational health has a potential impact on teacher efficacy.

- Perfect world scenario: Invite principals in Induction programs into the university setting. Consider ways to effectively involve union support.

- Give back to the process: principals also must be heard and enabled (feel valued) to add to the process, by allowing for mutual growth. Induction programs could benefit from the collective wisdom of the system ...

- Foster organizational growth mindsets:
- Only two types of employees in a school – teachers and those who support them.
- Only two types of employees in a school board/district – principals and those who support them.

## Concluding Remarks and Reflection

*"I am of you*
*You are always in view*
*And I, I am my will*
*You are in everything I do"*

In many ways, the idea and ideal of proper induction into a school, a job, a grade level, a relationship of any kind, has become paramount in the level of successes we achieved as a school. My transformation into a more effective school leader, still with many faults, that placed the well-being of all his staff and students at the heart of his decision making, transformed the school. In 2006, our school was ranked 19/20 of the public schools in our region (rankings based on the Fraser Report). In 2015, the school ranked 2/20 in our region, and in 2016, we ranked 1/20. The academic rankings were one thing; the data we cared most about were school climate surveys that we conducted that served to give us feedback from staff, students and parents. What we found was that we were an evolving organization that planned for the individual successes of all our students and staff. We were encouraged to hear from others that we were listening to them, that we cared about them, and that we cared about their overall success. Essentially, the well-being of the students and staff, whether newer or experienced, young or older, continued to be the guiding principle in everything we did. And it made the difference.

Finally, the most important thing that I learned in the process boils down to this – much can be done with the knowledge that every year a school must re-induct, re-introduce and re-socialize its staff and students into "the way we do things around here" by offering the challenge and providing support for everyone's needs to grow within the school culture.

# References

Bickmore, S. T., & Bickmore, D. L. (2010). Revealing the principal's role in the induction process: Novice teachers telling their stories. *Journal of School Leadership, 20*(4), 445–469.

Csikszentmihalyi, M. (2003). *Good business: Leadership, flow, and the making of meaning.* New York, NY: Penguin Books.

Darling-Hammond, L., & Sykes, G. (2003). Wanted: A national teacher supply policy for education: The right way to meet the "highly qualified teacher" challenge. *Education Policy Analysis Archives, 11*(33), 1–55.

Ganser, T. (2002). *Supporting new teacher mentor programs: Strategies for principals.* Paper presented at the annual meeting of the International Mentoring Association, Ft. Worth, Texas.

Hope, W. C. (1999). Principals' orientation and induction activities as factors in teacher retention. *The Clearing House: A Journal of Educational Strategies, Issues and Ideas, 73*(1), 54–56.

Gold, Y. (1996). Beginning teacher support: Attrition, mentoring, and induction. In J. Sikula, T. J. Buttery, & E. Guyton (Eds.), *Handbook of research on teacher education* (2nd ed., pp. 548–616). New York, NY: Macmillan.

McCann, T., & Johannessen, L. (2004). Why do new teachers cry? *The Clearing House: A Journal of Educational Strategies, Issues and Ideas, 77*(4), 138–145.

Roberson, S., & Roberson, R. (2009). The role and practice of the principal in developing novice first-year teachers. *The Clearing House: A Journal of Educational Strategies, Issues and Ideas, 82*(3), 113–118.

Wang, J., & Odell, S. J. 2002. Mentored learning to teach according to standards- based reform: A critical review. *Review of Educational Research, 72*(3), 481–546.

## Chapter 24

# Supporting New Teachers on the Road of Teaching: The Role of the Elementary School Principal

*Jenny Gonyou-Brown, Katina Pollock*

A teaching career is analogous to driving a long road. On that road, school principals can function as roadside assistance dispatchers who develop and facilitate supports for teachers navigating new careers. New teachers have prepared for the journey with pre-service university education, which includes pedagogical knowledge and some student teaching experience. Despite this preparation, however, the journey can include unanticipated obstacles and detours, such as high performance standards from stakeholders who expect new teachers to navigate the journey with the same competency as veteran educators (Stansbury & Zimmerman, 2000). As new teacher-drivers will manoeuver the road conditions with different levels of expertise, principals can offer the experience and available resources required to support these novice educators as they begin their journeys.

In 2016, we conducted a qualitative research study that sought to understand how elementary principals support new teachers (Gonyou-Brown, 2016). In this chapter, we have interwoven the principals' interview responses and perceptions with research from the existing literature to present our findings. The study was comprised of semi-structured interviews with 12 elementary school principal participants (seven female and five male, with an average of nine years of experience) from Southern Ontario who developed and facilitated supports for new teachers in their schools. The interviews averaged 50 minutes in length, plus two interviews lasting approximately 25 minutes; the study used data from these interviews. Participants shared observations and strategies gleaned from years of professional practice; specifically, they discussed their prior experience supporting new teachers and the strategies they employed to do this work. Many principals also shared the impact of their own early teaching experiences on their development and facilitation of new teacher supports.

To begin, this chapter addresses the expectations around how principals support new teachers within the Ontario context. Next, we discuss how principals understand new teacher supports and their role as resource facilitators; we then use these understandings to contextualize and review the strategies these principals employ. Third, we examine the challenges that principals face when developing and facilitating supports for new teachers. Lastly, this chapter concludes by addressing the positive influence that principals can have when supporting new teachers, and considering other potential supports that can help all new teachers successfully merge into their careers.

## The Road for New Teachers in Ontario

To begin a merge onto the teaching road in Ontario, all teachers are required to possess, at minimum, an undergraduate university degree and a Bachelor of Education qualification from a recognized university (Ontario College of Teachers, 2016b). After completing a teaching degree and gaining certification through the Ontario College of Teachers (OCT)—the governing body of teachers in the province—teachers are able to complete additional, specialist teaching qualifications through accredited universities. To qualify for this additional training, they must possess a strong knowledge base in the subject area and have at least two years of successful teaching experience, including at least one year of teaching in the specialist subject area in Ontario (Ontario College of Teachers, 2016a). Principals in Ontario typically begin as experienced teachers with a minimum of five years of teaching experience, certification in at least three divisions (primary, junior, intermediate, and/or senior), and two specialist qualifications, or a Master's degree (Ontario Ministry of Education, 2016). Principals are also required to complete the Ontario Principal's Qualification Program (PQP), which is designed to provide teachers with the background and skills required to become school administrators (Ontario Ministry of Education, 2016). Principals are also members of the OCT.

The educational job market in Ontario has changed in recent years. New teachers now find themselves entering a teacher-supply-surplus environment: There are now more available qualified teachers than there are teaching positions (Ontario College of Teachers, 2016c). New hiring practices are also now in place with Ontario's *Regulation 274/12* (also known as Reg. 274). Reg. 274 requires school boards to establish and maintain two *occasional teacher* lists: a roster of occasional (short-term) teachers and a long-term occasional (LTO) list. The two lists are seniority-based, with new teachers requiring a minimum of 10 months of occasional teaching with a minimum of 20 days teaching prior to applying to the district's LTO list (Elementary Teachers' Federation of Ontario [EFTO], 2013). The combination of the teacher-surplus situation and the extended hiring process guidelines of Reg. 274 has resulted in new teachers often waiting years before gaining long-term and/or permanent employment in Ontario.

In Ontario schools, principals are expected to offer educational supports to novice teachers entering the practice (Ontario Ministry of Education, 2010). Principals develop and facilitate, rather than directly implement, these supports. The principals in our study discussed developing these supports by building professional relationships and rapport with new teachers. The supports evolve based on the resources the principals have available to them as school and district leaders. The participants also discussed the unique perspective they have when developing new teacher supports, as they can draw upon their own years of teaching experience. Further, principals often have previously served as experienced teacher mentors. Scholars have found these experiences can lead to the increased likelihood that principals will value open communication, and use it to build trusting relationships. (Feiman-Nemser, 2003; Leithwood & Beatty, 2008). Educational scholars also recognize that principals, by facilitating new teacher supports, are essential in welcoming new teachers into the practice (Hope, 1999; Jorissen, 2002; Protheroe, 2006; Roberson & Roberson, 2008). Principals can consider the resources available and effectively oversee the assistance provided to teachers in need.

# Role of the School Principal in the Journey of New Teachers

Principals have unique insight into the experiences of new teachers. How principals understand the new teacher journey influences the ways they develop and facilitate different supports. Our study organized principals' understandings of new teacher supports into three themes (work, support, and policy) and identified connections between the concepts.

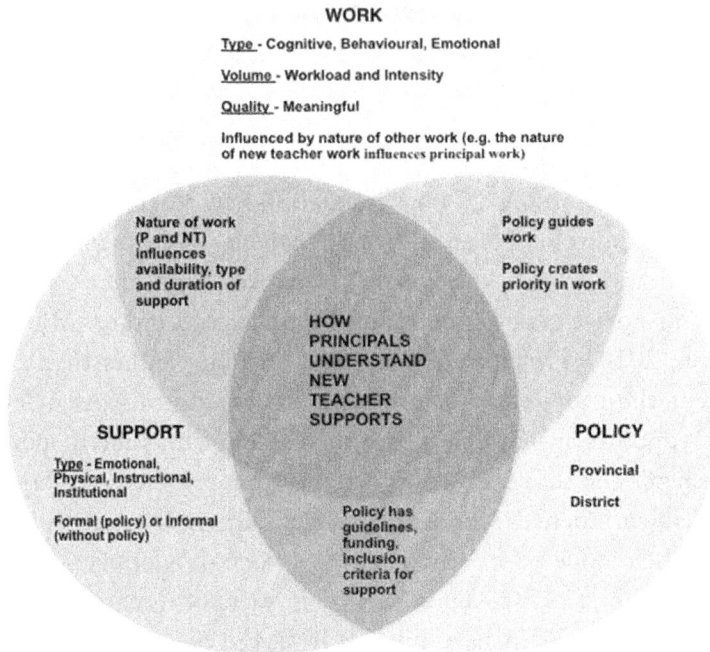

**WORK**

Type - Cognitive, Behavioural, Emotional

Volume - Workload and Intensity

Quality - Meaningful

Influenced by nature of other work (e.g. the nature of new teacher work influences principal work)

Nature of work (P and NT) influences availability, type and duration of support

Policy guides work

Policy creates priority in work

HOW PRINCIPALS UNDERSTAND NEW TEACHER SUPPORTS

**SUPPORT**

Type - Emotional, Physical, Instructional, Institutional

Formal (policy) or Informal (without policy)

**POLICY**

Provincial

District

Policy has guidelines, funding, inclusion criteria for support

*Figure 1:* Principals' Understanding of New Teacher Supports

## Principals' Understandings of New Teacher Supports

**Work.** Principals' work is comprised of many responsibilities. A typical principal works with students, teachers, and other educational stakeholders, including school district personnel, families, and the school community.

According to the principals interviewed in our study, the volume and intensity of their workload influences how they support new teachers. Principals' work has been continually increasing and intensifying; it now commonly extends beyond the usual workday into the hours before and after school (Alberta Teachers' Association & Canadian Association of Principals, 2014; Leithwood & Azah, 2014; Pollock, 2014). Specifically, technology has extended principals' workdays and increased expectations of their availability (Haughey, 2006; Petrecca, 2013; Pollock, 2014). While principals' work is intense, they still consider supporting new teachers to be a meaningful component of the job.

Due to the highly personal nature of work, scholars have found that it can provide meaning and purpose in life (Jackson, 2010; Krahn, Hughes, & Lowe, 2015; Mindzak, 2016). Research has also shown that meaning in principals' work emerges from two intrinsic sources: comprehension and intention (Brief & Nord, 1990; Morin, 2008). Scholars have linked the individual connection between meaning and work (or work environment) with a sense of personal identity (Pratt & Ashford, 2003). Principals derive meaning from providing new teacher supports, and this meaning impacts their work.

The length and type of new teacher work also informs how principals develop supports. In Ontario, most new teachers will be engaged in a variety of short-term or daily teaching work prior to gaining long-term employment. Short- and long-term teachers have different types of work arrangements: short-term teachers work with other teachers' planning and assessment models and frequently move between classes and schools, whereas long-term teachers develop effective programming and assessment with consistent teaching assignments (Chalikakis, 2012). These different arrangements (daily, short-term, or long-term) influence how principals understand their role in developing and facilitating different supports.

**Support.** In terms of categorization, Lipton and Wellman (2003) have identified four distinct types of support that principals provide to new teachers: emotional, physical, instructional, and institutional (p. 2). *Emotional supports* target the isolation (Ingersoll & Strong, 2011) and range of emotions that new educators can experience as they enter the practice (Lipton & Wellman, 2003). The range of learning needs that new teachers encounter may result in a phenomenon called "praxis shock," as new educators discover how the realities of the work challenge their previous beliefs and ideas about teaching (Kelchtermans & Ballet, 2002). *Physical supports* include classroom setup and providing teaching resources such as art supplies and physical education equipment (Lipton & Wellman, 2003). *Instructional supports* include content-area resources and practical professional suggestions that are specific to new teacher work arrangements (Lipton & Wellman, 2003). Lastly, *institutional supports* include information shared with new teachers; this information is based on work expectations and rooted in policies and procedures within the school and school district (Lipton & Wellman, 2003).

The type of supports that principals offer may be formal in nature and/or guided by policy, or informal. Informal supports may have similar characteristics to formal supports, but are not outlined in a policy or program and do not have corresponding available funding.

**Policy.** Principals must be aware of the policies related to new teacher supports. Scholars have described policy as a normative notion that expresses both an ends and a means to steer the actions and behaviours of people (Rizvi & Lingard, 2010). The access that school principals have to available funding and resources for new teachers is designed to support policy. Accordingly, these policies inform principals' approaches toward the development and facilitation of new teacher supports.

In Ontario, the New Teacher Induction Program (NTIP) is a program of professional learning supports. This policy-sanctioned program is outlined and funded by the Ontario Ministry of Education and managed by school districts. The program provides guidelines and funding that outline specific roles and offer resources, such as experienced teacher mentoring, Teacher Performance Appraisals (TPA), and work-specific professional development sessions. New teachers qualify for NTIP with a new teaching contract (permanent) position, or their first long-term occasional teaching position of 97 consecutive teaching days or longer.

Many new teachers, however, work in daily or short-term teaching assignments, following other teachers' plans and working in a range of classrooms. Notably, the inclusion criteria of NTIP do not include teachers first entering the profession in Ontario. Ontario's Reg. 274 indicates that an occasional teacher may only apply to be placed on a long-term occasional (LTO) teaching list once they have taught at least 20 days during the previous school year (EFTO, 2013). The regulation further stipulates that only occasional teachers on the LTO list who have completed a minimum of one LTO assignment of at least four months, and have the required qualifications and highest seniority ranking, can be considered for permanent positions. Prior to Reg. 274, school districts did not rank occasional teachers by seniority and new teachers applying for positions did not have to complete a minimum number of days in order to apply for long-term or contract teaching positions. The extended hiring process of Reg. 274 has resulted in most newly hired teachers spending years in daily and short-term occasional teaching work prior to gaining long-term teaching employment and qualifying for NTIP supports.

### Roadside Assistance for New Drivers

Similar to drivers having the potential to experience a broad range of vehicle issues on their journey, according to the principals in our study the support needs of new teachers are complex and multifaceted. In their pre-service education experience, the new teachers could demonstrate and practice professional skills in regular and predictable conditions. However, these teachers will encounter unknown conditions or challenges as they enter professional practice. The responsibilities of new teachers include planning lessons that meet a diverse range of student learning needs, developing rapport with students, building lines of communication with families, developing effective assessment and reporting, conducting work according to school district expectations, and meeting professional practice guidelines. The participants also considered these professional learning needs to be linked with the duration and type of teaching assignments (short- or long-term, teaching one class or covering multiple classes and/ or teaching subjects). Considering the many factors that make teaching a complex profession, every teacher has unique and individualized support needs.

Beginning a career in teaching can be lonely. The principals in our study expressed concerns, confirmed in the existing research, that many new teachers may experience a range of emotions in the first few years of teaching, including feeling overwhelmed, isolated, inadequate, or feeling unaware that others experience similar problems or challenges (Brock & Grady, 1998; Camp & Heath-Camp, 1991; Lieberman & Miller, 1994). Given their previous teaching experience, Ontario principals are able to relate to new teachers and recall the obstacles and challenges of their own early years. Upon entering the practice, many new educators discover they have learning needs they had not anticipated (Rust, 1994; Wong & Wong, 2009). One principal expressed feeling isolation in an early teaching experience: "Having been one myself, a brand new teacher, entering that classroom with a piece of chalk in the room and nothing else, you don't know where to go for support, even when it comes to actual resources in the classroom." While new teachers may not realize the value of having available supports, principals understand that there will be challenges ahead. Several of the principals expressed empathy for the plight of new teachers first encountering the complexities of professional teaching practice; all of the principals in our study agreed that a successful entry into the teaching profession is critical to a teacher's career and that providing support to new teachers is "one of the most important things that [principals] do." As such, effective and appropriate principal-developed supports can help new teachers succeed in the classroom (Fantilli & McDougall, 2009).

### Dispatching the Most Effective and Appropriate Supports

Comparable to roadside assistance dispatchers, principals develop and facilitate, rather than directly implement, supports. Principals assess the support needs and learning goals of new teachers, consider the resources available, and provide timely and efficient assistance. In our study, the principals identified themselves as *support facilitators* and discussed using their professional networks and capacities to engage the most appropriate supports for new teachers. Specifically, the principals identified engagement in collaborative school culture as a key support strategy. According to the participants, building relationships and learning with colleagues on the job offers productive, high-engagement, and practical learning opportunities for new teachers. The principals also identified conferencing, co-shadowing, and co-teaching with experienced educators as beneficial learning strategies that can only be acquired on the job (Gold, 1999; Feiman-Nemser, 2001; Ganser, 2002; Ingersoll & Strong, 2011). One principal discussed the value of new teachers working with experienced teacher mentors, emphasizing that: "[new teachers] need to see somebody doing it," and having someone "coming in and [seeing and discussing] teaching is really critical for [new teachers] to get to that understanding." Several other principals in the study discussed their belief that time out of the classroom had rendered them less current on pedagogical practices. For example, one principal shared: "I've been out of the classroom for 20 years now. I'm not the best person for [new teachers] to talk to about instructional approaches." However, while the interviewed principals did not see themselves as directly supporting new teachers, they did identify their significant amount of influence over the establishment of the school climate and culture (Cherian & Daniel, 2008; Drago-Severson, 2007; Hope, 1999; Richards, 2004; Stockard & Lehman, 2004). In our study, the principals identified engaging different individuals within the school to offer direct support to new teachers—including experienced teachers, instructional coaches, and learning co-ordinators—and working within school-based networks as key strategies they could employ within a collaborative school culture to indirectly support new teachers entering the profession.

## Challenges in Supporting New Drivers

As new drivers may hesitate to call a roadside assistance dispatcher, for the principals in our study, the supervisory nature of their position creates challenges when developing the open and trusting relationships they view as integral to supporting new teachers. One principal shared, "I remember being in those first couple of years [of teaching] and you could hear the principal coming down the hall, or walking in the room and it brought up anxiety. I understand that anxiety." The principals expressed the value of building relationships with the new teachers in their school, but felt they lack the time and opportunity to develop relationships with beginning teachers that only work at their school intermittently.

The principals in our study also viewed their workload requirements as limiting the time they have available to meet with and build professional relationships with new teachers, especially those with short-term work arrangements. One principal shared, "I would love to be able to be out in the classroom as often as possible to see new teachers in action. It doesn't happen as frequently as I would hope." Another participant explained that she has difficulty developing rapport with new teachers doing temporary teaching work within her school, but that "once you have the people [occasional teachers] who come into a building regularly, those are the ones that are automatically looked at as being part of my staff." Another principal described the difficulty of developing sustainable supports for short-term teachers: "If they are only there for those [couple of] weeks, it's more of a maintenance thing," rather than prolonged duration of supports. Not only does the time-consuming nature of principal work limit their ability to develop relationships that foster new teacher supports, but the short-term work arrangements of many new teachers, including extended periods of transient and temporary work, also make the development of open and trusting principal–new teacher relationships and rapport challenging.

During research interviews the principals in our study also discussed both formal and informal support structures for new teachers. The principals recognized formal supports, such as NTIP, as being guided by policy and having available related funding, and saw informal supports as those they developed when new teachers did not qualify under formal policy or program inclusion. One participant explained: "The NTIP program, in and of itself, is a nice program. It allows new teachers to get support from their peers, it gives some system-level support, and it gives them some material to think about and bounce [ideas] off." One of the supports within NTIP is Teacher Performance Appraisal (TPA). The Ontario Ministry of Education has described TPA as a process that provides teachers with meaningful appraisals that encourage professional learning and growth (Ontario Ministry of Education, 2012). The process commences with a meeting between the principal and new teacher to discuss professional learning goals. One principal described the TPA process as "our chance to actually really unpack what is happening in the classroom. What is really happening in their teaching?" Following the initial meeting, the principal observes the new teacher in the classroom environment and prepares reflection feedback. The principal discusses the classroom visit with the new teacher at a follow-up meeting, where they also devise next steps in professional learning. The principals viewed the TPA process as a useful strategy to support new teachers on their journey.

In addition to policy-sanctioned supports, principals can develop informal supports for new teachers who regularly work in their schools but who do not qualify for NTIP. According to the participants, the lack of funding and guidelines available for new teachers that do not qualify for NTIP can hinder principals' efforts to offer supports, such as providing the opportunity to meet with experienced teacher mentors, or attend professional learning sessions during the school day. The principals explained that developing informal supports required them to be creative with available resources and developing supports that do not require funding. A key strategy that principals discussed for both informal and formal supports was to engage new teachers within the collaborative school culture. The principals highlighted how a collaborative school community can offer a variety of new teacher supports—for example, new teachers benefit from working within a teaching network with experienced colleagues. Further, they expressed the belief that providing the opportunity for new teachers to work consistently and collaboratively within a school is also crucial when developing sustainable supports for teachers in long-term, consistent teaching employment. Overall, however, the principals found meeting the support needs for some of the newest teachers in daily and short-term teaching work in their school to be challenging.

Some new teachers without available supports may attempt to self-direct their own development. As a result of their work being temporary and intermittent, daily and short-term teachers' engagement in school culture is often limited. Some of the principals in the study observed that some new teachers self-direct their professional learning, especially when there is a lack of district- or school-based supports. Some new teachers develop their own professional and emotional coping strategies, which can negatively influence their instructional practices (Cherubini, 2010; Henke, Chen, & Geis, 2000; Youngs, 2007). Some principals in our study found it challenging to help new teachers overcome the lack of job-embedded collaborative learning. As one principal noted, new teachers "are highly educated in that they have done a lot of courses and coursework, but they haven't necessarily had the time that they need to go over and put what they've learned into practice ... it's not fine-tuned or refined." While several principals identified potential benefits of new teachers directing their own professional learning, they also viewed experience and collaboration as essential aspects of the learning process for new teachers. According to one principal: "Matching new teachers with a mentor teaching the same grade or subject is a very positive learning experience for new teachers." Overall, the participants emphasized the energy, passion, and dedication of teachers entering the profession, and see establishing early supports as essential to new teacher success and keeping quality educators in the profession.

### Promoting New Driver Confidence

Roadside assistance services strive to reassure their clients that support is available in times of driver need. The principals in our study discussed their desire to develop supports that promote resiliency and confidence in new teachers entering the profession. Each participant shared vivid recollections of their early teaching experiences. Several spoke of specific principals and experienced teacher mentors who offered support on their early journey. A couple of principals, however, discussed the sparse, negative, or nonexistent supports available during their early years. The principals who experienced a positive and supportive entrance into the profession described their motivation to "pay forward" their own experience by supporting new teachers. The principals who described experiencing a lack of available supports also expressed wanting to offer individualized support to the new teachers in their school in an effort to help them to avoid the obstacles they had encountered on their own journey. Throughout the study, the participants repeatedly expressed their aim to develop individualized and sustainable supports that make a positive, memorable impact for new teachers beginning professional practice.

As they advance in their careers, teachers will remember who offered them early and ongoing support. As experienced teachers themselves, principals have personally experienced how support can build confidence and collaborative skills. One participant expressed the belief that, as principals, they "cannot support [new teachers] enough in those first couple of years, because [principals] are shaping the profession [by providing support to new teachers]." The principals in our study were aware of how valuable the supports they develop and facilitate can be to new teachers entering professional practice. Often, principals can tangibly see teachers benefiting from these supports: As one principal said: "When [new teachers] are being successful, I have people that are so happy [that] they are coming to me and showing me what they have done." For the participants in the study, developing and facilitating these supports is not only a requirement of their job, but also an important responsibility that they connect to their own prior experiences.

According to the principals, the supports can have a broad-ranging influence on new teachers' short-term teaching experiences, and a positive, lasting impact on teachers' future experiences in the profession.

## Planning for Success on the Road

As a successful merge can be critical for teachers to experience a positive and confident teaching journey, a variety of roadside assistance options could be developed at the district level for the newest teacher-drivers who do not yet qualify for the more formal means of support—namely, meeting the inclusion criteria of NTIP. For example, daily and short-term teachers could potentially access supports more successfully through their employing school districts, or associated teacher federations. These broader networks have the potential to reach the teachers who move frequently between schools and therefore struggle to build rapport and professional relationships with principals and collaborative school communities. School districts and teacher associations could establish broad professional learning communities for new teachers to set professional learning goals and gain collaborative support for their individual needs. By considering the unique professional learning needs of the newest hired teachers in short-term teaching work, access to individualized supports outside the purview of school principals can be made more widely available. Granting new teachers access to a broader range of supports will build their confidence, preparedness, and focus to facilitate a smooth and successful merge into professional practice.

# Conclusion

The analogy in the introductory paragraphs of this chapter conceptualizes the important role school principals have in helping new teachers successfully enter professional practice. In this analogy, teachers are new drivers beginning the long journey of their careers, and principals function as roadside assistance dispatchers. Like assistance dispatchers, the principals have experience in traveling the road and are aware of road conditions. Their prior experiences help them to connect their networks of services with clients.

Principals develop and facilitate, as opposed to directly implement, supports for new teachers. As roadside assistance dispatchers don't usually change flat tires, principals consult with new teachers and employ their available resources and network connections to ensure that someone capable and qualified aids new teachers with their professional learning needs and gets them back on the teaching road. Similar to offering drivers specialized assistance that is effective and efficient, principals that develop supports for the new teachers in their school call upon others with the right tools and experience to directly support new teachers. This also keeps the principal available to dispatch help to others.

A challenge exists for principals to support new teachers that are not regularly in their school. Similar to some new teachers developing coping skills and self-directing their professional learning, if novice drivers do not have access to contact a roadside assistance dispatcher they may attempt to self-diagnose and repair their own vehicles. While these drivers may temporarily get back on the road, without access to the proper tools and lacking experience in repair, they will eventually need reinforcement. Similar to new teachers that do not yet qualify for NTIP, self-directed learning can become job-embedded if new teachers can gain access to informal supports by engaging in a collaborative school culture, or receive supports through a school district or teacher federation. If the new teacher can have access to professional support through a dispatcher, be it a school principal, district or federation leader, then some assistance can be employed to connect new teachers with other educators that have experienced success in driving the teaching road. The collegial support of a collaborative culture instills a sense of confidence in new teachers and reassures them that the road should not be lonely. Akin to roadside assistance dispatching support to ensure the experience of a pleasant road trip, school principals serve to aid the new teachers that are regularly in their school in merging into professional practice. If all new teachers can gain assistance in maneuvering the bumps and turns of the road from school, district or teacher federation support dispatchers, they will benefit from increased confidence, professional learning and a meaningful journey.

# References

Alberta Teachers' Association, & Canadian Association of Principals. (2014). *The future of principalship in Canada: A national research study.* Retrieved from https://www.teachers.ab.ca/SiteCollectionDocuments/ ATA/Publications/Research/ The%20Future%20of%20the%20 Principalship%20in%20Canada.pdf

Anhorn, R. (2008). The profession that eats its young. *Delta Kappa Gamma Bulletin, 73*(3), 15–19.

Baker-Doyle, K. (2011). *The networked teacher: How teachers build social networks for professional support.* New York, NY: Teachers College Press.

Brief, A., & Nord, W. (1990). *Meaning of occupational work.* Toronto, ON: Lexington Books.

Brock, B., & Grady, M. (1998). Beginning teacher induction programs. *The Clearing House, 71*(3), 179–183.

Camp, W., & Heath-Camp, B. (1991). *Becoming a teacher: They just gave me a key and said "good luck."* Berkley, CA: National Centre for Research in Vocational Education.

Chalikakis, A. (2012). *Short- and long-term occasional teaching work arrangement differences* (Master's thesis, University of Western Ontario). Retrieved from Electronic Thesis and Dissertations Repository. (Paper No. 406)

Cherian, F., & Daniel, Y. (2008). Principal leadership in new teacher induction: Becoming agents of change. *International Journal of Education Policy and Leadership, 3*(2). Retrieved from http://journals.sfu.ca/ijepl/index.php/ ijepl/article/view/97/35

Cherubini, L. (2010). An analysis of the implications between the theoretical framework and the policy context of provincial education policy in Ontario. *Journal of Contemporary Issues in Education, 5*(1), 20–33.

Drago-Severson, E. (2007). Helping teachers learn: Principals as professional development leaders. *Teachers College Record, 109*(1), 70–125.

Elementary Teachers' Federation of Ontario. (2013). *Understanding Ontario Regulation 274/12.* Retrieved from http://www.etfo.ca/Resources/ForTeachers/ Documents/Understanding%20Ontario %20Regulation%20274-12.pdf

Fantilli, R., & McDougall, D. (2009). A study of novice teachers: Challenges and supports in the first years. *Teaching and Teacher Education, 25*(6), 814–825.

Feiman-Nemser, S. (2001). From preparation to practice: Designing a continuum to strengthen and sustain teaching. *Teachers College Record, 103*(6), 1013–1055.

Ganser, T. (2002). The new teacher mentors: Four trends that are changing the look of mentoring programs for new teachers. *American School Board Journal, 189*(12), 25–27.

Gold, Y. (1996). Beginning teacher support: Attrition, mentoring, and induction. In C. B. Courtney (Ed.), *Review of research in education* (pp. 548-594). Washington, DC: American Educational Research Association.

Gonyou-Brown, J. (2016). *The work of elementary principals in supporting new teachers in Ontario publicly-funded, English speaking schools* (Doctoral dissertation, University of Western Ontario). Retrieved from Electronic Thesis and Dissertation Repository. (Paper No. 4317)

Haughey, M. (2006). The impact of computers on the work of the principal: Changing discourses on talk, leadership and professionalism. *School Leadership and Management, 26*(1), 23–34.

Henke, R., Chen, X., & Geis, S. (2000). *Progress through the teacher pipeline: 1992-93 college graduates and elementary secondary school teaching as of 1997.* (NCES 2000-152). Washington, DC: U.S. Department of Education Office of Educational Research and Improvement. Retrieved from the National Center for Education Statistics website: http://nces.ed.gov/pubs2000/2000152.pdf

Hope, W. (1999). Principals' orientation and the induction activities as factors in teacher retention. *The Clearing House, 73*(1), 54–56.

Ingersoll, R., & Strong, M. (2011). The impact of induction and mentoring programs for beginning teachers: A critical review of research. *Review of Educational Research, 81*(2), 201–233.

Jackson, A. (2010). *Work and labour in Canada: Critical issues.* Toronto, ON: Canadian Scholars' Press.

Jorrissen, K. (2002). Ten things principals can do to retain teachers. *Principal Leadership, 3*(1), 48–54.

Kelchtermans, G., & Ballet, K. (2002). The micro politics of teacher induction: A narrative-biographical study on teacher socialization. *Teacher and Teacher Education, 18,* 105-120.

Krahn, H., Hughes, K., & Lowe, G. (2015). *Work, industry & Canadian society.* Toronto, ON: Nelson.

Leithwood, K. & Azah, V. (2014). *Secondary principals' and vice-principals' workload study: Final report.* Retrieved from the Ontario Ministry of Education website: http://www.edu.gov.on.ca/eng/policyfunding/memos/nov2014/FullSecondaryRepor tOctober7_EN.pdf

Leithwood, K., & Beatty, B. (2008). *Leading with teacher emotions in mind.* Thousand Oaks, CA: Corwin Press.

Lieberman, A., & Miller, L. (1994). *Teachers, their world and their work.* Alexandria, VA: Association for Supervision, Curriculum and Development.

Lipton, L., & Wellman, B. (2003). *Mentoring matters: A practical guide to learning-focused relationships.* Sherman, CT: Mira Via.

Mindzak, M. (2016). *Exploring the working lives of unemployed and underemployed teachers in Ontario* (Doctoral dissertation, University of Western Ontario). Retrieved from Electronic Thesis and Dissertation Repository. (Paper No. 3668)

Morin, E. (2008). *The meaning of work, mental health and organizational commitment* (Research report R-585). Retrieved from the Institut de Recherche Robert-Sauvé en Santé et en Sécurité du Travail website: http://www.irsst.qc.ca/Media/documents/PubIRSST/R-585.pdf

Ontario College of Teachers. (2016a). Additional qualifications: Honour spccialist qualification. Retrieved from https://www.oct.ca/members/additional-qualifications/schedules-and-guidelines/schedule-e

Ontario College of Teachers. (2016b). *How teachers are certified.* Retrieved from https://www.oct.ca/public/professional-standards/how-teachers-are-certified

Ontario College of Teachers. (2016c). *Transition to teaching 2015: Early-career teachers in Ontario schools.* Toronto, ON: Ontario College of Teachers.

Ontario Ministry of Education. (2010). *The new teacher induction program handbook for principals.* Retrieved from: http://www.edu.gov.on.ca/eng/teacher/NTIPPrincipal.pdf

Ontario Ministry of Education. (2016). *I want to be a principal.* Retrieved from http://www.edu.gov.on.ca/eng/teacher/directobe.html

Petrecca, L. (2013, March 7). All work and no play? Mobile wipes out 8-hour workday. *USA Today.* Retrieved from http://www.usatoday.com/story/news/nation/2013/03/06/mobile-workforce-all-work/1958673/

Pollock, K. (with Wang, F., & Hauseman, D. C.) (2014). *The changing nature of principals' work. Final report.* Toronto, ON: The Ontario Principals' Council. Retrieved from http://www.edu.uwo.ca/faculty_profiles/cpels/pollock_katina/ OPC- Principals- Work-Report.pdf

Pratt, M., & Ashforth, B. (2003). Fostering meaningfulness in working and at work. In K. Cameron, J. Dutton, & R. Quinn (Eds.), *Positive organizational scholarship: Foundations of a new discipline* (pp. 309-327). San Francisco, CA: Berrett Koehler.

Protheroe, N. (2006). The principal's role in supporting new teachers. *Principal, 86*(2), 34–38.

Richards, J. (2004). What new teachers value most in principals. *Principal, 83*(3), 42–45.

Rizvi, F., & Lingard, B. (2010). *Globalizing education policy*. London/New York: Routledge.

Roberson, S., & Roberson, R. (2008). The role and practice of the principal in developing novice first year teachers. *The Clearing House, 82*(3), 113–118.

Rust, F. (1994). The first year of teaching: It's not what they expected. *Teaching and Teacher Education, 10*(2), 205–217.

Stansbury, K., & Zimmerman, J. (2000). *Lifelines to the classroom: Designing support for beginning teachers*. Retrieved from the WestEd Organization website: https://www.wested.org/online_pubs/trchrbrief.pdf

Stockard, J., & Lehman, M. (2004). Influences on the satisfaction and retention of 1st year teachers: The importance of effective school management. *Educational Administration Quarterly, 40*(5), 742–771.

Wong, H., & Wong, R. (2009). *How to be an effective teacher: The first days of school*. Mountainview, CA: Harry K. Wong Publications, Inc.

Youngs, P. (2007). How elementary principals' beliefs and actions influence new teachers' experiences. *Educational Administration Quarterly, 43*(1), 101–137.

# The Bliss and Blisters of Early Career Teaching in Canada: Where Do We Go from Here?

*Keith D. Walker, Benjamin Kutsyuruba*

In this final chapter we will offer a couple of emergent themes, a retrospective tour of this volume, and we will briefly share two of our aspirations for this book.

## Evidence of Bliss and Blisters

Of course, readers come to books like this with different shopping bags, different interests, sensibilities, and anticipated "take-aways." As editors, when we first read through the chapters of this book, among other smaller things we saw two gigantic themes.

**The first theme** related to just how passionate, idealistic, enthused, and energized early career teachers tend to be – as they seek to change the world, perhaps one student or one classroom at a time. It is impressive to us to read of the persistence and stick-to-itiveness of many of the teachers represented in the research. But this applied not only to teachers; we have seen similar characteristics amongst those who work to support beginning teachers and who are dedicated to efforts that will benefit those new to the profession. All and each of these educators want to make a positive difference. Likewise, the contributors to this collection have written in solidarity with the cause of well-delivered and experience-based education. Being integral to and becoming a contributive partner in this noble and sacred profession is quite apparently a driving force for many, many new teachers. The exhilaration that accompanies the creation of the space and the conditions for transformative engagement of students in learning are almost unmatchable. Then, there are also the experiences of the special breakthroughs or "overcoming the odds" moments, the steady stream of re-tellable student stories and the ever-growing inventories of "before your very eyes"-type transformations. These are the grist for and substance of the beginning educator's best moments. These are breath-taking, optimal, and beautiful times; these constitute what we've called the beginning teacher's bliss.

**The second theme** is embodied in the daunting assignments taken on by new teachers, their feelings of eroding confidence and competence, the sense of abandonment and depreciation, dashed or sabotaged plans, enduring temporary and occasional placements, missing out on some (even lots) of the fun of life, surrendering to the progressive revelation that being perfectly prepared is an illusion, the disappointment entailed in the realization that not every student "gets you and that being everyone's hero is fiction," the trauma of vulnerability, the unintended misunderstandings, the micro-politics of schools and staff rooms, over-estimation of capacities, chronic compassion fatigue, worrying, frustrations and even despair. Snakes-and-ladders or roller-coaster metaphors come to mind as we read through those experiences. Going from out of control to more out of control as a routine (that is where images of the Groundhog Day movie come to mind). This litany of experiences and emotions constitute the beginning teacher's blisters.

These bliss and blisters moments are inherent in the nature of the role, dependent on circumstances, and evidently negotiable with appropriate attention. Bliss and blisters go together, and are even, strangely, connected in the constellation of variables that define beginning teachers' lives. Rarely, it seems, do they experience all bliss or all blisters, but how to reduce the blisters and accentuate the bliss is a project worthy of consideration. We have found that an early career teacher's well-being and resilience, together with various reliance structures and human support initiatives, do make a difference in terms of whether a teacher is roughed up to the point of quitting or is polished up to the point of shining, during his or her first five years in the profession.

# Editors' Retrospective Summary

As promised, this book represents a window into the outstanding work and the reflections of our assembled group of experts from across Canada and the various programs and research efforts they represent. They have sought to shed light on the experiences of early career teachers, to offer perspectives and insights on promising induction and mentorship practices, to describe the timely and multi-dimensional means for "neophyte educator" supports, and to offer ways for us to plainly see the varieties of challenges faced by these beginning educators. Of course, there is an easy tendency "to be down on what we are not up on." We might be tempted to just assume that every new teacher needs to suffer through their first years of "trial by fire", as some of us did, and hope that there will be enough of them who are left standing after the "boot camp" or who can hold their breath through these "sink-or-swim" times to survive before they thrive. Alternatively and preferably, our focus in this volume has been on what is working and what is not. If we can better understand the challenges and find tailor-made, and even routinized, ways to encourage, exhort, and equip beginning teachers to live into their chosen profession in ways that might be described as flourishing, then everyone in the learning community will be better for it.

We think there will be people who will read this book and be astounded by the amount and quality of research and innovative practice in the domain of mentoring and supporting early career teachers in Canada. The authors in this volume provide a rich set of descriptions, narratives, and prescriptions for anyone wanting a sampling of the "state of the art" of early career teaching in Canada. As editors, it has been a privilege to work with these generous authors and with Word and Deed Publishing, under the funding of the Social Science Humanities Research Council of Canada. Also, we are grateful for the giftedness, intelligence, and energies of our co-enthusiastic graduate students who have worked on the various elements of this book and the larger project with us. We are especially excited about the conversations, provocations, and the generative benefits that this book might afford to those seeking encouragement, renewed hope, the good company of like-motivated educators, and a source for an abundance of innovative ideas for effectively coming alongside Canada's promising early career teachers. We think that investing attention on those with the longest professional careers still ahead of them, in what is surely one of the most important functions that there is (i.e., being an educator), is beyond necessary – it is simply a wise, prudent, and reliable long-term investment.

To recap, we have sought to explore the unique pan-Canadian landscape for the differential impact of teacher induction and mentorship programs on the early-career teachers' retention. We continue to learn much about what is going on in teacher induction programs across Canada. Teacher educators (pre-service and early career), teacher mentors, school and school system administrators (including recruiters and HR personnel), and early career teachers themselves, will have heard their voices throughout this book. And they will have heard from practitioners and scholars who have lent their uniquely Canadian and pan-Canadian perspectives to this project.

In the book, there are descriptions of the experiences of early career teachers, research analyses, personal narratives, poems, comics, the voices of beginning teachers, and those who have been highly invested in the development of systems, structures, supports, and programming to assist early career teachers. While pan-Canadian in breadth, beginning teachers' deep, wide, and complex perceptions of induction and mentorship programs and their experiences with permanent and non-permanent work have been uncovered in this book. We have shared what is working and what is not working for over 1300 new teachers from across Canada. We have heard the poet-voice of a beginning teacher's search for opportunities to teach and to learn, together with his expressions of yearning for mentorship, owning his teaching, enduring and hoping for more of what he loves - teaching. Another poet's voice speaks of her longings to be a teacher, as a fulfillment of a long-cherished dream. Our authors have unpacked how the various contexts and cultures of schools make a difference for the novice teacher, and how early career teachers have gained insights into their own agency, struggled with the influence of social class, and realized the importance of developing a professional identity. A refreshing break from regular text was provided as our readers were invited to explore the carefully designed layout and messages contained in the graphic depictions of teachers' stories that touch on typical challenges and professional growth.

The lenses of a beginning teacher who had navigated the new teachers supports provided to them, and the impact that various induction programs had on them, were informative. Three dozen phone conversations with a geographic sampling of Canadian beginning teachers offered their direct descriptions of highlights and low points in their early practices as educators. We have had the opportunity to read about the lived experiences of early career teachers, along with the colleagues who have supported them on their route to steady teaching employment and full professional citizenship. In these chapters, there are practices and relationships woven in the narratives that provide hints about how early career teacher optimism has been sustained and how self-agency has been discovered. We have been privileged with first-hand accounts of what has spurred them on to continued growth, even in challenging circumstances

Given the uniqueness of Canada's independent jurisdictions, the pan-Canadian overview of teacher induction and mentoring policies and programs provided an interesting set of descriptions. We have reviewed or "audited" provincial, territorial, and local jurisdiction documents and mined from these the varieties and inconsistencies of teacher induction programs, the role of mentorship as an aspect of teacher induction programs, and the mandated roles, duties, and responsibilities of school administrators in teacher induction and mentorship processes in each Canadian jurisdiction. The current professional realities of job insecurity, teaching subjects outside their specialty, professional instability, feeling incompetent, and the obvious need for support in the first years of teaching, have been thoroughly described. It is interesting that some support efforts are appreciated and others – not so much. The difference that listening to beginning teachers and their mentors has made in program and initiative design becomes self-apparent when reading the accounts portrayed in this book.

What a privilege it has been to be invited into the stories of new teacher induction, socialization, and mentorship programs: some in constant and continuing development and some well-institutionalized and embedded in school and school system cultures. As new teachers prepare for and grow their competencies to assess student learning, our authors have proffered implications for both teacher education and induction programs. In this book, we've read about the key factors that have contributed to the growth of new teachers, along with the emerging understandings of the power produced by building "mentoring webs," not just for new teachers but for all educators. We have heard about the values and benefits of a formal learning partnership model of mentorship for early service teachers (ESTs); wherein trusting learning relationships evolved over time with their trained mentors, and ESTs acquired a range of pedagogical acumen which markedly improved their teaching practice.

Where there were high levels of new teacher migration and where beginning teacher wellness presented personal and professional challenges, we have looked at a study that examined the provision of release time for mentor-teachers to work one-to-one in classrooms. These researchers demonstrated that co-learning and sufficient support systems do ameliorate many issues. Another longitudinal study of the impacts of school cultures and induction supports may have prompted us to ask how one conserves spaces that encourages new teachers to become themselves as educators, while honouring the diversity and significance of the places they inhabit, and building collaborative opportunities for organizational leadership. Our authors have explored ways that a provincial mentorship framework created and held generative space for 'new' teachers to become ethical educators and decision-makers.

School districts' mentorship programs are highlighted in this book and, we hope, they will spark conversations and uncover possibilities for tinkering with other mentorship program designs. It was interesting to observe how districts aligned and integrated new teacher mentorship with the vision and goals of the district in order to build the leadership capacity of teachers, respond to learner needs, and promote innovative teaching practice. We have read about the role of the school principal in self-directed professional development from the perspective of early career teachers, and have been brought into the inner reflections of principals' descriptions about how they have used their own learning journeys and resource networks to facilitate supports that seem to best fit the lives of beginning teachers, and all teachers. We have noted that principals are also experiencing an intensification of their workloads, with ramifications for early career teachers' support.

For the most part, this book focused on the Canadian scene. We realize that not all parts of Canada's educational terrain have been directly represented within this book's chapters; in the true, pan-Canadian spirit of collaboration, we envision that this book affords opportunities future interactions with scholars, practitioners, and policy makers from those jurisdictions. In addition, insights from other parts of the English-speaking world and from particular countries (i.e., Israel) have provided numerous interesting points of comparison and resonance. It is important to appreciate that the contextual challenges and opportunities afforded by the formative years of educators are universal, and that insights are gained by going beyond our current jurisdictions to other parts of Canada and the world. Valuable comparisons in this book offer food for thought for international policy makers and educational leaders about effective programmatic design, and the roles of mentors and school administrators in supporting beginning teachers in ways that may, in principle, be adapted into particular organizational and contextual settings.

## Two Fairly Modest Aspirations

Why have we bothered to spend energy and effort to draw together experts, teacher educators, mentors, and beginning teachers to share their experience, scholarship and wisdom on the lives of early career teachers and various initiatives aimed to support them? From the beginning, we have aspired to both **encourage** those involved in the all- important facet of quality education (i.e., nurturing those entering the profession) and to **foster hope.** Despite the challenges, we can get better at supporting early career teachers in their work, adding huge value to their personal and professional lives. We love the simplicity of the word "encourage." "En" means "to put in" and "courage" is what is needed to pursue both the professional calling of being an educator *and* to be an effective mentor to educators. Written and verbal words can *en*liven and *en*courage or *dis*parage and *dis*courage. When this book is read in context and in the spirit of trying to be both rigorous and helpful, we think the words offered should provide overall encouragement. We have noticed that there has been a discernable intensification in both teacher workplaces and in the demands placed on schools, teacher education providers and those working to support teachers. There are many wonderful examples of investment, development, creative design, and early career teacher-focused initiatives to come alongside these new professionals. It is said that leaders help others to define reality *and* then they say thank you. This book has certainly brought colour and texture to the realities of beginning teachers. As editors, we are thankful for those whose voices have been represented in this book and those who have offered their encouragement to its readers.

Keeping hope alive without denying the realities, building confidence without sugar-coating, and helping those new to the profession to anchor themselves in authentic and accurate professional identities and the great goods that are attained in the noble work of educators, has been crucial for us. We can live for hours and days without water, but hope and meaning are essential for professional lives to be seen as worth living. We have aspired to edit a book that feeds our hopes, rekindles or lights our fires, and yields a sense that there are many warrants for the promise of future developments in the field of early career teacher mentorship and support. We suggest the need for more sharing, the use of some of the brilliant ideas and insights found in this book, the more focused research and reflection on early career professional lives, and the continuing exercise of investment in the people who are able to make such positive differences through relationships and programs. All of the above would contribute to a good cause of the enhanced futures for beginning teachers. The multiplier effect of investments in beginning teachers' well-being and the resultant benefit for thousands of Canadian families, and into several future generations, ought to give hope to all of us. We believe that we get more of what we give attention to. Therefore, we need to continue to draw encouragement and hope from what our authors have shared about the ways and means, tried and true, that make a qualitative and organic difference for individuals and cohorts of beginning teachers.

The worth and merit of our ongoing awareness, attention, and responsiveness to these new educators' ought to be evident through these pages. The hope that there are those who have made and continue to make significant commitments and progress in their efforts to ensure that beginning teachers flourish rather than flounder has been encouraging to us as editors, and, we trust, to our readers as well.

# Editors

**_Benjamin Kutsyuruba_** (Ph.D., University of Saskatchewan) is an Associate Professor in Educational Policy, Leadership, and School Law and an Associate Director of Social Program Evaluation Group (SPEG) in the Faculty of Education at Queen's University, Kingston, Ontario, Canada. Throughout his career, Benjamin has worked as a teacher, researcher, manager, and professor in the field of education in Ukraine and Canada. His research interests include educational policymaking; educational leadership; mentorship and development of teachers; trust, moral agency, and ethical decision-making in education; international education; school climate, safety, well-being, and flourishing; and educational change, reform, and restructuring. His areas of teaching are educational leadership, school law and policy, educational policy studies, and policymaking in education.

✉ ben.kutsyuruba@queensu.ca

🌐 www.earlycareerteachers.com

*Keith Walker* (Ph.D., University of Saskatchewan) is a professor in the Johnson-Shoyama Graduate School of Public Policy and in the Department of Educational Administration in the College of Education at the University of Saskatchewan. He believes in the fundamental importance of robust systems of early childhood, K-12 education, and post-secondary education for the well-being of civil societies and has a wide-angle focus on lifelong and life-wide education in his work. To his way of thinking, organizational-community and leadership learning and development in all three sectors (public, social and private) are critical. His academic expertise in educational administration, executive leadership, organizational development and applied ethics match well with his public policy research interests (governance, leadership-constituent relationships and social policy). Walker's present projects range from an examination of trust – why it is important, how it can be sustained – to how we might further engage public and social sectors to become flourishing and engaging organizations.

keith.walker@usask.ca

http://KeithDWalker.ca

# Contributors

**Keith Alcock** is an early career teacher in his fourth year of teaching with the Limestone District School Board and a Masters student at the Faculty of Education, Queen's University.

**Maha Al Makhamreh** is a PhD student in the Faculty of Education at Queen's University in Kingston, Ontario. She is involved in different research projects at Queen's, and for her PhD dissertation Maha will be exploring leadership in Higher Education in Canada. Maha completed her MBA at Henley Business School in 2008, and in her dissertation she looked at the leadership role that facilitators play in face-to-face problem-solving groups. Maha holds an education degree (UAE) and a GDPI degree (Canada), and started her career as a teacher and principal before she began her independent career as a management/educational consultant.

**Sarah Barrett** is an Associate Professor in the Faculty of Education, York University. Her research centres on two themes: (1) teaching for social justice (especially in science and math), and (2) the impact that the core beliefs and values of teachers have on their classroom practice. That research has involved working with teachers in the first 5 years of their careers, many of whom struggle to reconcile their conceptions of the ideal teacher with the demands of the job and their commitments to social justice and equity. Consequently, sociological approaches to professional ethics and professional identity are central themes in her work. Her current research revolves around teachers' conceptions of what constitutes professional ethical practice, and the role of unions and the media in their sense of professional identity.

**Jaime Beck**, PhD, completed her doctoral work in the Centre for Research for Teacher Education and Development (CRTED) at the University of Alberta. Her dissertation, *Teachers Experiences of Negotiating Stories to Stay by*, continued to explore themes taken up in her award-winning Master's thesis, *Breaking the Silence: Beginning Teachers Share Pathways*

*Out of the Profession* (completed at UBC). Jaime's unique insights into the experiences of teachers have inspired her current commitment to developing/delivering professional development supports around issues of teacher induction, mentorship, and teacher professional growth. Jaime's published works also reflect her additional research interests, which include arts-based and narrative methodologies.

**John Bosica** is a PhD student in the Faculty of Education at Queen's University. With a BScH from Queen's University and MSc in Mathematics from the Royal Military College of Canada, John is focused on Mathematics Education. Specifically, his research is focused on a teacher's mathematical self-efficacy and how that corresponds to their teaching practices.

**Kathryn Broad**, PhD, is a faculty member at the Ontario Institute for Studies in Education, University of Toronto, where she has served in many roles supporting Initial Teacher Education, including as Academic Director, ITE. She has been an elementary teacher and administrator, and recently completed a secondment to the Teaching Policy and Standards Branch at the Ontario Ministry of Education. In every context, she has had the privilege of learning with and from colleagues. These experiences have deepened her understanding and commitment to collaborative professional learning, mentorship and researching to inform and support teacher learning across the continuum.

**Kathy Collis**, B.A., B.Ed., is the Program Director of the Professional Learning and Leadership Centre in Winnipeg School Division. She previously served her school division as a classroom teacher, curriculum consultant in Literacy Development, and support teacher for Inner City Schools. Her current work includes promoting and facilitating quality adult learning that supports new teachers and mentors. Ms. Collis has lead learning sessions at both the provincial and national levels in the areas of K-12 literacy development, assessment for learning, and teacher induction and mentorship. Currently, she is a member of the Pan-Canadian Expert Panel on Teacher Induction and Mentoring.

**Jean-Claude Couture**, PhD, coordinates the research activities of the Alberta Teachers' Association. His recent research included a national study of the influences shaping the work-life of school leaders. His ongoing work involves supporting the Association's international network of innovative schools and strategic planning. Couture completed a PhD from the University of Alberta that applied cultural psychoanalytic theory to the analysis of the intensification of teachers' work. He has published numerous articles on school development and accountability and continues to advocate for role of teacher organizations in contributing to educational development.

**Katharine (Kate) Creery** is the New Teacher Induction Program coordinator and School Effectiveness Lead for the Upper Grand District School Board, in Guelph, Ontario. Kate is a teacher and school principal who has worked with students grades kindergarten through to grade 12. She is most hopeful about the future of education in Canada when she sees the dedication and passion of our newest teachers.

**Alison Davies** has been coordinator for the BC New Teacher Mentorship Project since its inception in 2012. Alison's two interests of mentorship and teacher inquiry were developed through her years as an elementary teacher and 8 years as a Faculty Associate with Simon Fraser University. Alison understands mentorship as a core process of teacher professionalism, and is committed to developing systemic supports for new teachers across BC.

**Carol Demchuk-Kosolofski** is an educator with regular classroom experience from K-10. During her career, she has also worked as a Home-based Education Program Facilitator, an Early Literacy Facilitator, an Instructor/ programmer for vulnerable youth and a Field Experience Consultant during a secondment to the University of Saskatchewan. Working with many talented mentors during her various roles has spurred a deep interest in mentorship in education.

**Tracy Dollansky**, PhD, is an Educational Consultant and former Superintendent of Education (retired) for a rural Saskatchewan school division. Prior to becoming a superintendent in 2009, she worked for 27 years as a teacher, vice-principal, and principal in rural schools. Tracy is currently a sessional instructor at the University of Saskatchewan in the Department of Educational Administration. Tracy is recognized for her research and work in the areas of beginning teacher mentorship, teacher supervision, and administrative/instructional leadership. She supports rural schools and school community councils as they build capacity to ensure student achievement.

**Sylvie Fontaine**, PhD, a été directrice des programmes de formation des enseignants (2012-2015) et des études supérieures (2006-2008) au département des sciences de l'éducation de l'Université du Québec en Outaouais. Elle enseigne le cours d'évaluation des apprentissages au premier cycle et des cours de développement de la recherche aux cycles supérieurs en éducation. Elle a dirigé ou collaboré à des recherches sur la préparation des enseignants en Nouvelle-Zélande et au Québec. Actuellement, ses recherches portent sur le développement des compétences des enseignants en évaluation des apprentissages et sur la fraude en milieu universitaire, à savoir le plagiat et la tricherie.

**Annette Ford**, PhD, teaches in the Intercultural Studies department at Ambrose University in Calgary, Alberta. She recently completed a Ph.D. in Curriculum and Teacher Development at the University of Toronto's Ontario Institute for Studies in Education (OISE) with a concentration in Comparative, International, and Development Education (CIDE). Her Ph.D. thesis was entitled, *Who Mentors the Mentors? Curriculum and Development for Mentors of New Teachers in Israel.* While at the University of Toronto she served on OISE's Faculty Council and Executive Council and coordinated the CIDE program's Student Association. She continues to serve on the board of the International Christian Community for Teacher Education. Annette's research interests include mentoring in education; educational leadership; teacher preparation, induction, and development; community-based education; and education in conflict-affected contexts. As a citizen of Canada and the United States who grew up and worked in India, USA, Canada, Italy, Germany, Hungary, and Kazakhstan, Annette has a unique understanding of intercultural adaptation in teaching and leadership.

**Lorraine Godden**, PhD, is an Adjunct Assistant Professor at the Faculty of Education, Queen's University. Lorraine was the pan-Canadian teacher induction and mentoring research project's manager for 5 years. Lorraine's research is rooted in understanding how policy actors interpret policy documents to implement career/life planning, and experiential learning policies across multidisciplinary environments. Lorraine is interested in how stakeholders are supported, and policy implementation facilitated, through these complex interpretive processes. Lorraine has undertaken many collaborative, empirical, and community-based research projects informing theory, policy, and practice-based initiatives for at-risk youth. Lorraine's doctorate was funded by the Social Sciences and Humanities Research Council of Canada (SSHRC).

**Jenny Gonyou-Brown**, EdD, recently completed the Doctor of Education (EdD) program at Western University in London, Ontario. Her research interest in investigating the supports available for early career teachers has evolved from her work with the Thames Valley District School Board (TVDSB) as a lead mentor and professional learning facilitator for the New Teacher Induction Program (NTIP). Alongside her research work, Dr. Gonyou-Brown is a music specialist and special education teacher and has been working with students, their families and other educators in schools for the past fourteen years.

**Anne Hales** is a doctoral candidate in the Department of Curriculum and Pedagogy at the University of British Columbia. Anne is currently serving as Senior Researcher at the British Columbia Teachers' Federation, and as a teacher educator and lecturer in Simon Fraser University's Faculty of Education. She chairs Teacher Mentorship BC, a grassroots educator network advocating for early career teacher mentorship. Her research interests include teacher education, beginning teacher mentorship and critical theory.

**Laurie-Ann Hellsten**, PhD, is a Professor in Educational Psychology and Special Education in the College of Education at the University of Saskatchewan. Her teaching areas include applied measurement and evaluation, assessment, statistics, and research methods. Laurie-ann's research expertise includes instrument development and validation, survey methodology, program evaluation, mixed methodologies, and the application of advanced quantitative techniques. Most of her research is conducted with adolescents and emerging adults in the health (physical activity, stress, self-regulation, and well-being) and education (beginning teacher, teacher identity development, mentorship, and higher education) domains.

**Trista Hollweck** is a PhD Candidate and Part-Time Professor in the Faculty of Education at the University of Ottawa. Her SSHRC-funded research examines the impact of a mentoring and coaching community of practice on Mentor-Coaches and the culture of a school district. Trista completed her Post Graduate Certificate of Education (PGCE) from the University of Edinburgh in 2000. Since then Trista has been a secondary teacher, teacher trainer (Tribes TLC, Restorative Practice & Instructional Intelligence), administrator, and consultant for the Western Quebec School Board. In 2009, she became involved in the development and coordination of the WQSB's Teacher Induction Program (TIP), focusing on professional growth, mentoring and coaching fellowships, and teacher evaluation.

**Rita Irwin**, PhD, is Professor of Art Education and Curriculum Studies, Faculty of Education, The University of British Columbia, Vancouver, Canada. She is Past President of UNESCO-affiliated InSEA (International Society for Education through Art, CSEA (Canadian Society for Education through Art) and Principal Editor of the International Journal of Education through Art (2017-2020). Her major research interests include practice based research, participatory and community engaged research, and a/r/tography set within questions related to sociocultural issues, teacher education, inquiry based learning, and contemporary art. She is the principal investigator of a SSHRC-funded research project: Pedagogical Assemblage: Building and sustaining teacher capacity through mentoring programs in British Columbia (2014-2017).

**Ruth Kane**, PhD, is a Full Professor and Director of Graduate Studies at the Faculty of Education, University of Ottawa. She has worked in Teacher Education in New Zealand and Australia before moving to Canada in 2006 as Director of Teacher Education. Her research interests focus on Teacher Education, and beginning teacher induction, particularly as related to preparing teachers for urban schools. Ruth has lead a number of national (NZ) and provincial (Ontario) research studies and is currently part of the team evaluating New Zealand's postgraduate teacher education programs (2014-2017). She is principal investigator in a five-year study of how school boards, teachers, and students take up citizenship within urban schools that serve youth from indigenous and first generation immigrant communities. This project funded through a SSHRC insight grant investigates the development of mobile media spaces for civic engagement in urban priority schools. She supervises a number of doctoral and masters students in the areas of teaching, teacher education and teacher professional learning.

**Terry Kharyati** is a Secretary General/Director of Human Resources at Western Quebec School Board. Having struggled through high school and CEGEP himself, Terry began his university training with the goal of becoming a teacher, to give back to the leaders and teachers who had helped and mentored him along the way. His drive and passion for helping a range of students and staff to learn and grow was evidenced early on, and he seized leadership opportunities whenever they presented themselves. Terry was a teacher, vice-principal, principal for 23 years and is now working at central office. He has recently graduated from the MEd Program at Queens University where he immersed himself in the study of the impact of leadership on school climate, the impact of leadership of student and staff efficacy and the belief that systems need to support and nurture all school leaders. He is a proud husband and a father of three beautiful girls and lives in the community he proudly serves.

**Tashi Kirincic** is the Coordinator of Teacher Mentorship for the Delta School District, the Coordinator of Technology for the New Teacher Mentorship Project (BC), and a member of the Provincial Mentorship Resource Team (BC). In all of these roles, she is a learner first. She is passionate about learning and teaching and is particularly interested in cultivating and sustaining communities of learning for all teachers at all phases of their careers. She believes that effective mentorship is reciprocal and should nourish all participants. She is also the mother of two young boys who challenge her to grow and learn every day.

**Thursica Kovinthan** is a doctoral candidate, part-time professor, and Vanier scholar at the Faculty of Education, University of Ottawa. Her research interests include citizenship, refugee education, gender equality, and post-conflict education. Thursica is also an elementary school teacher with the Toronto District School Board where she works with special education students and English language learners.

**Julian Lawrence** is pursuing his Master's degree in the Department of Curriculum and Pedagogy at the University of British Columbia. Growing up an isolated English kid in separatist Quebec, he quickly discovered the world of comics and even taught himself to speak French through reading Tintin, Asterix and Lucky Luke. These were formative years as he has dedicated his life to learning about comics, making comics, reading comics and teaching comics. He is a research assistant of the Pedagogical Assemblage research project, using comics to portray teachers' professional growth through mentorship.

**Lynn Lemisko**, PhD, is an associate professor in the Department of Educational Foundations in the College of Education at the University of Saskatchewan. Her teaching experience includes work in Alberta in the Calgary and Ft. McMurray public school systems where she taught students in grades four through nine, and many years of teaching post-secondary student courses in Canadian and European history, trends and issues in curriculum development, social studies curriculum-making and the history of education. Her research interests include explorations of issues in citizenship education, teacher education, mentorship, and the history of education.

**Ching-Chiu Lin**, PhD, is a Research Associate in the Department of Curriculum and Pedagogy at the University of British Columbia. Her research interests lie in community arts education and teacher development and in maintaining her scholarly experiences of collaborative partnership in a cross-disciplinary environment. She works closely with Dr. Rita Irwin on a SSHRC-funded Partnership Development Grant exploring how teacher mentorship can support and strengthen teacher practice in British Columbia.

**Amber Lum** is a Psychology major student with a minor in Education at the University of British Columbia. Amber is a strong mental health advocate with a passion to pursue either Counselling or Clinical Psychology. Working as a research assistant in both Psychology and Education has given

Amber a unique perspective that has cultivated her interests in mental health literacy and safe space facilitation. Amber works closely with the Pedagogical Assemblage research team to produce comics and videos of teachers' narratives.

**Ian Matheson** is a graduate student in the PhD program in Education at Queen's University with a focus in Learning and Cognition. His research is focused on students with high-incidence hidden exceptionalities, and he will be starting a position in Inclusive Education as an Assistant Professor at the University of Regina in the summer of 2017. Along with teaching and research experience at Queen's University, Ian also has experience as a teacher at the elementary and secondary school levels in a variety of classroom settings.

**Joséphine Mukamurera**, PhD, psychopédagogue, est professeure titulaire au département de Pédagogie, Faculté d'éducation, Université de Sherbrooke. Elle enseigne dans les programmes de formation des enseignants pour le secondaire. Chercheure régulière au Centre de recherche interuniversitaire sur la formation et la profession enseignante (CRIFPE), elle est spécialiste des questions relatives à l'insertion et à la carrière en enseignement. Ses recherches portent principalement sur les réalités vécues par les nouveaux enseignants et leurs besoins de soutien, sur le développement professionnel ainsi que sur les programmes d'insertion en enseignement.

**Matthew McIntyre** is a 2nd year elementary teacher at the Western Quebec School Board. With a background in Outdoor and Physical Education he began teaching at the elementary level with a hope of impacting young students in new, active and engaging ways. As a new teacher to the WQSB he is in the final stages of completing the two-year induction program at their board. Matthew has enjoyed representing the induction program this year and sharing his experiences with administration, ministry reps and other new teachers from across the country.

**Carmine Minutillo** is currently a principal within a school board in eastern Ontario who has served in three schools in this capacity over the past ten years. Prior to becoming a principal, Carmine was a classroom teacher for four years and a special education teacher for another four years. He has been involved in the Ontario New Teacher Induction Program (NTIP), working alongside several novice teachers and his school board and has been a member of his school board's NTIP Committee in the past. In addition to his professional association as a principal working with new teachers, Carmine has recently completed his Master of Education degree at Queen's University where his research focus and thesis work primarily centred on how principals can motivate and support new and more experienced teachers with respect to participating in professional development pursuits.

**Francine Morin**, PhD, Professor at the Faculty of Education, University of Manitoba, is a leading authority in Canadian arts education and teacher professional development. After serving two terms as Department Head of Curriculum, Teaching, and Learning, she has now been appointed Associate Dean Undergraduate Studies. Dr. Morin has conducted several action research studies aimed at improving educational experiences and programs for children, teachers, and school administrators. Presently, she is working in collaboration with field-based partners to improve and refine a two-year induction program for new teachers, and an after-school orchestral program for children who live in disadvantaged school communities.

**Stefanie Muhling**, PhD, is a teacher, teacher educator and researcher. She has taught elementary students in the Eastern Arctic, rural Ontario and Toronto, and has supported professional learning for teachers in a number of leadership positions. Prior to her current role as an Education Officer for the Ontario Ministry of Education's Teaching Policy and Standards Branch, Stefanie coordinated a bilingual teacher education program in Toronto. She is delighted to be working with educators across Ontario to support and promote teachers' professional learning. Stefanie passionately believes that mentorship is essential to teachers' professional learning at every stage of their careers.

**Aggie Nemes** is the New Teacher Induction Program (NTIP) Coordinator for the Toronto Catholic District School Board, working with new teachers in the areas of Orientation, Professional Development, and Mentorship. She has also worked as an elementary vice principal and a Math Resource Teacher. As a classroom teacher, she worked with Primary and Intermediate students for 15 years.

**Katina Pollock**, PhD, is Associate Professor of Educational Leadership and Policy in Critical Policy, Equity, and Leadership Studies at the Faculty of Education, Western University. Katina has received a number of research awards. Her most recent grant (with Dr. Fei Wang) explores Secondary School Principals' Understanding of Work Intensification. In addition to her traditional scholarship efforts, Dr. Pollock has also been involved in large-scale knowledge mobilization initiatives that connect research to practice. She is currently Co-director for the Knowledge Network for Applied Education Researcher (KNAER), an initiative supported by the Ontario Ministry of Education.

**Gail Ruta Fontaine**, B.Ed., M.Ed., is the Support Teacher for the Professional Learning and Leadership Centre in Winnipeg School Division. Her career has encompassed early years teaching in high needs urban schools as well as working as a Learning Support Teacher with teachers and administrators from three urban school sites. Ms. Ruta Fontaine's expertise as a mathematics and literacy educator has led to opportunities to serve on provincial curriculum development committees. She has training in Cognitive Coaching and Learning Focused Relationships which informs her work with early service teachers, mentors and school leaders.

**Laura Servage**, PhD, completed her masters and doctoral degrees at the University of Alberta. Her research has spanned K-12 and higher education, with a particular emphasis on the relationships between education, work, and social mobility. In public education, Laura has been conducting research on teacher professional learning, teacher professionalism, and teachers' working conditions for ten years. Dr. Servage presently holds a postdoctoral fellowship at Ontario Institute for the Study of Education (OISE) at the University of Toronto.

**Cathryn Smith**, PhD, has been an educator for over 30 years working at all levels from elementary to post-secondary. In the summer of 2016 she assumed the position of Assistant Professor in the Department of Leadership and Educational Administration, Faculty of Education at Brandon University. She is a frequent facilitator of workshops for the Manitoba Teachers' Society and the Manitoba Rural Learning Consortium. Her research focuses on developing the capacity of teacher leaders and administrators to function as agents of change within various educational contexts and the facilitation of adult learning with a focus on navigating change and conflict.

**Jim Strachan** is an Education Officer with the Ontario Ministry of Education where he supports mentorship across the province. He has been working with (and learning from) children for 33 years as a social worker, classroom teacher of grades 2 to 8, instructional leader for ICT and program coordinator for beginning teachers in the Toronto District School Board. By modeling caring, compassion, cooperation and humour, Jim believes we can contribute to the success of all children. It is his daily challenge to live these beliefs! His recent publications include *The Heart and Art of Teaching and Learning: Practical Ideas and Resources for Beginning Teachers* (ETFO, 2011), *Flash Forward! Rethinking Learning* (Lantern Resources, 2012) and *Mentoring for All* (Ontario Ministry of Education, 2016). Jim starts each day in his kayak watching the sun rise of Lake Ontario.

**Rebecca Stroud Stasel** is a PhD student at Queen's University. Her research interests include educational policy and leadership, international education, and performance arts-based pedagogies. She is part of the pan-Canadian research team that examines teacher induction and mentoring. She has also worked at the Queen's Teachers Overseas Recruitment Fair, and she teaches a B.Ed. course at Queen's Faculty of Education. Rebecca has worked for twenty years as a high school teacher, primarily in drama, debate, and language arts, both locally and abroad. Her master's thesis explored transformative pedagogy using a variety of theatre forms that intersected with social action.

**Jennifer Watt**, PhD, is a recent graduate of the doctoral program in Education at the University of Manitoba. She is currently a Sessional Instructor in the Department of Curriculum, Teaching, and Learning at the University of Manitoba teaching courses primarily in the area of Language and Literacy Education. In addition, Dr. Watt continues to work as a Research Assistant or Contract Researcher on a number of interesting education projects.

CPSIA information can be obtained
at www.ICGtesting.com
Printed in the USA
LVOW13s0336150617

538200LV00001B/1/P

9 780991 862696